Oprah

This book was published with the assistance of the Frederick W. Hilles Publication Fund of Yale University.

Oprah

The Gospel of an Icon

Kathryn Lofton

UNIVERSITY OF CALIFORNIA PRESS
Berkeley · Los Angeles · London

306.609
Lofton

Parts of this book appeared previously in different
form in the following publications and are printed here
by permission of their original publishers: "Practicing
Oprah; Or, The Prescriptive Compulsion of a Spiritual
Capitalism," *Journal of Popular Culture* 39, no. 4
(August 2006): 599–621; "Public Confessions: Oprah
Winfrey's American Religious History," *Women &*
Performance: A Journal of Feminist Theory 18, no. 1
(March 2008): 49–67; "Reading Religiously: The
Ritual Practices of Oprah's Book Club," in *The Oprah*
Affect: Critical Essays on Oprah's Book Club, ed.
Cecilia Konchar Farr and Jaime Harker (Albany: State
University of New York Press, 2008), 55–71.

University of California Press, one of the most
distinguished university presses in the United States,
enriches lives around the world by advancing
scholarship in the humanities, social sciences, and
natural sciences. Its activities are supported by the UC
Press Foundation and by philanthropic contributions
from individuals and institutions. For more
information, visit www.ucpress.edu.

University of California Press
Berkeley and Los Angeles, California

University of California Press, Ltd.
London, England

Library of Congress Cataloging-in-Publication Data

Lofton, Kathryn.
    Oprah : the gospel of an icon / Kathryn Lofton.
        p.   cm.
    Includes bibliographical references and index.
    ISBN 978-0-520-25927-0 (cloth : alk. paper)
    ISBN 978-0-520-26752-7 (pbk. : alk. paper)
    1. United States—Religion.   2. Religion and
culture—United States.   3. Popular culture—Religious
aspects.   4. Celebrities.   5. Oprah Winfrey show.
6. Winfrey, Oprah—Influence.   I. Title.
    BL2525.L65   2011
    306.60973'090511—dc22   2010022319

Manufactured in the United States of America

20   19   18   17   16   15   14   13   12   11
10   9   8   7   6   5   4   3   2   1

This book is printed on Cascades Enviro 100, a 100%
post consumer waste, recycled, de-inked fiber. FSC
recycled certified and processed chlorine free. It is acid
free, Ecologo certified, and manufactured by BioGas
energy.

For Susan and John Lofton

The false Messiah is as old as the hope for the true Messiah.
He is the changing form of this changeless hope.

—Franz Rosenzweig

Contents

Acknowledgments

Every writer has an imagined audience. For me, this audience is four people who disciplined my thinking from there to here. Catherine Brekus, Laurie Maffly-Kipp, Jonathan Smith, and Thomas Tweed define a set of problems that have become in my work the ones worth solving. Not because they can be solved, but because the process of their solution is the very thing that defines our professional obligation.

There have been many readers for this book, first and foremost my departmental homes, including the Department of Religious Studies at the University of North Carolina at Chapel Hill, the Department of Religion at Reed College, the Department of Religious Studies and Program in American Studies at Indiana University, Bloomington, and the Department of Religious Studies and Program in American Studies at Yale University. Papers related to this project were presented at annual meetings of the American Academy of Religion and the Society for the Scientific Study of Religion, as well as before audiences at Baylor University, Hofstra University, Manhattan College, North Carolina State University, the University of Rochester, the University of Texas at Austin, the University of Toronto, and the University of Utah. Finally, I received support during my research and writing through the History of American Christian Practice Project, the Young Scholars in American Religion Program (both funded by the Lilly Endowment), and the Center for the Study of Religion at Princeton University, where I received feedback from the Religion and Culture Workshop as well as from the American Religious History Colloquium.

Tracy Fessenden, Marie Griffith, and Leigh Schmidt have not only written the books that fostered this one but also encouraged argumentative improvement at several intersections. I stayed in graduate school because Randall Styers and Ruel Tyson convinced me, in their words and their models, that this was a life of elegance and verve. And over the long course of this book's contemplation, I have enjoyed and been improved by the critical knowing of Wallace Best, Jason Bivins, Anthea Butler, Julie Byrne, Martha Crunkleton, Edward Curtis, Heather Curtis, Amy DeRogatis, Kate Carte Engel, J. Spencer Fluhman, Philip Goff, Paul Harvey, Martin Kavka, Laura Levitt, Shanny Luft, Shaul Magid, Melani McAlister, Colleen McDannell, Lynn Neal, Amanda Porterfield, Sally Promey, Susan Ridgely, Nora Rubel, Roberto Lint Sagarena, Chad Seales, David Shefferman, David Delgado Shorter, Matthew Sutton, Mark Valeri, Grant Wacker, David Harrington Watt, Judith Weisenfeld, and Tisa Wenger. In the final round of writing, Courtney Bender, Daphne Brooks, Eraina Davis, Joshua Dubler, Daniel Hanna, John Lardas Modern, Anthony Petro, Sam See, Harry Stout, Stephen Teiser, and Moulie Vidas provided savvy readings and new collegiality.

The growing body of literature on Oprah Winfrey includes scholarship written from a variety of disciplinary enclaves. The citations in my backnotes offer acknowledgment of the formal variety. Here I would like to mention Cecilia Konchar Farr, Jaime Harker, Eva Illouz, Kathleen Lowney, Marcia Z. Nelson, Janice Peck, Trysh Travis, and Eitan Wilf for their energizing intellectual commiseration, on the page and in person.

Eventually conversation becomes text. At that point, Reed Malcolm and my anonymous reviewers for the University of California Press offered impeccable counsel that transformed this manuscript for the better. Heather Scherschel supplied timely final research assistance. And during the earlier days of this book's consideration, Theo Calderara, Martha Hoffman, and Gary Morris supplied questions about style and argument that persisted to its final completion. Robin Whitaker and Laura Harger stewarded the manuscript to careful completion.

As much as this book is an analysis of an academic object, it is also a profoundly personal story—personal to the millions of women who watch Oprah, and personal to the hundreds of women with whom I discussed this work. Unspecified in this text are the women I met in church groups and book clubs who shared with me their feelings about Oprah under the auspices of a guest lecture on my research. Since this project did not unfold as ethnography, these interactions go unmentioned in my rendering. Nevertheless, those moments of exchange were formative for my own sense of Oprah's pervasive appeal, and I remain humbled by the stories shared in those formal and informal contexts.

In addition, this story is personal to the sphere of friends and family who buoyed me through many drafts of living, modeling the fraught quagmires between gender identity and work, intellectual labor and parenthood, partnership and presence. I thank my compatriots here for allowing me in their worlds: Megan Biddinger, Barb Candy and Chuck Pruitt, Kit and Rob Chaskin, Denise Cruz and Jordan Blackman, Jay Dickson, Jacqueline Dirks, Mary and Doug Earle, Veronica and Jason Fickel, Nancy and Clark Gilpin, Erika Hagen, Rebecca Hamlin, Carrie Heitman, Scott Herring and Shane Vogel, Nancy Hiller, Joy and John Kasson, Ken and Margrethe Kearney, Sandra Latcha, Helen Lee, Susan Lepselter, Joan Lounsbery, Kim Luft, Mimi McNamee, Esther and Victor Meksin, Ellen Millender, Kyriell Noon, Kevin O'Neill and Archana Sridhar, Zach Pruitt, Nick Quattrocchi, Mary Ritchie and Tom Cunningham, Emily Seales, Martha Tyson, and Tara Ward.

If Ms. Winfrey has taught me anything, it is that the enemy to intimacy is spectacle. Banality is the thing, the scrubbings and tugging of interrupting calls, subway strategy, grocery store excursions, and unruly dogs. Some of those with whom I share this life have already been mentioned. To that list, I will thank those who propel all joy at relational possibility: Jennifer Connerley, Jason Earle, Constance Furey, Matthew Guterl, Dana Katz, Brian Lofton, Lauren Lofton, Kathryn Lounsbery, and Mary Ellen O'Donnell. Each of you deserves a paragraph soliloquy on your grace and on your quick editorial splice on subjects textual and interpersonal. Nancy Levene found me amid my sentences, and for that and more I will always be glad. Leeza Meksin is the Oprah to my Gayle and she knows it; I am as we made, as we wended, as we share. Finally, this book is for the only two people I know who don't need anyone—not anyone, not no how—to tell them how to live their best life. They just do. Thank you for every ingredient of your practice, every piece of your love.

Introduction

What is Oprah? A noun. A name. A misspelling. Oprah is a person we know because of her publicity, a pioneer we recognize because of her accolades, and a personage we respect because of her embodied endurance, her passionate care, her industrious production. First and foremost, though, Oprah is a woman. An African American woman with a story broadcast by her own engines, with ideas inspired by her unceasing consumption, and with a self magnified by the media mechanics that make tabloid her every gesture. Before that broadcast, before that spectacle, she did possess particularity: a place of birth, a date of origin, a story of parentage, abuse, and utter destitution. The terms of her subsequent uplift are so ritually inspirational as to be mythic; the results of her rise are so idiosyncratic as to be impossible. What is Oprah? Oprah is an instance of American astonishment at what can be.

From the start, it should be clear: this Oprah is maybe not *your* Oprah. She is most likely nothing like the Oprah you recollect, the one who hugs and helps and heals the world, one sympathizing smile at a time. For the purposes of this work, the materiality of Oprah Winfrey—her body, her biography, and her singularity—is interesting only insofar as it documents and creates *Oprah*.[1] Shifting from *her* to *it* is not easy, since Oprah is a professionally lovable sort of she. But the move is necessary if we are to know just what it is, exactly, that she sells. Because whatever Oprah is, it will be, in perpetuity, a product. This book examines a person who is also a product, a woman who blends, bends, and obliterates the line between private practice and public performance and whose aesthetics completely ignore what we have historically conceived as a great divide between what is properly religious and what is not. This is the space between the eighteenth-century itinerant preacher George Whitfield and the twentieth-century incorporation of Coca-Cola; it is the charisma between the formation of churches and the formation of empires. *Oprah: The Gospel of an Icon* argues that the products of Oprah Winfrey's empire offer a description of religion in modern society. Within the religious pluralism of contemporary America, Oprah extols what she likes, what she needs, and what she believes. These decisions are not just product plugs but also proposals for a mass spiritual revolution, supplying forms of religious practice that fuse consumer behavior, celebrity ambition, and religious idiom. Through multiple media, Oprah sells us a story about ourselves.

Before we can understand the story she sells, however, the seller must be described. Inverted to Harpo, Oprah is a corporation, an employer of nearly a thousand people, a distributor of an internationally recognized brand.

> Oprah, *The Oprah Winfrey Show, Oprah & Friends,* Make the Connection, Oprah's Book Club, Use Your Life, Live Your Best Life, Oprah's Favorite Things, Wildest Dreams with Oprah, and Oprah Boutique are registered trademarks of Harpo, Inc. Harpo is a registered trademark of Harpo Productions, Inc. The Oprah Store, Oprah.com, *Oprah's Big Give,* The Big Give, Give Big or Go Home, Expert Minutes, the "Oprah" signature and the "O" design are trademarks of Harpo, Inc. Oprah's Angel Network®, Angel Network, O Ambassadors, and the corresponding "O" design are trademarks of Oprah's Angel Network. Oprah Winfrey Leadership Academy for Girls is a trademark of The Oprah Winfrey Leadership Academy Foundation. O, *The Oprah Magazine* and O *at Home* are registered trademarks of Harpo Print, LLC. All Rights Reserved.[2]

These titles and imprints are not just trademarks. They are cultures of expression, a supply chain of self unmatched in the history of industry, celebrity, or charismatic authority. The kernel was a studio of televised rhetoric: *The Oprah Winfrey Show.* Not an object you could hold in your hands, but a process of conversation, a didactic community.[3] This is what started it all, spiraling quickly into brand compulsion: *The Oprah Winfrey Show* entered national syndication in 1986, becoming the highest-rated talk show in television history. In 1988, Oprah established Harpo Studios, a production facility in Chicago. Produced by her production company, Harpo Productions, Inc., the show, as of 2009, is seen by an estimated forty-two million viewers a week in the United States and is broadcast internationally in 147 countries.

The spin-offs were inevitable, as the republic of the daily show became the empire of a transnational O. Not surprisingly, change happened because she changed, and she changed because the market changed. Or is it the other way? Did the market change because of her? Did her spirit shape the world, or does she manifest the world in her spirit? The answer will be (in her voice, on her terms) intertwined, always. "You become what you believe."[4] What we know is that by the mid-1990s, her genre was changing. The talk show television market was flooded with hosts offering carnivals of absurdity: encounters between incestuous relations and criminals consorting with their victims. Violence and mayhem seemed to be the visual intent, a blending of professional wrestling and soap opera, dressed as therapy in drag. Just as her expressive medium seemed bent upon new extremes of exhibitionism, Winfrey found herself in the midst of multiple personal transitions.[5] As with everything in her, as with everything of her, as with everything (eaten, read, thought, felt, bought, met, seen) by her, these plot points were publicized as open-door national psychological exorcisms.[6] Yet this time, with a product tie-in, with a mass-distributed print culture twist. Oprah is someone who objectifies her mistakes, casting the commodification of those mistaken objects as seemly despite their confessional graft. Harpo, Inc., doesn't understand *sellout* as an epithet. It just sells more, more ardently, under the banner of self-love.

As such, Oprah is an effect and an affect, a product that responds to a marketplace as well as an imagined marketplace to which the products reply. In 1996, a group of Texas cattlemen sued Winfrey for twelve million dollars after she proclaimed that she would never eat another burger. Cattle prices plummeted and kept falling for two weeks in what beef traders called the Oprah Crash. Winfrey found herself in Amarillo, Texas, fighting a defamation suit.[7] Her experience in Amarillo, the sharp shift in talk show tastes, her own psychological awakening, and a midlife professional restlessness coalesced to a metamorphosis of her own programming. "I really am tired of the crud," she said.

> The time has come for this genre of talk shows to move on from dysfunctional whining and complaining and blaming. I have had enough of people's dysfunction. I don't want to spend an hour listening to somebody blaming their mother. So to say that I am tired—yes, I am. I'm tired of it. I think it's completely unnecessary. We're all aware that we do have some problems and

we need to work on them. What are you willing to do about it? And that is what our shows are going to be about.[8]

The despair is reflexive, as Winfrey repudiates herself as much as the medium. She calls upon herself, and her viewers, to invent practices of reply and to *do* something about the problems that pervade. Elsewhere, she fantasized: "I dream about finding a new way of doing television that elevates us all." She can't bear to hear another disgruntled daughter or beleaguered wife, nor can she stand to be associated by genre with the fistfights and sexual extremities of her déclassé subphylum. "I started this because I believe people are ultimately good," she said, "I think television is a good way of opening people's hearts." To claim the good, to silk the sow's ear, she recanted: "I've been guilty of doing trash TV and not thinking it was trash."[9] She confessed to come clean, creating over a four-year period (1994–98) a corporate makeover worthy of the converting rites she herself would come to master. Programming would now, late in the neoliberal heyday, focus on the reformation of the world in her own image, on what she called "Change Your Life TV."[10]

"Originally our goal was to uplift, enlighten, encourage, and entertain through the medium of television," Winfrey explained. "Now our mission . . . is to use television to transform people's lives, to make viewers see themselves differently, and to bring happiness and a sense of fulfillment into every home."[11] To transform, to bring happiness, to create a "sense" of fulfillment: these are callings of a higher order. "I am talking about each individual having her or his own inner revolution," Winfrey explained. "I am talking about each individual coming to the awareness that, 'I am Creation's son. I am Creation's daughter. I am more than my physical self. I am more than this job that I do. I am more than the external definitions I have given myself. . . . Those roles are all extensions of who I define myself to be, but ultimately I am Spirit come from the greatest Spirit. I am Spirit.'"[12] Much of the content for her show stayed the same, as celebrities continued to sell their films, mothers continued to weep about their wayward daughters, and amazing pets still strutted their special stuff. Now, though, it was enchanted with a straight-backed righteousness of the spiritually assured. "I wanted to help people think differently about themselves and pursue ideas about spirit and balance and the possibility of a better life," Winfrey would recollect later. "It was a decision that was bigger than money or material interest."[13] Winfrey's narrative of this program shift expresses an indifference to profit margins. Yet what matters here, what matters to understanding what makes *Oprah,* is that this explicitly missionary maneuver to help people was her empire's ascent. Her spiritualization programmed her incorporation.[14] This is how Oprah Winfrey became Oprah, how she became a product. Oprah Winfrey can be canceled, boycotted, and condemned. *Oprah* cannot.

Once Change Your Life TV changed *The Oprah Winfrey Show,* so too was her O brand altered, quickly multiplying forms to cajole new thought, new selves, and new lives. Oprah was seemingly everywhere, exploding media formats that themselves exploded the bounds between text and image, studio and audience, world and stage. On September 17, 1996, Oprah's Book Club began with the announcement of Jacquelyn Mitchard's *The Deep End of the Ocean* (1996) as the first pick. Within its inaugural year, Oprah's Book Club was the largest book club in the world, attracting approximately two million members. In April 2000, Oprah and Hearst Magazines introduced *O, The Oprah Magazine,* a monthly magazine credited as being the most successful magazine launch in recent history; it has a circulation of 2.3 million readers each month. In April 2002, Oprah launched the first international edition of *O, The Oprah Magazine* in South Africa, extending her "live your best life" message to another broad audience. In 1997, her Angel Network encouraged others to become involved in volunteer work and charitable giving. Oprah.com, the Web site of her amalgamated productions, averages 96 million page views and more than 6.7 million users per month and has more than 1.8 million newsletter subscribers. In 2003, Oprah.com launched Live Your Best Life, an interactive multimedia workshop based on Winfrey's sold-out national speaking tour that featured Oprah's personal life stories and life lessons along with a workbook of thought-provoking exercises. Through a joint venture, Oprah launched Oprah & Friends satellite radio channel in September 2006. Oprah & Friends features a range of original daily programming from Harpo Radio, Inc., including regular segments hosted by popular personalities from *The Oprah Winfrey Show* and *O, The Oprah Magazine* and her exclusive thirty-minute weekly radio show, *Oprah's Soul Series.* And finally, Oprah and Discovery Communications announced plans to create OWN: The Oprah Winfrey Network. The new multiplatform media venture will be designed to entertain, inform, and inspire people to "live their best lives." (All rights reserved.) OWN is slated to debut in more than eighty million homes. With Change Your Life TV, Winfrey found a way to make the message of her life the substance of the show, and, simultaneously, a way to make the message of her life the impetus for further market development.[15]

What has Oprah become? No longer merely a therapeutic idiom, Oprah has become an insignia, supplying a stylized economy that includes multiple print cultures (magazine, literary, cookbook, self-help, medical, and inspirational), multimedia programming (podcasts, weekly and daily electronic updates, weekly and daily television programs, radio shows, television networks, movies, movies of the week, and stage productions), educational philosophies, international philanthropies, interpersonal counseling, self-care workshops, and product plugs. Tracking the product amid all this making and recasting is hard. What is this, the object that she sells within these many productions? "Look, I know that to you guys the Oprah name is a brand. But for me, it is my life, it's the way I live my life, and the way I behave and everything I stand for."[16] She is, of course, more than this, more than just her life. The brand supersedes her biography, progressing from "everything I stand for" to recommending an Oprah that can stand in for something, filling a space where before there was something missing.

This seems odd to say, since what *can* be missing? The late twentieth century might have been a moment of extreme income disparity and global trauma, but in the country of Oprah's ascent, the problem seemed not deprivation but excess: so many options, so many stores, so many ambitions, and so much of absolutely everything. For scholars of religion, this late modern moment is also described as similarly redolent. Although some theorists posited it to be a "secular" age increasingly lacking certain forms of religious polity and ideation, for religionists this description misses the diagnostic mark. Religions are everywhere, available to everyone, in every color of the conceivable theological, ritual, and experiential rainbow.

Amid all this abundance, Oprah nominates herself as cheering section and signifying arbiter in an economy of revelation that she constructs. The revolutionary imperative pervades. "Become the change you want to see," she says, offering herself as the model and mode to that change.[17] Every maneuver and claim by Harpo Productions suggests that change must happen, now; that inspiration is needed, now; and that our lives require revision, now. In her discursive profusion, Winfrey posits a world that seems stunned before plenty, dumbly stalled in one section of the grocery store rather than selecting, moving, changing, and acting. Breaking the impasse of her viewers, Oprah interrupts their silencing.[18] She offers a discriminating plenty in the form of her own biographic freight: "When you get me, you are not getting an image, you are not getting a figurehead. You're not getting a theme song. You're getting all of me. And I bring all my stuff with me. My history, my past. Mississippi, Nashville. I'm coming with the sistahs in the church, I'm bringing Sojourner Truth with me. And then there we all are, sitting up in your meeting, at your table, with the marketing directors."[19] The subject makes herself here more than one thing, more than one woman or one history. Rather, she casts herself as a spiritual gathering, a collection at the table of iconography. She eschews branding (herself as brand) even as she gathers in her presumptive pervasiveness a past and present that can be described only as ubiquitous, insistent, and universal.[20] After all, the products of Harpo, Inc., supply that which people want to hear and to know; they create an opportunity to be heard and to learn; and they seat her audience at her long table of memory and market might. Oprah replies to the want of her imagined people with the voluminous convenience of herself. Her products, her ideas as her product, seep into every nook and cranny and become common sense.[21] Such sense is needed (urgently, daily, now); it is wanted (podcasted, downloaded, papered) to rectify silences, to offer assurance to an unnamed restlessness (for the missing, for the needed, for the silenced).

One way to imagine her presence, her repeated iconic referral and reproduction, is to say that Oprah supplies the way to survive this thronged silence, a way to endure the plenty before which bearings seem hard to find. "Something like a transnational public sphere has certainly rendered any strictly bounded sense of community or locality obsolete," Akhil Gupta and James Ferguson have written. "In the pulverized space of postmodernity, space has not become irrelevant: it has been reterritorialized."[22] Transforming pulverized space into a produced consumer caress, Oprah defines a territory where clarity may be found. Sense in a style, a therapy, an irresistible first person; sense in the form of soothing trademarked adages: "Make the Connection," "Use Your Life," and "Live Your Best Life." After a survey of the optional glut, Oprah selects the life to which you seek connection. In so doing, she frames the nature of a public sphere in which the subject is *you* in a clearinghouse counterpublic she has defined.

Do not be deceived: this is no discursive ephemera. Oprah is the product that sells a self in order to surpass its singularity and enter, repetitiously, the marketplace of products. Harpo, Inc., fills airspace with her body, with the sense of her sense, well beyond her time. Iconic comparisons (Elvis, Jackie O, Marilyn, Jesus) limit as much as they encourage. What we know is that (as with Elvis, as with Jackie) we don't need any more of her; we don't need any more than what we already have, to make of her the pieces that we need.[23] But of course: we'll keep taking. Oprah is an instant of overflowing cultural iconography, providing stuffing for every nook and cranny of your psychological gaps and material needs. This redolence seems singular, offering few neat comparisons. Yet Oprah, like her iconic predecessors, is also very much a production of taste cultures, race cultures, gender cultures, and economic cultures that append and assist her existence. She is in a moment that she made and that made her. Before this moment, she could not be. After her death, nothing will be quite the same.

This is another way of saying that Oprah Winfrey is not forever. Her death (the death of the founder) will be the end of the body but perhaps not of her. Although she is franchised and globalized, she remains limited by her materiality. Oprah makes Harpo, Harpo makes Oprah, and Oprah will die. Is she so pervasive as to transcend that end? The recent announcement that she would cancel her show in 2011 inaugurates her public incorporation of her charisma, her own consciousness that the person of Oprah must diminish if the Oprah product is to endure.[24] This transience of the subject is not unheralded in the history of industry; charisma and corporations have always had a codependency, with the generations following the founder struggling to keep, for example, Wal-Mart without Sam Walton, Kentucky Fried Chicken without the epicurean approval of Colonel Sanders, or the Church of Scientology without the steering hand of L. Ron Hubbard.[25] But here we introduce a new image, one seemingly far-flung from the company. Imagining the necessity of the founder, and her problematic continuance, requires reaching for other metaphors. I speak of the religious.

"My show is really a ministry," Winfrey tells us, "a ministry that doesn't ask for money. I can't tell you how many lives we've changed—or inspired to change."[26] By definitions currently codified in law and supported by scholarship, Oprah does not constitute a religion.[27] But Oprah tempts study by scholars of religion, because her productions overspill the imagined bounds of "economy" and "popular culture." Her success, and the modes of her branding, cannot be easily cordoned by macroeconomics, nor can the "culture" of her occupation be understood outside some interactive conception of "religion." Her religious aspects are literal (episodes of her shows addressing "everyday miracles," her satellite radio *Soul Series,* her issuing of *Spirit Newsletters*) and iconic. Oprah, *the* Oprah, is always telling you what to do, always telling you how to do it, always telling you to buy, and always telling you to save. Even if you want to avoid her, even if you have avoided her, you have not (you cannot). She looms. She haunts the supermarket (endorsing food, hawking magazines, bloated on tabloids), she helms national initiatives, and she endorses presidential candidates. So even if your consumption resists her recommendations, even if you have only laughed at her caricature on late-night satire, you laugh on the premise of her cultural suffusion.

This domination transfixes *Oprah: The Gospel of an Icon*, because her suffusion is familiar, and her modes are recognizable: she preaches prosperity gospel, she advocates books as scripture, she offers exegesis, she conducts exculpatory rites, she supplies a bazaar of faithful practices, she propagates missions, both home and foreign. She opines repeatedly on the meaning of existence, the seat of the soul, the purpose of your life, and the place of a higher calling. Oprah plays religious even as she is, most adamantly (by scholarly classification and by her own), *not* a religion.

For some critics of pop culture and its money-milking strategies, the religious idiom deployed by Harpo, Inc., may be seen as a clever angle on a profitable product, a product that uses spiritual discourse to smooth its solipsism. These critics might believe that any study of Oprah should be a study of scheming financial genius in which, by some fluke of capitalistic dispensation, one woman was given the instinctual gifts of ninety Wharton graduates. Is she, to borrow from another observer, just practicing "another capitalist enterprise that thrives on social dislocation, privatization, and feelings of disempowerment and disenchantment"?[28] This is a tempting demotion, allowing cultured despisers to admire that genius, to sneer wickedly at the duped consumers, and, most disturbingly, to imagine the producing agents (Oprah, Harpo, Hearst) as motivated neatly by one ambition. Yet, to describe any endeavor—legal or governmental, business or religious—as sourced so singularly is to refuse the multiplicity of cultural experiences, artifacts, and products.[29] The competitive performances of masculinity and the glamour of American dreaming have compelled many a financier to choices neither obviously moral nor assuredly profitable. There were many ways Enron could have made money, as there are many ways Oprah Winfrey could make money. That they did as they did (and that she does as she does) tells us more about what is human about them than what was perfected from their microeconomics coursework.

More important, to name Winfrey's spirituality as a financial scheme is also to evade critical engagement with the process of consumption itself, with the why of purchase, the seductions of sale, and the sorts of beliefs that compel American women to watch, and watch again, this African American product. Reducing Winfrey to a profit grab misses an opportunity to observe the symphonic way in which consumption and religion are categories not in opposition to each other but rather in collaboration. That we scholars in cultural studies and religious studies have for so long resisted this impression says a lot more about what we think is sacred and what we think is profane than about what believers (and consumers) consider sacred and profane. What is revealing from a scholarly vantage is that most studies of religion and popular culture establish three basic relationships between those two terms: religion appearing in popular culture (like a crucifix in a pop music video); popular culture appearing in religion (the use of blogs by believers); and popular culture as religion (fandom as religion).[30] This neat troika perpetuates the sense that religion and culture are categories that can be untangled from one another, that "religion" and "popular culture" are separable components of a recipe for "culture." Furthermore, by imagining that popular culture is an ingredient of religion (or religion an accessory to popular culture), one encourages estimation of the interaction, such as an evaluation of the tastefulness of Passover action figures or graphic novels depicting Muhammad. This is why, for many, "religion in popular culture" can be seen as a profanity (the furor over Madonna videos), and, likewise, popular culture in a religion (malls at a megachurch, for example) may be estimated as crass commercialization. No matter what one's ethical instincts on such deployments might be, to imagine that there could be a moral verdict on that interaction is as much a categorical problem as it is an ideological one. If only we didn't imagine culture and religion as neatly divided, we may be less surprised by their ceaseless commingling. There have, as it turns out, always been pigeon sellers, in every temple.[31]

No neat equation of expenditure and commodity would explain all religions or all consumer behavior. Oprah, however, emerges as the exemplar of their fusion, of the combined categorical freight of religion, spirituality, commodity, and corporatism. To study modern religion—to study the modern American economy—requires thinking of these categories as conjoined, and not distinct. Writing this resists Winfrey's own desire: Oprah sees herself as a product not of calculation but of inspiration: "I never took a business course. I run this company based on instinct. I'm an instinct player, an instinct actor—and I use it to guide me in the business."[32] Oprah dominates tabloid culture more than business reports; more magazine covers address her weight and cloth-ing than breathlessly account for her stock portfolio. This is precisely as she wants it, away from products and into people: "I've been successful all these years because I do my show with the people in mind, not for the corporations or the money."[33] Claiming that she operates with no strategy, no bureaucracy, and no spreadsheets, Oprah controls one of the most successful conglomerates in modern America.

As we will see, this anti-institutional and anti-creedal discourse sur-rounding her business acumen echoes her critiques of religious subjects. Just as she dismisses descriptions of her as a businesswoman, she also resists any attributions of herself as a leader of her own church. She eschews the category of religion, always, since to her religion represents hierarchy, rules, and male manipulation. Oprah won't let the chroniclers press her into one category or another, slinking sweetly between corpo-ration and religion, celebrity and common gal. She isn't Warren Buffet, and she isn't any demigod. She's the lemonade stand gone global.

You cannot box her because, she claims, she has not boxed herself: "People would be stunned to know how little calculation has gone into the creation of my life," she explains. "My brand developed deliber-ately by accident. . . . Just daily choosing to do what felt like the right thing to do."[34] This is the accidental deliberation seeking precision in *Oprah: The Gospel of an Icon.* This book addresses imperatives applied outside the realm of the specific tax-exempt sect, turning instead to the imperatives of comfort nestling modern women in a language of self-service. That language is the secular that Oprah creates.[35] Schol-ars define the secular as a way of conveying a condition in which the-ism is an option, rationalism is the logic, and liberation is the universal ambition. This is no slick revelatory steam engine: the secular, in such cataloging, is freighted by its own plurality. To be secular is to be con-fronted with seemingly unending difference over and against the assimi-lating forces of doctrinal religious identity.[36] Winfrey's media empire is an exposition on this religious context, an exposition on her allegedly irreligious society. Scholars of American religious history have mapped the polyglot expressions of this society, showing the gregarious religios-ity within the absence of an established faith. Historians, sociologists, and theorists of religion have filled many books with explanations for this passionate personal pluralism and public secularity, but none of them has adequately acknowledged the new forms of discourse—con-sumer, religious, celebrity, market—that have emerged in this unfocused sectarian landscape. These forms are unfamiliar to students of history and religion, as they are without bounds, without permanent structure, and without imprinted creed. These are religions without religion, faith without bounded social structure and clear membership rules. These are religions for an age in which markets make custom, consumption is the universal aspect, and celebrities are ostensible gods.

Oprah offers to us a way to see a mechanism, up close, strings demonstratively exposed, of how contemporary mass culture convinces us of its conveyances. Is it a religious culture? A consumer culture? Simmering beneath the particulars of this study is the proposition that to force a difference between the two is to compel a false distillation from a quagmire of commingling processes. These processes are partly what make the analysis of Oprah so instructive to students of late modernity. Whatever definitions of religion we develop must speak to the dynamism of the invention of religion as a category without reifying a checklist of classifications premised on a scientific posture complicit with religion's eradication. When we define religion through a list of attributes (creed, code, ritual, community) or aspects (mediated, transcendent, sacred), we demonstrate just how enfolded we've become in the supposition that we are, somehow, without it; that we are, somehow, apart from it; that we can, somehow, separate ourselves from it. Oprah is a climax of multiple intersecting histories, as well as an exemplar of many modes and manifestations of modern religion.

A certain plotline of American religions exists here, one upon which I rely even as I question its checkmate. The overarching patterns of U.S. religious history draw a picture of the past that concludes with the storied religious buffet distinguished by the plurality of option and the individual's move toward a nonsectarian identity. To turn to Oprah as a figure in that history is not to dismiss the triumph of pluralism; rather, it is to emphasize the holism in which that pluralism was, and can be, folded. As the culture wars came and went (then came and went, again), questions of ethnic, racial, or gendered identity became muddied. In the economies of popular culture to which Oprah has contributed (talk shows, women's magazines, televisions specials, musicals, and Monday night melodramas), claims of ethnic and sexual identity are not grounds for ideological formation but rather accessories to a proposed assimilation of the postmodern self.[37] This self is not a production inured of recognizable religion. "Far from being a neutral matrix," Tracy Fessenden has written, "the secular sphere as constituted in American politics, culture, and jurisprudence has long been more permeable to some religious interventions than others." A presumptive Protestantism guides this American secularity, Fessenden concludes.[38] In this, Winfrey again serves as a secular exemplar, advocating for her biographical past drenched with Protestant idiom and Christian coherence:

> By the time I was three, I was reciting speeches in the church. And they'd put me up on the program, and they would say, "and Little Mistress Winfrey will render a recitation," and I would do "Jesus rose on Easter Day, Hallelujah, Hallelujah, all the angels did proclaim." And all the sisters sitting in the front row would fan themselves and turn to my grandmother and say, "Hattie Mae, this child is gifted." . . . In the fourth grade was when I first, I think, began to believe in myself. . . . I felt I was the queen bee. I felt I could control the world. I was going to be a missionary. I was going to Costa Rica. I used to collect money on the playground to take to church on Sundays from all the other kids. At the time, in school we had devotions, and I would sit and I would listen to everything the preacher said on Sunday and go back to school on Monday morning and beg Mrs. Duncan to please let me do devotions, just sort of repeat the sermon. So, in the fourth grade, I was called "preacher."[39]

Of the many cultures that compose Oprah's personae, her Christian preamble bronzes the naming of her nonreligion religious. She is the ideal subject for her moment: palatably diverse, commensurably civilized, folksy populist, and previously Protestant.

It is perhaps not mere coincidence that such an era—the era of Oprah's ascent—includes not only processes of corporate internationalization and governmental privatization but also the ascent of the celebrity as an exchange value and of the public confession as a necessary exfoliation of celebrities' charismatic might. Oprah is all of it and none of it: celebrity and everywoman, corporate chairwoman and smart shopper, black woman and white woman, straight and queer, religious and spiritual, megachurch and shopping mall, seminarian and psychologist.[40] She was and is the amalgamation of her epoch's exposition, reducing enormous global change to one woman, with one weight problem, in one midwestern talk show studio. In order for us to understand contemporary American women and their discontents, in order for us to access the ways public religion has melded to consumer compulsion, Oprah is our optimal guide.

How, then, do we approach such an objectified Oprah? *Oprah: The Gospel of an Icon* is a study of the good news (gospel) related by a symbolic figure (icon). In the fields of religious studies and art history, the study of icons has a long history, including everything from Marian statuary to Andy Warhol's series portraiture. Icons are multivalent objects and ideas, simultaneously engendering ritual worship and being engendered by such ritual adoration. This double valence (the icon is made by the very thing it makes) invites many different sorts of scholarship, from studies of those ritual processes (ethnographies of pilgrimage, for example) to studies of iconic construction (such as iconographic readings). Oprah is an icon both because she invites ritual processes toward her and because her iconography fosters produced rituals. In order to study this synecdoche, then, we must see what it has rendered and read what it has made. Focusing solely on the last twelve seasons of Change Your Life TV, we can tally 1,560 transcripts of original episodes; 105 issues of O, The Oprah Magazine, 17 issues of (the recently defunct) O at Home; 68 Oprah's Book Club selections; 52 Spirit Newsletters; and literally hundreds of books hawked by her spiritual advisers, domestic organizers, and body therapists. In addition, there are her series of reprints (Oprah aphorisms, "What Oprah Knows for Sure" compendiums, anthologies of magazine highlights), her endorsed products, her advertising TV specials, and her films produced and endorsed. Finally, there are the thousands of newspaper clippings, magazine mentions, journal profiles, blog entries, and amateur online archives; the secondary material outweighs the primary. Reading, watching, comparing, and collating this material with an eye toward her dramatic structures—her iconography—made up the documentary effort of this study. "In the dreams of those in charge of mummifying the world," Adorno wrote, "mass culture represents a priestly hieroglyphic script which addresses its images to those who have been subjugated not in order that they might be enjoyed but only that they might be read."[41] This is a process of removing the mummy's wraps, seeking instances of discursive production, the production of power, and the propagation of knowledge.[42] The researcher, then, does the triplicate process of reading the scripts, of pressing to the ways they are marked as (in Adorno's terms) so "enjoyed."

Much of the challenge of such a work is to convey the content of the object (in this case, Oprah) in order to encourage cultural criticism from the reader as much as the author. For this reason, I have included a lot of Oprah's words in the pages that follow. I do this not only to demonstrate the nature of the icon but also to encourage a reply. If the Oprah created herein by me is not recognizable to you, then I encourage you to use this material to respond. With the productions of Oprah, how might you interpret her iconicity? This is no flippant encouragement: at stake is the interactive value of popular cultural studies. I do not own Oprah any more than any viewer or consumer of her empire does. My task, as

I saw it, was to sift through the determined contingency and incurable excess of Harpo Productions in order to find its patterns. Oprah hasn't just been consistent; she's been repetitive. This is not shocking since the nature of the corporate entity requires product control, and Oprah is the total incorporation of her totalized self. If brands were not reliable, they would not be brands; when brands evidence inconsistency the audience parries, complains, or even abandons. The success of the product relies upon its predictability. What patterns I found I documented and, with the assistance of scholarship described in the footnotes, I interpreted. But I surround these interpretations with as much of her as the page will tolerate precisely so that viewers and scholars may not only come to know what I think I have seen but also can come to decide, too, what they might see in this corporate clarity. *Oprah: The Gospel of an Icon* should not close the book on Oprah; my hope is that it will foster other readings, encouraging viewers to wonder at the repetitions they see and scholars to think about the cultures and discourses this volume parallels and explains.

By establishing a catechism from Oprah that is codified and corporate, I diminish two important aspects of her enterprise. First, Winfrey (*the* Oprah) undoubtedly opines more diversely than her empire, which assimilates her human complexity into a brand resolution. Many students of cultural history will rightly inquire about Oprah's intention and her editorial process, wondering what might be discerned from interviewing her, knowing her, inquiring about her producer's objective. Such an inquiry is understandable considering the subject herself: Oprah believes such inquiries about the authentic self are what matter. She encourages her consumers to wonder about her actuality and to consider her intentions. "I believe intention rules the world," she regularly repeats. Second, by focusing on the products of her enterprise, one might also suggest that individual practitioners are eclipsed. Her audience consumes more creatively than she produces, contradicting at times her monolithic advice. Ethnographic pursuit of Oprah's viewers would demonstrate the wide variety of experiences gleaned from her prescriptive hegemony, showing how people fit some of her counsel into their lives, redact other parts of her counsel, and dismiss altogether whole swaths of her enterprise.

Oprah: The Gospel of an Icon does not seek to reckon with Winfrey's biography, nor does it focus on the reception of her message in the pews. Such research could answer compelling questions. But these are questions already entertained abundantly by Winfrey. Wherever you turn in the world of Harpo, you will find opportunities (onstage, in articles, and on message boards) where individuals may share their experiential truth and, possibly, be selected by Harpo to include their story in Oprah's multimedia productions. Moreover, within the bookshelves devoted to religious subjects, one may find many a treatise considering the multi-faceted detail of an individual's religious imagination or a community's complex practices. On this bookshelf, and on those message boards, critical ideas are conveyed. Yet I have become increasingly concerned that in our scholarly ambition to translate our subjects—to, as the phrasing often goes, take our subjects *seriously*—we have become sycophants to our subjects, reframing every act as an inevitably creative act. Within religious studies, this has meant a diminishment of studies attempting to explain broad themes in religious history out of a fear that to do so may violate the granular greatness of any subject's contradictory expression. We have become so worried that we will contribute to the bigotry of caricature that we have become lost in pointillist profusions, dividing our material by decades, our sects by geography, and our rituals into practices. We have become Borges's cartographers, who, in their effort to map accurately the crevice of every mountain, created a map the size of the territory. No longer representative of ideas, the cartographers produced a "Map of the Empire whose size was that of the Empire," one that no longer represented digested composites, only reproduced likenesses.[43]

My tone should not be taken as condemnatory. The last decades of scholarship have included studies and monographs as diverse as its religious objects, and to speak summarily about its summaries is to repeat the very problem of caricature its production sought to combat. Moreover, with genuine empathy (and complicity) I can say that in this pursuit of particularity and creativity, we are in broad company. The combinatory discourses of secularism and consumerism are infectious, persuading modern observers to believe the relentless agency of that shower curtain or this one, that prayer shawl or this one, that worship or this one.[44] Our very cultural context—a context of which, I argue, Oprah is an icon—presses us to cajole tales of liberation from every source, from every subject, no matter the structural contours that surround, determine, and occupy that subject. It *is* the case that Oprah viewers will and do make of her what they will, responding critically and borrowing ad hoc. But we do a disservice to patterns in production and to the pervading, prescribing influence of corporate structures when we fail to account for the mass media's effect on religious life, on the ways this formats *against* improvisation. My gaze is arrested by that omnipotence more than by that idiosyncrasy, by the consistency of consumers' consumption rather than the agency of their application.

Furthermore, to study the meanings of these productions does not remove us altogether from Winfrey's pews. As each chapter will relate, because her viewers are so integral to her every ritual and gift, the celebrants of her empire cannot be excised from interpretive scrutiny. Precisely because Oprah Winfrey discursively posits and ritually incorporates carefully selected candidates from her viewing audience, the student and scholar of Oprah Winfrey's manifold productions will never be able to deny their diversity, adamancy, or critical participation. She draws these congregants with a powerful vision of who they are, a vision that returns them again and again to her gaze and their imagined and lived reciprocal, commercial relationship. Oprah needs these stories of others to validate her story; she consumes their confessions as much as they consume hers. It is the management of those stories by her, and through the formatting media of her productions, that focuses this retelling, rather than the possible "reality" of their usages of her. In the conclusion, I return again to this question and consider some cases that demonstrate the relative freedom of an Oprah consumer.

This is, therefore, not an exposé of Oprah, telling why she does what she does or whom she loves and how she loves him (or her). Instead, this is the definition of a performance ecology, one that has transformed from local chat room into a lacquered international distribution operation. The burden of this project is not to prove her weight in the world but to pursue the tactics of her production and postulate some of its consequences to the study of modern religion. As Thomas Tweed has explained, religion can no longer be seen as some static set of objects and ideas but as mobile reconfigurations by individuals also migratory in places also transient.[45] Thus, the task of the book before you is to climb through the material of Oprah's world and convey its contents despite the obvious categorical conundrums. *Oprah: The Gospel of an Icon* seeks to find religious studies' stride again within and through studies of the secular that made the "agent" its hero and "choice" its creedal cry. How, now, in these ways (monograph, media, maven) and in this time (postmodern, postsecular, postcolonial) can we speak about products and people? Such a climb will not prove Oprah's corporate intransigence but will encourage a view of its multiple consequences, real and imagined, virtual and lived, political and domestic.

In each chapter, I will examine material from Oprah's corporate production alongside comparisons with a category of religious studies analysis as well as with examples from seemingly nonreligious culture. In chapter 1, "Practicing Purchase: The Prosperity Gospel of a Spiritual Capitalism," I study the practices advocated within Winfrey's recommendations, focusing in particular on the relationship between consumer culture and prosperity gospels. In chapter 2, "Celebrity Spirit: The Incorporation of Your Best Life," I pursue the relationship between celebrity culture, contemporary evangelicalism, and discourses of spirituality. In chapter 3, "Diverting Conversions: The Makeover as Social Rite," I focus on the subject of ritual and contemplate the ways daily television shows concoct ritual productions of identity formation. In chapter 4, "Preacher Queen: The Race and Gender of America's Confessor," I consider Winfrey as an inheritor of a long line of American preaching women and analyze the correlation among her race, her preaching, and her celebration of the mother as an ideal gender type. In chapter 5, "Reading Religiously: The Reformations of Oprah's Book Club," I pursue the post-Reformation Protestant textual tradition, especially as it manifests in Bible studies and book clubs. And chapter 6, "Missionary Gift: The Globalization of Inspiration," I relate the story of the Oprah Winfrey Leadership Academy for Girls, in South Africa, to a longer trajectory of African American missions, as well as to the unfolding process of global corporate markets. In each chapter, the point is not to name Oprah a preacher or to propose that Harpo is just a missionary agent. As we will find, these categories are representative of Winfrey's Christian preamble, as well as her nation's suffused Protestantism. The analytic space is as much the distance between her practices and those categories as it is the similarities found between the two. *Oprah: The Gospel of an Icon* seeks to explode the tenuous wire between secular occupations and religious ones in order to highlight the constituent nature of each. In the epilogue, "Political Spirituality, or the Oprahfication of Obama," the domestic programs of Oprah are connected to a national political event.

To join together analogical object—like the Bible study—and the present subject—like the Oprah's Book Club—is not to make precise the comparison but to encourage viewing the religious enchantment of capital as much as the enchanting capital of religion. This is not posing historical precedents for Winfrey, nor is it a recasting of Winfrey as a secular messiah. It is to comment upon modes (styles, social groupings, conversational idioms, theological imperatives) that surpass classificatory purity as soon as they may satisfy them. Winfrey's success is not a craven remark on spirituality's successful sale, nor is it a woeful statement about the female complaint. In her narcissistic production of the inspirational moment, Winfrey posits nothing more, and nothing less, than a culmination of the religious now. It is Oprah's world. We're just buying in it, buying into it, and believing it.

CHAPTER I

Practicing Purchase

The Prosperity Gospel of a Spiritual Capitalism

The long story of free markets in the West deposits us at the door of Oprah Winfrey. Even in the face of such an anesthetizing clearing-house as Harpo, Incorporated, the nature of capitalism is too ubiquitous to say anything simple about it. Capitalism may be adjudicated on numerical grounds; it may be observed as a historical factor; it may breathe and it may beget; it may manifest and exclude; it may transfix and enchant; it may be magical, cruel, relentless, calculating, incoherent, and organizing; it may produce certain sociologies, certain anthropologies, and certain ecologies; likewise, it may be seen to have been produced by these social sciences and natural sciences; it may be gendered and racial, colonial and postcolonial, sexual and neutered; it is radical egalitarianism and imperfect hierarchy; it is the ultimate morality and the egregious immorality; it is lionized and defamed; it is liberation and it is oppression. "Capitalism—in the diverse range of needs, dependencies, affective investments, self-pathologies, and long-ings it promotes—gets personal," Joel Pfister has written.[1] Capitalism is everything even as "it" is nothing—nothing singular, at the very least. It is the condition of possessing its productions (capital); it is a position of its participants (capitalists); and it is a system that produces more of itself (capitalism). Yet this generic is inadequate to the narratives of its particular. If we are to take up the structural contours in which the empire of Oprah found its footing, then this specificity must be found and named.

To approach this modern moment, we might best narrow its capitalism to the modes of life that it produces and that produce it. The easiest way to accomplish this winnowing is to emphasize the transactional character of society. Commodities are things produced as articles of commerce. Not all objects are commodities, as the category of commodity lexically marks the difference between an object and an object as merchandise. A consumer society is one in which the commodity orients social activity. "Consumption" then categorizes the conceptualization of the purchase and use of such objects. In this rendering, capitalism is the overarching narrative process, commodity is the distinguishing designation of that process, and consumption is the framework for the experience and engagement with that history and its products. To distinguish these categories (capitalism, commodity, and consumption) so cleanly is to miss, in some vital sense, the dazzling, Technicolor mess of the whole shebang. Yet scholarship tends to huddle on the flavored dynamic of this troika, trying to determine how some commodities have surpassed others, how some strategies of consumption have displaced others, and how the methods of capitalism have pervaded the rationalizing irrationality of nation-state formation, global market saturation, and the large-scale violence of labor negotiation.

Oprah presents an instantiation of the overlapping nature of these categories. She is capitalist and capital; she is a commodity and consumer. Oprah is a product, but Oprah's product is not individual objects. Her patents are not mechanical innovations or engineering improvements. She does not design fabric or copyright personal recipes. Rather, her taste is her product.[2] Her O is what she sells. The O is her signature, her initial, and her trademark. It is a sound, a reminder of her televised exclamations: "Oh, no." "Oh, yes." "Oh, please." "Oh, I never." "Oh!" "Oh?" "Oh." Awed, orgasmic, thrilled, worried, and converted, an O is the noise of emotional presence and ready delight. Such instinctual display (what I feel right now, right here, before this new thing, new experience, or new encounter—Oh!) should not confuse the consumer with its earthy sheen. The O is never unscheduled or chaotic. It is cadence. For every girly (womanly, interviewing, ministerial, listening, awakening) "oh," there is a corporate O labeling a magazine, a book, a bracelet, or a piece of stereo equipment. The O circles her consumer selections with her emboss, bequeathing her halo upon her beloved choices.[3] The O envelops the commodities that she has chosen expressly for herself and, now, expressly for you. She is a pitchwoman of her own consumption; her consumption is her commodity.

As the charismatic entrepreneur of her consumer choices, Oprah may seem to embody the enemy of the ascetic Protestants cast in Max Weber's *The Protestant Ethic and the Spirit of Capitalism* (1904–5). Cashmere-coated and ribbon-ringed, the *O* frames a quality of abundance that Weber named as oppositional to the appearance-of-saintly-restraint component of Calvinist bourgeois business acumen. "As long as his moral conduct was spotless and the use to which he put his wealth was not objectionable," Weber wrote of that ideal Protestant worker, this man "could follow his pecuniary interests as he would and feel that he was fulfilling a duty in doing so."[4] Protestants can, unlike their posited religious forerunners, contribute centrally to the new capitalism. They can make money and, according to Weber, they have made it incredibly well. But the manner in which it has been made and spent has determined the sanctification of the buyer (and the producer's) spirit. "Man is only a trustee of the goods which have come to him through God's grace" is a description of the limited array of goods that should come, not an endorsement of every graceful cup, chair, or pen.[5] Weber argued that certain stripes of Protestantism have provided spiritual agency to the Western rationalization of capitalism, yet he, and his elected Calvinists, were clear: those stripes are not to be bedazzled.

If Weber's version of capital practices required faithful capitalist labor by ascetic Protestants with limited possessions, Winfrey's revision reclaims those abandoned possessions from the condemnation by Protestant reformers. Scholars have differentiated between charismatic capitalism, a capitalism that sells itself through the autonomy of direct solicitation, and millennial capitalism. Charismatic capitalism is driven by the image and reality of door-to-door persuasions, whereas millennial capitalism presents itself as a "gospel of salvation" that supersedes any storefront operator to become itself a discourse of possibility.[6] On *The Oprah Winfrey Show* and in *O, The Oprah Magazine*, a combination of the two succeeds, as a singular door-to-door, page-to-page, day-to-day peddler finds her voice in a regular dispersal of a good news materialism. In Winfrey's capitalist modernity, this materiality is a *spiritual* practice. Since spirit is deployed abundantly and to great affirming gusto by Harpo, it receives its own specific attention in a later chapter. For this perusal of practices and purchasing, "the spiritual" will be deployed in the sense used by Winfrey herself, namely, that for Oprah the spiritual is uninhibited ineffability. Spirituality is the application of this ineffable pursuit of revelation, of the divine, and of your authentic Best Life through regimens of practice. That these practices are largely oriented around consumption should not be seen as hypocrisy. Spiritual capitalism is a redundancy, not an irony of history. Oprah is a component of the persistent spirituality of capital and not a spiritual mountebank in an imagined secular capitalism.

In the world of this *O*, little practices are little pleasures that garner direct, material connection to your spirit. "A strong cup of coffee . . . going for a walk through the woods with all five dogs unleashed . . . working out . . . sitting under my oaks, reading the Sunday papers . . . hanging out at Quincy Jones' kitchen table, talking about everything and nuthin'," these are the practices of celebrity consumption and self-servicing pleasure that Winfrey regularly relates to her audience. "The enjoyment comes from knowing the receiver understands the spirit of the gift."[7] Winfrey's gift giving dominates her enterprise, so much so that every chapter of *Oprah: The Gospel of an Icon* narrates a genre of gift encircled by Winfrey's *O*. Distribution and the celebration of the distributive act are difficult to divide in Winfrey's world. But in this she is not alone. To divide advertisement from entertainment was never a clean classificatory effort, all the less now, as the development of commodity image is requisite for everything from novels to starlets to new vacuum cleaners. Infomercials are increasingly hard to differentiate from prime time television programming. Celebrities are indistinguishable from corporate brands. Product placements drive fictional televised plots. The line between cultural consumption and consumer culture is seemingly impossible to draw.[8]

What separates Winfrey's work is the soul-salving signification attached to her recommendations. Much of her persistence has been premised on the unaffected joy she takes in fusing her charisma with a product's image and with connecting the message of her show to the slogan of a new brand. Her real-time economic consequences have produced a market result, as financial observers named an "Oprah Effect" to describe the market upswing resultant from any Winfrey endorsement. She recommends so that you too may consume, so that you too may share in the decadence of her self-celebrating life. Show formats ("Oprah's Favorite Things," "Transform Your Closet," "Instant Room Makeovers") and columns in her magazine and segments of her Web site ("Food and Home," "Mind and Body") recommend countless objects, from lipsticks to tank tops, honey to books, pens to sedans, computers to butter trays. These holiday and springtime Favorite Things bonanzas distribute to audience members "all the things I love to give and receive." This gifting has biographic origins preceding her fortunate financial position. "Since I was a kid," Winfrey explains, "since I was like bare foot on a red dirt road in Mississippi whatever I had always felt better to me if I could share it with someone else."[9]

This is the differentiating mark of Winfrey's parceling process. She gives not just to display the gifted product but also to encourage other practices of self-appreciation. She gives to remind her selected viewers that their spiritual election correlates to their donating abilities. The right goods, according to Winfrey's advocacy, encourage self-indulgence and relaxed reflection among individuals who spend too much time on others, not enough on themselves. This is how products become practices in the land of O. Every product of Winfrey's empire combines spiritual counsel with practical encouragement, inner awakening with capitalist pragmatism. Although in this chapter the practices of purchasing, buying, and shopping will be emphasized, the enjoinder to practice—practice anything collaborative with her middlebrow ambitions—covers a far wider swath of habits. "Behave your way to success" is one of the oft-repeated maxims recited by Oprah Winfrey and her cohort of guest psychologists, columnists, and spiritual gurus. Any study of the products of Harpo, Inc., reveals that prescriptive behavior dominates the substance of Winfrey's message. "Live Your Best Life" columnist and meditation teacher Sharon Salzberg wrote in O, The Oprah Magazine, "To be able to make an intense effort—to heal, to speak, to create, to alleviate our suffering or the suffering of others—while guided by a vision of life with all its mutability, evanescence, dislocations, and unruliness, is the particular gift of faith."[10] Viewers and readers are told to follow slogans that instruct them to "make the connection" and "get with the program" in an effort to "change your life" or "live your best life." Such connections are made, programs are designed, and lives are changed through Oprah's multimedia advocacy of specified, routine practices.

After watching an episode of *The Oprah Winfrey Show,* leafing through the magazine, or scanning the official Web site, one finds it imperative to *do* something. Inevitably, the stories of triumph make you wonder why you haven't; the endless precise advocacies (eat breakfast, spot prevaricators, write more letters, choose a better dentist, employ more flora as a decorating strategy) and psychological counsel (discover your relationship sin, reconcile with your estranged relative, find your dream, love realistically, work passionately) make you decide to vow to do something—even if its something small—somehow better.

For example, saying "thank you" becomes, in the world of Oprah Winfrey, not an act of reciprocal etiquette but a demonstration of communion, a gift to someone you love. "I am Miss Gratitude. I preach gratitude, I live gratitude, I am gratitude, I am Oprah 'Gratitude' Winfrey," she comments.[11] Gratitude doubles as a practice of healing *and* a practice of purchase. Responding to a New York City police officer who was at Ground Zero, Winfrey offered a gift: "When we heard that you were writing in your gratitude journal at Ground Zero, I wanted to give you this. This is my favorite writing journal that I created for myself. And this is one of my favorite pens from Rebecca Moss, that store that carries beautiful pens."[12] Closing with a recommendation of Sarah Ban Breathnach's *Simple Abundance,* Winfrey binds it all together: "We see how we're all connected." The connection emerges from the fusion of genteel revival (say "thank you" more), regular practice (record your gratitude daily), and purchased garnish (these fine pens, those better notebooks). The product is a practice, and her practice is her product.

Winfrey's voice pervades throughout these instructions, modeling her suggestions through the order of her singular life. It is her face peering from the corner of every Web page, from the cover of every magazine, and from the center of every television screen. This cajoling omnipresence reminds the viewer that the teleology of these practices is no abstraction; the end is in her. She is the paradigmatic result of her prescriptions: it is her body, her business, her couture closet, her favorite novel, and her latest breakfast marmalade that stand as the ideal demonstrations of the successful enactment of her advice. The message is made manifest in each of her media modes: here's what to do; here's some sage testimony as to the utility of your newly chosen habit; here's where to go to get it done; and here are some smart products to assist and decorate your process of self-realization. And in case you don't remember all Winfrey has told you to do, she provides three modes of reminder (televised, print, and Internet). The point of this media assault is clear. Don't just watch, *do.* This advocacy of action replies to the practical attentions of her viewers, since they turned to her in the beginning for some story, some answer, and some commiserating community that their own lives had not yet found. The products of her empire are the trail pointing her audience to the correct path back to *her* success.

Not only does Oprah programming incorporate an avalanche of practical encouragement, but her episodes and articles also serve as paradigmatic articulations of the spiritual practice of a capitalism simultaneously millennial, charismatic, and relentlessly quotidian. By leaning so heavily on a reading of Winfrey's consumer injunctions, I may seem to offer an undifferentiated materialist critique of her enterprise. Yet the supposition of her encouragements is never merely to acquire but also to transform. "If it is true that the grid of 'discipline' is everywhere becoming clearer and more extensive," Michel de Certeau has explained, "it is all the more urgent to discover how an entire society resists being reduced to it."[13] Gathering the prescriptions of Oprah points us to those moments in which ideology feeds action, in which her rhetoric of change might manifest in individual lives.

O, The Oprah Magazine is the how-to manual for these prescriptions, with every page singing a song of revolutionary self-improvement, first-person fable, and consumer choice. The magazine arrived deep into Winfrey's reign, in 2000. "Why do I need a magazine?" Oprah relates later, recalling her conversation with Hearst Magazines. "I already have a full-time job that speaks to women all over the world." In response, Winfrey reported that the editor-in-chief of Good Housekeeping cited the permanence of the written form: "The written word is lasting, and women pass it on."[14] In 1999, Hearst representatives flew to Chicago "armed with three sample tables of contents, a book of page layouts and a self-shot video of women on the street professing their desire for an 'Oprah' they could hold in their hands and keep." One Hearst representative later recalled, "We knew we had to engage her in a mission, not just a magazine." They even had a name for the new product: Oprah's Spirit. Winfrey hated it. "The word 'spirit' was too loaded," she explained.[15] Less loaded was her O, offering iconic assurance without assigning some obvious spiritual essence: O, The Oprah Magazine. Nonetheless, her spirit suffused the magazine from the outset, as it exhibited Winfrey's taste and energy, as an extension of "her self service to the world." "Oprah has never been content with mere voyeurism," one Time reporter explained. "O is also a workbook wherein you can apply what you learn."[16] The first editor of O agreed, describing the magazine as a "personal-growth guide for the next century—almost a workbook." Winfrey concurs, repeatedly referring to the material in the magazine as a textual translation of items treated briefly on the show and as a detailed exegesis on modern women's lives. "It's the book I never wrote," she would say.[17]

It may be tempting to toss Oprah Winfrey's multimedia expansion into the pile of contemporary lifestyle outlets, including magazines like Real Simple, channels like the Food Network, and stores like Pottery Barn and Metropolitan. Those businesses share Winfrey's knack for affiliating individual products with holistic lifestyle fantasies, but they do not offer the same spiritual injunction to consume. Spirit ambition suffuses every consumer practice. For example, if you have trouble find-ing ways to schedule your personal revolution, each issue of O magazine includes a calendar. Such a document should be familiar to anyone who has picked up a contemporary magazine named for an iconic female. Rosie O'Donnell and Martha Stewart also opened their eponymous magazines with similar schedules of daily aspiration. Whereas Stewart emphasizes the right day to tend perennials or varnish porch chairs, and O'Donnell satirized the genre, Winfrey uses the calendar as a framework for enacting her message in coherent steps.[18] Approximately half of the days of any given month include either inspirational quotations or pre-scriptive counsel. In the latter category, one might find suggestions about the formation of a support group, or a topic to focus on during medita-tion, or an idea for extending your generosity into the world. On July 28, 2002, the reader is told, "Dare to go out alone (and enjoy it). Start with a play or concert; work up to a dance club or singles bar. After that, who knows?"[19] On June 26, 2002: "It's a privilege to hear someone's confidences. Practice 'open' listening, without interrupting or passing judgment."[20] The calendar is a map of suggested practices, littered with details about the precise, minor ways that women can order their time more around themselves and their goals than around merely servicing those who surround them. There is even a dotted line with a scissors icon on these monthly maps—a place for readers to cut it away from the mag-azine and post it on a refrigerator. The days of the calendar are prayer beads for Oprah, with each day offering the possibility of difference.

Throughout this book, I will take up different sections of this maga-zine as they pertain to different aspects of the modern religious spec-trum. For us to consider her spiritual capitalism, however, one section requires special highlight. Every O magazine includes "The O List," a three-page assemblage of a "few things" that Oprah thinks are "just great." Every object posted on the list is accompanied by photo and short quote, ostensibly straight from Oprah, describing the highlights of the product and, frequently, a recommendation of the ideal way to use it. All of the actions proposed alongside objects on "The O List" correspond to propositions of self-discovery, self-indulgence, and the set-up of an ideally accessorized moment. Deluxe footwear appears near-monthly on the list, often with an assignment of when to wear the never-sensible selections, like Spa Fleurs sandals, so "you can breeze out of the salon without that extra hour of nail drying," or the Nike Kyoto sneakers, which are "great for peaceful walks to and from yoga sessions." Winfrey culls her selections from the distributing company's broader array, choosing the toile-print loafers ($99) from the canvas Chou Chou selections and the patriotic red, white, and blue Manolo Blahnik sandals ($465) from among the many other Manolo sandal options.[21] Through this representation of one from the possible many, O conveys the exclusivity of a list that could only be Oprah's: she has decided, for herself, what looks good for her. It's up to you to decide if her choice is a look you want to emulate. The presumption of the sale, as well as its success, is that you do want to, that you don't just copy, but that you partake not only of the footwear purchase but also of the pedicure that preceded your breezing exit from the salon.[22]

O emulation doesn't end at her feet. "The O List" conveys more than clothing, including in its luxury sampler linen-covered journals, jasmine candles, brightly colored umbrellas, and cellulose towels. Gourmet snacks (cheese, olive oil, olive oil potato chips, dried-fruit boxes, cinnamon-walnut coffee cake, key lime pie, caramels, thin crust black truffle pizza, whoopee pies) and tea time accoutrement (water kettles, thermoses, demitasse cups, black button sage honey) suggest that meal staples are satisfied, leaving the luxuriating lady available to consider the perfect break buffet. Reading the list suggests that living like Oprah involves a lot of delicious repose, repose with dogs (collapsible water-and-food bowl, wireless mike dog collar, wood stand with double ceramic food bowls) and repose with electronics (video cameras, portable DVD players, cordless phones, wireless phones, universal remotes, battery rechargers).[23] It also suggests that many other goods are lying about, goods designed for containment. Terracotta olive trays, metal cutlery caddies, designer leather luggage tags, sunglasses holders, eyeglasses coasters ("for a person who has every *other* thing"), MP3 player cases, embossed leather tampon cases, and firewood bags celebrate the showcasing of the casing.[24] Indeed, containers—from carafes and decanters, plates and nesting trays, cruets and champagne flutes—occupy a controlling share of the list, more than even lotions and soaps. This is especially true if you include handbags, which, like footwear, make a monthly appearance, including a Kate Spade tool bag ($200), a Versace sunflower tote, leather duffel bags ($495), nylon and leather holiday bags ($790), and a Tod's orange leather bag ($1,100).[25] The existence of potential containment encourages the purchase of products to properly fill the space temptingly glamorized. If you have the container, the contained will come. Related to this is the array of *Oprah* show episodes devoted to decluttering the space and razing the homes of hoarders. Careful containment is a sign of an ordered mind, whereas an excess of unsequestered objects suggests a mental morass. You need these containers to contain not only your goods but also your domestic and relational wellness.

Nothing in the world of O is ever about merely framing or containing the good, however. It is also always about betterment *through* the frame, the improvement of the interior through exterior reformations. So, if you decide to pursue the September 23, 2002, O magazine monthly calendar recommendation to "create a notebook labeled Big Dreams. Give each dream its own page and action plan. Every day take a step toward realizing one of your dreams. Track your progress," you will need a notebook to complete this recommendation.[26] Of course, you could use a ninety-nine-cent Mead notebook. However, should you want to feel the dream as you draft it, you may want to splurge on the practice. Check out the August 2002 "O List," which includes just the right "launch pad" for such a journal: alligator-embossed leather notepads with interchangeable pewter snaps, twenty-eight and fifty-four dollars. "These were a gift from my pal Robin McGraw," Oprah writes. "The small one is just right for jotting notes, the big one for jotting dreams."[27] Now you need a pen for jotting. In January 2002 Oprah recommends a stationery set for thirty dollars that includes a mock quill pen: "Who knew stationary could be so sensual?" reads the accompanying quote. "Each sheet of paper is handmade, and the quill pen somehow makes writing more interesting."[28] Every object is listed with its price, as well as the toll-free telephone number or Web site for the business that sells the good. Buying is not a mandated practice but a suggested accompaniment to your overall practice of self-indulgence. "You owe it to everyone you love (including yourself) to find pockets of tranquility in your busy world," reads Oprah's introductory comments to her October 2002 issue.[29] Purchasing O-endorsed products is one way both to legitimate independent time (goods must be bought to tend the home) and to construct a situation of comfort in your leisure (you deserve a home as loving as you).

It would be inaccurate to elect O magazine as singular in its production of enjoined consumption. Hearst Magazines produces several volumes sharing proximate interests to O (including *Cosmopolitan, Good Housekeeping, Redbook,* and *Town & Country*), and bookstores frequently shelve O nearby *Real Simple* and *Martha Stewart Living* as analogous lifestyle publications. Pausing briefly to compare these publications will show the topical overlap and affective differences that emphasize O's market share. Consider, then, a set of these magazines, all issued the same month (January 2009). Sex and working-girl sass climax in *Cosmopolitan,* the magazine for the single set, offering the "Fun Fearless Female" monthly sections like the Man Manual (e.g., "How I Got Him to . . .") and the monthly report in "Fun Fearless Fashion" ("Get Sexy Cleavage").[30] The single gal's desires are preserved and revived in the more mature and domesticated *Redbook,* which neatens the avenues of a mother's life into four sectional attributes: Your Pretty Life ("Mega-Moisturizers"), Your Healthy Life ("No-Workout Weight Loss"), Your Love Life ("How to Have Just-Met Sex"), and Your Home Life ("pantry" meals, "quick and easy coq au vin").[31] As purveyor of its own seal of approval, *Good Housekeeping* has, over the last decade, experienced a glamorizing makeover. The presumed *Good Housekeeping* reader is exhausted, deep in playroom messes and den difficulties, seeking easy hints to solve the solvable problems of mothering and home management, from responding to messy beds to designing "pretty pomegranate centerpieces." "Why water is a dieting Do" and "nondrying dish soap" indicate the readers' focus and worries, as does the "subject-by-subject guide to this issue," organizing topics under categories of beauty and skin care, celebrities, cleaning and organizing, decorating and crafts, diet and exercise, fashion, food and nutrition, testing and tips, giveaways, good reads, health and wellness, parenting, psychology, recipes, saving money, and tech.[32] These categories not only list an index but also present a commanding profile in the presumptive mother's self-expectation.

If *Good Housekeeping* salves the spastic midcentury matriarch, then *Real Simple* soothes the aspirant cool-headed postmodern queen. It's all about "simple" rendered in primary colors, Scandinavian lines, and containers for every conceivable paper you have to sort. *Cosmopolitan*'s lexicon seeks to shake, rattle, and roll, deploying the word *sizzle* as much as possible. *Good Housekeeping* supplies emotional commiseration ("could work for you," "your family will love," "think yourself happier"). But *Real Simple* makes it all a matter of numbers, nominating "seventeen fresh beauty essentials," "twenty-five annual home-maintenance suggestions," and "five easy dinners" among the many recent interventions. If it can't be counted off, if it is not easy, if it's not neat, if it's not saving you something for something else, *Real Simple* says, "Why on earth would you do it?" Simplify, save, find time, and discover "new uses for everyday things."[33] *Town & Country* cools the anxious, task-oriented dial, offering fewer Hearst hues of fuchsia and teal and more deep sea blues rimming discussions of large game painters, exclusive fashion, apartment design, and society weddings. *Town & Country* is a guidebook to genteel taste more than a handbook to female survival.[34]

Martha Stewart Living blends this *Town & Country* class with *Good Housekeeping* specificity and *Real Simple* cleanliness with *Bon Appétit* detail. There are the predictable closet organizing strategies and multiple uses for citrus, but the Martha twist is ratcheting up the self-made woman to accomplish new heights of domestic capability in the era of her greatest emancipation. If viewers watch Oprah for ritual healing about the situations of their lives, readers turn to Martha for the ingredients of the crafts in their lives.[35] "Although they require little more than sugar and egg whites," readers learn from Martha, "ethereal meringues have always had the power to enchant." All of it is made first by Martha, just as all in Harpo's world was consumed first by Oprah. "Martha prepares marmalades made with a variety of citrus," we learn; "Martha's fitness and beauty routines address all aspects of health, inside and out." Psychological self-understanding is closeted for someplace else, somewhere else.[36] The Martha reader arrives, like Martha, ready to make, to run, to breed, or to grow. She does not need to think about the *why* of her making, just that it is delightful to do so, with care, with tools rightly selected, and with the appearance of khaki-pants ease: "Making cache-pots from pumpkins for Thanksgiving, sewing button holes into linen napkins, turning staircase balusters into candlesticks, growing and drying herbs, and laying dinner-party tables with individual place cards drawn from the clip art on the Martha Web site, Stewart—cool, blonde, poised, and efficient—offered a vision of a light, bright, spacious home where there was a place for everything and everything was in its place."[37]

Martha and Oprah frequently find themselves in the same comparative breath, even as their shared commitment to domestic counsel stops short of a strong similarity.[38] "Martha is about what you can have, and Oprah is about who you can be, and there is the difference," remarked one *Oprah* show viewer.[39] Martha is a charismatic capitalist of the highest order, soliciting every viewer to participate in the same pleasures that she takes from her do-it-yourself production. Yet Martha's capitalist practice has none of Winfrey's good news, none of the millennial prospect of self-transformation: "*O* is a glossy rendering of Winfrey's on-air motivational crusade, encouraging readers to revamp their souls the way Martha Stewart helps them revamp their kitchens."[40] Martha develops product lines to fill your life with beauty and order, and Oprah selects products to remind you of *your* beauty and *your* order. In Martha's world, these products and their correlating task assignments may be therapy, but therapy is not the prescriptive underpinning to task.

This race through contemporary magazine culture emphasizes the gender location (married, heterosexual, parenting) and psychological condition (needful, anxious, dissatisfied) of the postulated readership. Many signifiers might be taken to summarize this array, but spotlighted clothing reifies the price point and customer base of each publication. *Cosmopolitan* hawks "7 Boyfriend Looks to Borrow—Rock these sexy guy styles (no walk of shame required)." *Redbook* reveals "what we found at . . . L.L. Bean" with its "well-priced preppy pieces that scream 'winter weekend.'" *Good Housekeeping* sells sweater coats: "these bathrobe-comfy dusters flatter when they're slouchy but not sloppy (avoid angle lengths and chunky cables)." *Town & Country* advocates "a rainbow-hued selection of the season's best resort wear," *Real Simple* suggests "flattering pieces for your shape," and *Martha Stewart Living* describes "stylish knitting projects" to make "winter woolies" like mittens to "suit the wearer."[41] Sexy boyfriend jeans, L.L. Bean winter weekends, slouchy sweater coats, resort watches, homemade gloves, and skirts for bodies of every shape: the clothes stand in for selves, for sensual mornings-after and weekday carpools; Sunday family brunches and women alone, working on their knitted love. "Magazines . . . provide a fairly predictable emotional formula," writes one scholar of magazine literatures, "a balance between the fostering of anxiety that draws readers to seek out advice and the offering of positive messages that encourage them to return the following month."[42]

For *O,* the encouraged return is the persistent pursuit of personal growth as a transcendent possibility. The January 2009 *O* fashion recommendation does not suggest a single type of clothing (sweater), a location for clothing (resort), a sensible brand (L.L. Bean), a mode of production (knitting), or a relational result (boyfriend thievery). Rather, the *O* recommendation is an emotional transaction with a problematic type. "Things are looking up in the world of fashion," *O* proclaims. "Meet five women 5'10" and taller who love every inch of themselves and dress with incredible confidence."[43] The *O* difference is a consumption swathed with her application, her need, for the best individual (quirky, too tall, smartly confident) self.

Consumption threads this wave of contemporary magazines into one expression of what many have referred to as a late-twentieth-century New Gilded Age, with reference to the nineteenth-century apex of late industrial expansion and individual acquisition. The "gild" suggested in part the Beaux Arts architectural idiom and the doily décor contained within the ornate homes of the nouveau riche. On the heels of the turn from the nineteenth to the twentieth century, economist Thorstein Veblen defined "conspicuous consumption" in *Theory of the Leisure Class* (1899) to describe the urge to demonstrate status through personal expenditure. "That social emulation expressed through extravagant personal display—not the purely rational economic motive to enrich oneself—motivated all social classes within the capitalist society of the Gilded Age to aspire to the standards set by the elite."[44] That Gilded Age included the celebration of singularly displayed objects in ethnology museums, department stores, world's fairs, and local color fictions, each of which attributed to goods a sort of "animism." And this "animation of material objects makes it seem as though there is something hidden within them."[45] Hidden within them was a class accomplishment, a moral suasion, and, in later years, a certain sort of citizenship.

Fast forward to the later twentieth century, and you find historian Lizabeth Cohen arguing that the nation has become overrun by this model of citizenship. It is now a Consumerized Republic, she proclaims, where "self-interested citizens increasingly view government policies like other market transactions, judging them by how well served they feel personally."[46] Consumption in this valence offers "more social egalitarianism, more democratic participation, and more political freedom." It can provide jobs and supply purchasing power all while "allowing Americans . . . to exercise their cherished freedoms by making independent choices in market and politics."[47] To be sure, a host of treatises, such as Robert Frank's *Luxury Fever* (2000), argue that our consumerist culture creates an unquenchable thirst for more things, driving the middle class into deep debt and dark spiritual terrain. But in the women's magazines studied above, consumption was and is an articulation of female freedom, of the possibility of ceaseless self-making amid the disappointing travails of social circumstance and domestic failure. No matter the market changes, no matter the spousal disappointments, the shop window remains open and available, inviting a girl to be free.

Advertising the thing—from wall paint to bedding to boyfriend's Oxford shirt—grounds the Oprah consumer exhibition. "The tale of possessions—of being possessed by possessions—is something stranger than the history of a culture of consumption," Bill Brown writes.[48] Scholars of marketing often separate magazine content pages from advertising pages, using the latter to construct a profile in market share.

Every page of every magazine is component to a comprehensive marketing plan. Picking up any magazine, you find it impossible to evade the overlap of advertised products and editorial content. What is an article? What is an ad? What is O apart from her list? Women on a nighttime doctor's drama dance drunkenly to the latest pop single; men on a sitcom joke about shaving mishaps with old-fashioned straight razors; children play coolly with new dolls amid soap opera din. And these manifold advertisements for the bonding reverie, for male beauty, for the more peaceful parenting life do not lack for spiritual meaning, either in the descriptions of advertising historians or in the spirit flavoring of Winfrey's world. "Through advertising and the interactions of the modern consuming crowd," Gary Cross argues, "products . . . assumed 'spiritual' roles."[49] The contentment the product brings is in no small way connected to its sale, to the conveyance of the product by a particular salesman, be she an actor, a homemaking Connecticut doyenne, or a Chicago maven. In his history of advertising, Jackson Lears writes, "Like the traditional conjurer multiplying rabbits, doves, or scarves, the peddler opened his pack and presented a startling vision of abundance." Lears suggested that this "emissary of the miraculous" was particularly adept at influencing women.[50] These travelers knew who ran the home and just what messages would compel them to buy. As one such emissary relates through therapeutic dialogue:

Gary Zukav: Do you like yourself?

Winfrey: I don't just like me. I adore me.

Zukav: What do you adore the most?

Winfrey: I adore that I feel a connection to other people that really makes me feel like a part of something that is bigger than myself. . . . And I adore that I have a great generous spirit. That's the best thing about me. Everything I get, gets better when I share it and I know it does. The moon over the water the other night was glorious. It lit the whole ocean. I called everybody. "You gotta see the moon. Have you seen the moon? Go out right now and look at it." Last week I found some slippers that felt wonderful, so I bought them for all the women in the control room at the studio.[51]

The particular sale of our particular subject, Oprah, is undeniably female. If "the thing seems to name the object just as it is even as it names some thing else," that something else is, in Winfrey's empire, a promise of female care in an uncaring world, slippers and moonshine against grimness and sore feet.[52] In his definition of "invidious comparison,"

Thorstein Veblen warned of the gratification that comes from the price of an object, of what he referred to as "costliness masquerading under the name of beauty."[53] As Winfrey selects objects for others, she endows their gathering as a moral venture, one knit with "something bigger" than herself. Purchasing objects thus becomes feminist practice.

"Advertisement endowed goods with a language of their own, a language of promise radically new in the history of man-made things," Alan Trachtenberg wrote. "If the advertisement aimed to make consumption of a particular product habitual, it also aimed to make habitual the identification of products with something else, with ideas, feelings, status."[54] In Winfrey's idiom, the difference between habitual consumption and the identification of products with "something else" is the difference between the gerunds *buying* and *shopping*. If buying is to gain possession of something by giving an equivalent value, shopping is a locality for this purchase process. "Shopping is different than buying . . . by the time we've actually exchanged money for something, we have already begun to possess it—examining, touching, thinking about what we'll do with it. . . . Shopping is a way of examining the world," O magazine encourages its readers. "If variety is the spice of life, shopping provides it . . . the best kind of shopping is as delicious and satisfying as love, and like love, it has less to do with *having* (and accumulating) than with thoughtful appreciation and delight."[55] Again, recasting the process of consumption as a moral imperative ("shopping provides it") and an emotional expenditure ("like love"), Oprah prescribes a capitalism that is more than millennial and more than charismatic.

Women are told to buy and save, accessorize and restrain. They are told that their purchasing power is correlated to their moral merit. Individual shopping choices offer moments of possible piety: "Our simplest shopping decisions can protect the environment, save family farms, lift villages from destitution, and restore dignity to war-torn communities."[56] Consumption is advised to be controlled, but the borders of that control are unclear. Hoarders are worrisome, fashionably dressed women are not; control freaks need treatment, but clean freaks do not. The difference between the practices that constitute the two is a gray area in Harpo productions. "Whether you're in the market for a credit card, a doctor, a piece of art, a car that won't drive you into bankruptcy, or phone service that won't drive you crazy," the editorial staff of O writes, "O's experts steer you right." This steerage contains command forms aplenty: "don't choose a lousy plan"; "ask friends"; "avoid roaming charges"; "read the fine print"; visit, go, send, start, make, wear, consider, check out, find out, shop for, shop for, shop for.[57] Shopping savvy involves more than quick glances at store windows. It is a major aspect of the daily rounds, an integral component of living your Best Life. "We're on the mission in search of the very best," Winfrey declared at the outset of an episode, "Only the Best," which included the pursuit of the best peanut butter, stain remover, macaroni and cheese, pie, TiVo, diamonds, and small luxury automobiles.[58] As with the exhibiting challenge of "The O List," such episodes only magnify the products to reify the world of practices that enshrine the ideal object and its ideal setting in your potentially ideal life. Even the insistent practice of thrift in O and on the *Oprah* show does not restrict consumers, ascribing them instead a creativity of practice compelling further expenditure. "Being thrifty is an art form," one columnist explains. "Making do takes ingenuity. . . . Being thrifty never means sacrificing taste."[59]

Oprah viewers are presumed members of the ever-amorphous American middle class, a class defined by its unending desire for goods that authenticate their class position. The costs of careless shopping pockmark Winfrey's money makeover episodes, helmed largely by her primary financial adviser, Suze Orman, author of *The Courage to Be Rich: Creating a Life of Material and Spiritual Abundance* (1999). Although Orman's consultancy will be explored further later in this volume, here it is pertinent to note the way even financial recovery from the brink of bankruptcy is framed as a product. "Stay a Step Ahead: Meet Four Real Women Who Achieved Fiscal Fitness," advertises one January 2009 four-page spread "brought to you by Chase." Chase—as a bank, a credit card, and a financial counselor—resolves financial trouble in part by reinstating its central position in the life of consumers. This corporate collaboration ("visit Oprah.com/chase for the resources and inspiration to help you embark on your own financial makeover") simultaneously sells Chase, sells Oprah, sells Orman, and sells the wise liberation of women unafraid of facing their financial problems, corporate logos in tow. Through the production of this spiritual capitalism, Oprah is not simply hawking a self-satisfying shopper's possibility. She manifests also the American market ideal. What else defines the American middle class than the desire to simultaneously maintain, exhibit, and advance within their caste? In her show, Oprah speaks directly to middle-class anxiety, by offering suggestions on how to keep up class occupation ("welcome financial adviser Suzy Orman!"), show it off (Winfrey suggests that the best hostess gift is *At Home with Carolyn Roehm*, sixty dollars), and move on up (advice from career planner Ronna Lichtenberg: "Dress for the job you want, not the job you have!"). Everything about the Oprah spiritual project requires a delight in luxury and an aspiration to material prosperity.

Oprah's encouraged practices of consumption are not only intended to improve an aesthetic or to perfect social position but also are means to change the experience of living for her viewers. The practice of buying feeds internal and external change for such women, dressing and surrounding them with a material beauty that should be reflected in their spiritual interior. Through the whole practical promotion, Winfrey stands as the shopping ideal in practice and pocketbook. "I feel blessed to be in the unbelievable position of being able to buy anything, *anything* I want," and yet: .

> I still think twice before I buy anything. How will this fit in with what I already have? Am I just caught up in the moment? Can it be of real use to me or is it just something beautiful to have (which, if one can afford it, is a very legitimate reason)? I *loooove* beautiful things. Last month I was in an antiques store and the dealer was showing me a gorgeous 18th-century dressing table with mirrors and hidden drawers. . . . But as I stood pondering whether to purchase it, I said to the guy, "You're right, it's beautiful and I've never seen one quite like it, but I don't really need a dressing table with all that razzle-dazzle." He took a pretentious breath and replied, "Madam, no one buys anything here because of their needs—these are treasures to be enjoyed." Indeed. Well, let me get down to the "needs" store, I thought, because what I'm really looking for are fireplace utensils. Not only did I not need a dressing table, I hadn't the space for it. But Mr. Dealer had a point. Some things are just to be treasured and enjoyed. And I know for sure that you enjoy everything a lot more when you're not overreaching. This is how you know you've shopped smart: You bring home a purchase and there's not a tinge of remorse, and whatever you got feels better to you ten days later than it did when you first bought it.[60]

Winfrey promotes individuality and creativity while affirming the necessity of treasures that are "to be enjoyed," that will, ultimately, make you feel better than you did before you had them. There are pretentious sorts who believe in beauty for beauty's sake; Winfrey dismisses such snobs (even as she buys their wares, repeats their taste) and promotes beauty for self's sake. "On a good day, shopping can be glorious—the thrill of the hunt, the triumphant score (fabulous shoes! in your size! on sale!)," describes one O magazine writer. "On a bad day, there's nothing like a cruelly lit fitting room or a hit of sticker shock to make you feel fat, old, anxious, and broke."[61] Being pretty, feeling thin, standing under right lights, American women can stand back and feel the glory of transient consumer power, swathed in objects made priceless by their self-celebratory acquisition.

The *O* purchasing climax is, then, the opening of the Oprah Store in 2008. The Chicago store invites shoppers to select from nine hundred Oprah-selected products "that reflect her consuming interests."[62] In her online tour of the Oprah Store, Winfrey explains some of the decorative choices: "When you come to shop, I also want you to feel inspired as you leave, so we call this the inspiration wall. Everything you'll see here has a quote from my 'What I Know for Sure' columns in *O* magazine." Like the ex-voto wall at a shrine, the "inspiration wall" reveals the prayers of the supplicants, named by Oprah on their imagined behalf. Quotations like "Always lead with the truth," "Love what you've got," "Live your own dreams," and "Become more of yourself" swirl around store areas devoted to workout clothes, pajamas, men's clothing, *Oprah* show souvenirs, and *O* baby paraphernalia. Along one wall is a reliquary showcasing Winfrey's outfits, Oprah's Closet: "This is the closest most humans will ever get to Oprah Winfrey."[63] Never far from the sight of the customer is that niggling *O*, the one that offers more than any circle, ever. "Now, this section of the store is very dear to my heart. . . . Proceeds from all these items with the Oprah Winfrey Leadership Academy logo will go toward the education of my girls," her voiceover deepens the emboss. "When you wear this logo, you are literally helping me realize a dream of limitless possibilities for all the girls. It's a cool logo too."[64] A magazine description of the Oprah Store places the customer in that section as a particular sort of ethical consumer. "You can also feel like a philanthropist while indulging yourself: Profits from the sale of clothing with Oprah's Angel Network or Oprah Winfrey Leadership Academy logo go to benefit each of these worthy causes."[65] The process of visiting the store, like the purchasing process it provides, ritualizes the spiritual capitalism of Oprah. "It's a ritual that plays itself out nearly 200 times a TV season," writes one *Chicago Tribune* reporter, describing the stream of women who cross Washington Avenue and Carpenter Street after each *Oprah* show so that they might "bring home a piece of Her—even if she comes in water bottle form."[66] Now her audience has relics from their pilgrimage to remind them, daily, not only of the studio rituals but also of the shopping prowess it prescribes.

The Oprah Store opened in a moment in which stores were increasingly converting from a sectional departmental array to a narrower commodity scope. Oprah was not the only one branding such a single-product holism for shoppers. Just three miles from the Oprah Store one can find the American Girl Place, a multivalent shopping experience for American Girl doll owners that also pairs promises of uplift alongside a collector's expenditure. The American Girl collection is a line of dolls that includes books and accessories for those dolls and for the girls that own them. Introduced in 1985, the initial set of three historical dolls arrived in girls' mailboxes in the same mid-1980s moment that Winfrey began peering through the television screen. Before Winfrey entered the lifestyle racket in the 1990s, American Girl dolls tried to bring "history alive and provide girls with role models."[67] There are currently nine historical dolls, representing different cultural vantages for history lessons, ethnic exhibitionism, and girl power. Josefina, for example, is sold for ninety dollars and includes the doll that arrives "in a blouse (or *camisa*) with a skirt, moccasins, a hair ribbon, earrings, flowers, and a *Meet Josefina* paperback book. Her accessories set includes a shawl (or *rebozo*), pendant, pouch, hankie, and a pretend coin." The description of the product reiterates that this purchase encourages indigenous creativity, and not corporate consumption. "As a New Mexican girl growing up in 1824, Josefina is trying to preserve what is precious after her mother's passing," the Web site explains. "Josefina is overjoyed when her mother's sister, Tía Dolores, comes to live on the family *rancho*, but worries about her new ideas. Can Josefina welcome change and still remember the old ways?" The way American Girl consumers remember these old ways is through the reading of six books in the Josefina series (consistently titled with every doll, *Josefina Learns a Lesson, Kit Learns a Lesson, Samantha Learns a Lesson*, et cetera), as well as the purchase of historical dioramas. These dioramas establish ordered universes of food preparation, birthday parties, schoolwork, and recreation. "Josefina's Oven & Food" includes Josefina's outdoor oven, which "comes with a wooden paddle, two pretend loaves of bread, a door and a hide, a cloth mat, a *mano* and *metante*, or grinding stones to 'grind' corn, and two bunches of chiles in a basket" (forty-two dollars). All the dolls have similar pieces of furniture or appliances with the requisite adjoining utensils and chilies. Felicity Merriman, representing the revolutionary year of 1774, has a "Colonial Stable Set" (seventy-five dollars), and the Nez Perce girl Kaya, from 1764, has a tepee, "Kaya's Tepee" (seventy dollars), with "two tule mats and a wood fire that really lights up!" The girls have outfits, too, for birthdays, major holidays, key moments in adventure, and formal wear. Since 1986, more than 14 million American Girl dolls have been sold, as well as 123 million copies of books about their adventures.[68]

"The point is that household material culture may express an order which in each case seems equivalent to what one might term a social cosmology, if this was the order of things, values and relationships of a society," Daniel Miller writes in *The Comfort of Things*.[69] The order sold through American Girl dolls maps a chronology of a girl's developmental ambition. Designers associate the dolls with liveliness and tenacity ("a spunky, spritely, colonial girl"; "a pioneer girl of strength and spirit"; "a loveable schemer and dreamer").[70] Even the slogan of American Girl, "Follow Your Inner Star," adds a bit of cosmic shimmer to the "Live Your Best Life" branded by Winfrey. "Who is an American girl?" asks each catalog and the Web site. "Together the answer is still 'you,' the same you who remains unnamed: consumer," write two scholarly observers of American Girl.[71] To that consumerist end, in November 1998, American Girl Place opened in Chicago with a photo studio, a doll hair salon, theater, and a café in addition to the shopping areas designated for books, souvenirs, Bitty Baby dolls, the historical character dolls, the Just Like You dolls, and the child-sized clothing, Dress Like Your Doll: "Now girls and their dolls can be a perfect pair . . . together, they're ready to go anywhere and do everything in American Girl style!"[72] Its musical review and restaurant require many months' advance reservation.

Like Winfrey, Pleasant Rowland, founder and original designer of the American Girls, has become engaged in reforming philanthropies, including the Rowland Reading Foundation to provide phonics-based reading programs and the urban rehabilitation of Aurora, New York. She bankrolled the aesthetic overhaul of that upstate New York town through the restoration of buildings, homes, and businesses. "It seemed to me then that if God's glory was expressed in the natural beauty of Aurora, man's glory was expressed in its handsome old buildings, the living legacy of a gracious past, a place of gentility, rare in the world as I had come to know it," Rowland said. "Aurora was a very special place, indeed—a treasure to protect."[73] Like the innocence of the girls themselves, Aurora needed care and remodeling to ensure it would not face the corruptive scabbing of modern life. The girl, playing with her doll and her doll's accessories, engages in more than capitalist practice; she reclaims an arrangement of the world that may be wrested from her if she does not wrest it back to herself, if she doesn't control the tea cups and tepee fire. Such a girl exemplifies "a self capable of transcending the accidents and dispersions of historical reality," Susan Stewart writes. "Not simply a consumer of the objects that fill the décor, the self generates a fantasy in which it becomes producer of those objects, a producer by arrangement and manipulation."[74] In his review of the film *Kit Kittridge,* an adaptation of one American Girl doll's story, film critic A.O. Scott writes that the experiential retail stores like American Girl Place are "like miniature, idealized versions of the urban department stores of yesteryear, where you can buy a new outfit for your doll (or a pair of snowshoes or sunglasses or crutches, or a collar for her dog) and then take a break for tea, finger sandwiches and even a show."[75] The nostalgia trades commercially even as it proffers a refined romance of gilded ages gone and Edith Wharton worlds where girls were aspiring ladies. Now, though, they can be more than debutantes: they can be tricksters and teacher's pets, simultaneously, so long as they're always properly accessorized.

The dolls propose play-time creativity and repeat consumption. But American Girl dolls have also inspired lay revision by their owners, including the making of handmade clothes and communal knitting sessions. Likewise, Winfrey's productions have created reams of message board debates and book club assemblages. This lived religion of American Girl dolls or Harpo does not dismiss the genius of the sale itself, slathered with girl power and preservations of female innocence in porcelain, in Josefina and in the O. Rather, consumer creativity suggests the many ways the objects may be rearranged upon removal from their corporate contexts after sale. Even in the brightest varnish of capitalism's Michigan Avenue display, something more may be walking out with the girl's new tea set and her mother's new O turtleneck, since "relative homogeneity" has always "given way to a mélange of disparate . . . ways of life."[76] Girls and their mothers play and accessorize with idiosyncrasy.

Before tracking that play too far into its private domains, however, let us remember that the girl did not invent the doll she clutches, nor did her mother get her own insignia embossed on her new shirt. These shoppers strut away with the taste of something, of someone, else. From this something else these shopping women may mold something new. But the study underway does not steer to the new made by the consumer; rather, it emphasizes the seller. I do so not to reiterate relentlessly the hegemony of the sale. Rather, I do so to observe the nature of the sale. Money is never money quickly or cheaply made in the land of O. The sale is a roundabout sale of prosperity, wellness, and individual wholeness. Oprah assumes her viewers' particularities of practice, yet also presumes her wholeness is a model for theirs.

Her 2007 celebration of *The Secret* underlines this investment. "Have you heard about it?" Winfrey asked her audience. *The Secret* began as a DVD consisting of a series of interviews with contemporary spiritual leaders reflecting on the "law of attraction." Subsequent to the DVD's distribution, Rhonda Byrne, entrepreneur of *The Secret,* compiled two books, *The Secret* and *The Secret Gratitude Book,* both published in 2007.[77] Byrne attributes her realization of *The Secret* to Wallace D. Wattles's *The Science of Getting Rich* (1910), with which she felt immediate synergy upon reading. According to her account, she then read widely in self-help and spiritual guides. In addition to quoting an array of contemporary spiritual leaders, many of whom Byrne eventually incorporated into the DVD and text, *The Secret* draws upon Carl Jung, New Testament sources, Ralph Waldo Emerson, Martin Luther King Jr., and Buddha for epigrammatic invocation. Dominating her bibliography, however, were figures unknown to the everyday spiritual browser. Although it poses itself as an "ancient secret," eternal and unchanging, *The Secret* references the writings of Genevieve Behrend (1881–1950), Robert Collier (1885–1950), Charles Fillmore (1854–1948), Charles Haanel (1866–1949), and Prentice Mulford (1834–91), as well as books such as Christian D. Larson's *The Hidden Secret* (1907). All of these authors belong within U.S. religious history under the rubric of New Thought.

Frequently referred to as a movement, New Thought is probably better understood as a potent combinatory trope, one that galvanized the formation of seminaries (the Christian Science Theological Seminary), federations (the International New Thought Alliance), and independent religious bodies (the Unity School of Christianity, the United Church of Religious Science, and the Church of Christ Scientist), even as its organizers expressed resistance to institutionalization. While Ralph Waldo Trine's *In Tune with the Infinite* (1897) has been canonized as the definitive New Thought best seller, the authors called upon by Byrne for her 2007 *Secret* also produced texts, all of which struggled with the problem of the body and the soul in light of new late-nineteenth-century science and encounters with religious ideas from abroad. Committed to philosophical idealism and mind cure, New Thought proponents were identifiable by a devotion to the possibility of physical healing through spiritual healing. Coming into consciousness with God produces health; likewise, coming into consciousness with God produces abundance. New Thought advocates shunned dogma and encouraged cosmic optimism. This is how New Thought contributes to the positive thought movement, which would exchange some of the divine oneness in New Thought for the exuberant affirmation of individual ambition sanctified by American thinkers such as Napoleon Hill (*Think and Grow Rich,* 1937) and Norman Vincent Peale (*The Power of Positive Thinking,* 1952).[78]

"The placebo effect is an example of the law of attraction in action," explains Rhonda Byrne. "When a patient truly believes the tablet is a cure, he received what he believes and is cured."[79] Byrne's source material derives from New Thought expressions, resisting as she does any creed or institution other than the imperative of the law and the institutions of media that propel her message. Byrne also echoes New Thought premises in her perpetual affirmation of wellness through strength of mind. The law of attraction will heal you ("Disease is held in the body by thought"), it will make you prosperous ("The only reason any person does not have enough money is because they are *blocking* money from coming to them with their thoughts"), and it will make you a beacon of positive confession ("When you think about what you want, and you emit that frequency, you cause the energy of what you want to vibrate at that frequency and you bring it to You!").[80] Winfrey's dream of best living coordinates harmoniously with this emphasis. "When I watch *The Secret,*" Winfrey remarked, "I realized I've always lived by the secret. I didn't know it was a secret."[81] Later, she repeats the point: "All my life, I wanted to be a teacher. . . . And for years on this show, this is what I have been trying to do, is to get people to see [the secret] through different ways manifested through the lives of other people." Another dialogue typical of the conversation revealed Winfrey's enthusiasm for Rhonda Byrne's project. As you track this discussion, note how Oprah's voice guides and overrides the diversity of her discussants.

> *Winfrey:* You know, for years on this show, I've encouraged people to do gratitude journals, because I say, you know, what we were talking about earlier, what you focus on expands. But I heard you phrase gratitude in a way that I never heard it before. You said . . .
>
> *Dr. Michael Beckwith:* Well, basically, nothing new can come into your life unless you open yourself up to being grateful.
>
> *Winfrey:* Isn't that—doesn't little hairs on your head . . .
>
> *Rhonda Byrne:* Right.
>
> *Beckwith:* I mean, if you think about it . . .
>
> *Winfrey:* When I heard that, Michael, for the first time, my eyes watered, 'cause I thought just the way you phrased that, it's connected so—nothing new can come into your life unless you're grateful for what you already have.

Beckwith: Absolutely.

James Ray: It's about powerful magnetic force . . .

Beckwith: Yeah.

James Ray: . . . in the universe.

Winfrey: Isn't that amazing? I think that is an amazing view.[82]

Opening up to gratitude allows energy into the believer, allows him or her the "amazing view," which may raise the hairs on your head and electrify the possibility of change. Winfrey's correction ("nothing new can come into your life unless you're grateful for what you already have") to Beckwith's remark ("nothing new can come into your life unless you open yourself up to being grateful") emphasizes the given products over and above the emotional disposition. This talk of energy and attraction resonates with Winfrey's beliefs about gratitude not just for personal prosperity but also for the world's abundance. "For me, money has always been about an energy exchange. . . . I give my energy to the work and in exchange am rewarded with the different form of energy—money," wrote Winfrey in an *O* magazine column. "This in turn lets me acquire, create, and build other forms of energy."[83]

The material promise of *The Secret* is one premised on the world's abundance. "There's enough for everyone," Michael Beckwith, a teacher from *The Secret*, remarks. "If you believe it, if you can see it, if you act from it, it'll show up for you. That's the truth."[84] On the *Oprah* show, Beckwith repeats, "The universe has more than enough to give to everybody who asks." On behalf of her viewing audience, Winfrey says that her viewers believe they are doing that: "I'm asking. I'm asking. I'm asking. I'm not getting it." Beckwith replies, "Well, people have a tendency to believe in lack, limitation, and scarcity. They may say, I want a beautiful life, a magnificent life full of love and harmony and prosperity, but underneath there's a belief in scarcity."[85] Spiritual adviser James Ray remarked in the follow-up episode to *The Secret*: "If you look at the root of wealth, it comes from the same root as well-being."[86] And *The Oprah Winfrey Show* has plenty of self-worth:

Winfrey: Nobody, including myself and Bill Gates (know him personally), was trying to make money.

Beckwith: Right.

Winfrey: We're not trying to have the great money. I have more money than I ever imagined.

James Ray: That's the added thing.

Winfrey: You know?

Beckwith: And shoes, too.

Winfrey: And shoes, too. And shoes, too. And shoes to boot. So you have to follow what is the thing that gives you your juice.[87]

We return to the shoes, perhaps to those recommended monthly on "The O List," the ones that viewers know how to buy, know how to budget to buy, and know why to buy. "Although I'm grateful for the blessings of wealth," Winfrey remarked in a 2004 issue of the London *Times,* "it hasn't changed who I am. My feet are still on the ground. I'm just wearing better shoes." There is no line between the O and you, between her and her Spirit, between her and her shoes. She is the secret, connecting your dreams to your humdrum choices in her colloquial ways.

Critics conflate Winfrey with a posse of charlatan prosperity purveyors. "As promoted by Oprah Winfrey, scores of megachurch pastors and an endless flow of self-help best sellers, the idea is to firmly believe that you will get what you want, not only because it will make you feel better to do so, but because 'visualizing' something—ardently and with concentration—actually makes it happen," wrote Barbara Ehrenreich in a *New York Times* column. "You will be able to pay that adjustable-rate mortgage or, at the other end of the transaction, turn thousands of bad mortgages into giga-profits if only you believe that you can."[88] This description rushes to presume that Winfrey sells one prosperity gospel as any other is sold—one like that of any megachurch or any self-help guru. There is something specifically resonant here, something that fuses visualization with hungry American materiality.

For the past several decades, this strain of Christianity has gone by several names (Word of Faith, The Faith, Faith Formula, Health and Wealth, Word Movement, Name It and Claim It, Prosperity Theology), but no matter the particular invocation, the pastor espousing its ideas emphasizes the same dream of physical and spiritual wellness invoked in New Thought, with just a more full-throated sectarian belief in Christ's promises and the ability for believers to access God's abundance. Such prosperity gospel or prosperity theology has its origins in Andrew Carnegie's *The Gospel of Wealth* (1889) and Russell Herman Conwell's "Acres of Diamonds," a sermon that the Baptist Conwell delivered on more than six thousand occasions and published in 1915. Whereas Carnegie emphasized the philanthropic responsibilities of the rich, Conwell advocated that every individual had what he or she needed—enough diamonds in his or her own backyard, to profit while living rightly by the gospel. In the mid-1950s, leading purveyor Oral Roberts created a blessing pact, in which subscribers who contributed a hundred dollars to his work were promised a refund if they did not receive an equivalent gift from a totally unexpected source within one year.[89] Contemporary evangelists such as Creflo Dollar, Joyce Meyer, Joel Osteen, and T.D. Jakes espouse variants of the same prosperity gospel, the belief that material wealth is God's desire for the faithful. The luxurious lifestyles of these evangelists are, then, not ironic contradictions to their Christian proposals but material rewards of their model spiritual lives.[90] This theology knit well with the American Dream and the ruthlessness of its failure: if you believe that the right thoughts and speech will prompt divine repayment, then it follows that those who experience poverty have only themselves to blame.[91] Several biblical passages inform this prosperity gospel, including John 10:10 ("I came that they may have life and have it abundantly") and 3 John 2 ("Beloved, I pray that all may go well with you and that you may be in good health, just as it is well with your soul"). Appealing to the disadvantaged and the middle class alike, this is a global theological trend. In Ghana, for example, new Faith churches pray for a God-fearing leader who brings his people prosperity.[92]

In America, the biggest megachurches in the country—including Joel Osteen's Lakewood Church in Houston, T.D. Jakes's Potter's House in south Dallas, and Creflo Dollar's World Changers near Atlanta—advocate prosperity to their believers. Joel Osteen, author of the best-selling *Your Best Life Now*, insists that one of God's top priorities is to "shower blessings" on Christians and that believers should expect nothing less. One follower of Osteen stated the case clearly: "I'm dreaming big—because all of heaven is dreaming big. Jesus died for our sins. . . . Because I want to follow Jesus and do what he ordained, God wants to support us." Elsewhere, Joyce Meyer, a popular television preacher and author, asks, "Who would want to get in on something where you're miserable, poor, broke and ugly and you just have to muddle through until you get to heaven?"[93] On the subject of salvation and purchase, leaders vary. Writing of his Pentecostal forbears, evangelist T.D. Jakes writes, "How much more impact these good Christians could have had if they availed themselves of the riches the world offered?" Elsewhere, Jakes repudiates materialism among believers: "Christianity's foundation is not built upon elite mansions, stocks and bonds, or sports cars and cruise-control living. . . . To make finances the symbol of faith is ridiculous."[94] Yet Jakes himself lives lavishly, living with his wife and five children in a $1.7 million pillared mansion, flying on charter planes, dressing in tailored suits, and sporting a large diamond ring.[95]

That these churches draw upon images challenging to smart economic practice has not gone unnoticed in the subprime debacle of the early twenty-first century. "The economic boom of the Nineties and financial overextensions of the new millennium contributed to the success of the Prosperity message," Jonathan Walton has written, noting that the sermons declaring "it's your season to overflow" supplanted messages of economic sobriety.[96] Seeing the excess of the advocates of this message and the persistent poverty of many of its followers, Ben Witherington, an influential evangelical theologian at Asbury Seminary in Kentucky, thunders against prosperity gospel, writing, "We need to renounce the false gospel of wealth and health—it is a disease of our American culture; it is not a solution or answer to life's problems."[97] In her anthropology of reception experiences among watchers of prosperity televangelism, Marla Frederick relates how one interviewee tells Frederick that she has stopped watching Creflo Dollar because she has tired of his money talk. "I don't listen to him anymore," the former viewer attests. "There's nothing different. . . . You know sometimes you need to hear something more than prosperity."[98]

Amid this religious din of prosperity expression, Winfrey offers a parallel project of restraint and expenditure. In 2006, the Oprah show launched "America's Debt Diet," invoking a weight-loss metaphor that immediately familiarized viewers with the process, the stakes, and the potential self-celebrating rewards. Within ten months, one million people had downloaded the "diet" from Oprah.com/debtdiet.[99] The diet commanded practices strung with imperative verbs: *calculate, stop, repay, create, prioritize, earn, make, supercharge.*[100] Here, shopping with care—elsewhere an Oprah recommendation—can become vulnerability. "Her Achilles' heel turned out to be bargain hunting," financial consultant Jean Chatzky reported about one woman on the Debt Diet. "She'd go into Wal-Mart three times a week, intending to buy what the family needed for dinner; she'd come out with groceries, plus a cute outfit or two for the kids, and maybe a planter for the house."[101] For Harpo, Inc., the pecuniary failures of its customer base—suckered in by the multipurpose excesses of Wal-Mart and Target—only supply more customers for O. Like Oprah's weight fluctuations, like her every program and advocacy, the Debt Diet relies on failure. Even savvy shoppers and fiscal managers need her advice, so her crack crew of counselors are there, ready to advise those who save too many things ("Inside the

Lives of Hoarders with Peter Walsh") and those who can't handle what they've saved ("Julie Morgenstern hand-delivers a solution to in-box overflow").[102] Through it all, Oprah is the irrepressible exemplar, telling friends to return borrowed Tupperware for fear of any money-losing waste ("It makes me crazy to waste anything. I even save toast").[103] She somehow does it all right, spending right, spending smart, while the rest of us flail and turn to Chatzky. "Every day the path to your own spirituality starts with clarifying who you are and what you want," Winfrey reminds readers. "Not just *things*—things are easy. I mean the stuff that really matters."[104]

Stuffing stuff that matters into magazine pages and televised gifting events, Winfrey orients her consumers around her structures of choice and freedom. The promises Oprah makes aren't contingent on membership or creed. She eschews denomination and hierarchy, pressing viewers instead to grab hold of *their* lives, with their individual stories and whatever gods in tow. Bring all that with you, she says. The only expectation—the only need—is that you find her, again, in whatever multimedia format you prefer. Buy these things, find her purchases, and join an insistent, immediate prosperity. The now is nigh: the millennium is upon us, and it will be well-clad. This is not shopping as salvation but inspirational shopping as brand.

What, then, becomes of religion, or the religious, in this world? The October 5, 2001, episode of *The Oprah Winfrey Show*, "Islam 101," included an interview with an American University professor of Islamic studies, a teleconference with Queen Rania of Jordan, and a profile of a reporter with the *Chicago Tribune*, Noreen. Introducing the segment on Noreen, Winfrey said, "Take a look at how Noreen incorporates Islamic traditions into her modern life." The audience then followed a day in Noreen's life, observing her affinity for rock music and commitment to family, her observance of *hijab* and careful application of makeup. Noreen used the phrase "just like any other American" four times in her video monologue. After the Noreen montage, Winfrey opened the discussion to the audience, which included several other Muslim women in analogous professional and domestic situations. Their conversation emphasized the universality of women's issues regardless of religious affiliation and the prejudicial threats facing Muslim American communities since the September 11 attack. As Winfrey closed her show, she thanked all of her guests, giving particular attention to her Muslim women:

Winfrey: And thank you, Queen Rania of Jordan, Ambassador Maleeha Lodhi; Noreen and Minal, thank you modern Muslim women. *[Smiling, hands outstretched]* Modern Muslim women. Join us online at Oprah .com. *[Fist in the air]* Modern Muslim women!

Any regular viewer of *The Oprah Winfrey Show* could report that "modern" is not a standard Oprah idiom.[105] More to the point, her *enthusiasm* about the adjective was noteworthy. On this day, being modern mattered. These women were not ordinary Muslims; they were *modern* Muslims, Muslims who worked and raised children and bought Victoria's Secret lingerie. Religious yet accessible, faithful yet earthly, moral yet hip: modern Muslim women!

While the scholar of religion might find several questions appropriate about the phrasing of Oprah's exclamatory, here the adjective is specifically compelling. The juxtaposition of *modern* with *Muslim* is intriguing, suggesting that for the speaker, not all Muslims are modern. What differentiates a modern Muslim from a Muslim without such an adjectival honorific? Recall the focus on Noreen's career, her egalitarian marriage, and her enjoyment of Bruce Springsteen. Noreen is "just like" any other Oprah viewer, with sweet but exhausting children, a demanding but meaningful job, and a passion for the perfect lip color. Thus, not only is the *modern* Muslim woman not a Muslim who would hijack a plane or toss a pipe bomb, but she is also a religious believer who does not allow religion to interfere with her consumption. Oprah's Muslims are "just like any other American," except with different accessories.[106] Religious difference in Oprah's America is a fashion choice rather than a theological commitment, a translatable cultural context rather than an exclusivist worldview. The difference between a "modern" Muslim and a Muslim lacking modernity is that modern Muslims don't do anything that would disrupt the primacy of democracy and the cult of capitalism. For Oprah, modern religious identity is an afterthought to middle-class life.

Oprah's disavowal of religion and religious doctrine is a sleight of hand: she endorses some modes of theological existence but condemns many more. For her, *religion* implies control and oppression and the inability to catalog shop. The only way religion—and religious belief— works for Oprah is if it is safely couched within a girl-power democracy and capitalist pleasure. Thus, the turn to *spirituality*: the nondogmatic dogma that encourages an ambiguous theism alongside an exuberant consumerism. All religions can be "spiritual" through the right O reformatting. In Oprah's religious cosmos Buddhism isn't about meditation and renunciation; it's about beaded bracelets and yummy incense. Christianity isn't about Christ's apocalyptic visions or the memorization of creeds; it's about a friendly guy named Jesus and his egalitarian message. As long as you can spend, feel good about yourself, and look good, your religious belief will be tolerated on Planet O. The spiritual Oprah supplies is the incorporated optimism, the redemptive certitude, and the millennial promise of late-capitalist America.

CHAPTER 2

Celebrity Spirit

The Incorporation of Your Best Life

Any story of American religions over the last quarter of the twentieth century would necessarily need to acknowledge the aftereffects of
Sixties political radicalism, the domestic consequences of demographic
shifts, and the plurality of options available for the wandering believer.
Scholars contributing to the study of Oprah Winfrey have pointed to
the symbolic date of her origins, sitting as she did in the immediate
backwash of these changes, in the heart of the Reagan Revolution.[1]
From her 1986 syndication, it is possible to perceive hers as a climax in
a certain history, one that includes the civil rights movement, the wom-
en's liberation movement, the gay liberation movement, and the palette of critical experimentation that made up the imagined, advertised,
and lived counterculture. The subsequent sociological transformations
included women entering the workforce en masse, the reconfiguring of
the nuclear family, and a rampant diversification of American racial and
ethnic populations. Religious history cannot be understood separately
from these social and political dynamics. For example, in partial reply
to Woodstock abandon and women's liberation, antifeminist factions
within the evangelical subculture advocated a return to full-time homemaking. The same nondenominational outfits restricted church leadership roles for women in direct response to the success of women clerics
in other, mainline Protestant denominations, as well as the increasing
prominence of women within the reigning economies of secular power.[2]

Newly unbound women were being told to recapture their essential role as the pious epicenter of a well family. They were being told to return to the nest with newly educated, happily resolved gusto.

African American Christianity experienced similar tugs and pulls from the culture wars as black Christians continually reconsidered the consequences of desegregation and the legacy of the civil rights movement. Some denominations turned to theologies that reconstituted respect for black culture within a race-based interpretation of Christianity. Other majority-black religious outfits joined with white denominations that seemed to coordinate better with particular worship patterns and ecumenical aspirations. Meanwhile, non-Christian groups contested Protestantism's majority among African Americans, and the ongoing reality of a socioeconomic underclass in the black community caused many to turn to nondenominational prosperity gospels and televangelists rather than historical traditions or nationalist theological inclinations. Any definition of a controlling "Black Church" collapsed as the critical political agency of that entity was diffused by atomizing sectarianism and economic realignments.

Finally, religious seekers across the racial and gender divides found their options only multiplying. The so-called New Age religion, which took shape in the late Sixties and Seventies, introduced to the mass culture an eclectic mix of world religious traditions, pop psychology, quantum physics, and occult practices. Practices that before had been seen either solely in other parts of the globe or on the far margins of U.S. religious creativity found cultural success in paperback editions. Channeling, visualization, meditation, and alternative healing methods became available at the local bookstore and community college.[3] Longstanding religious denominations discovered that talk of angels, miracles, and psychic phenomena had mainstream appeal. This success of the New Age palette is the product of multiple histories and cultures, including the popularization of Native American rituals, the incursion of Southeast Asian immigrants, and the slow medical approval of some holistic healing practices.[4] Whatever story you want to tell about religion in the last quarter of the twentieth century, it will not be neat. It seems, from the outside, to be determined by a riotous marketplace of possibility in a culture ceaselessly editing its structural limits. And even as this age seems a riot of the new, it repeats patterns of diversification, competition, and social discord seen throughout American religious history. This era is only as new as its packaging.

To point to these histories is not to argue them as neat antecedents to Oprah Winfrey, nor is it to identify a pattern to point to specific correlation. Oprah is nothing if not a rebuttal to simple historical causality and a revision of many dominant trends. Still her exceptional way is predicated on religious formats, and her success would become predictive of formats to come: Oprah's pronouncement would be prophecy. And so from whence she came, she became; whatever she liked, dominated; whatever she sold, would sell.[5] Therefore her prehistory becomes a *her*story, even in its inaccuracies. Even if her understanding of, say, the history of Black Power or the meaning of feminism were wrong, her interpretations did, in a sense, become history by the sheer will of her narrations, by the hegemony of her sway.

Within this historical imaginary, the products of Oprah Winfrey's empire offer a consolidated vision for your healthiest spiritual future in the relentlessly cheerful now. Consider the "Best Life Week" that inaugurated *The Oprah Winfrey Show* in January 2009. Each day of that week supplied classes to inculcate an ostensibly multifaceted Oprah ideal: Your Weight (Monday), Your Health (Tuesday), Your Spirit (Wednesday), Your Money (Thursday), and Your Sex Life (Friday). Much might be made of the categories absent from this best life overhaul, including as it does your sex life but not your home, your weight but not your children, your health but not your career. The Best Life Week emphasizes immediate change to foster an overarching, self-oriented revolution. Rather than reexamine the legal and labor structures in which the prescribing women partake, the Best Life Week focuses on the relentless importance of the quotidian, on what you eat, where you buy, and how you have sex. Each day reintroduced an Oprah familiar (such as Bob Greene, her trainer, who guest-starred on the day featuring Your Weight) to reply to a series of viewers' inquiries about that day's topic.

The day devoted to Your Spirit was therefore precisely like the scripts and schemata for Your Weight and Your Sex Life. On that day, Oprah's "best spiritual teachers" considered concerns of viewers like Tanya, whose business was failing; Nikki, whose mother had cancer; and Caroline, a forty-one-year-old stay-at-home mom from Pacific Grove, California, who joined Oprah and her counselors via Skype from her mother-in-law's den. For viewers, this array of other viewers volunteering trouble and the stock committee of counselors supplying advice would be rote. The day may be about your spirit, but it is Oprah's incorporating sociability that pervades. Winfrey asks, "Caroline, your question is . . . ?"

> *Caroline*: Hi. Twelve years ago I decided to give up my career and stay
> home with my kids, and I feel very blessed to do that, but there are times
> when I'm doing laundry and chauffeuring them around that I don't
> always feel appreciated. And what I realized after reading the Eckhart
> Tolle book [is] that I am identifying with being a mother. That was a big
> aha moment for me. And I would like to find a way to create a larger
> space between realizing when I'm in ego and identifying with the role of
> being a mother, so that I can be in the present moment and find the peace
> and the happiness that I would like to be able to attain while I'm doing
> laundry or having to clean the bathroom and that type of stuff.[6]

Insider O language swarms Caroline's self-description: the "aha moment,"
the reference to an Eckhart Tolle book, the conflation of "role" and
"ego." But the counselors don't translate her narrative, choosing instead
to seize upon her story with confirming replies. One reminds Caroline
that all her work is being done "for the sacred." Another tells her that
she's doing it all, even the laundry, "for the divine." "You're doing it for
the divine," he summarizes, "even if it's something as mundane as the
laundry." The other spiritual guide remarks, "A wonderful thing happens
when you show up fully 100 percent with your kids or with your husband or with the laundry." Oprah, too, chimes in with a ribbon of praise,
remarking, "I just want to say that for you, Caroline, and for every other
woman out there who has made the choice to be at home and take care
of your kids . . . that that really is God's holiest work." Agreeing with
the counselors' emphasis on the importance of banal tasks, she underlines, "There is no . . . higher calling than raising children who are kind,
who live with grace, and are going to be generous human beings in the
world. . . . That is the sacred at work every day."

Despite the studio audience's nodding pleasure at Winfrey's coronation of motherhood, Caroline's trouble dangles unresolved on the
screen. She understands that there is sacred power in the laundry, and
she knows she is more than just someone's mother, but still, she's frustrated. She has done the O reading and found no answers:

> *Caroline*: My husband works full-time, and he's going to law school. So
> he's very busy, and we've made a decision to do this as a family, and
> I'm supporting him, but at the same time there's a part of me that feels
> like it's my turn. I want to do something. And I've done enough, I think,
> soul-searching and in reading some of these books that part of my issue
> was with identifying with that role and not even realizing until I kind
> of looked at it and got that space between my thoughts . . . thinking,
> wow, you know, I'm identified as a mother. I know that a lot of people
> planned on being at home, but that wasn't my number one goal.

Perhaps sensing the scriptural specificity and the orthodox override of Caroline's reading, Winfrey interrupts. She provides, finally, some clarification on the nouns and self-diagnosis that Caroline and her team of advisers have been bandying:

> *Winfrey*: Let me just interrupt you here, Caroline, because a lot of people haven't read Eckhart Tolle's book *A New Earth,* which is another really great spiritual teaching. So they will hear you saying, "I'm identified with being a mother," and say, well, what's wrong with being identified as a mother? There's nothing wrong with being identified as a mother. What you're saying is if that's the only way you see yourself, that if . . . your complete and total identity is only as being a mother, then you start to lose yourself. And I know that there are millions of you who are listening to us right now who identify with what Caroline's saying. You've lost yourself, because you think that's all that you are.

In the early years of *The Oprah Winfrey Show,* pundits used the word *Oprahfication* to describe a rhetorical idiom in which the interviewer restates what her subject has said in order to affirm its truth through association with a universal that she, Oprah, represents. *Oprahfication* in that sense refers to a dialogical process by which the individual becomes enfolded into the interviewer's experiential whole. "You've lost yourself," Oprah responds, hearing what Caroline has described, noting that "millions of you" have, too. Caroline is not alone. Winfrey is not only listening, she is encompassing.

For viewers, the task of the episode is to improve; for Oprah and her committee, the task is to help viewers find their spiritual path. How then will Winfrey and her trio of counselors help Caroline? Their therapies are, in the end, less a therapeutic cure than a pastoral hug, as the team confirms and commiserates. "Everybody has a true self, and that's how it starts to feel. You start to feel itchy. You start to feel irritated," Winfrey continues. The studio audience audibly assents, and Oprah proceeds:

> *Winfrey*: You know, you're at a job and you know that you really should be doing more. It doesn't fulfill you. And that's why you're really here. Being a mother obviously was a part of the calling, but why you're really here is to fulfill that thing that you're now feeling.
>
> *Caroline*: Absolutely.
>
> *Winfrey*: Thank you, Caroline. We'll be right back. You're on the way. You're on the way to that.

The show breaks for a commercial, and Caroline's televised Best Life problem concludes. The next segment introduces a different viewer with a different problem. Caroline's O gift bag included approval for her choice to be a mother, confirmation that her problem is real, and affirmation that she is on her way to ongoing holiness because of her motherhood and because of her problems with motherhood. She is further told that her awareness of her discomfort is important, that she should think about how "to fulfill that thing that you're now feeling" through ongoing reflection. Her instructions are to follow the spirit as she launders underwear, to unhook from the laundry and then retether herself to it with the caressing language (aha!), texts *(A New Earth)*, and comforting spiritual center (the O) provided by this line of products.[7]

Caroline's episode began with a promise that the pursuit of spirituality was, as Winfrey defined it, the pursuit of "feeling more alive." Talk of spirituality, and of the Spirit's fulfillment, pullulates in the world of Harpo.[8] This talk links Oprah's positioning as a guru, her reliance upon strategic outside advisers, and her hunt for what she terms "spiritual" solutions to "everyday" dilemmas. In the academic historiography of Oprah Winfrey, scholars insert Oprah's invocations of the salved spirit into broader discussions of modern consultancy culture. This interpretive maneuver shoulders the spiritualized Oprah into a "therapeutic gospel" that gained increasing sway in the twentieth-century American public sphere. This gospel sets psychology as the engine of historical change, elevates happiness over all other goals, and celebrates the potency of individualism.[9]

Categorizing Winfrey as just a particularly grandiose therapist shunts her titular stand to only one professional trope. Oprah encompasses more than a therapist's couch, or a woman's purse, or the revival preacher's bench. Rather, she claims, on behalf of her postulated flock, to be that flock's Spirit.[10] Her therapy is not coincidentally or cynically a "gospel," glazing a science with a hymn or a psychotherapeutic silence with a commercial break. Her gospel *is,* whether or not it is therapeutic. Describing Harpo, Inc., as just an exhibit of the therapeutic gospel in American culture suggests that the connective tissue of the shows' episodes, magazine issues, Web pages, and endorsed books is one of *psychological* improvement.[11] But neither Winfrey nor her products claim to be so medically bracketed in their teleology of healing. Even as Oprah pushes on to the next client, Harpo, Inc., pulls the customer back into her fold. Emphasizing then the *gospel* of an Oprah over and above the therapeutic *process* of an Oprah is not to negate the scholarship recording the psychological idioms of her episodes. Rather, focusing on her search for women's spiritual revivification returns us to what she sets out to accomplish and what she says she has to offer. The viewers may or may not notice that Caroline was left dangling, questions unanswered and therapies unresolved. *O* consumers like Carolyn are taught—through every word, every transition, and every exhibit of this empire—not to linger in the questions but to revel in the certitude surrounding this gospel of change. Scholarship adjudicating Winfrey as a therapist would most likely decide that she has failed Caroline. However, if estimated as a preacher of a gospel of change, she has succeeded. "If you don't know the answer to why you are really here, your whole life will be out of sorts," Winfrey explains to another group of women. "Your purpose is the spiritual thread that connects all of your life experiences."[12] No matter what she may feel now, Caroline will—if she wills it, if she is unafraid to find herself, if she will just listen to Oprah—feel the power of inspirational invocation. This is not change itself but change as affect. Psychology may supply some of the modes, but spirituality is the medium.

The scholarly tendency to lean away from Oprah's spiritual self would be unsurprising to her. "A lot of people think when I talk about spirituality that I'm talking some pie-in-the-sky stuff. But it's not. I'm talking about how you get women to look at their lives differently and see that through the stories of people."[13] Winfrey seeks to make women look at their lives differently, an optimistic result of therapy. But the processing of Winfrey's programs demonstrates what historian Christopher G. White has termed an efflorescence of religious ideation buttressed by psychological notions.[14] Had Winfrey emerged in the mid-nineteenth century, she most certainly would have been incorporated into William James's roster of awakened spiritual heroes in *The Varieties of Religious Experience*.[15] But the combined effect of scholarly classificatory inhibition and the morass of contemporary spirituality has muted appraisal of those products that fuse therapeutic scripts and spiritual desire.

Such spirituality scripts abound in the land of O. "We're not asking for much," explained one *O* magazine writer, "just a sense of meaning and purpose in our lives. A higher level of awareness. A feeling of being linked to something greater than ourselves. And how about a side order of uplift and joy?"[16] Such a statement contains the shibboleths of contemporary spirituality, emphasizing as it does a vague dispositional result, an undifferentiated higher something, and an image of spirituality as a platter you might order from a restaurant. In part because of this market taste, no one has ever wanted spirituality to succeed.[17] Within religious studies, for instance, spirituality as an object of inquiry has been consistently pressed to the margins of intellectual appraisal. Many factors contribute to this position for the study of spirituality, including the difficulty of tracking believers when they practice outside the ordering confines of denominations. "The trend toward spirituality is real," one seminarian said to O magazine; "it's just hard to gauge because there isn't a church of being spiritual."[18]

The best work on spirituality within the academy has explored the emergence of seeker spirituality alongside the triumph of liberal democracy and free market capitalism, showing how spirituality smoothed the edges of modern industrialization to offer retreat for the factory laborer at a peaceful pond where he or she might remember social reform, divine immanence, and universal brotherhood.[19] But spirituality has also struggled against a barely disguised disdain within the modern academy for anyone who could really believe this "pie-in-the-sky" stuff. Especially because participants in spirituality culture are often educated members of the bourgeoisie, spirituality has seemed like some adolescent rebellion against the disciplined logic of secularization. Spirituality has figured as a muggy third in the clean space between theism and atheism. Following such a dualism, definitions of spirituality tend to be framed in opposition to orthodoxy, adjudicating some freedom between self and institution, belief and practice, the masculine and the feminine. As British sociologists Tony Walter and Grace Davie have explained: "Since women have been particularly subject to the male authority of churches, it is not surprising that women are to the fore in developing postmodern discourses of 'spirituality' nor that some experience these new discourses as liberating."[20] Rather than term this gendered inflection the feminization of American culture, I find it more useful to define this shift as the *spiritualization* of American culture, specifying a cultural revolution supplied through wildcat faith, lavish female enshrinement, and no small amount of earnest capital.[21] Winfrey describes spirituality as a set of choices within a broad banquet of rejuvenation: "We can choose whether to go to church or not, we can worship as we please— or we can lounge in bed on a Sunday morning, wearing the very cutest underwear."[22] Abundant consumption and liberal selectivity while consuming pose no moral threat to this spiritual collector. Indeed, consumption and spiritual choice often supply the only comfort a Caroline might have.

Pursuing the market mélange within Winfrey's empire might lead to some productive exploratory ends. We could parse the spiritual genealogy of Winfrey's spiritual products to find shards of nineteenth-century experimental metaphysics, African American worship strategies, Eastern spirituality, and American free thought. Or, we could follow her readers, raiding their carts for a sense of the contemporary cornucopia: "We're browsing the spiritual marketplace, dropping new ideas and philosophies into our carts—a smidgen of Buddhism, some New Testament, maybe a little tai chi tossed in."[23] In other words, one research route would be to describe what Catherine Albanese has called the combinative quality of metaphysical religion in America, the habit of combining different ideas and practices into a practicable pastiche.[24] Emphasizing this diversity of sources, however, misses the important combinative result: Winfrey's whole. "Like all seminal creative figures," Lee Siegel has written, Winfrey's "essential gift lies in her synthesizing power."[25] For Winfrey, the only point in diversity is to assemble a resolute spiritual truth. To study her spirit is to examine a singularity composed of important pluralities, but the assemblage is her hopeful tour to truth. The icon of the O is her spirit. It is her ability to speak for, and to, everyone.

Pursuing spiritual counselor Eckhart Tolle's recycling of *advaita* won't supply a point critical to the Harpo line of products. Rather, it will supply the snarky sense that something pure has been put to unabashed commodity use. Historian Leigh Schmidt warns against such reductive material talk: "A cynical narrative about commercialization is hardly the primary story of modern interiority . . . as if religious seekers were little more than spiritual gluttons gobbling up anything and everything that they can heap on their plates."[26] Focusing on the iconic aspects of Oprah's spiritual messaging, then, turns us away from delineating "purer" sources from an imagined debasement and turns our attentions instead toward the larger cultural processes that format her spiritual spectacles. Oprah brands an iconic, reproducible, born-again promise of the pervasive majority. Any concerns you may have that all of this is some sort of bastardization of real religion—or a corruption of an enlightened secularity—are concerns that underline premises of purity, of authenticity, and of origins that have little valence in the land of Oprah. The only authenticity (the only originality, the only purity) is the You that you will find through the tools she supplies.

To begin any study of Oprah's spiritual labor is to discover that the word *Spirit* is itself the centerpiece: Spirit walks, Spirit bags, Spirit books, Spirit memories, and Spirit candles. *Spirit* becomes itself an italicized mark of Oprah's presence—if it doesn't have Spirit somewhere, it isn't

O. Backtracking through the longer history of religions, one finds that the category of spirit has a strong etymological link to the Holy Spirit, the third person of the Christian Trinity, which serves to connect God and the world. The relationship between God and the world through spirit is maddeningly diverse, as usages of *Spirit* and *the Holy Spirit* vary as much as all of their lexical progeny. Everyone from Transcendentalists and Spiritualists to Lutherans and Pentecostals have applied talk of spirit to their individual selves and communal theologies. In the history of religion, the ineffable and the sacred have often been expressed through descriptions of spirit. Spirit has been synonymous with energy, consciousness, quiet, holiness, life source, interiority, and animating principle. In many religious traditions, one finds spirit guides, spirit possessions, and spirit mediums. People speak of the spirit filling them, calling them, possessing them, and changing them. Spirituals are sung, and spirituality is practiced. Trappist monks have spirituality; Jewish feminists have spirituality; Tibetan Buddhists have spirituality; womanists, queer theologians, Zuni poets, and Celtic priestesses have spirituality. The Holy Spirit pursued by Pentecostal worshippers in Corpus Christi today isn't the same spirit invoked by the Shaker Mother Ann Lee in the eighteenth century; the "emptiness" sought through Buddhist spirituality is not the same as the liberation of transgender spirituality. Quaker spiritual disciplines are different from Methodist ones, and the ordinary spirit of Ralph Waldo Emerson is different from the extraordinary spirit by Rabbi Zalman M. Schachter-Shalomi's Jewish Renewal movement.[27]

Perhaps one thing that can be said to link all usages of *spirit* in its variant forms is that it names something that crosses the laws of daily life to transport the individual believer to a different sense of self, a different connection to divines, or a different location. To speak of s/Spirit is to speak of a transcendent difference in contrast with the life you live. In this spirit-filled capacity, Oprah supplies an array of products connecting you to the life you want and, more specifically, to the self you need to become to create the life you want. She has said, "Spirit is not a religion; it's just about what is really great about yourself and remembering to live that way."[28] The reminders to live that spiritual way are multiple. For example, on May 9, 2008, she began e-mailing the *Spirit Newsletter* to her online constituency. The first issue prepared readers, viewers, and listeners for Oprah's *Soul Series,* a radio broadcast on her XM satellite station, also available for postshow download on Oprah.com. "Get in Touch with Your Soul!" the copy encouraged. Subsequent newsletters announced these broadcasts, repeatedly described as the "most powerful conversations Oprah's ever had" with her favorite spirit advisers, including Sarah Ban Breathnach, author of *Simple Abundance;* "Prayer pioneer" Larry Dossey; dream therapist Rodger Kamenetz; inspirational speaker Byron Katie; psychic and author Ainslie MacLeod; and psychotherapist Jenny Phillips, among others.

Quickly, the newsletter became more than a promotional outlet for the radio *Soul Series,* supplying redacted summaries of content available on Oprah.com. It was itself a little spiritual intervention in your electronic in-box, expressing in its range of quotations, recommendations, and sectarian sources the infinite palette of the universe itself. The newsletter is a thumbnail advertisement for the whole, crafted as a reminder to connect to your spirit just as you connect to Oprah's *Spirit* through the virtual mediation of the World Wide Web. Each newsletter contained a series of hyperlinks to the "Spirit" segment of the Oprah.com site, which itself links to episodes, articles from the magazine, books recommended on the show, and other Oprah products. Familiar Oprah idioms appear in these newsletters, such as links to "Aha! Moments Revealed" ("get inspired and motivated by people's aha! moment and let their experiences guide you along your personal journey") and "Extraordinary Makeovers" ("What's better than a fabulous makeover? One that's well-deserved!"). There are encouragements to break out of yourself ("Step Out of Your Comfort Zone," "Express Yourself," "Escape Your Rat Race") and advice on how to take a break (the "Breathing Space" connects you to "awe-inspiring photographs"). Most relevant to the "spirit" in this newsletter are links to "Breaking Open Your Spirit," "Your Life's Purpose," and "How to Maintain a Spiritual Connection."[29]

If the newsletter recipients click on these link titles, they will be transferred to the main page of the "Spirit" segment of Oprah.com, a page that has been variously subdivided over the years but always includes several generic headings of need (Know Yourself, Inspiration, Emotional Health, Body Image) and some spotlighted counselors from the Oprah stable (e.g., Marianne Williamson, Elizabeth Lesser, Martha Beck). Counsel on these pages openly offers to help you toward a more enlightened you. The pathways to enlightenment are sets of enumerated cheer: "4 ways to instantly find bliss," "5 great films that will stir your soul," "31 *free* ways to get happy," and "10 ways to transform your life." The content exhibited via slide show is abridged and axiomatic. To track the "10 ways to transform your life" is to learn ten Oprah ideals, again: "Big changes come with small choices" or "Nothing hurts you more than your expectations." The bulleting belies possible concentration elsewhere. Viewers know if they look longer they'll find book-length treatments of those subjects by her spiritual posse or magazine articles that concentrate in more vivid detail. But this concentration is deferred, because the women consuming this product don't have a lot of time. There are spirit videos, spirit photographs, and spirit quotations. Blips and bits and pieces of spirit serve to transcend the overworked normalcy into a momentary calm. As indicated already, management of time—through handsome watches, refrigerator calendars, and an orderly disposition—is a central conquering practice of an Oprah sort of spiritual woman.[30]

"The unexamined life may not be worth living, but who, outside of an ashram or a cloister, has the time—and space—for contemplation?" asks one O magazine article. "You do, despite daily e-mail invasions and phone-message pileups, despite kids under 2 or loquacious friends or an in-your-face boss or husband who wants to see you once in a while."[31] In the Harpo spirit landscape, spiritual practice and religious idiom encourage separate spaces for spirit rejuvenation amid this-worldly mayhem. "We believe in meditating," Winfrey related during her 2001 Live Your Best Life Tour. "I believe in meditating in the tub with some very nice bath products." She regaled the crowd with her meditative process, explaining that as she inhales and exhales she repeats, "Oh, God, my heart is open to you. Come sit in my heart." To the audience, she says, "If you're not comfortable with the word God, it doesn't matter," offering then a series of alternatives.[32] Winfrey doesn't force anything, not even God. God could be "future," it could be "divine" or "love" or "grace" or "joy." "God" is an exchangeable category, mattering only insofar as it sets the stakes. "I think God doesn't get hung up on the titles. It's the people that get hung up on the titles."[33] She sets her meditation at a divine height and offers to everyone else the option to set his or her own deity. "You come from a power source and therefore you have great power," Winfrey explains. "And the moment you recognize that power, you will recognize that power is God."[34]

Saddling that power is the process by which you Live Your Best Life, how you Change Your Life, how you Use Your Life. "Life is an exchange of energy," Winfrey remarks in episodes on *The Secret*, in conversations with Eckhart Tolle, and in editorials on money management ("and currency is one of the biggest energy forms").[35] Energy is the force that guides spirit, motivating disciplined practice and compassionate embrace. Categories like spirit and energy dance, then, with other corollary ventures to encourage regular ritual and spiritual exploration; they pulse the veins that sample a new yoga practice, try their hand at foot washing, weigh the meaning of their horoscope, and consider the healing power of prayer. Energy and spirit align to supply the miraculous, from a 2001 episode of the *Oprah* show advertising miracles showcased on the PAX network's *It's a Miracle* to a 2008 radio series *Course in Miracles*, offering a daily lesson with Marianne Williamson.[36] Ranging over ritual and discipline, individual power and personal seeking, energy and spirit tug at the corner of the viewer's eye. The O spirit calls them to expect more from their daily life, and energy presses them to expand into the unexplored beyond. "I've learned that the more stressful and chaotic things are on the outside, the calmer you need to get on the inside," Winfrey says. "It's the only way you can connect with where your spirit is leading you."[37]

Articles in O magazine showcase the "spiritual" as a solution to your deadlock. Spirit steps in to explain why you get listless, why you get irritated, and why you can't lose those last pounds. For Oprah, the spirit replaces politics, economics, psychology, and sociology as explanatory mechanisms. The spirit is anything keeping you from being the best You. "Why is it that every time you shed a few pounds, you gain them back?" asks one author. "They focus on what goes into their stomachs instead of what's going on in their heads." Spotlighting a megachurch with a weight-loss ministry, the report includes one woman who has successfully beaten back the tide of temptation through such a "spiritual solution." "It's not like I see an apple pie and get down on my knees to pray that I don't eat it," she writes. "I do my Bible studies in the morning, and I feel refreshed for the rest of the day. . . . People who are not Christians would probably say that I had an inner voice before this program and now I can hear it." It is impossible to find an O magazine article not ringed with talk of motivation and aha connections to the spirit's unstoppable sway. "I was with God," Dr. Jill Bolte Taylor recounted in her description of a personal medical trauma. "My spirit was huge."[38] Spirit slices through any and every complaint with the vagaries of revelation cast as a ready-for-the-taking revolution. Whenever you have arrived at an impasse—with your weight, your sex life, your money problems—spirit will tunnel you through.

This set of examples suggests the divergent paths through which the spirit flows within Harpo. But the road through s/Spirit has not been without its bumps. One of the program changes associated with Change Your Life TV was a segment that closed the daily *Oprah* show called

"Remembering Your Spirit," in which individuals testified to the ways they enacted spiritual self-care. A *Newsweek* reporter recounted with a critical eye, "The touchy-feely vignettes, pre-produced with soft light and new-age music, were testimonials from people around the country who had, usually as a result of crisis like the death of a child or a divorce, stumbled onto some simple truth about life."[39] Critics abounded, with many citing "Remembering Your Spirit" as they reacted adversely to what they called the new Deepak Oprah. In 1997, *Newsweek* reporter Wendy Kaminer commented that the "pop-guru business is certainly flourishing" and quoted Oprah Winfrey saying that gurus are here "not to teach us about their divinity but to teach us about our own." Kaminer cynically eyed this role, arguing that gurus "are paid to talk while we pay to listen."[40] A year later, the *New York Times* columnist Jeff Mac-Gregor underscored Kaminer's point, arguing that *The Oprah Winfrey Show* was "about nothing so much as Ms. Winfrey herself, and her pilgrimage toward a more rewarding state of Oprahness." MacGregor further indicted Winfrey's format switch from standard talk show fare to Change Your Life TV as a "psychospiritual Reformation, in which any attempt to entertain has been abandoned in favor of a search for Truth, Wellness and Reduced-Fat Snacks That Still Satisfy."[41]

In interviews and on the show, Winfrey showed that she heard these criticisms and replied. "Many years ago, I did a segment called 'Remembering Your Spirit,' and I was challenged and talked about and ridiculed because people thought I was trying to tell them how to be religious," Winfrey would later reflect. To reply to the ridicule, she dropped the repeated invocation of Change Your Life TV and rejected initial proposals by Hearst to call her magazine *Oprah's Spirit*.[42] "In the beginning, someone proposed a story idea about some healer women," Winfrey recalled. "I'm not interested in that . . . [and] it's not going to reach a mass audience."[43] It is the mass audience that she wants, and it is to that audience the suitably inscrutable Spirit serves as a catchall designate for her renovations. She knows she can't light too many candles, or her audience will abandon her. Reflecting on Remembering Your Spirit, she commented:

> Regardless of whom we're talking to, they have a candle lit. Every single person. There was a woman sitting beside the stove paying her bills, and there was a candle on the stove. . . . I saw a segment about a woman who was reconnecting with her spirit by fishing. She was casting her line with this euphoric look on her face. I mean, come on. Get real, right? I'm with ya. We need to pull that back, so we don't end up being a caricature of ourselves.

That sort of thing was good at the beginning, when we needed to spell out our message. But now let's evolve to the next level. Your holiest moments, most sacred moments, are often the ones that are the most painful. And we need to get with that. You know, feel some spirit when you're sitting there arguing with your husband and children.[44]

Everything about this passage shines with Oprah styling. The colloquial invocations ("Get real, right?"), the quotidian detail (arguing with family), and the humor ("I mean, come on"). But note too the self-scrutinizing appraisal of the CEO. Her spirit is savvy, knowing what we need to do in order to maintain a market share.

The consistency of the product—spiritual and otherwise—is the O, circling and containing an individual's awakening in her capacious narrative imprint. The girlfriend and the CEO, the guru and the therapist: it is the O as a combination effect that became *Oprah* the icon. In an essay examining the nature of contemporary stardom, critic David Denby observes something telling about the nature of recent film productions. He notes that among the thirty-five top-earning films of all time, all but two can be classified as spectacle, fantasy, or animation. "In these movies, stars are reduced to burbling voices, or get shoved aside by scaly creatures, digital convulsions, or magical columns of light." Noting the diminishing privacy of twenty-first-century celebrities and the parallel diminishment of their iconicity, Denby suggests this may have something to do with those sorts of films. "The 'concept' for a big movie, or its special effects, may be the true star," he remarks.[45] While Winfrey's spiritual substance derives in part from her parliament of advisers, her effective result occurs as a media effect. She is the concept of herself, offering Spirit in between breathless flights to Maui and South Africa, between fund-raising parties and weight-loss strategies.

To speak of Winfrey's spirit within history, then, is not only to specify her launch within a post-Sixties racial landscape or the religious backdrop of Reaganomics but also to witness precisely how her charismatic star was born. Scholarship on celebrity has suggested that in a secular age, celebrities are replacement divinities. "With the death of God, and the decline of the Church, the sacramental props in the quest for salvation have been undermined," Chris Rojek has written. "Celebrity and spectacle fill the vacuum."[46] The cultural function of celebrity parallels that of religion, since both share certain relationships to communities of believers reliant upon icons who dwell within the realm of possible experience.[47] Through celebrity exemplars, social communities find sites for parasocial interactions and modes of gossip that supply common terms for examinations of individual life, morality, and social change.[48] Designating celebrities as merely new divines inadequately addresses the particular ways different celebrities establish themselves and the peculiar charisma of Winfrey within that galaxy. Winfrey emerged as a syndicated serial titan—and an Oscar-nominated actress—during an epoch of rapidly accelerating celebrification. *Celebrification* refers to the way social interaction and identity formation are inflected by celebrity culture. Through instantaneous data transmission, new media forms accelerated celebrity story lines as live experiences. Trapping individuals in paparazzi hoards—or in panoptic reality show dens—heightens the relationship between viewer and star, suggesting that no matter your obscurity, you too may fit the formats of stardom.

In scholarship on contemporary media cultures, the celebrity is repeatedly described as a commodity, as a media effect reliant upon the acquisition and publicity of that individual's private life. Current incarnations of that rabid pursuit include tracking the celebrities: "They're just like us!" "They Select Veggies!" "They Buy in Bulk!" "They Rest on Benches!"[49] Private domestic needs, like walking pets and shopping for toilet paper, become objects for consumption. Those performances become infomercials selling the toilet paper or the purebred pet ostensibly under the genre of documentary reporting. The stars, now so relatable (they rest on benches, too!), become also more easy to mimic. The girl in the magazine or on the screen could be me, if only I bought like that. When David Denby suggests that a film's profits now seem dependent not upon individual talent but on a concept, he may be explaining what happens when celebrities become so accessibly democratic, namely, that their products are no longer theirs. Rather, their products, their films or serials or songs, must become replicable hooks, images, and brands that supersede the stone of their benches, their dog poop, and their ugly squint.[50]

Within the hyperrealism of celebrity consumption, the appeal of Oprah is that she has absorbed so many flashbulbs that she has surpassed their glare. Or, perhaps more exactly, she has become such a consumer of herself that there is nothing the bulbs can capture that she has not already made commodity. When asked, "Are you ever concerned about oversaturation?" she responded, "Actually, no. I'm not concerned about that. Nope."[51] She is incandescently everywhere, illuminated by her own engines and by engines that surpass her touch, with bloggers noting her every maneuver and news wires baited for her next step. "As the star and the diamantine reduce to the celebrity and the logo, the public secretly longs for that rare charismatic figure whose auratic values are not reduced but magnified," Daniel Herwitz explains.[52] Who is more magnified than she? She repeated, with increasing confidence, the catechism of her specificity: I am black. I am woman. I am fat. I am lonely. I am in need. Over the years, this talk smoothed to a hum of universal humanity: I am your spirit. I am Spirit. Through her relentless public journaling and exposition, she has transfigured herself from woman to celebrity to star to holiness. It is perhaps not coincidental that the movies that cultivate the strongest lay following as sacred artifacts, such as *Star Wars* and *The Matrix,* are vehicles dependent on the concept of an everyman self knit into a technological enormity. In these films, individuals pose as universal signs resistant to the rules and laws of everyday life. Or, as Peter Brown wrote about late Roman society: "The holy man was deliberately not human."[53]

Oprah's stratospheric humanness has been made deliberate, time and again, in her own retelling. In this, she echoes traditions of charismatic translation in the history of American religion. The modern American holy man made himself human through constructions of his self-invention. Late-nineteenth-century evangelical preachers, for example, propelled their notoriety through promotional biographies. Including financial records, seating charts, architectural plans, and stagecraft descriptions, these documents rhetorically integrated the minister and his tactics, demonstrating that he was no con man but also that he was no miracle worker: this holy work took human sweat.[54] Winfrey shares this proclivity, relentlessly revealing her process. Examples abound, from a behind-the-scenes *Oprah* show episode describing "what happens behind the scenes at Harpo" to Winfrey's recent display of photos proving "this is not a weave; this is my hair!" While parts of her private life seem off-limits—for example, her relationship with Stedman Graham, which makes only fleeting discursive appearances—most of her existence seems available for video feed. Whether she's exposing her weight gain on her magazine cover or offering a preparty tour of an event at her Montecito, California, estate, Winfrey's life on screen and in print is manufactured for parable form. Her weight is a prime topic of embarrassment and recovery. "Standing between Tina Turner and Cher," she would relate, "I felt like a fat cow." Winfrey deconstructs herself so that she may save herself. "I have to focus on being fully alive, awake, present, and engaged, connected in every area of my life. Right *now.*"[55] In case you're tired, she is too, but she is still working harder. She is the icon of the problems her iconicity resolves.

Oprah would say that any description of this iconicity is meaningless without her spirit. It is, she believes and she regales, her spirit that concocts, inspires, and energizes her singular glow. "I feel that I am spirit-led: my own spirit and the greater spirit."[56] From whence this spirit? Her personal faith is both excessively confessional and oddly secreted. Everyone knows, for instance, about her childhood success in the church, the way that her Baptist church cast her early in the role of orator, of minister, of scriptural entertainer.[57] But the reality of her adult practice and congregational participation remains generalized by her productions. When Winfrey left Jeremiah Wright's United Church of Christ, she cited "her fatigue with organized religion and a desire to be involved with a more inclusive ministry."[58] On the *Oprah* show, she testifies about her struggles against authoritarian faith and her own commitment to an omnipotent higher power. "I've been on the spiritual path for a very long time," she summarized, "probably since, you know, the mid-'80s." Breaking with the United Church of Christ was, therefore, a part of a broader pursuit of the truths of the spirit, albeit always in the context of Protestant presumption. "I was raised a Christian," she says. "I still am a Christian."[59] She frequently mentions "God" and the "power of God" on her program, at her inspirational workshops, and in her *O* magazine column. During her Live Your Best Life Tour, Winfrey wrapped up a marathon session by pressing her hands together "worshipfully" while intoning, "I pray for you! I pray for you!"[60] She prays every day and, for many years, claimed to read a passage of scripture every morning. To elaborate the drama of a particular biographic moment, she will detail specific prayers she has offered to God, such as her recitation of "I surrender all, I surrender all, I surrender all, all to my blessed savior" when she was waiting to hear whether she was cast in *The Color Purple*. She persistently tells employees and audience members, "God can dream a bigger dream for you than you can for yourself."[61]

Oprah's transcendent stardom is bound up in her symbolism as a healer, a prophet, a peculiar form of human holy woman. During a 2005 interview, Lisa Marie Presley remarked to Winfrey, "You're like Mama Moses." Her viewers ascribe to her a potency that only religious metaphors can access. "She's a billionaire and a sister," said one, adding that meeting Winfrey was "like meeting Jesus."[62] One viewer explained that Oprah gives her "the tools to find" herself. "I'm not there yet," says Mary Madden, thirty-seven, a suburban housewife from West Islip, New York. "But she gives me the inspiration and the courage to take the journey." Madden, who has three young sons, watches the talk show

religiously, buys Oprah-recommended books, has a subscription to O magazine, and writes in a daily gratitude journal, as Oprah instructs.[63] With her viewers following her taste, her books, and her practices, "Oprah's work has been her own life. That is her ministry."[64]

Most fans posting to Winfrey's message boards would not reach for divine analogies to describe their feelings for Winfrey, and such invocations of Oprah as Jesus should be seen as outliers in the overall classificatory reception of her signification. Moreover, all celebrities to some extent or another engender their fandom through demonstrations of connection and care. For Winfrey, though, the product of her labor *is* her fans' transformation. She is not a religion, she repeats, but she does want you to change your life as she has changed hers. "I'm constantly reading, trying to figure out how the world works," she explains. "I've been a student of spirituality and metaphysics."[65] Her learning, her self-schooled spiritual maturation, is exhibited for their modeling. Even when she defers to another spiritual authority (here, Eckhart Tolle), it is *her* story, her celebrity demonstration that supplies text for her audience's transformations.

> *The Power of Now* has saved me many, many times. As a matter of fact, this has been one of the most hectic days. I just got back from Africa. I'm sleep deprived, and I woke up this morning thinking, Oh my God, I'm going to be so stressed. But I let that go and just thought, "I will be present now." I taped four television shows today, and I was very excited about being able to talk to you, but I kept saying to myself, Don't think about how many other things you have to do. Just be present now. And that is what has gotten me to the end of the day, in this moment.[66]

The monologue supplies a sliver of Winfrey's spiritual life, paraded with an election not merely religiously sacred but also connected to celebrity. Everyone can relate to being sleep deprived—stars *are* just like us! No matter that her deprivation was due to a school and a talk show with her name on them. The point is that her quotidian need is designated as her audience's spiritual recommendation. Eckhart Tolle humbles her mightiness, showing the audience that even she needs a helping hand to interpret her enormity. What connects her to her crowd is the practice bridging his text to her, her to her spirit, and her spirit to you, those seeking care.

The celebrity of her spiritual work is not limited to her sui generis self. Interviews with her celebrity friends and film-promoting pals turn to the deeper matters of the heart. "I'm always on five different spiritual paths at any one time, you know?" Jim Carrey explains.[67] When she encounters guests with differing religious practices (such as John Travolta, a practicing Scientologist, and Wynonna Judd, an evangelical), Winfrey asks them to describe their faith, then quickly affirms the universal elements of this foreign set of beliefs. In her September 2003 interview with Madonna, Winfrey aggressively pursued Madonna's newfound interest in kabbalah. Madonna explained that kabbalah involves two "fundamental principles." First, "we're responsible for everything that happens to us." And second, "we have to take responsibility for everything that happens to us." To both statements, Winfrey nodded her head.

> *Winfrey*: Well, this is what I believe. I didn't know I believe in kabbalah, but these are my beliefs.
>
> *Madonna*: Good.
>
> *Winfrey*: Yeah, these are my beliefs.
>
> *Madonna*: Well, you are. You're a—you're a closet kabbalist.
>
> *Winfrey*: I'm a closet kabbalist.[68]

This dialogue occurs in different forms every time Winfrey encounters someone who professes a particular faith. Winfrey is a "closet" anything that incorporates easily into her universalizing vision, a chameleon shifting colors even as her O remains the same. "A conversation with Sting and his wife, Trudie Styler, got Oprah thinking," the *Oprah* show relates. "If tantric sex works for them, maybe it can work for you!" The narrative quickly supplies information about the practice, summarizing that "Tantra sexuality, a seven-thousand-year-old tradition from India, is about connecting with your partner in such a deep way that the two of you become one through breath, sound and movement." For Winfrey viewer Lisa Schrader and her husband, Rick Schlussel, Tantra was just the answer to their sluggish sexual relationship. They began with "soul gazing," staring deep into each other's eyes. The next step is the "heart salutation," touching foreheads and breathing. "Your orgasmic energy will increase tenfold if you breathe and vocalize," Lisa said.[69] Winfrey's spiritual selections are not gossamer fantasies. They are pragmatic, step-by-step strategies to resolve the difficulties of your bedroom, your laundry room, and your kitchen. Anything that coordinates with your domesticity and makes it more alive, more present, is acceptable spirituality. Anything that does not is framed as oppressive, limiting, and *religious*.

Oprah is involved in her own study of religion, whether or not she wants to be a religion. The very fact of her charismatic sway attracts indictments classifying hers as the "Church of Oprah" or the "Cult of Oprah." To be sure, many aspects of Winfrey's project coordinate with definitions of what scholars call new religious movements, or NRMs. Her promotion of affective bonds among her audience members, for example, alongside her proposal of direct rewards to followers, puts her in the company of other leaders who have capitalized upon seekers needing the comfort of authoritarian interventions. Yet, as sociologists of religion have described the NRM, it becomes clear that leaders of new religious movements are usually figures with few close friends and unpredictable personal behavior and that for an NRM to inaugurate it must demand considerable sacrifices by its followers. Profiles of new religious movements emphasize the importance of boundary maintenance, dividing members in their new order from their old ways of life.[70] Whatever offhand remarks might be made about the modes of the celebrity culture around Winfrey, her ascent does not match patterns observed in the comparison of other religious sects at their outset.

Like women leaders across denominations, however, Winfrey suffers the pins and arrows of female empowerment, criticized in her early years of monomaniacal business practices and an ambiguous sexual identity. The most adamant observers of Oprah accuse her of watering down Christian orthodoxy, using a gendered accusation that she has transformed a tough and masculine religion into an ephemeral and feminine spirituality. "I wish she'd go on and say 'God' and stop talking about a higher being," says Fertina Bell, a church administrator in Los Angeles. "She can say 'Jesus.' She has enough money. If they cancel her show, she can still live."[71] Bell's description of Winfrey's freedom repeats in other Christian descriptions of Winfrey, as critics cite her indifference to additional profit as a reason to fear her.[72] Moreover, her eagerness to incorporate new things shows her disloyalty to Christian ideas. Writing for *Our Sunday Visitor*, Amy Welborn highlighted Winfrey's "un-Christian" elements: "So, in short, here's what Oprah's spirituality is about: a higher power, spirit, soul, 'authentic power,' meaning, healing, affirmation, helping, miracles, meditation, journaling, and angels. An unremarkable New Age hodgepodge. Here's what Oprah's spirituality is not about: sin, redemption, sacrifice, conversion, humility, worship, holiness, and Jesus Christ."[73] For Welborn, what Winfrey isn't, is precisely what she *should* be. Other Christian observers have produced passionate treatises—self-produced and sold online—to describe in scriptural detail just how Winfrey's promotions contradict the teachings of Christ. "Marianne Williamson uses *A Course in Miracles* to teach her

Oprah & Friends listeners how to systematically dismantle the supposedly fear-based worldview of biblical Christianity," one writer explains. "Please pray for Oprah & Marianne, that their eyes will be opened."[74] Elsewhere, another critic, David J. Stewart writes, "Oprah teaches and promotes New Age heresy." She is "so dangerous . . . she has massive influence over millions of people and is tragically using it to lead them straight into the fires of Hell."[75] Carrington Steele produced a video and booklet to counsel Protestant pastors on how to guide their flocks away from Winfrey, whom he reads as a sign of the end times. "What you have here is evil doctrine, persuasive and subliminal techniques, sudden rises in power and even the latter day peace alliance," Steele explains, noting that "the pieces of the puzzle are coming together." Focusing on Winfrey's combined promotional work for Barack Obama and Eckhart Tolle, Steele believes this is the fulfillment of prophecy and that "false teachers" walk among us, bringing in "damnable heresies."[76] For these worried writers, Winfrey's productions construct a cult of the New Age.

In a 2002 *Christianity Today* article, "The Church of O," Winfrey's work was carefully broken down into the particulars of her biography, her magazine, the book club, the journaling, and spiritual counselors and interpreted as a wholly new spiritual movement, led by a "postmodern priestess—an icon of church-free spirituality." After reviewing several interpretations of her religious contexts, Latonya Taylor determined that the brand of spirituality Winfrey advocates is ultimately unsatisfying. "The question for Christians is this," Taylor writes. "What can we do to help Oprah and her disciples find what they are ultimately seeking—the power, grace, and love that can only be found through a personal relationship with Jesus Christ?"[77] Taylor casts Winfrey as the nemesis to persistent Christianity, a Pied Piper distracting her flock from their righteous work.

Self-designated born-again Christians have been among Winfrey's heartiest critics, even though Baptist Winfrey might be included among their numbers. Since her childhood memorization of biblical passages, Winfrey has departed from the formal contours of any church while still retaining aspects of evangelical performance. Before I proceed with such a parallel, a brief outline of what evangelicalism is may be useful. *Evangelicalism* is a term with several descriptive usages: first, it summarizes a large theological subset of Protestantism; second, it titles a social movement that was inaugurated in the Reformation and continues to the present day; and third, it describes a mode of religious expression in which missionary activity is the primary objective. The word has its origins in the Greek word *evangelion,* meaning "the good news" or "the gospel." From this root, we get the verb *to evangelize* and the nouns *evangelist* and *evangelical.* As one historian has noted, the only test to determine whether a Christian is an evangelical is whether he or she possesses a strong Christian identity that supersedes denominational location. Although many Christian theologians might be described as evangelical, evangelicalism does not possess a systematic theological genealogy. Most evangelicals would describe their world as crowded by the supernatural and suffused with the active and gracious presence of a triune God. God is the ultimate arbiter and source of evangelical salvation: He directs lives, motivates history, heals loyal followers, and empowers the many toward righteousness. Indeed, it is this "power of the Holy Spirit" that leads many evangelicals to distinguish themselves from "Churchmen," who they believe rely more on grace through sacraments than on grace personally experienced. Such talk of the sanctifying Holy Spirit infuses evangelical rhetoric and is used by believers to measure themselves against other Christian adherents.

Despite the sense of some that she may indeed be the Antichrist, the work of Oprah and the work of an evangelical in the last decades of the twentieth century are not so dissimilar. First, they share a mutual emphasis on expanding into new forms of mediation, especially in the development of television and the Internet as sites for engagement. Second, Oprah and evangelical advocates focus on lay piety and communal worship in gargantuan virtual communities. Third, evangelicalism and Winfrey cultivate parachurch ministries for type-specific pastoral care. Relying on personas and drama, the storied televangelists capitalize upon domestic broadcasting to become major celebrities with national followings.[78] These "electronic churches" have attracted large followings of believers who come from a variety of denominational contexts but now elect to watch these programs in addition to, or as a replacement of, church attendance at a specific denomination or church building. Like the televangelist's broadcast church, the megachurch emerged after the Sixties under the leadership of an often unaccredited charismatic authority who emphasized worship uncommitted to stock liturgies. Describing Joel Osteen's Lakewood Church in Houston, Texas, one reporter writes, "Gone are traditional religious dogma, rituals, and symbols, replaced by uplifting songs and sermons. Congregants are taught that—through God—they are victors, not victims." It is "Jesus meets the power of positive thinking," and, according to Boston College professor Alan Wolfe, the message is fittingly "upbeat, one of empowerment."[79]

Nothing in this ceaselessly renovating evangelicalism is built to last. Of his arrival at one Dallas megachurch, Jonathan Walton writes: "The actual church building is more instrumental than architecturally inspiring. Like a sports complex or convention center, it seems built more to accommodate huge crowds than to impress."[80] Critics of megachurches and their Las Vegas architecture conflate these structures with histories of white flight and decentralized postsuburban landscapes. Like the service industries within which so many of their congregants work, megachurches represent in such critical renderings another part of a "fast food nation" seeking quick spiritual rehab and caloric intake.[81] Yet the ease of the megachurch is not merely a product of recent history. In its exacting pursuit of answers to the particularities of real life, it is component to the longer history of evangelical emphasis on usability. As Candy Gunther Brown has explained, "Usefulness, rather than genre or form, was the primary characteristic that marked texts as evangelical."[82]

Usefulness and usability motivated the development of parachurch and local ministries to serve particular outlets of congregant identity. These smaller subsections of church gatherings constitute a significant part of contemporary Christian religious organization. Joel Osteen's Lakewood Church, for example, comprises over twenty ministries, including ones organized for children, teenagers, single parents, singles, married couples, and men or women exclusively. Problem-oriented ministries, too, exist, like the Financial Ministry (providing "a pathway for people to move into a financial covenant with God") and the Celebrate Recovery ministry ("to help those struggling with hurts, habits, and hang-ups"). These ministries trade in idiom familiar to any *Oprah* show viewer, promising to offer time "away from the everyday details of life with an opportunity to deepen your walk with Christ" and to "take a break from the busy demands of everyday life and invest in what is really important: your relationship with God and your relationship with the people around you."[83]

"I'm not trying to be some evangelist," Winfrey would say to these evangelical manifestations, arguing that her "intention is to try and get people to feel some illumination."[84] Like her organizing and subdividing evangelical compatriots, however, Winfrey has realized that her charisma can stretch only so thin. So she's increasingly incorporated a "stable of regular on-air experts to lighten her on-air responsibilities."[85] Each of these assistant pastors deserves book-length treatment of his or her own, since each of them has cultivated an elaborate online, televised, and textual empire of his or her own as a result of the association with Winfrey. For the purposes of this discussion, however, it is necessary only to note their assistive ministerial role, assigned subcategory of topical responsibility, and reiterated presence in the empire of Oprah. The magazine includes two regular on-air counselors (Dr. Phil McGraw and Suze Orman), as well as the small stable of regular commentators, such as Martha Beck and Sharon Salzberg (offering insight into spiritual matters), Valerie Monroe (makeup), and Lisa Kogan (comic domesticity). On the Oprah & Friends radio network, more *Oprah*-show regulars receive air time, including designer Nate Berkus (who "reveals the secrets to great style"), Dr. Mehmet Oz (who offers "information on how to live the healthiest life possible"), Bob Greene (who "tells you the truth about how to lose weight"), Dr. Robin Smith (who helps solve "the biggest problems in your life"), Jean Chatzky (who "shows you how to make money and keep it"), Marianne Williamson (who "shows you how to create miracles in your life"), and Oprah's own best friend, Gayle King (with whom "nothing's off limits"). This cast perpetuates the diverse sameness Winfrey repeatedly parades, blending black faces and white ones, men and women, degreed and amateur voices who specialize in the classic Oprah roster of concerns: spirit, body, self, money, beauty, family, and change.

No matter their specialty, however, these counselors share three attributes: a gift for the clarion one-liner, a commitment to the blended pastiche, and an ambiguous self-presentation. No one would be invited back to the *Oprah* show again if he or she couldn't declare something efficiently before commercial break or something salable in a magazine cover headline. Moreover, no one could return if he or she didn't represent ease with the world's diversity—in appearance, race, situation, and financial need. All of Winfrey's compatriots articulate a bourgeois populism, seeking, as she does, to assimilate the plurality of the world's problems into sound-bite wellness, smart hair cuts, and proper body odor. "A cashmere throw is so versatile," explains Nate Berkus in his advertisement of "perfect presents" for the 2006 holiday season. "On your couch it will aid and abet frequent nap-taking; on extra-cold days (or on an airplane) it doubles as a quick shawl."[86] Every object can be used multiply, and every multiple represents a holistic view of the necessary usability of your life and taste. This sense of the domestic reality of the postulated *Oprah* viewer is intriguing, since each of her counselors, like Winfrey, seems a little cut off from normative family contexts. Of the entire crew, only Dr. Phil presents a nuclear family of his own in regular discursive intervals; the rest are single, single mothers, partnered in same-sex relationships, or private about their personal lives. This contributes to an overarching sense of disconnection, of a queer dynamic with the Middle America they console. Like Winfrey, they share an ardent belief in the possibility of change. "Changing Your Life Is a Journey," exclaims one advertisement for the *Dr. Phil* show, while another proclaims, "Every Day Is a Turning Point." But against Winfrey's profile in tough love tenderness, her counselors give a little more toughness. She hires them to play her foil, to say the things she can't say, but, as she tells her audience over and over again, "I'm thinking."

To pull just one example from among many, consider Suze Orman's September 23, 2008, appearance on the *Oprah* show. With a nation on the brink of financial disaster, Orman explained the mammoth, labyrinthine disaster in domestic terms:

> *Orman*: All right. You built, you know, you bought homes you couldn't afford. You put things on your credit cards you couldn't afford. You took the equity out of your homes to buy other things you couldn't afford. You leased your cars. You bought new cars. You went on vacation. You bought clothes. You spent money like it was going out of style, and it wasn't your money to spend, because why? They were borrowing it. When you borrow money, you leverage yourself. The United States of America leveraged itself so high that when it started to come down, the whole thing now has fallen down. Is this serious? I have to tell you, ladies and gentlemen, this is more serious than it has ever been.

Winfrey is pleased with this explanation, replying, "As you're speaking I'm thinking, 'It's just like the law of cause and effect. It really is more spiritual than financial, and it is reflecting the spiritual consciousness. The spiritual consciousness is just being reflected back to us.' That's what I'm hearing." Invoking the law of attraction also advertised in Winfrey's episodes on *The Secret,* Orman agrees immediately, relating the problems of an international economic situation to the everyday vulnerabilities regularly rehearsed by her, in mantra form:

> *Orman*: That's right and . . . these corporations, the banks, the brokerage firms, all insurance companies are made up of people. People, whether they're CEOs or they're you, people are people . . . and . . . there's a consciousness or a lack of consciousness where those people didn't care about these people—because those people cared about money before people. Do you not hear me say it all the time? What is my mantra? People first, then money, then things. Have you all ever wondered, "Why does Suze Orman say people first, then money, then things? What does that mean?" It means, if we cared about people more than we cared about money, we would not be having what happened today, because

the people who run the corporations, if they had cared about all of you, they wouldn't have created loans that you couldn't afford, loans that would eventually, you know, just totally dissolve.

If the people in the corporations had cared about you, if they had, as Suze instructed, put "people first," then this story would not be as bad as it is. Suze's regular sound bite—her mantra, to invoke the religious idiom—isn't just something she says; it is something that could, in its easy triplicate, save the world:

> *Winfrey*: So, what do we do?
>
> *Orman*: So, what we do is—this is the time to be, truthfully, safe and sound and to stop living . . . the financial lies that you have been living. Stop doing what we have been begging you [to do] on *The Oprah Winfrey Show* now for ten years. Start doing what we have been begging you to do, which is—if you don't have the money to pay for something, can you just not buy it? Can you wait? Can we start looking at keeping our cars for ten years rather than getting a new one every three? To downsize rather than have this dream of wanting more and more megamansions?[87]

The circumstances of Orman's sermon are unique. Normally, Winfrey's assistant pastors counsel individuals or single families, not the entire American public. Nonetheless the themes of the sermon are familiar: you've been doing something wrong, we have your solution, if you watch this show, you'll improve. With the solution distilled to a portable Orman nugget ("People first, then money, then things"), the viewers may then return to everyday life slightly reproached, still angry at the abstract unconsciousness of corporations, and certain that they need to rethink their monetary lives somehow. Fortunately, the Web site guides you to Orman's products and ideas, so you will not, and should never be, alone in your struggle.

The entirety of Winfrey's enterprise is connected by such missionary camaraderie. "You Just Have to Dust Yourself Off and Move On," bellows one O magazine headline. "5 Things You Should Never Do If You Want to Feel Beautiful," promises another. What to do, what to say, what to wear, what to hear, how to listen, whom to date, whom to dump, when to dump, when to buy, what to buy, how to improve, what to practice, what to read, when to take a break. Consultants swarm the pages of the magazine, the episodes, and the Web content, informing you of "21 Things You Can Stop Worrying about Right Now" and advising you of the best things you can do for your relationship, the books you should read just once, the types of friends every woman should have, ways to get a life, places to see in your lifetime, and ideas that could fix the world.[88] Spiritual leaders supply a rarified brand of counsel, as in the article "Soul Mates: A Primer," which includes counsel on dating from "religious leaders" and "metaphysicians."[89] Buddhist monk Pema Chödrön, Archbishop Desmond Tutu, the Dalai Lama—these are Oprah's counselors, and so they are yours, too.[90] Receiving the same page-length (but rarely the same screen time) treatment as Julia Roberts and Tom Hanks, her "memorable thinkers" reconcile the numbered (six ways to, five ideas about, nineteen moments to) counsel of her glossy advertisements with the thoughtful spiritual seeker Winfrey longs to be. Beneath the spectacle of her products and their genre-appropriate surfaces, she sneaks long stares at the spiritual revelators who have spent their lives in less ornate confines than she propagates.

Over the years, of course, she has invited a variety of spiritual counselors from the establishment perimeter. Plucking books from the self-help section of the bookstore, Winfrey has invited their authors, minor celebrities on the inspirational speaker circuit, to append her offerings and supply new classifications for her self-diagnosis. Most recently, and most globally distributed, was her March 2008 ten-week classroom discussion with Eckhart Tolle of his book *A New Earth*, but Tolle's appearance was only a recent installment in a two-decade parade of spiritual pets. Included among her invitees have been Deepak Chopra, head of the Chopra Center for Well Being in La Jolla, California; Iyanla Vanzant, founder of Inner Visions Worldwide; and Gary Zukav, founder of Genesis: The Foundation for the Universal Human. In addition, Winfrey has focused episodes on makeovers and viewer problems solved through the key words of the Insight Meditation advocate Martha Beck, the Unity minister Eric Butterworth, the creative visualization doyenne Shakti Gawain, and the medical intuitive Caroline Myss. Each life coach, makeover manager, and spiritual guide comes bearing books and dreams of O-embossed spin-offs. These leaders represent ideas flecked with Buddhist, Hindu, Christian, Toltec, and Yoruba interpretations and practices. Of the existent troops, Marianne Williamson has endured the longest with her latter-day New Thought expositions. Through their appearances, many of these counselors would gain spots on Winfrey's co-owned Oxygen Network or radio network; some would return several times to elaborate their central concept (e.g., "sacred contracts," "shadow beliefs"); a few would acquire space in the magazine. Even at their most celebrated, however, these consultants have remained advisory, threading their ideas through an O-shaped needle.

If we were to profile each of these leaders, we would discover the diffused backdrops of the New Age movement, a category that ties together the loose affiliations of proponents and practitioners of channeling, psychic healing, past-life regression, and holistic health. "Instead of monthly or weekly ritual groups, like covens," writes Sarah Pike, "New Agers are typically more comfortable in specialist-client relationships." For the conglomeration of purchasers gathered beneath the generic promise of a New Age, practices of spiritual and physical healing facilitate the shift to a new level of consciousness.[91] There are some intentional communities, some patterns in workshop attendance, some signal texts, and some ritual practices (visualization, astrology, meditation, Reiki) that herald a New Age outlook. Those associated with New Age seeking frequently search for connectivity to the divine inner self through techniques earned and learned and bought from experts, experts who proffer their skills through self-authored texts, in community college classes and weekend retreats, and in small-group gatherings. According to one historian of religions, what unifies New Age beliefs is an optimistic view of the future, a rejection of any form of authoritarian doctrine or hierarchy, an ethic of self-empowerment, an eclecticism of beliefs and practices, and a press to use science for spiritual ends.[92]

In any such description, Winfrey's products are an obvious document, offering, as she does, a showcase of the spiritual generality and the purveyor placards of postcounterculture seeking. "Spirit to me is the essence of who we are," Winfrey explains. "That essence doesn't require any particular belief. It just is." There is variety among these thinkers and their writings, and there has been variety in Winfrey's duration of interest with each of them. But the take-home is always the same: find the spirit inside yourself that will connect you to a better understanding of your true self. Rid yourself of all blockages in order to find you, to be you. As Winfrey will repeat, "Spirituality is about paying attention to your life—always asking, in every moment, *What can I learn from this?*"[93] Everyday life is the site of a possible Winfrey-named sacred, precisely because attentiveness to your world— your world, now—is the binding concept of her many visitors. "There are no ordinary moments," Winfrey remarks. "To be alive is the most extraordinary thing we know."[94]

The success of Oprah is not this message. It is that she—she as Spirit, celebrity, commodity, charismatic, evangelical—*is* the product. The modes of Harpo command certain abbreviations, leading to exclamations over sartorial triumph ("Hallelujah! JEANS THAT FIT!"), religious allusions run amok ("*O*'s Bra Bible"), and spiritually assured puns ("The Power of Positive Dressing"). Noting that the mode is a commodity is, by now, redundant. But to note that the mode is therefore necessarily smoothing, transferable, and commensurable takes us to a stronger description of the religious now. It is Winfrey's spiritual nondiscrimination, not her spiritual peculiarities, that have made her successful in the broad marketplace. To say there is a unity between mind and spirit, a purpose to our indwelling, a hope for spiritual rejuvenation isn't particular; it's generic. Evangelicalism and Orthodox Judaism may not advocate these ideas, but they do not condemn them, either. Let us not make precious this convertible pastiche: universal sells, universal converts, and the universal consoles.

Wade Clark Roof once offhandedly remarked, "Much of what passes as spirituality is as thin as chicken soup and as transparent as Celestine profits."[95] Roof is perhaps too abrupt with this thinness, since to name a width suggests that "thickness" is possible, that somewhere a denser thicket of religiosity and ideation might be found. These are dangerous suggestions, since against what religious baseline could we measure the relative complexity of Harpo's enterprises? As religionists celebrate our plural climes, as sociologists tally the trips of fundamentalist to the psychic, as historians catalog the liberalism of seeking, we must remember that what makes Oprah Winfrey work is the incorporation of her audience into the spiritualization of herself as the sale. This is not hoodwink. This is a product that postulates how much time its audience share can take for its consumption, and it serves up morsels specially prepared for frenzy and balm.

She cannot stop the abbreviations, because they serve her so very well. Before hitting the treadmill and jumping into her day, Winfrey pulls out a piece of personal stationery inscribed with one of her favorite quotations, one by Ralph Waldo Emerson: "What lies behind us and what lies before us are tiny matters compared to what lies within us."[96] From the "Thought of the Day" quotation posted to her Web site and e-mailed to you in her *Spirit Newsletter* to the pull-out quotations in the magazine, discerning mantras for daily usage becomes a critical practice of O. "Throw yourself a line," puns an article title. "Call them mantras, mind tools, or—our favorite—O-phorisms. They're the soothing, energizing, sanity-restoring phrases that can get you through any situation."[97] The mantra, the axiom, the abbreviated cut-to-commercial cataloging of what has already transpired: these tools make up an Oprah sense of spirituality.

Toward the end of her 2008–9 season, Winfrey joined the micro-blogging service Twitter. Users on Twitter broadcast messages of 140 characters or fewer to note where they are and what they're doing or sometimes to submit meaningful quotations to a cadre of readers who track—for amusement, for sociability, for self-expression—their words as banners of their day. "When someone like Oprah, who is a very smart businesswoman, sees that a new media platform is worthy of her engaging on it, it signifies a real sea change," one marketer commented. "The mega-celebrity marketing machine that is Oprah seems like the next level of adoption."[98] Oprah transitions the product: moving through the O is a funnel to the next level, transcending to the spiritual and material big time. She offers and composes the difference that transcendence makes. With all her words for spirit and all her celebrations of spirituality, Oprah is not a message seeking complication. She is a voice seeking microphones to amplify her permeating presence in your survival song.

CHAPTER 3

Diverting Conversions

The Makeover as Social Rite

It was just another episode, a day like so many other days with *The Oprah Winfrey Show*. This particular show in 2003 devoted itself to crowning four women as princesses. "I love surprising people," Oprah said in her opening voice-over. "I love making them happy." And make them happy she did. The first princess, Ashley Smith, earned an audition for *American Idol;* the second, Fannie Eugene, received weekly Merry Maid service, a $23,700 Ford Windstar minivan for her long workday commute, and a deluxe trip for two to New York City, accessorized with new luggage; the third, Linda Feinstein, received a total home makeover, including wall-to-wall carpeting, a new dining room set (matching china, silverware, linens, pots and pans, all courtesy of Crate and Barrel), and a new washer, dryer, dishwasher, refrigerator, and microwave; finally, Laurie Mullick received a complete wardrobe from Dana Buchman.[1] None of this was unusual, and despite its relentlessly dramatic reveals ("a *complete* wardrobe?"), none of it was very surprising. All resonated with what had come before: the goods, the excess, the gifting, and the spectacular casting. The *ritual* of her generosity is what is so resonant to the cultural observer: the care of the managers, the timing of the process, and the seriousness of their steps. The room knows what to expect from Oprah, and they know how it will come.

To begin, the *Oprah* show conducts the event with giddy ritual care. Each time a new princess is announced, she receives a large tiara and a sash (e.g., "PRINCESS FANNIE"), and she remains on a center-stage throne as her montage screens overhead. The proper nouns of the stories change even if the narrative arc does not vary. Every princess possesses the same attributions: she is overtaxed, unendingly kind, marvelously deserving, and somehow financially needful. Though the princess bevy appears diverse (including a sixteen-year-old white high school student, a middle-aged African American nanny and housekeeper, a worn-out white small-town waitress, and a soon-to-be-a-spinster schoolteacher), their montages show them to be uniform in their generosity and financial poverty, in their kindness to others at material cost to themselves.[2]

The making of such queens echoes other forms of televised events. In their research on the ceremonial modes of televised history, Daniel Dayan and Elihu Katz name three sorts of media events: competitions (e.g., the Olympics), conquests (a moon landing), and coronations. The coronation includes rites of stillness and seriousness, as coronations are often solemn forms of glorifications, of "beatifications and canonizations."[3] The coronations of Oprah Winfrey's "Princess for a Day" canonize women with a winking solemnity in which Winfrey is the sieve and celebrant. She coordinates this ritual reiteration of their daily sacrifice. Through the Oprah-produced montage, average women become minor saints in the landscape of America, deserving of some divine intervention. The world simply cannot be the sort of place where such goodness goes without its deserved, and previously overlooked, reward.

Scholars of religion emphasize that any definition of ritual ought to include some consideration of the relationship between the human actors involved with the ritual and their relationship to superhuman beings. Although debates about just what ritual is and just what it does vary, most religionists agree that ritual is a process of actions ordered into a beginning, a middle, and an end. These actions often enact stories that retell the metaphorical and literal organization of the world, its hierarchies, origins, or central principles, or all of these. Some social theorists though have persistently set aside the explicit citation of a divine figuring, focusing instead on the material manifestations of ritual action. In such ritual descriptions, talk of divinity is implicit within communal behavior and not explicitly invoked in its ritual performance. This is how some scholars have defined Thanksgiving dinner and Super Bowl Sunday as "ritual events," even though the superhuman beings at such occasions are more conjurations of the observers than incantations of the actors. Other religionists resist the dilution of the category ritual with such vague instances. This book traffics in the excessive specifics of these vagaries, looking to the rites of Oprah to discern the spiritual ambition of her secular conveyances. Her coronations present a pervasively divine icon extending, with unstoppable gushing, gifts to those who remind us of the order of things in an overlooking world.

Once the montage concludes, the cameras return to Oprah and her princesses. Now the unveiling begins. A Vanna White lookalike pulls back a curtain to reveal Sears appliances; an army of models files out in Laurie's new wardrobe; Paula Abdul, then a judge on *American Idol,* takes a seat in the front row, awaiting Ashley's performance. Each gift appears with a touch of irony: Aren't these crowns extreme? And where did the elflike helpers come from? Winfrey is never anything less than demonstrably self-deprecating. The sincerity of the donation and the honesty of its reception cannot be denied. "Wow," Oprah says after viewing Princess Fannie Eugene's montage, "so it sounds like—you deserve a break, ma'am." And after all that you've heard (Fannie has adopted seven children orphaned by relatives, she nannies two wealthy white New Orleans families, and she tends to her ailing husband), you believe she does. Not only does she deserve a break, but she deserves an *Oprah* break, including luxury hotels, indulgent respite, and virtuous self-satisfaction. The moment of personal, spiritual release, after which everything will be truly different, comes only after submission to the O.

Every guest on *The Oprah Winfrey Show* is similarly blessed: she is praised in her greatness and offered bounty as her reward. This individual reformation is the hallmark of the *Oprah* show. "In all cases," wrote anthropologist Claude Lévi-Strauss, "ritual makes constant use of two procedures: parceling out and repetition."[4] This is the ritual Oprah offers her guests and her princesses: a repeated recognition. Whether it is within the confines of an episode (the process of coronation) or a redundancy among her episodes (the pattern of "make a wish"), repetition is the necessary condition of her message. Conducted within the walls of her Chicago studio, Winfrey's ritual process offers a corrective to the despairs and inequalities of the world outside her kingdom. Writing about ritual, historian J.C. Heestermann describes an analogous process: "[The ritual] has nothing to say about the world, its concerns and conflicts. It proposes, on the contrary, a separate, self-contained world ruled exclusively by the comprehensive and exhaustive order of the ritual."[5] The world of Oprah Winfrey is that self-contained world, that world apart from the mundane and arbitrary rules of ordinary existence. When women enter her studio, they are merely mothers, wives, and workers. They leave as princesses. Every woman—even those in the audience, sitting without crowns—can now imagine the possibility of coronation if they give just a little bit more. Or, if they shop at the right places:

> *Winfrey*: We have so many people to thank for helping us pull off our very first ever Princess for a Day extravaganza—Joe Rizza Ford, Sears, Roebuck and Company, . . . Crate and Barrel, and NYC and Company for putting together Fannie's trip to the Big Apple. Thank you to Debi Lilly from Perfect Event for making our studio look so beautiful. Also our thanks go to Tiaras.com. And get yourself a crown yourself. It makes you feel very special just to wear one.

Winfrey closes nearly every show with this brand of product recognition. During the show, all the products are revealed without elaboration or back story, offered as if in a dreamscape. But at the end, we must, briefly, return to earth. Everything comes from somewhere, and there is no such thing as a free gift.

By the conclusion of any episode, Oprah has provided the necessary program guide. *These dreams are yours for the taking.* All you need is the money or the right family member writing the right sort of letter and the right profile of martyrdom. "Fannie's majestic air and noble heart are legendary, according to her friends and family," Winfrey explains. "Just listen to this. Listen to this." The "listen to this" is a suffering testimony in montage form. Marcel Mauss has explained that the economy of the gift is reciprocal, obligating the receiver to respond to the donor.[6] Another observer elaborates, "While having the appearance of being free and gratuitous, the gift in fact evokes a countergift."[7] In Harpo Studios, the "countergift" is the first-person testimonial. The recipient receives blessings only after she has exposed the extremity of her need to a viewing audience, to the wheels of production that rely upon suffering for their process.[8] The transaction of the gift is the transformation of the recipient, the story of sorrow proffered for products that may ease that sorrow. The procedure of the ritual recalculates a balance between confessor and confessed, host and needful parasite, queen and princess. Yet it should be clear: Winfrey's tiara is the largest of them all. She offers the designation, she mediates the negotiation, and her life organizes the moral equation. These rites are hers.

Examining the gifting bounty of the "Princess for a Day" episode emphasizes the nature of the gift that organizes so many episodes of *The Oprah Winfrey Show*. As one reporter rhapsodized, "Her show is one big childhood-surprise party, only instead of a pony, she's bearing a Pontiac G6." Giving away 276 new Pontiac G6 cars at the start of her nineteenth season in 2004, Winfrey gushed over the model's satellite radio, the sun roof, and its powerful engine.[9] But she remarked about the give-away, "My favorite part was when I announced the first 10 who really, really needed cars because they had such old clinkers, and they were so excited. I wasn't so sure that was gonna happen. Sometimes people just don't give you any kind of reaction. When I saw their reaction and how overwhelmed they were, I thought, 'Oh, I got 'em!'"[10] "Getting" these recipients when they really, really were in need, she gives to them, and she gives to you, prescribing a studio process for home use. "You can reach out. You can be a princess, a queen in your own life by taking what you have and extending it to other people," she reveals elsewhere.[11] If you give to the world, you will receive. But your gift is never merely the generosity of your gift; it is never just about being Fannie to those other children. It is the testimony of your Fannie-hood, your confession of your good within an ungrateful, broken-down jalopy world that gives you gifts that balance the scale of your daily, womanly giving.

The gift Winfrey gives is the ritual makeover, including in its various incarnations rehearsal and reward, confession and redemption, intimacy and spectacle. The makeover is not only material—including the dispersal of new cars, new clothes, new dryers—but also spiritual. You are made over with the compliment the goods supply, with the galvanized ambition they provide to pursue, now, your even better life. Observing the rituals of this gift procedure returns us to an affect of the religious, namely, the distributive function of the ritual. But watching Winfrey's makeover rites also turns our attentions to the religious affect of a secular rite. Although our object is Winfrey's parceling of gifts and gab, the aspects of her process resonate throughout her medium (television) and her genre (the talk show). This is some sort of secular rite, one that we pursue to name (what variation of "secular"? what stripe of "rite"?) through a move in Winfrey's confessional paradise of memoir. Other makeovers exist in the contemporary American televisual landscape, including *Extreme Makeover Home Edition, The Swan, The Biggest Loser,* and the literature on these comparative examples suggests an affinity between Winfrey's work and theirs, as those shows, too, propose that external change assists internal wellness. The distinguishing mark of a Winfrey makeover is she herself, which makes her case less singular than indicative. What might be said here about Winfrey's transformation circus may be seen elsewhere with the same aspiring hunger to change who we are.

Each makeover elicits from the audience a response, posted to message boards and expressed in on-air exclamations. Harpo employees and producers review this material, frequently revisiting figures of renown in subsequent episodes or finding new guests from these volunteered comments. Fannie Eugene, one of the nominated princesses, received abundant accolades for her sweetness and her sincerity of appreciation for the coronation:

> *Winfrey*: It is all yours, Fannie. God bless you.
>
> *Fannie*: God bless you.
>
> *Winfrey*: God bless you.
>
> *Fannie*: God bless you.
>
> *Winfrey*: God is blessing me right now. He's blessing me right now. It is a blessing to be able to do this for you.
>
> *Fannie*: God bless you. Oh, my God. My God, this is unreal. Oh, my God.
>
> *Winfrey*: I know. But you have the tape. See, you can play it back. It's really happening.

Of the four princesses, Fannie Eugene suffered from the most extreme poverty and offered to others, according to her montage testimonies, the most excessive generosity. The racial story harkened to images of spiritualized black care and white pleasure in black care that reverberated with Winfrey's relationship to her own audience. Recall that Fannie worked for two very wealthy white families. And if taken as truth, the montage exhibited a lot of other family members and friends praising Fannie's magnanimity. It was hard then not to wonder why none of those people assisted Fannie, why one of her employers didn't buy her a car, and why someone didn't give Fannie a day off. The instinct to appeal to Oprah tells us again something about what Oprah provides. She fills the space that her postulated audience is too tired, too guilty, or too unimaginative to conjure.[12] At the end, Fannie will have a minivan, a three-day vacation to New York, and red luggage. She has fabulous luggage even as if nothing else has ostensibly altered. The structures of Fannie's world are not edited; the existent ones are just better accessorized.

The tiara endures through the travails of a life still struggling. Princess Fannie subsequently "moves back home" in an episode of that title (February 9, 2009), produced as a follow-up to Hurricane Katrina. In that episode, Fannie is described as "one of our all-time favorite guests," who was, after the hurricane, found living in a FEMA trailer. The 2003 Oprah van receives a special accolade as the way by which Fannie and her family escaped Katrina.

Fannie: Well, we found out Katrina was coming. I was able to pile twelve
of my relatives into the van that Oprah gave me. We was able to get out.
When we were leaving, I made sure I had one very important thing, my
tiara that Oprah gave me when I became princess for a day. And being
the van was as crowded as it was with kids, I didn't want it stepped on,
so I put it on. I made sure it was safe.

Two years after the storm, Fannie still has her tiara, wearing it as she
exits the stormy Crescent City with children in tow. The strength of
the tiara might buoy her spirits, but it couldn't offer shelter, and the
contractors have slowed in the rebuilding of her home. Winfrey finds
this unacceptable: "I think . . . for me, Fannie represents, you know, the
multitude, the thousands and thousands of people whose FEMA trailers
are still in their yard and didn't have this opportunity, and she represents, you know, the struggle and the hope." Before Nate Berkus, Winfrey's favorite in-house redecorator, can work his hopeful magic, they
must survey the damage, noting how tiny the bathroom in the trailer
is, just how many children are stuffed in its tiny metal confines. "Can
you imagine trying to be a family in this space?" Oprah asks from her
Chicago studio. You *can* imagine it once you've had the montage tour,
once there has been a paced exploration of the damage and reblessing
of the sanctified site.

When Hurricane Gustav struck, Winfrey and Nate teleconferenced
to check the damage again:

Winfrey: Well, you know, Fannie, I was thinking about you and, obviously,
the people of New Orleans and Mississippi and the Gulf Coast, but, you
know, during that whole Gustav, I was thinking, "How's Fannie's house?
How's Fannie's house?" How was the house when you came back?

Fannie: The house is great. When we left I knew they would have a little
debris with the wind and all. But somewhere in my spirit, I just knew
that my house would be okay, because God had already blessed me to
have it done, which was a huge blessing. And I knew it wasn't going to
be taken away from me just that easily.

Winfrey: I heard you also—you took the crown with you again?

Fannie: Everywhere I go my crown goes. It's very important to me. It keeps
me grounded and let's me know that good things do happen and it will
happen.

Winfrey: Yeah.

The crown is the memory of a makeover self. When Fannie explains
that she no longer has her PRINCESS FANNIE sash, Nate Berkus makes

her a new one. "I thought, 'We're the ones who gave you the sash, so we should be able to make another one.'" Harpo cannot remake the politics of disaster, nor will it enter into an examination of Delta economics. Its accessories signify a self but not a society that can be transformed. And Harpo will repeat this makeover whenever the right victim, with the right narrative potency, prostrates herself before the queen.

Exposure is therefore a necessary component of the makeover procedure. Such disclosing testimony defines talk show television and is, many observers have argued, a variety of "evangelical disclosure."[13] Winfrey's subjects are women who have celebrated others but have not revealed or reveled in themselves. "Maybe you're like so many women I've talked to over the years who have suspended their deepest desires in order to accommodate everything and everyone else," Winfrey writes in O magazine. "You ignore the nudge to finally get on with what you know you should be doing."[14] To know what you should be doing requires revealing not only your deepest desires but also what you've done during their suspension. The Oprah confession elicits not only promises of new days and better cars but also the revelation of what had been hidden before, during their "suspension," during your servile Fannie days.

This is where the confession and the makeover meet, with the first as a prerequisite for the pleasure in the second. An hour-long interview with former New Jersey governor Jim McGreevey (September 19, 2006) provides a porthole to Winfrey's proclivity for rolling in such hidden trouble prior to awakened alacrity. Viewers trained by Winfrey's now redundant narrative expect a nostalgic opening segment, the picture-perfection of a hidden life. "Just two years ago," Winfrey explains, "he was a family man with a beautiful wife and two daughters by his side. He was one of the most powerful governors in America, with dreams of one day perhaps living in the White House." The Oprah Winfrey Show regularly begins such scenes with sepia-tinted visuals: "Michael was a Cub Scout leader, a high school tennis coach; everybody said he was a good father," another episode begins, "until the day all hell broke loose." Hell breaks loose usually within Winfrey's first monologue, where she tracks the tale from pretty family portrait to postapocalyptic devastation, from ideal type to squalid collapse. "You know what? That is a false perception that all of us have," Winfrey relates during an interview with child-actress-turned-drug-addict Tatum O'Neal. "We think when you're that good-looking and you live in that kind of life that you can't be violent or neglectful."[15]

The habit of the show is compulsive revelation through confession of the dark side of pretty faces, of the hidden desires of public men, and the hungry needs of laboring women. This Oprah arc is so expected that we anticipate her tales before they're told. If I tell you a New Jersey governor was on the *Oprah* show, you can predict that his was a narrative of struggle, not a narrative of ceaseless cheer and happy hopscotch. You would predict that he had experienced trial—painkiller addiction, perhaps, or a wretched childhood, or a life-changing moral moment in sub-Saharan Africa. You would predict from the outset the eventual Oprah-endorsed conversion, the moment in which she translates metamorphosis as commodity. Winfrey's consumer base watches not because they expect surprise but because they recall the pleasure of hearing the surprise before, the simultaneous knowing of salacious details and a certitude of a triumphant return. Ideals are established, destruction occurs, and the subject is moved away from the deceptions of the pristine picket-fenced exterior to the hard truths of interior self-knowledge. The deviant here is offered rectitude and reentry into the social order.[16] It is then utterly predictable, so predictable as to be ritual, that being Governor Jim McGreevey wasn't all it was cracked up to be. Viewers know before they are told that McGreevey had a hard time being the all-American man, that he had ascended to great power only to have it thwarted by unexamined desire, and that his narrative of that trial—the book he is selling, the interview he is strolling through with somber charm and eager triumph—is so made for *Oprah* that you almost believe it happened so he could meet Oprah. That the minute he confessed before his electorate, "I am a gay American," was the minute he knew that his was a story so predictably tragic that Oprah's studio would be the only place to crown his suffering.

Pressing McGreevey for his confession, goading him to name the minute he knew he was gay, and speaking of his suffering quicken the creation of Winfrey's "wow" climax. In his study of the emotional impact of popular culture, Henry Jenkins defines the "wow climax" as the "moment of peak spectacle" in vaudeville acts. Winfrey's "wow" is less often a "wow" than it is an "aha!" Conjured awakenings of body, mind, and spirit center the enterprise. Advertisements for the show state simply, "Aha! The Power of a Moment," and suggest that if you watch you will see "One Aha! Moment after Another." Varying from realizations about wrong bra sizing to childhood abuse, the aha moment has several names (light bulb, goose bumps, turning point) and several ejaculations (Bingo! Got it! Bing-bing! Shazam!), but no matter the invocation, it serves as the climax of the *Oprah* show experience. Like the orgasm in pornography, the terrified scream in a horror film, and the anguished deathbed weeping in a melodrama, the aha moment moves the plot to denouement. It screams and wails, and then it exhales. You have been branded.[17]

Each month the "Aha! Moment" column in O magazine spotlights an author or a celebrity testifying to a formative incident in their life story. Octavia Butler recounts her realization of the wholeness of others by looking into her dog's eyes at age three. "He wasn't like any of the people in the house," Butler remembered. "He was *someone else* entirely."[18] Edwidge Danticat hit her head while entering an airplane, and Dorothy Allison's mother threatened to burn their childhood house down; these are minor moments made "aha" by the sectional divisions of a magazine.[19] If writers tend toward miniscule discernment worthy of their vocations, then celebrities narrate stories a bit more like soap opera: actor-writer Tyler Perry's father tells him, "I love you," or Donald Trump meets his wife.[20] These moments become requisite hinges, moving a life from misunderstanding to clarity. "We are here, it seems, to be transformed, and transformed again, and again and again," novelist Michael Cunningham summarizes.[21] Through memoirs and expository nonfiction, O magazine supplies a location where you might not only experience the wow of someone else's transformation but also mull the possibility of your own aha.

If the magazine narrates subtlety in biographic minutiae, the show spotlights a gargantuan arc and cartoon revelation. Winfrey repeats often that every time the television is turned on, a life can be changed. On the *Oprah* show, the aha moment achieves hyperbolic stakes, revelation now made for TV as a commodity form. Winfrey frequently recommends the usage of Post-it flags to mark aha passages in book club selections; e-mailed book club newsletters and Oprah.com Web pages similarly advertise these Post-its, making the highlighting of text a commentarial "aha!" Readers and viewers are thus instructed to seek the aha as a requisite accomplishment of consumption. "This story will change your life," Winfrey temptingly promises at the outset of many an episode. A story, not an experience, will change your life—the Word makes your world. "I started to realize the show was more than a show," Winfrey reflected later. "You are affecting the way people see themselves." Clear sight is the ambition; change is the imperative. "You always have the potential to get better," wrote Oprah in the first issue of O, *The Oprah Magazine*. "That, as I see it, is one of the purposes of your life: Not to be good but continuously to get better, to constantly move forward, to create the highest, grandest vision and to be led by that vision every day."[22]

Such change requires confession at the outset, confession that lays bare the troublesome obstacles that may prohibit living your best life. "A confession is an admission of fault: *I am sorry because I did wrong. I sinned*," Susan Wise Bauer has written. To begin a new life, confession requires absolute exposure and total humility. The confessor must set down his or her power in order for it to be handed back.[23] This is "risky," O editors tell us, since it exposes truths that may alienate those with whom you seek to connect. "Perhaps our secrets struggle to be revealed because they know that confession can perform a miracle: It can make dark secrets bright . . . into beacons of hope for others."[24] The speaking of true stories does more than reveal an individual's interiority; it also supplies exemplars of survival for others. This is an exchange, as novelist Mark Leyner elaborates in the pages of O magazine: "We confess to a priest to gain absolution, to a therapist to facilitate healing, to the police in the hope that it will mitigate criminal prosecution."[25] On the *Oprah* show, confession admits no shameful costs or excesses. Televised confession produces—or is produced to produce—only relieving revelation. "Think of confession as life's strategic opening move," O magazine editors advise. Before you can live your best life, you must confess to your worst. "Everyone has dark corners," the O Calendar recommends for June 3, 2002. "To explore yours, keep a journal. 'Confess' what/who stirs your anger, fear, jealousy, revenge fantasies."

Winfrey places writing at the center of her commentaries on the exploratory spirit. Journaling is invoked frequently as the agitating practice to elicit confession, as the first step in an overall process of transformation and self-actualization. On her Web site and in episodes of the show, the practice of journaling has been promoted by Oprah and her team of testimonial experts as a way for women to "discover what you love and then find a way to offer it to others in the form of service, working hard, and also allowing the energy of the universe to lead you."[26] Oprah's Web site includes extensive descriptions of the journaling process that might assist this discovery. There, women can read how to get started, what to write about, how often to write, and the benefits of journaling.[27] As women follow Winfrey's writing assignments, they are told that they will "find" themselves on the page and discover their truest selves. Winfrey recommends writing as a central motif in the interrogation of the spiritual self. Winfrey's Web site suggests that you keep *six* different journals: the daily journal (for "general daily thoughts"), the gratitude journal ("write five things you love every day"), the Spa Girls journal (for your exercise regimen), the discovery journal ("get to know yourself by looking back"), the health journal, and the "create your own journal" ("you can name it whatever you like. It's yours!"). Obviously, for Winfrey, journal keeping is a practice necessary for any viewer seeking spiritual awareness and revivification. The ultimate benefits of all this writing are bulleted on the same Web page: discovering yourself, experiencing less stress, finding the courage to pursue your passion, understanding your past, acquiring a greater sense of peace, and achieving general awareness.[28] Daily writing exercises function as the local catechism within the broader auspices of lifestyle makeovers, improvements in attitude, and the pursuit of female empowerment.

In the hundreds of online journals posted by Oprah viewers, certain tropes appear that mirror the paradigms established within Protestant conversion narratives. Scholars agree that these narratives have had an analogous structure, moving from contrition ("I'm sorry for my wayward ways") to humiliation ("Everyone can see how awful I am") to volition ("I must and can be better") to exaltation ("Glory to the God that placed me on this holy path").[29] Religious journals are thus a primary tool of volition within Protestant circles, as they facilitate the process of committing to a better life. Addressing colonial journals and conversion narratives, Gregory Jackson summarizes, "Interpretations of the discrete events of life helped weave a larger fabric of meaning and shape a spiritual destiny, transforming the personal idiom into a universal message for community consumption."[30] In the world of Oprah Winfrey, journals function similarly, as viewers are instructed to write and rewrite in an attempt to demonstrate their loyalty to this new mode of spiritual revelation. On the show, these journals are condensed into conversion narratives by show producers, Winfrey's voice-overs, and the guests themselves. The journal writers read from their journals as the voice-over narratives are redacted into montages. Spiritual counselors are then called upon to provide interpretations of these testimonial texts. The guests thus serve as confessors to priestlike spiritual counselors, who in turn defer to Oprah, the divine queen, who supplies affirmation and the confirming self-referential anecdote to illuminate how every story connects to hers.

The pattern of exhibition and commentary repeats in show after show. For example, on November 3, 2006, viewers tuned in to watch "Why 15-Year-Old Jessica Coleman Killed Her Baby." By the show's ending, viewers not only understood why she killed her baby but also had a program of action to prohibit such future deaths. To begin, the setting needs to be established: "In 1999, the residents of Columbia Station, Ohio, woke up on a Tuesday morning to a horrific headline: 'Newborn boy found stabbed in duffel bag in quarry.' The community named him Baby Boy Hope and gave him a memorial service." Quickly, the camera pans to a pretty face, a former cheerleader, star athlete, and honor student. This is Jessica Coleman, and the implication of her photo montage is made clear: she could be your daughter. Your friend's daughter. Or maybe your town's Friday night cheerleader.

Oprah travels to prison for her interview with Jessica, homing in on Jessica's prematurely aged face, lacking any makeup or cheer, frequently streamed with tears. We learn that Jessica's happy teenage facade covered a pattern of bulimia and codependent male relationships, including a fatal one with Tom Truelson, a popular basketball star who impregnated Jessica when she was just fifteen. The largely female audience gasps audibly when Jessica informs Oprah that Tom would sit on her protruding belly to squash the fetus he and she kept secret. The death of their child is described in graphic detail, from her birthing into a toilet, to the barrette applied to the umbilical cord, and the knife wound Jessica inflicts after leaving the baby exposed on her bed during dinnertime. We listen to Jessica describe how she placed her baby in a duffel bag, stored the corpse in her closet, then watched as Tom absconded with it. "Tom took the duffel bag and he ended up tossing the duffel bag in a quarry near where we lived at the time," Jessica says. "I felt scared. I didn't know what he was going to do beforehand. And after he told me what he had done, I felt terrible then, too." Jessica's crime is not discovered immediately, and the *Oprah* show drags her criminal history out for full dramatic effect, replete with a team of characters to pile on the pain: Jessica's fiancé, Matt; the investigating officer, Detective Karl Yost; Jessica's mother, Jennifer; her sentencing judge, Edward Zaleski; a visiting newspaper reporter, Suzanne Hobbs. Each contributing voice is trotted out to amplify the moment, the location, and the crime, to sensitize viewers to the details of Jessica's choice and the manifold consequences.

If it isn't enough that Jessica has committed a crime against her infant, the show forces the audience to acknowledge that this is a crime against the fabric of her loving family and community. The death of Baby Hope is not just the death of Jessica's youth—it is an assault on civil society.[31] Why are viewers forced through this detail, this tragic teenage irrationality? Only once viewers have been taken to the pit with

Jessica can they fully appreciate Oprah's hand extended into the well. Only she can pull the drama from its hopeless sentiment into the optimism of her perfect success:

> Did you know that at the age of fourteen, I hid a pregnancy? I was raped at nine and sexually abused from the time I was ten to fourteen. At fourteen years old, I became pregnant. I hid that pregnancy from everybody. One day my ankles started to swell. I was taken to the hospital and the doctors said, "Are you pregnant?" I didn't even know what pregnancy was. I'd been abused all this time, but I really wasn't even sure that the outcome was you have a baby. So I confessed that I had been having sex with people who had been abusing me for years. The stress of that confession caused me to go into labor, and the baby died. And my father said to me at that time what I'm going to say to you: "What you have done is the past, and you alone get to determine what your future will be."

Just when viewers believe the world is too awful to endure, too imperfect to resolve, Oprah arrives with connective biographical balm.[32] Winfrey is not a particularly gifted interviewer. Known for soliciting dramatic confessions, the gift of Winfrey has always been more mechanical than slyly seductive. As her celebrity surpassed all quotidian access, she became even worse at interviewing, exhibiting boredom more obviously with tedious interviewees and offering more "uh-huh" replies than piercing follow-up inquiries. Her gift is not her interviewing strategy but her confessional promiscuity. "In television's perfect world, Winfrey is flawed. It is these blemishes that seem to make her less-than-perfect audience love her," writes one reporter. "Winfrey is an imperfect woman who has bared her imperfections for all to see on national television."[33] This publicly expressed frailty separates Winfrey's stagecraft. She possesses the uncanny ability to know when to reveal her poignant first person. "Every *Oprah Winfrey Show* has about it the aura of Oprah's own life," remarks Lee Siegel.[34] This aura is, like the biography of a religious founder, the canonical comfort of a haunted heroine to rely upon as iconic certitude amid the disappointing daily of normal life.[35] Winfrey has said, "If there's a thread running through each show we do, it is the message that 'you are not alone.'" She parcels hope, reminding viewers that through her show, her public ritual, through her, we may be made whole, again.

Rewind two hundred years and you find that Oprah's studio is not the first American site of such charismatic comfort, ritual confession, and repetitious spectacle. In the early years of the nineteenth century, itinerant Methodists developed a common floor plan for their camp meetings. Dominating this tableau was the "mourners' altar" or "inquirers' bench."[36] During his 1830 revival campaign in Rochester, New York, the headlining preacher and evangelical strategist Charles G. Finney formalized the altar call around a singular "anxious bench," where business and professional people were forced to come "to a stand." Finney had found that the greatest obstacle to conversion was the "fear of being known as anxious inquirers." The embarrassment of their own anxiety prohibited prosperous worshippers from truly engaging with Finney's gospel message. The anxious bench was unveiled to force individual renunciation of their sins and a "public committal of themselves to God."[37] The anxious bench was part of a larger set of new measures established by Finney to goad more conversions, to excite the spirit of the parishioners toward Christ through communal gatherings. The bench was the climactic site in the revival process, setting sinners physically apart from the audience as symbols of sin and of their own failure to make a break with their sinful past. They were separated by their failures and by their failure to cease their failing. Members of the congregation, including family and friends, would shout and wail supplications and impromptu prayers on behalf of the exhibited soul. Supporters would sometimes circle the bench, urging the seated to rise in the light of the heavily signified Lord.

Scholarship on the bench has been crowded by appraisals of antebellum evangelicalism more generally. On this front, opinions are divided, with some arguing for the social coercion of the anxious bench and others claiming it was a profoundly democratic theological force, educating young Americans to their republican opportunities.[38] Leonard I. Sweet summarized the perspective of the former: "The open invitation of the anxious bench, which ostensibly symbolized the democratization of new measures evangelism where all classes stood united in their common sinfulness, was actually designed as a device to attract the higher classes . . . new measures revivalism did not overthrow status, but provided new status symbols for the elite."[39] From the perspective of Finney and other revivalists, however, the anxious bench was a site for instruction, where the anxious could "be addressed particularly, and be made subjects of prayer, and sometimes conversed with individually."[40] The intense interview conducted by the preacher forced sinners to face themselves publicly. After all, asked one proponent of the bench, "if no test-questions are presented, how can they ever act or determine whether they will serve God or not?"[41] The bench, then, was a formal prop in the script of conversion. It required several steps of sinners' self-selection: first, to separate themselves from the crowd; second, to parse their sins from their virtues; and, third, to devote themselves to a singular godhead. At each stage, the preacher forced a public narration of their ritual processing: the walk to the bench, the narrative of sin from the bench, the surrounding calls of their community, the recognition of a right path, and a final commitment to Christ. At every point, the preacher prodded, focused, named, and decried that which was, for the sinner, as much an emotive act as a cognitive one. Finney himself admitted it was emotion, and not reason, that brought men to the bench; the preacher's job was to play reason against the roused spirit of the anxious.

"Ritual is above all a pattern of action," Theodore W. Jennings has written.[42] The *Oprah* show invokes the ritual of the anxious bench both in its daily ritual presentation and in the particular set-piece of the "bench." Just as the attendees at a Finney revival knew what they were about to receive, so do the talk show viewers know what they are about to see. Despite the surprise gifts and the diverse topics, this episodic format is habitual in the extreme. The show's arc is so commonplace, so unsurprising, that it is the premise of the viewers' rapt attention: they watch to experience the familiar ritual turn of daily confession and rejuvenation. One month of Winfrey's programming offers the easiest entrée to this summation. In February 2007, there were twenty new hour-long installments of the *Oprah* show.[43] Included in that twenty-episode series were "Moms Who Made Millions"; comedian Martin Lawrence promoting *Wild Hogs;* home organization expert Peter Walsh advising how to declutter a home; confessions of a once-upon-a-time Haitian child slave; and Dr. Mehmet Oz answering questions on feminine douches.

Closer inspection of the plots driving these February episodes reveals Winfrey's devotional habit. Her ongoing emphasis on everyday miracles codifies a version of domestic spirituality. "Nate's Small Space Miracle" (February 20, 2007) advocates more than a small-space revolution through the purchase of Akemi Tanaka Tagei and Futaba coffee tables, an IKEA Cyril secretary, or JCPenney's leather armless chair with hidden storage; it also hawks a salvation of self through this materiality. Nate says his "biggest challenge ever" was rewarding because it made him reprioritize some things in his life. "I mean, how much space do we really need?" he explains. "I thought to myself, there was so much joy coming out of those four walls that it really motivated me to do the best I could do—literally the best I could do." Nate Berkus's self-improvement mirrors and refracts throughout the month. From "This Is the Year to Live Well with Colin Cowie" to "The Best Life Diet Weight

Loss Challenge," Winfrey repeats the principles of personal faith (faith in self, faith in the solar system to serve self, faith in the market to supply the right goods) and social celebration. Episodes on the phenomenon of *The Secret* (February 8, 2007) and popular television psychics are exceptional in their explicitly metaphysical bent and still utterly familiar in their party favors. The show processes viewers' problems into shopping cart choices and climactic psychological expulsions.

Viewers of the *Oprah* show will also easily recognize the Finney floor plan in Winfrey's stage setup, with Oprah sitting at a ninety-degree angle to her participatory guests, their knees pointing toward each another as Oprah prods and her guests respond, narrate, and confess.[44] First, guests are forced to admit their worst transgressions, to say precisely how they felt when they pulled the trigger, for example, or, in Governor McGreevey's case, to describe the sordid locations of his clandestine sexual encounters. Here the descriptions divide into two categories: the accused and the traumatized. McGreevey is among the accused, present to describe a criminal, immoral, or unloving act. Included in this category is a wide range of failures, from the murderess Jessica Coleman to Janet Jackson, who came on the *Oprah* show to respond to criticisms of her bare-breasted Super Bowl performance (September 25, 2006), and from a bipolar murderess mother (September 24, 2007) to a woman who cheated with her best friend's husband (May 18, 2006). No matter the severity of the action, Oprah's approach is regulated to a beige pitch of therapy for the admitted transgressor. If the accused are there to defend their actions and confess specific malfeasance, then the traumatized are offered to testify the healing powers of salvation. Recent trauma victims of this sort are Anderson Cooper, who described the details of his beloved brother's suicide, and senatorial spouse Elizabeth Edwards, who drew dramatic portraits of a son's death and a cancer diagnosis; more plebian were the airline worker who checked in the 9/11 terrorists and the French doctor who was first on the scene as Princess Diana lay dying. Although the doctor, aviation employee, journalist, and politician are not to be blamed for the genesis of their suffering, they, like the accused, must account for their subsequent self-management. They must say aloud just how bad things have been (or how very bad they were), then explain their planned or completed trajectory of self improvement to the absolving body of preacher Winfrey. Whether victim or perpetrator, audience or actor, the occupant of Oprah's anxious center is there for a reason: to instruct themselves. At the center of her ritual process is the awareness that all of us, no matter our cultural or criminal position, have some sin from which we must, and shall, be released.

A recent year of benched sinners included several murderous spouses, adulterous partners, listless housewives, and, perhaps most notorious, one rather deceptive memoirist. James Frey's dual appearances on *The Oprah Winfrey Show* offer a painful profile of anxious seating and unseating (and, seating again). Winfrey endorsed Frey's searing self-portrait of addiction, *A Million Little Pieces*, as a masterpiece of therapeutic nonfiction. In their initial book club interview, she walked viewers through his most painful experiences, including dental work without Novocain, the suicide of his rehab girlfriend, and a long jail time for drug-related charges. She marked studio time through the standard declarative script, asking, "Why do you think you're alive today?" In response, Frey explained that he was "blessed," adding, "Ultimately I'm alive because I wanted to stay alive." Endurance in the face of failure, fortitude before excruciating pain, creative resolve amid degrading chaos: Frey was a prime exhibit in Oprah's museum of contemporary converts.

Then, in a somewhat unusual turn of events, the cycle of self-destruction proceeded despite the sealant of an Oprah's Book Club sticker. Just four months after the original book club episode, Winfrey brought Frey back to the studio following intense allegations that he had embellished much of his story, including his criminality, the nature of his treatment, and his relationships with other addicts. Media observers spilled much ink in praising Winfrey's courage for this episode, for her willingness to admit her lapse of judgment. Regular viewers of the program were ready for her lambasting of Frey, the parade of incriminating evidence, and her own moral self-celebration. This episode was merely another altar call. "I made a mistake, and I left the impression that the truth does not matter," Winfrey began. "And I am deeply sorry about that, because that is not what I believe."[45] Her own sins acknowledged, Winfrey continued to James Frey and then to his editor, Nan Talese, pressing them to confess every lie, clarify every deception. The effect was excruciating to watch, as Frey stared and swallowed his sin, and Talese tried to defend the genre of memoir. Toward the close of the show, Winfrey forced Frey to differentiate between a mistake, which she had made, and lies, of which he had told many. "I believe the truth sets you free," she explained to Frey, proclaiming, "this is the beginning of another kind of truth for you."

Frey did admit this, but only after goading by the likes of Anderson Cooper, Maureen Dowd, and Frank Rich, all of whom Winfrey imported to circle the bench and taunt the anxious. The viewer is struck by the simultaneous exaltation of Winfrey (called a "savior of truth" and a "mensch" during the course of the episode) and the concomitant degradation of Frey. Critics of Charles Finney's nineteenth-century incarnation of the anxious bench focused on its false premise, its forced performativity, and its spiritual "quackery." Theologian John Nevin argued vociferously that "no conversions [were] more precarious and insecure than those of the Anxious Bench."[46] *The Oprah Winfrey Show* effects a similar fragility, as the viewer is forced to wonder how long the sinners will repent: Can they keep the weight off? Will they murder again? Can James Frey not tell a lie? The assessment of the content of Oprah Winfrey's conversions is best left to a more theological milieu. However, what is relevant to students of religious studies is Winfrey's evocative charismatic positioning. After all, despite the apparent universality of her message, it is Winfrey herself who poses the most thrilling occupant of the anxious bench. James Frey was not brought back to the show merely to display his mortification; he was brought back to demonstrate Winfrey's divine particularity.

If Charles Finney was pastor to nineteenth-century America, it is not an overstatement to suggest that Winfrey is his twenty-first-century parallel. Unlike Finney, however, who overtly proclaimed his "new measures," Winfrey is careful to obscure the rigged ritual of her episodes in an organic self-description devoid of ecclesiastical structures. She controls the dirt you see and the dirt you don't. Even as she repeatedly calls congregants to their interior, to exchange all exterior deceptions— those family portraits and their lying smiles—for interior truths, she still directs the discernment. Be not deceived: these are her truths; it is her perfected interior that is modeled by her much-narrated exterior. The show is her show, this show is her biography, and her biography is largely her body on discussed display.

No aspect of Winfrey's particularity receives more press, or more of her own self-appraisal, than her body. Winfrey's body is a central feature of her authenticity. "Oprah dresses conservatively," explained Princess Reema bint Bandar al-Saud, a co-owner of a women's spa in Riyadh. "She struggles with her weight. She overcame depression. She rose from poverty and abuse. On all these levels she appeals to a Saudi woman. People really idolize her here."[47] As a global media phenomenon, Oprah transcends cultural difference in order to communicate an authentic yet accessible ubiquity. Her body, along with her inability to control its size, makes it possible for Winfrey to sustain lay commensurability even as she achieves otherworldly status in fame, in funds, and in experience. "We, the people, have lived through Winfrey's weight-loss struggles. Her marathon was our marathon. We were her million-plus support system of chronic snackers who empathized as she wrestled her mashed-potato demons," Robin Givhan writes in the *Washington Post.* "Winfrey inspires her fans in part because she makes extraordinary accomplishments look possible. But as her weight continues to yo-yo, she confirms what folks have always suspected: Just being average can be quite a challenge, too."[48] The public discussion of her weight problem formed a constant opportunity for makeover of her and of others. As reality television in the Nineties replaced the talk show heyday of the Eighties, refashioning the body became a component to assimilating a national ideal. As Brenda Weber has written in her study of *Extreme Makeover,* the gesturing to "inner beauty" on such programming "clearly codes internal attractiveness as dependent upon external appearance," an appearance that "conforms to a fairly narrow palette of pleasing looks."[49]

Winfrey's dream of a body that matches her best self, a body that fits the best clothes and the best vision she has for herself, is not only for herself. It also connects her to other similarly suffering women. "The failure of hope is always an event between people," Robert Orsi has written. "Despair is relational."[50] Every time Winfrey sighs on the scale, she does so in a community that recognizes the reasons for her unhappiness. Her embodied torment brings her star to earth into a moment of extreme expectations for physical recasting. Scholars have begun to name the ways this suffering on behalf of physical reshaping possesses spiritual and ritual aspects. Although dismissed by many as additional indicators of the plasticity of postmodernism, plastic surgery and dieting emerge from a longer history of asceticism and self-flagellation, including figures like St. Francis of Assisi, who admonished, "I have no greater enemy than my body," arguing that "we should feel hatred towards our body for its vices and sinning!" In the American context, penitential practices have refigured in more genteel manners. In her research on the body in American Christianity, Marie Griffith has demonstrated the streams of religious ideation that constitute the perfectible female body, including New Thought and evangelicalism. She writes, "It turns out, then, that American culture's own purportedly secular doctrine of the perfectible body is deeply indebted to currents that have perceived the body as essential for pushing the soul along the path to redemption."[51]

This redemptive teleology for body betterment coordinates well with other descriptions of contemporary dieting practices as a rite of womanhood. Practices such as counting calories, consulting diet treatises, measuring body parts, and regulating physical movement indicate the wholesale lifestyles associated with female physical maintenance.[52] Processing the body into an ideal form becomes a ritual realization ("I am not as I ought to be") and confession ("I know I have failed the ideal that is possible"). During Oprah's January 2009 weight gain confession, she describes it as a process of "outing" herself, invoking a category of sexual-identity disclosure to explain the drama of her corporeal confession. The confession invokes prior confessions. She thought she had her weight under control, managed ritually through exercise and diet, but then "what happened was, um, life took over. Life took over. I, um, I started getting overwhelmed." The confession emphasizes the psychological disposition and the mental imbalance that destroys the ritual maintenance. "When you see me gain weight, it is not about I'm pigging out. It is always about my life is out of balance," she remarks, quickly flipping her particular to your universal. "Anybody who struggles with a weight issue, it is about . . . what you're really hungry for. It's not about food. It's about using food, abusing food."[53]

Episodes of "Incredible Weight-Loss Stories" reveal, then, not only her specific dreams for her body but also her penitential habits of ritual makeover. On an episode with such a transforming subject, the majority of that day's topic will be consigned to first-person testimonial montages, preproduced and collated into the program. On average, four testimonials are presented in any given show, each chosen for its diverse sameness—for its physical and cultural dissimilarity ("we all look different") unified through experiential similarity ("but we all have the same feelings"). Likewise, the narrative trajectory of each experience is programmed into analogy. A man or a woman struggles with obesity because of self-loathing as the result of childhood trauma. This man or woman has a "wake-up call" that motivates "change." The man or woman then loses an enormous amount of weight "the right way," through balanced diet, exercise, and daily journaling. He or she emerges spiritually enlightened and psychologically secure. Also, he or she looks much more telegenic as the result of a Winfrey-funded total makeover. These participants spend time thanking God and Oprah for their never-ending support but finally confess that, yes, they have themselves to thank for taking responsibility for their lives. Consider, for example, the story of this woman, who lost 190 pounds:

My name is Ginny San Pollard. I was a size 26 and XXX. Being over 340 pounds, it was miserable. Anything that I did in my life on a daily basis, whether it's pushing a grocery cart or going out in the street to get your mail, everything was a struggle. I let a lot of my life go by, and all from overeating. Then, I went to the doctor, and he told me I would die if I didn't make a change. Oprah helped me with my weight loss journey, because she encourages her audience not only for weight loss but to keep a daily journal. I wrote my daily caloric intakes, and I would weigh myself, and I would have different graphs of how I lost my weight. I would put pictures of me fat, and as I lost weight I would . . . put thinner ones in there. In one of my journals I wrote a letter to Oprah: "It amazes me that someone from so far away who has never met me could change my life."[54]

This testimonial is read over a set of photographs from Ginny, photographs that showed stages in her physical transformation as well as tools for her transformation, such as her journals and the motivational collages she made with photos of Oprah. This is a conversion narrative facilitated by Oprah's prescriptions and Oprah's symbolic omnipresence in Ginny's life. You could fit any sort of person into this narrative—a rich black woman, a poor Asian woman, an unemployed white woman—and still the story outline and regaled moral would remain the same.

The moral is, of course, that there is no magic other than the motivating, inspirational imprint of O. Only *you* can make the change you wish to see in your body, in this world. As one O magazine article summarizes, "In the world of dieting, which so often is full of guilt and self-loathing, recognizing that people have to be ready before they can have success is perhaps the best sermon of all."[55] Weight-loss challenges—placed by Oprah to herself, to her friends, to nominated viewers, self-selected Harpo employees, mothers, veterans, professionals—litter the seasonal landscape of the *Oprah* show.[56] In each and every one, a complex balance is sought between motivating physical reformation and dispositional self-satisfaction. "Actress Sheila Kelley believes every woman can benefit from uncaging her 'inner stripper,'" the Web site intones, "For her, stripping isn't for your guy—it's about celebrating you!"[57] There are confusions in all this clarity. "Good-looking individuals are treated better than homely ones" is a "Fact" submitted to O readers under the guise of relentless truth. "Get any makeover you believe will help," the magazine advises, just so long as you "realize that a makeover won't take unless you already know how to sustain self-esteem." "You'll always look like you," but you also might "look better."[58] An O article title advises you "How to Look (at Least) 10 Years Younger," yet you are also told that "we're all for accepting the march of time."[59] You are supposed to love your body, love your sexual self, but learn to strip and look younger; you're supposed to look better but not unlike yourself. "Know that another change is just around the bend," Martha Beck restlessly reminds us. "Don't attribute your happiness to your new identity; security lies in knowing how to deal with metamorphosis, whenever it occurs."[60] Strapped to Winfrey's dreams of change are anxious additional labors of physical assessment, mental discipline, and therapeutic self-love. At every turn, there is a hug of self-love and the slap of self-scrutiny. Being your self is what you are meant to be, but being yourself is never enough.

The point, however, is not to reconcile confusion but to revolutionize through change. Harpo and Winfrey do not encourage psychoanalytic disassembling. Instead, the instantaneous nature of their productions— televised and glossy, virtual and montage—come and go with a shifting speed typical of the new media age. The corresponding hyperactive expectations for change infer that the point is not to digest the tangled threads of advertised reasoning but rather to propagate compulsive awakening and transformation. "Today we're hearing stories of inspiration, hope, and perseverance," episodes begin. "Get out of your comfort zone," others preach. "Take Risks!" In January 2009 the magazine shouts "Fresh Starts" for the new year: "If you're ripe for a new beginning but aren't sure how to make change stick . . . If a little inspiration could help you roll up your sleeves, let go of the past, and get on with the new day—we've got all that and more."[61] Episodes "challenge" viewers "to step out of their box." "This is bold," Winfrey compliments one spotlighted shifter: "She's not just stepping out; she is setting the box on fire."[62]

Sleeves rolled up, boxes afire, lives made over: if you are doing it all, if you are making the rites of Oprah the rites of you, you probably don't have a moment to spare. Images of makeover frenzy abound in Winfrey's textual and televised world, because her posited viewers are women trying to have it all, be it all, make it all, raise it all, redecorate it all, all while embodying the possibility of the self-improvement she inscribes. However, another article worries, "You can . . . bring home the bacon, fry it up in a pan, do eight things at once, but as you'll discover, more is not merrier."[63] Worries over successful performance mesh with worries over personal wellness. "Why are you rushing?" asks one headline, as another prods: "Have you been burning the candle at both ends?" Every Winfrey watcher must, by sheer prescriptive necessity, be doing too much in too little time. "Wait! Stop! It's All Too Much!" yells one *O* magazine headline. A September 2008 *O* magazine piece simply announces: "TOO BUSY TO LIVE." "Our culture's definition of what women should be is fundamentally, irreconcilably unbalanced," an *O* counselor mourns. "Balance, schmalance."[64] Transformation exhausts, and equilibrium is impossible.

Amid the compulsive "aha!" the viewer must also pursue "things that make you go 'ahhh.'" "Sometimes I have to admit that I simply need to rest," confesses a columnist.[65] To encourage rest, *O* magazine recommends "disconnection strategies," it spotlights books like *In Praise of Slowness* (2004), and it advocates "patience" as the "cure for craziness."[66] If it's not enough that you're practicing Oprah through ceaseless makeover revolutions and accessories, you also find yourself developing practices to relax and soothe for relief from the overexcited agent of change.[67] "A little restoration goes a long way," Oprah cajoles, pressing readers to reenergize, schedule downtime, and refill your tank.[68] The practice imperatives for an "ahh" moment pile up quickly: declutter your space, relax to focus, take a steaming Jacuzzi bath, indulge in a manicure, dig in the garden, keep candles lit on the coffee table, splurge on strappy sandals, rent a romantic comedy, talk out your troubles with a golden retriever, sweep the floor, sip some red wine, sleep late, take off early on Friday afternoon, make a blender drink.[69] This is how even relaxing becomes something to manage ritually.

Only masters of time could handle this, only people who have, for example, completed the "friendly-reminder cards" from the April 2004 *O* magazine (theme: "Time") that remind you of "all the things you've been meaning to make time for." For this you need just one more accessory: a clock. "You're in good hands with these wall clocks," advertises one April 2004 array. One spotlight on watches sells $155 MoMA watches that are "modern, completely unexpected and seriously fun" (March 2005), while another highlights "the anatomy of accuracy" (September 2006), and one later sells rubber and plastic watches for "play time" (February 2008).[70] Watches for sporty days and glittery nights, violet watches and pumpkin-colored watches and light-up watches: on "The O List" and in Favorite Things episodes, Winfrey loves to endorse watches as ways of looking cute while maintaining an orderliness to her endeavors.[71]

Oprah practitioners are told that they not only will glean the spiritual lessons imparted in the experience of confessional production and product consumption but will also enjoy the triumph of successfully completing a prescribed productivity, of beating the demons of time and psychology to accomplish something outside the boundaries of normative routine. For all this, the revolution and the revelation, you'll need as many clocks, as many practices, as possible. "If you're spread so thin you're just about threadbare, gaze inward," suggests the July 27, 2002, *O* calendar recommendation. "Are you willing to address those problems so you can restock your vitality?" Staying vital while restocking vitality, the timekeeping reader relies upon the calendar to map daily ways to maintain the makeover mojo. Elsewhere on the same July 2002 calendar, the reader is told to do things that "replenish," to avoid complex carbohydrates, to exercise, to remember an energized moment, to get a blood test for low thyroid function and anemia, to stretch for five minutes after work, to sleep an extra half hour before work, to skip the caffeine during work, to "rock-out" to music on your way home from work, to turn off the TV, to flirt, to jump rope for three minutes, to grab an energy bar with no more than twenty grams of carbohydrates, to prepare a cucumber nosh as snack, have a slice of avocado, to "spend some serious, or not so serious, cash on yourself," to write down what your purpose in life is, and to call up a friend.[72] This is just one month of timed activity, just one-twelfth of your Oprah year. The expectation cannot be to change but to revel in the delicious details of change. This is makeover porn, watched as much to be reminded of what you're not doing, what you're not getting, as it is to inspire new ways to get what you want.[73]

The cornucopia of the magazine distills to the thematic spectacle of easy conversions on TV. "For the last few weeks," Winfrey announces at the beginning of another episode, "we have scoured suburban malls and city streets to find people who need to change just one thing, from clothes to glasses to the way they talk." Guests are taught to work with their cowlick, change glasses, and relinquish old nylons. These are changes of a significant order:

> *Linda*: My hair has ruined my life. It's consuming far too much of my energy and my thoughts. I have to plan my activities around my hair. I can't go on vacations. I hate going swimming. I can't get my hair wet. I hate when it rains. I get scared when it rains. Every time I have a shower or bath, I have to blow-dry it. I have to get all the right brushes. Takes about forty minutes to blow-dry. It's so time-consuming. And then I have to put this special serum on, and then I have to stick on this hat, which I've had for five years, because it's really tight on my head and it flattens it down. So I have to wear that for twenty minutes. If there was just one thing I could change about myself, it would be to straighten my

hair. That's all I want. When my hair is straight, I feel sexy. I feel confident. And I feel like the woman I want to be.

Is Linda the product of a Winfrey-induced mania? Or is she primed
for its soothing revolution? Harpo, Inc., may not be solely responsible for the manic self-expectations of American women, yet Winfrey
is uniquely situated to assuage the cycle of revelatory life makeovers
and body checking. But it seems impossible for her to relinquish the
wizardry of its elaboration. "Today, look around you. Is this the life
you imagined for yourself?" Winfrey asked in a 2001 episode. "If not,
now is your moment," she continues. "Open yourself up. Take a chance.
They did."

They did. They can do it; why can't you? "We hope to inspire you
today with stories of just incredible women who found the courage,
'cause that's what it takes, to create a better life for themselves." That's
what it takes, that's what they have, and that's what you need. But *this*
is the only thing the show can't sell. In order to go to your destiny, to fill
in the something missing and reply to the wake-up call, you must find
the resolve and the courage to make change and reinvent yourself in
order to live your best life. The products of Oprah are clear: your new
chapter will commence the minute you find out what the gift is that
you were "given at the cradle and sent to fulfill."[74] Harpo, Inc., enjoins
snack-time choices and physical fitness regimes, and it draws calendars
and suggests solutions. But this product does not and cannot concoct
the stamina—the spirit—that would make the regime your aspired reality. Only you can make you what you deserve to become. "With an
understanding of your strengths, your mental habits, and your dreams
comes both the resolve to hang tough when rewards seem elusive and
the courage to risk something new," an O magazine article concludes.
"Even in the most volatile times you can find opportunities, especially
if you're aware of what you really have to offer."[75] No moment should
be wasted, since every moment might be the moment you need to find,
finally, the inspiration to be you. "Nobody said it was easy," an article
comforts. "Whether you're reinventing yourself as a size 10, a marathon
runner, or a high-functioning ball of fire, the road to change is rough."[76]

Winfrey smoothes the road between desire and actuation with compatriot voices, such as that of Cheryl Richardson, author of *Life Makeovers,* and with adjunct productions, including her radio broadcasts
and touring speaker series. These tours schedule pricey all-day seminars designed to jump-start careers, like the Personal Growth Summit

of 2000 and the Live Your Best Life Tour of 2001.[77] Paying attendees of her Live Your Best Life Tour reflected upon the makeovers Winfrey has made for them. "She is an everyday kind of person," says a sales rep who explains that Winfrey helped her recover from a hysterectomy. "I feel connected to her like a friend," describes a schoolteacher who ascribes to Winfrey her "personal renaissance" after her divorce. "Oprah's life is the example," the teacher underlines. "If she can do it, anyone can." Winfrey's tour is her autobiography, filled with anecdotes of "her own struggles with poverty, weight, career setbacks, relationships" and recommendations that "the universe is always trying to get you to honor your calling."[78] The magazine enshrines women who start businesses (glassblowing and knitting), nonprofits (domestic violence prevention and Sioux Indian theater promotion), women who design tote bags for yoga mats, open African American bookstores, improve reading habits at Memphis high schools, and join orchestras late in life.[79] The tour and seminars seek to cajole women to find their passion and to make what is real for them, real now.

Your clear-eyed identity is the sleeping giant in all of this awakening to action. Throughout the years, Winfrey has trotted out hundreds of therapists and counselors to enact the confessional process in bite-size hour apportionments. Her therapies are designed to extract that which is hidden by you in order that you may, like her, begin to be as you are meant to be. "If you are not moving forward it is a shadow belief, because we become what we believe," Winfrey explains. "So at any given point in your life, you don't blame other people for wherever you are, because you are where you believe you should be."[80] These shadow beliefs are among the confessions Winfrey seeks. Through staged confession and exfoliating makeover, the subjects expose what they believe, truly, about themselves (I am unworthy, I am ugly, I am nobody). Their makeovers reciprocate the suffering with the hagiography of their new bodies, employments, and identities. These converting rites address an array of selves and sorrows, but the unifying principle is that they are conducted to create one-line "aha" revelations paired with a more flattering haircut. Hair color and bob length indicate just how true you are to yourself; you will look right if you are reconciled rightly to your interiority.

Among the many types of confession collected on the *Oprah* show, a significant subgenre is her gay awakenings in which she not only encourages women and men, such as Governor McGreevey, to admit their "real selves" as lesbian or gay but also deploys her own cast of queer-eyed makeover consultants to enhance the real self you've revealed. In 2005, the *Oprah* show hosted TV celebrities, public relations consultants, and fashion stylists—including some who had served on makeover episodes—to tell their surprising, charming, good-time gay "aha" moments. "Today you're going to meet people who grew up hiding the same secret," Winfrey begins. "For some it took years even to say out loud." The show was upbeat, with the participants telling comic coming-out plots that included childhood crushes on Lee Majors, wailing over the death of Judy Garland, anger over painted moldings, and mistaken heterosexual marriages, all related under the understated advertising auspices of Robert Trachtenberg's testimonial collection, *When I Knew,* and Carson Kressley's *You're Different and That's Super.* Emphasized is the clarity of the either/or: you know you are or you know you aren't. The inscription of the show is that when you knew, you knew—there was no if, and, or queer about it. These Winfrey-led dialogues are straight dichotomous differentiation, articulated often as mere difference in taste. Some boys like Judy Garland, and others like Metallica. The Judy-lovers may be called queer by some, but the discursive plot line is anti-queer, bent on keeping sexuality on the straight and narrow. Like all the makeovers in an Oprah world, the result does not contest normalcy; it enshrines an O bourgeois best.

Although used since the nineteenth century as a generic synonym for the male homosexual, *queer* was recast in last decades of the twentieth century to press against the cleanliness of dimorphic sexual descriptions. In this incarnation, queer became an invocation of multiplicity, a way to "question the stability of any categories of identity based on sexual orientation." Queer then might "denaturalize categories such as 'lesbian' and 'gay' (not to mention 'straight' and 'heterosexual') revealing them as socially and historically constructed."[81] Any queer found in Winfrey herself, or in her ritual process that she unfurls, is fleeting, nervous, and articulated by confessors seeking constructed clarity. In the context of religious history, such solicitation and instantiation are a familiar aspect of the pastoral conversation Winfrey evokes. Using the work of Michel Foucault, Mark Jordan has described the very queer space of confessionals, the desire to reveal while disclosing, to proclaim complexity while also territorializing proper form. "The *scientia sexualis* of Christian pastoral practice," Jordan elaborates, "is in reality not a science, but an art, a series of rhetorical or theatrical programs that elaborate and impose scripts for the performance of moral identities—most powerfully and consequentially, identities of sexual grace or sexual sin."[82] The conversions wrought by Winfrey do not include those toward queer ambiguity, since even the *Oprah* show "appears to challenge common sense assumptions about relationships, specifically heterosexual relationships." It nonetheless "often works to reinforce precisely the norms she seems to challenge."[83] Any queer irresolution encounters the sealant of her makeover brush, which smoothes them for the camera.

It should be clear that in these righting conversions Winfrey maintains her agnosticism to their endgame. She eschews any obvious moralizing about who they are. She claims, over and over again, that she has fallen so many times and made so many mistakes of self-care that she is no place to judge any of her subjects or their myriad confusions. Still she is an openly judgmental and relentlessly clarifying questioner, driving the interviewee to only certain types of self-aware classification. To pursue a shadow belief is to uncover something singular ("I am not worthy") or to name a simple secret ("I am gay"). In the quest for such singularity, ambiguity of identity—not to mention of psychic reality—may fall by the wayside. The sheer experience of finding the singular should feel so good that you won't mind that it's too neat by half. The catharsis is worth the compromise of complexity. "Keeping secrets is very hard," observes one psychiatrist in an O magazine article. "Revealing them can be like draining an abscess. There's often a great feeling of relief that comes afterward."[84] The relief is, on the *Oprah* show, not just for the revealer of the secret but also for the studio and television audience, who get their abscesses drained, voyeuristically, with the aha climax of disclosure.

In "Wives Confess They Are Gay," for example, Winfrey exhibits a series of women "having the best sex of their lives" after the "unexpected confession" of their deepest, darkest "secret." Winfrey shows how the women had been "repressing" their true identities, and by doing so she underlines an identity for each of the repressed. Each story is set up with familiar white-picket sentimentality ("she married, had two children, did the carpool thing, had an active sex life with her really loving husband") and harsh awakening ("but after seven years of marriage, Chris says she could no longer ignore some of her deepest desires"). Desires become desire, even as the questioned may resist such redaction:

Winfrey: You wanted to have sex with your husband?

Chris: I did. I did. We were—

Winfrey: You are a different kind of lesbian.

Chris: I know.

Winfrey: You are. I've never heard this before. You wanted to have sex with your husband?

Chris: I did. I did.

Chris's multiple desires confuse Winfrey. You wanted to have sex with your husband, too? Although Winfrey brackets the problem categorically—placing Chris in the camp of a *different kind of* lesbian—she finds the same difficulty in every converting queer she encounters. What Winfrey wants is the lightbulb moment, a moment of pure admission of "when I knew," illustrated by one confessing wife when she said, "I could not suppress that anymore . . . like something came out of me . . . my whole world changed . . . it was like a little lightbulb clicked on, and as much as I tried to click off the lightbulb, I couldn't get it to go off."

Addressing Winfrey's 2004 encounter with J.L. King, author of *On the Down Low: A Journey into the Lives of "Straight" Black Men Who Sleep with Men* (2004), literary critic Scott Herring writes that the *Oprah* show seeks "to solicit true confessions from King that will 'blow the lid off' the down low,'" yet since King refuses to offer any clean explanation of his desires or of his identity, the "exchange goes no where," becoming in Herring's rendering "an inarticulation that functions as sexual disarticulation."[85] Winfrey's "excavations," in Herring's interpretation, make King only more undetectable; the more she researches, the more he recedes. How her subjects *feel* is important to her, but in order to explain what they *are,* she will turn to the familiar.

Winfrey: So you don't feel that you're gay?

Kristie Joe: I don't feel that I am gay, yeah. I mean, well, I think to myself, I'm gay, because I'm with Amanda. So obviously I'm living a gay lifestyle. You know, I love her. But I don't look at a lot of other women and say—and I don't look at the—you know, women in general and . . .

Winfrey: Oh, this is just so darn interesting, I don't know what to say.

Amanda: It's that scale.

Winfrey: It's the scale. It's the spectrum.

Kristie Jo: It's a scale, yeah. And I struggle with that, too, because . . .

Winfrey: This is, like—who was Ellen's girlfriend's name? What was it?

Amanda: Anne Heche.

Winfrey: Anne He—this is an Anne Heche thing?

Kristie Jo: Well, no, I don't think so. I mean . . .

> *Winfrey*: No, I'm not trying to label it.
>
> *Kristie Jo*: Yeah. No, no.
>
> *Winfrey*: But I'm just trying to put it in my brain.[86]

As always, Winfrey stands in for her audience, being the singular that can conceive and contain their diverse whole. She remarks frequently that she asks the questions she imagines her audience asking on behalf of pragmatic middle Americans. So, is it an Anne Heche thing? Is Kristie Jo a temporary lesbian, bound to return to boys once the desire for this dame is through? The "scale" or "spectrum" of sexual desire is invoked, but it's hard to practice, hard to "put it" in Winfrey's "brain" without wanting a celebrity association and a teleology of sexual endgame. It's so interesting, she doesn't know what to say.

No one in recent years has been more maddening on this point than the infamous evangelist Ted Haggard, who posed a very real problem for Winfrey's scripting. Once the leader of the National Evangelical Association, Pastor Ted left his pulpit and his political affiliations after a man claimed to have had drug-fueled homosexual trysts with him. Haggard's downfall included years in evangelical exile with his family while comedians mocked his hypocrisy, off-Broadway actors developed a study of his Colorado Springs context, and a documentarian tracked his experiences for HBO. At the time of the release of the documentary, he appeared on the *Oprah* show and maddened her efforts to elicit clarity. First, he admitted to secret desire for men, but even in the light of that admission, he refused to accept the label of gay.

> *Haggard*: No, I don't think I'm gay. I did wonder about that. After this crisis, when I went to therapy, I said, "I need to know, am I gay, am I straight, am I bi? What am I?" And my first therapist said, "You are a heterosexual with homosexual attachments." So we processed through that. I wasn't sure what that meant. Then we went through a . . .
>
> *Winfrey*: Nor am I.
>
> *Haggard*: Yeah.
>
> *Winfrey*: Nor is the audience.
>
> *Haggard*: Is that it?
>
> *Winfrey*: Nor is—and certainly nor are the gay people watching right now, yes.
>
> *Haggard*: Well, yeah. It—and it is. I do believe I don't fit into the normal boxes. I do think there are complexities associated with some people's sexuality. I don't know about other people.

Winfrey: I would agree with you, yeah.

Haggard: But it just wasn't as simple as I wanted it to be, because I was so deeply in love with my wife, am so deeply in love with my wife. Our intimate relationship is wonderful and very satisfying. But I had this other thing going on inside of me, too.

"It just wasn't as simple as I wanted it to be" is a remark atypical of the evangelicalism in which Haggard has been a central proponent. It is a theological and social movement bent on vernacular clarity and bright-light conversions. Haggard's performance here suggests gray territory in the landscape of truth. He loves his wife, and he slept with her; he wanted to have sex with men, so he did that, too. A therapist offers an explanation ("a heterosexual with homosexual attachments"), and nobody seems satisfied. Winfrey certainly isn't ("nor am I"), and she, protective of her homo compatriots, intimates that the "gay people" may too be confused. She worries always about the representative meaning of her display:

Winfrey: Yes. And that you are, you know, you represent so many people throughout the world who are gay.

Haggard: Yeah.

Winfrey: Or, as you say, have these complexities and are inclined to want to have same-sex relationships and who are tortured . . .

Haggard: Yes.

Winfrey: . . . tortured by it.

Haggard: Yes. Yeah.

Winfrey: Why in this whole process could you just not make peace with that?

Haggard: I couldn't.

Winfrey: Why couldn't you just make peace with "this is who I am"?

Haggard: I think it was probably a combination of what I wanted to be, the ideal of what I—I wanted to be a great husband.

Winfrey: But how can you—but how can you—Ted. How . . .

Haggard: I know. I know. I hear you.

Winfrey: But how can you deny who you are? What you are?

Haggard: Because as a Christian I believe that I become a new man in Christ. And I believe . . .

Winfrey: And so you don't believe that Christ accepts homosexuals.

Haggard is a frustrating subject, since he won't let Oprah cajole him to peace. Not surprisingly, he is a savvy occupant of the anxious bench, having managed many before, to church-building and soul-saving effect. He does not sweat or squirm. He remains polite. He merely resists her version of his conversion. She wants him to find peace in an identity marker that he cannot claim, and she wants him to pursue freedom from the religion that she believes encourages his shadows to fester. It is, in her world, the religion's fault, since it forces men and women into structures and dogmas unnatural to their authentic selves. She presents beatific spiritual ease: she just wants you to be happy, to admit what you are, to live joyfully, in the light, after all your torture, after all your torturous self-denial of what is true. Just come to her. Before that peace, however, she'd like to hear your abreaction, the naming of just what you are. She'd like the "aha" to be made here, on her stage, for her consumer expectations to be fulfilled. Just say it, Ted. Stop denying it, Ted: you are tortured because you are gay.

> *Winfrey*: But what's confusing me, and I think confusing a lot of other people, is that you're saying the ideal was not to have those sexual inclinations. I think so many people are confused by that, because if that is who you are . . .
>
> *Haggard*: Yeah.
>
> *Winfrey*: . . . that is who you are.
>
> *Haggard*: I hear you. But it's got to be part of the process. I hid it.
>
> *Winfrey*: Yeah.
>
> *Haggard*: So it actually became a problem. Actually . . .
>
> *Winfrey*: The ideal would be not to lie about that.
>
> *Haggard*: The ideal would be not to lie about it, that's right.
>
> *Winfrey*: Would you say you are completely heterosexual?
>
> *Haggard*: No.
>
> *Winfrey*: And would you say you're gay?
>
> *Haggard*: No.
>
> *Winfrey*: You're . . .
>
> *Haggard*: I would say I'm a heterosexual with issues.
>
> *Winfrey*: Okay.[87]

Okay. This is not the truth Winfrey sought. Failing to submit to his sexual makeover, Haggard deflates her ritual process. No matter, though—it is, Winfrey would claim, his loss. He is the one evading his authenticity. Winfrey can't stand the inauthentic mess of this, leaving issues on the table rather than solving the case, finding the shadow and setting it free. Haggard, too, appears to be straining, as the lights of Winfrey's stage make the translucency of his sexual narration seem self-denying and self-deceptive. "Action can be coerced," Erving Goffman has written, "but a coerced show of feeling is only a show."[88] Even as it seems that Haggard presents a portrait of complexity recommending compassion, he receives the naming of better ideals and the dismissal of his beliefs. Winfrey's advice consolidates complexity into her born-again clarity: "I would just say to anybody, whatever secret you're holding, live your own truth; life is really short."[89] Haggard cannot quite meet that standard, or rather can never meet it to her satisfaction, so long as he interprets his truth within a system of religious logic that tells him what he should want. By his evangelical God, he's told to be with his wife. By his Oprah, he's told to be true, be merry, and be gay. The space between the two is the dialectic of religion in an age described, too easily and flatly, as a secular one.

"So it's really having compassion for your internal world," remarks one guest, Debbie Ford, author of *The Dark Side of the Light Chasers*. "Anything you can't be with won't let you be."[90] However does one find the real, or the best, life with all this televised reboxing of identity? If life is meant to be perpetual transformation to more clear-cut versions of you, however can any semblance of stillness, of intimacy, of squalor be found? The magazine offers more promising queer ambiguity. "Sexuality does fall along some kind of continuum," one column explains, later noting that the very forced clarity of confession may force things into cleaner chaos than necessary. "Once he announces he has homosexual feelings and may or may not have acted on them, his wife and often a therapist get on his case," which is called "shaping behavior." "The guy is turned into a liar and a louse," the piece continues. "The man . . . follows the program, gets divorced, adopts a gay lifestyle, and then he's in the shower fantasizing about sex with his ex-wife."[91] The problem is that such a *guy* is hard to convey on the TV screen spectacle of the talk show. Winfrey's makeover rites are redactions premised on a commodity genre that expects climax. The horror movie needs its scream, and Winfrey needs her "Yup, I'm gay." A vanilla orgasm for an afternoon spent watching talk show TV.

"Television does not vary," George W. S. Trow once explained. "The trivial is raised up to power in it. The powerful is lowered toward the trivial. The power behind it resembles the power of no-action, the powerful passive. It is *bewitching*."[92] We are bewitched into passivity by the quickening mayhem of that spectacle, the society Guy DeBord has described as organized around the production and consumption of images and staged events rather than intimate connections and local work.[93] During the heyday of scholarship on talk show television, these programs were made to be the prime exhibit in that society, as they were linked analogically to tabloid journalism, the stigmatized freak show, the capitalist carnival, the Depression-era hunger for early televised game shows, and the pervasive triumph of liberal democratic therapy culture.[94] The *Oprah* show's turn to Change Your Life TV was a civilizing maneuver meant to gentrify this grotesque. The television, however, remained the same: "A single week of Oprah takes you from bondage to all the violent terrors of life, to escape through vicarious encounters with celebrity, to visions of charity and hope, to hard resolve, to redemption and moral renovation."[95] The show would, under its new banner, become a reply to the closing of the confessional and the failure of pastoral psychology. It would become a public sermon and a therapeutic rite. But it would do it all in the confines of a Nielsen rating and commercial intervals. "This is secular charisma," Richard Sennett has written, "a psychic striptease."[96]

From this Nineties reformation, *The Oprah Winfrey Show* lassoed religious idiom for a purportedly secular space. "Media exposure serves as a kind of *accelerant* to religious discourse, providing the 'oxygen of publicity' to ideas and movements that may not have been able to achieve prominence before," Stewart Hoover explains. "Religion also acts as a kind of *accelerant* to media, acting as something outside the realm of normal media discourse that exists, intervenes, and contradicts that discourse with a kind of portentous possibility."[97] This emphasis on acceleration resonates with any viewing of the *Oprah* show even as it creates a false distinction between religion and media. Is media only the mechanism, only television? Or is it not also the mode, the staged confession and reappointing of new selves? Where do the media end and the religion begin in the world of televised spectacle? The talk show possesses the cadences, breaks, and crescendos of ceremonies accelerated for your allotted efficiency and your commanding pleasure. With the right purchases, the right assemblage of counselors, the right story, and the right resolution, we can transform. In makeover, we trust.

Meanwhile, the whole endeavor is insistently devoted to the removal of the self from any authoritative binds in order to recommend that you—you on behalf of yourself, you modeled after Her—pursue *your* authentic body, *your* authentic practices, and *your* matching accessories. The woman at the center of every television screen and the screen framing the woman at its center cannot be separated; they have become the same. The frame is the woman, the woman is the frame. And that woman is, as we continue to find, not just *any* signifying woman. The media and the religion are codetermining and contingent. On the *Oprah* show, the ritual spectacle is scripted by a most particular self, by a most pressing preacher. Winfrey, the talk show preacher, is a "story drama-tizer" with her confessional prodding, with her attempts to "heal the guest and the greater society whose 'problem' he or she supposedly rep-resents."[98] As with every other description of her structural role, Winfrey disavows it, distancing herself from any notion of charismatic centrality. "I'm not here to change your life," Winfrey remarks. "I am just here to present an idea and perhaps get you to think differently about it. And if that changes you, fine, fine. And if it doesn't, that's okay too. But do I get you to think differently? Do I get you to think at all? Do I get a moment where you go, 'Ahhh, I never thought of it that way before'? That's all I'm looking for."[99] Winfrey argues she is the conduit, the genre, the medium of your revelation. The confession is the thing, and she is just its context. That it may have aftershocks is just a collateral pleasure. "Honest confession always has this double effect," an *O* contributor explains. "It benefits not only the one who confesses but the rest of the world."[100] Viewers and readers testify to this consequence. "This helped me think about where I wanted to go in my life," one attendee of a Live Your Best Life Tour remarked. "Oprah is a good messenger."[101]

To emphasize Winfrey's centrality is not to undercut the potential revolutions of her assignments. Rather, it is to underscore that in her capacity as interpreter, as channel from your ugly, lying place to your prettier, rectified, awakened one, she does more than merely "present an idea." She converts you to an idea, to the idea of her biographical revelations as a model for the world. She *is* the divine pervasion. She offers up her body as bridge to a nation, the traversing of which will transform sinners into the saved, mere viewers into consumer converts. Oprah's viewers tune in to this experience hoping for the same pro-cessing she offers her guests. Through encounter with her weighted form, all believers dream of salvation. It is her biographical body that absorbs the memory of pain, the realities of pain, and the ongoing nar-rative of pain. As sinners prepare for their appearances, as the murder-ers and memoirists anticipate their sound bites, all are made perfectly aware that she is the encompassing force of their confession; she is the template against which all complexity will be resolved. Her body is the bench.

CHAPTER 4

Preacher Queen

The Race and Gender of America's Confessor

On September 23, 2001, mourners gathered at Yankee Stadium to remember the missing and the dead. Just two weeks after planes crashed into the Twin Towers, organizers assembled a five-hour interfaith ceremony titled "A Prayer for America," which offered a series of speeches, benedictions, and songs. The *New York Times* would call the Bronx rally akin to an Olympic event, as the crowd broke into chants of "U.S.A.! U.S.A.! U.S.A.!" Pleas for tolerance blended with prayers for unification by a cornucopia of religious representatives, who sat on the dais in rows alongside the governors and mayors. Included in the collected congress of America's faithful was Cardinal Edward M. Egan, of the Roman Catholic Diocese of New York, Imam Izak-el Mu-eed Pasha, of the Malcolm Shabazz Mosque in Harlem, and Rabbi Arthur Schneier, as well as several other leaders of Christian, Muslim, Jewish, Sikh, and Hindu faith. There was no apparent cynicism about the scripted religious buffet in this posttraumatic moment, as families who had lost loved ones wept while hearing Greek Orthodox, Catholic, and Sunni prayers.[1] This was a portrait of an America assimilated into national resolve.

Who would be the right person to steer this collective? Who could best organize the assorted religious vestments and somber political suits into a soothing visual and spiritual clarity? At the dawn of the twenty-first century, there was but one nominee. Oprah Winfrey was America's middle ground. No Protestant preacher dominated the airwaves, no other celebrity ruled over the flyover country, and no CEO transcended her executive office to dwell among the consuming populace. And certainly no one person combined all three roles, fusing spiritual leadership, celebrity recognition, and consumer popularity into the ideal summary icon. As master of ceremonies at the "Prayer for America," Oprah Winfrey opened the event with this description: "We each came here as one, but we stand as thousands. . . . What was meant to divide us has drawn us together. . . . May we leave this place determined to now use every moment that we yet live to turn up the volume in our own lives, to create deeper meaning, to know what really matters." On her show and in her print and Internet productions, Winfrey rarely speaks of a collective *we*, focusing instead on her inimitable *I*. In her service as the liturgical center of this diverse parliament, however, it was her iconic obligation to name that which really matters to the "we" that we are, together. "What really matters," she reminds us, "what really matters is who you love and how you love."[2] The messages of her show coordinated with the message of her nation's needed unification. She was America's assembly, she was America's love, and she was America's preacher queen.

This patriotic podium calls for consideration of Winfrey's representative meaning. How had she become the right symbol of diverse assemblage? How had she, an African American television talk show host, become the ideal assimilation of American spiritual strength? To some extent, as this chapter will show, the answer is in the question. It is *because* of her commitment to an image and strategy of assimilated diversity, her particular description of herself as a black American, and her interpretation of the role of women in national culture that meant she would not sit on the dais as a sectarian representative but meant she would front the consortium as its representative whole. Her consumption of products, people, and ideas possesses an impressive diversity, yet she assimilates all those characters into herself, into her incorporated individual "she." Oprah toys publicly with her racial identity, constantly searching for a way to include more (more people, more ideas, more confession, more objects) and exclude fewer from her particularity. Preachers and saleswomen share the common ambition to convert the multitudes under their advertising slogans proposing exclusivity. The product must do something that no other savior, and nothing else, can do. Oprah is the one picture that tells the whole story, affirming the virtues of plurality while representing a corporate and biographical singularity. She conjures a religious space in regard to her country's mythic dream, becoming a site of ritual and moral transaction for a nation possessed by the idea of a plural marketplace for everyone's dreams.

Before considering the sort of self Oprah Winfrey projects, we must wrestle with her national identity. How requisite is the specific American flag for her specific pastoral ascent? Could Oprah *only* be American, or might she have easily been from Ghana or Taiwan? Considering the media methods and consumer cultures upon which she has relied, by the mid-1980s few other national television contexts would have been able to collaborate to such symphonic success. Yet, by the beginning of the twenty-first century, the spread of Holiness-Pentecostal worship patterns and evangelical denominations enthroned charismatic leaders in Africa, Asia, and Latin America. Is this profligacy of preacher kings and some stage queens indicative of Winfrey's influence, Winfrey's replication, or of the inevitable patterns of certain Protestant programs? The observations of this chapter lean toward the last, suggesting that the effects of Holiness-Pentecostal idioms cannot be overstated. In the United States, the success of this Holiness-Pentecostal sectarian cluster has relied in no small way on race and gender paradigms that were contingent upon a national story, a story that includes everything from anti-lynching legislation to women's suffrage, the strange notion of religious freedom and the perpetuation of a Protestant domination. In this chapter, not all aspects of Winfrey's racial and gender preamble will be pursued. However, through the comparative study of iconic instances and individuals from within U.S. religious history, her multivalent cultural position might be mapped. Oprah is the result of racial, gendered, and denominational histories that she celebrates and repudiates, dancing as she does in the promise of a postracial paradise that she believes will, through her naming, appear. She seeks to be the pluralist preacher, extolling a universal vision that only she can offer. Her genius is this first-person communitarian embodiment, how she makes herself the center of a story that she claims is a compilation, and not a monologue.

Oprah establishes the aesthetic that balances her diversity on our behalf. She has become famous as a result of her universality, because she accepts individuals as they are refracted through her paradigm, not as they are infected by history or race or denomination. In a *USA Today* article, Winfrey stated the case clearly: "I've been able to do it because my race and gender have never been an issue for me. I've been blessed in knowing who I am, and I am a part of a great legacy. . . . I am the seed of the free, and I know it. I intend to bear great fruit."[3] Her great fruit would be to pose herself as inclusive of the world's abundance. This is a somewhat muddy discursive turn, however, since despite her claim that race and gender are nonissues, she invokes them perpetually. Oprah simply wouldn't have become *Oprah* if she hadn't lived the life of a black woman in America. Her race and her gender supply the premise of her unifying form.

A plea for national unity amid the nation's demographic diversity is a trope reflected through U.S. religious history. Believers have worried constantly about how to convert the different, how to compel others to a sectarian side that attempts, always, to represent its mission as an encompassing whole. In 1893, these conversations climaxed among a leading group of American liberal Christians in Chicago. The same city that would later host Winfrey's plurality offered a parliament of difference—the World's Parliament of Religions.[4] Faced with an astonishing influx of immigrants and their foreign faiths, the attendants at the parliament in Chicago provided a thorough rebuttal to the corresponding nativism that festered in American industrial centers. Historians of American religion have spotlighted this parliament as a rite of passage from a predominantly Christian one to a more religiously plural America. There, representatives of over a dozen faiths (including twelve Buddhists, eight Hindus, two Muslims, two Zoroastrians, two Shintoists, two Confucians, one Taoist, one Jain) converged in the pursuit of world religious unity, or, in the terms of its participants, "to unite all religion against all irreligion"; to set forth "their common aim and common grounds of union"; to help secure "the coming unity of mankind, in the service of God and Man"; and "to indicate the impregnable foundations of theism."[5] Through a grand exhibition and discussion of a plurality of traditions, organizers of the World's Parliament of Religions hoped for a converging unity in which all faiths would meet in a common quest for reconciliation and peace.[6] Their photographed assemblage eerily mirrors that of the Yankee Stadium gathering in 2001, with rows of religious leaders in full ceremonial regalia staring out from a Gilded Age stage into a witnessing American mass.

Despite the showy display of elaborately costumed foreigners, the majority of participants in the parliament were American Protestants, and the majority of speeches by these Christians openly aspired to a "reunion" of Christendom that would dominate the globe.[7] As historian Richard Hughes Seager has demonstrated, the parliament failed in this ambition. Although it was an unprecedented gathering of religious leadership, it did not produce the global theological ecumenism celebrated in its presentations.[8] The following century saw the triumph of consumerism, and not Christianity, as the dominating ritual ideology about which all humanity revolved. Yet, the intellectual and social paradigm of the parliament is a powerful one. In its racial interpretations and plural promises, the parliament predicted a century of political and cultural performance premised on a pervasive Protestantism.[9] Parliament leaders believed that if they could define the parameters of our essential spirituality, they could define the future of a unified human race.

Some time later, in the same city, Oprah Winfrey would host a similar sort of dreaming. Believing that the removal of religious sacraments (such as exclusive rituals, legislating hierarchies, codes of membership) encourages spiritual commonality, Winfrey advocates a deracinated religiosity and racial collaboration. "Oprah has created and appeals to a kind of fourth race—the Oprah-people—which is not white, black, or celebrity," Lee Siegel has written. This is "a racial utopia based on the exchangeability of colorless human pain."[10] Thus the assemblage of acceptable differences, of palatable diversity, is done around themes of communal agreement. The kaleidoscope splays into abundant diversity, then coheres into familiar strands of human desire. From her explorations of self to her celebrations of color swatches, Winfrey's goal is a cohering portrait of wellness. "My heart's deepest desire is to align the energy of my personality with that of my soul and become a whole, complete, glorious human here on earth," Winfrey told Gary Zukav.[11] This alignment echoes throughout her efforts, as she draws the diffused energies of the world into a whole that she defines. "The new diversities ensuing from transnationalism and the flow of populations and cultural goods have not only opened possibilities for new pluralities and hybrid identities," Arlene Dávila has written, "but, most significantly, created new demands for establishing 'belonging.'"[12] To establish belonging, Oprah assimilates the diversity of the universe into transferable sameness. "Their stories are unique," Winfrey remarks again and again, "but the situation is universal."[13] The story is the thing we tell to find our way to common ground, to a situation in which we all might belong.

The images of organized abundance resonate beyond parliaments and makeover contestants. Consider, for example, the way that fashions are paraded in periodical literature. As you page through any fashion magazine, you encounter thematic sets of photographs. Perhaps the theme is a season (summer) or a place (Cape Cod); an article of clothing (shorts) or a particular style within that genre (formal shorts); a color (red) or a color as emotional narrative (passionate red); a character type (professional woman) or a character twist (professional woman

of the future). In any such spread, the seven or eight dramatically photographed images coordinate in tone and coloration, offering a sampler as a set. Perhaps one photo shows a passionate red skirt, another
a passionate red velvet jacket, or just a passionate red bracelet on a
carefully shadowed nude form. The unifying point of this constructed
array is to sell the magazine reader (from *Vogue* and *Woman's Wear
Daily* to *Redbook* and *Good Housekeeping*) on a new consumer particular ("This month, I'm looking for more passionate reds . . . more
futuristic jacket silhouettes . . . more formal shorts"). This innovative
aha! has been encoded as a new perspective on the humdrum. If *Vogue*
is more likely to pursue the diverse avant-garde ("peacock headgear
for winter!"), *Redbook* reduces any avant-garde to a plainclothes garnish ("three ways to accessorize your favorite basic black dress!").[14] No
matter this difference in an imagined audience—the *Sex and City* aspirations of *Vogue* readers, the maternal practicality of *Redbook* mothers—the purpose of the exhibiting proclivity is the same. You should
now pack differently for whatever shore you visit, whether or not it is
on Cape Cod. The point is to encourage aesthetic conscientiousness for
consumer creativity.

The *O Magazine* fashion spread and *Oprah* show fashion makeovers
mirror this exhibiting pattern but do so with two multicultural twists.
Here *multicultural* infers the duality that is the *O* difference, since *O*
magazine and the *Oprah* show pursue a rigorous multiculturalism of
subjects (models, body types, clothing styles) and a multiculturalism
of sensitivities (to physical flaws, problematic fashion needs, character
quirks).[15] In an *O* magazine story titled "Suits: The Female of the Species," eight different actresses (different ages, different races, different
hair styles, different gender performances) get suits selected to match
their special stylistic flavor. Thus, the woman seeking "discreet sex
appeal" finds a suit with a "dramatic, immensely flattering neck line."
The woman whose goal is "keeping it simple" wears a "chic knit getup
that evokes the pleasant tension between the genders." Sex and simplic-
ity have easy getup solutions. The text alongside these real-life man-
nequins admits in their first-person voices to a preferred informality, so
that actress Kate Walsh wearing a Kenneth Cole suit wishes in the copy
that she could instead be in "workout clothes" and actress Gabrielle
Union, with a Chanel bracelet and Naum suit, longs to be wearing "flip-
flops" and doing "that L.A. casual thing."[16] Encased in formal expectations yet dreaming of down-time casual, the Oprah fashion perspective
is a ruthlessly contrived balance, the balance of aesthetics in order to

enjoin the individual model's spirit. Hence, every printed or televised fashion array shows different types of women with the same type of clothing problem or women wearing different styles of clothing with the same desire for an everyday, informal opposite. The reconciliation is to a balanced woman, the sort who has suits, has reasons to wear said suits occasionally, is made equal to her sisters (across races, across income brackets, across backgrounds) by the desire to look good in said suits, but really wants to sink into a couch in casual cotton and dig into some Häagen-Dazs. The woman who does not have the need for the singular item, the calling to reconcile a wardrobe with down-time flip-flops, or the impulse to make every outfit a story line is just not an Oprah sort of woman.

The Oprah woman is prepared, always, to assimilate her renowned diversity into a spiritual unity and to cohere her closet contents into daily constructions of this reconciled She. Inside, she's a girl ready for all occasions, needing many different things, desiring many different lives, all while pursuing the Best Life holism propagated by Winfrey prescriptions and makeovers. Outside she finds accessories and pieces to represent the diversity, make it neatly commensurable. She becomes a costuming myriorama, a moving panorama that no matter the order of the diverse pieces—skin coloration, ethnic bracelets, T-shirt fabrics—forms the same woman.[17] This is woman as *tableau polyoptique,* a woman as a oneness that Oprah exemplifies. "Uniqueness" is a diversity deserving spotlighted exhibition (your unique nose, your unique inherited garment, your unique scar). Uniqueness requires leavening accessories and balancing shoes to underline uniformity while still heralding the special. "What makes us different from one another is so much less important than what makes us alike," Oprah extols in a "What I Know For Sure" column.[18] The cosmetic consequences for this eclecticism are exuberantly deliberate. In a spread titled "The Bold and the Beautiful," another set of "eight creative women" are shown equalizing their quirk (Piper Perabo likes "secondhand clothes . . . because they're unique"; Marisa Berenson likes "wonderful, big" antique accessories) through overall equations of equilibrium (Perabo mixes vintage pieces with new Ungaro; Berenson balances large jewelry with sleek Donna Karan lines).[19]

Lest all this balance and coordination seem incorporating, Oprah reminds you: you do this for you, and not for me. In her study of the *Oprah* episode "Around the World with Oprah" (October 6, 2004), Sharon Heijin Lee identifies how Winfrey's framing of an ideal self feeds into a neoliberal politics of beauty that celebrates choice as the

attitudinal gauge of quality.[20] Are you choosing to do this plastic surgery because it makes you feel like your more authentic self? Or are you
having this plastic surgery to coordinate with an idea of beauty determined by some other gaze? In Winfrey's world, women are supposed to
tell the difference ("I choose this bracelet because *I* choose it") even as
she selects—on the show, on the pages of her magazine—the taste that
defines an authentic self, tastefully cohered for mass acceptability. "It's
the illusion of free choice, but it's actually an absence of choice," performance artist Robyn Okrant has remarked.[21] Because she is so careful with her best life, Oprah's productions suggest you shouldn't mind
her in your life. This is just what unmarried, childless, wildly successful Oprah enjoys. Maybe you will, too? She presents her presumptively
peculiar features (her segregated suffering, her nouveau riche tastes, and
her monetary excess) to convert her viewers from their provincial limits
to her cosmopolitan expanse.

She is the queen of the human buffet, counseling a disposition of sen-
sibly monitored free will. You make your world, you make your beauty,
you make your accessories, and you make your composite self. When
you do this, and do it in earnest, palettes of plural perfection emerge.
Balanced beauty is, of course, the prime principle when adjudicating an
outfit, a life story, or a biracial appearance. "A stylish mix of easygoing
basics with evening-ready separates will take you everywhere," reminds
an *O* magazine spread.[22] Talk of legislative policies and global economies is for other locations, for magazines printed for other parts of ourselves and television shows at other times of day. The talk that matters
most for this location, for this medium, is talk of surfaces. We cannot
manipulate the interior, but we can pose and position the exterior. Her
representation of ethnicity therefore becomes an "option," to quote Rey
Chow, an accessory to her corporeal and intellectual constancy.[23] The
promise is that, because of these decorating choices, the reformation
bleeds inward. No aspect of the human exterior escapes arrangement.
For example, another *O* magazine spread uses racial and ethnic profiling
to glamorous effect, reporting about six families who model "harmonic
convergences." "Take one parent (Asian? African-American? Hungar-
ian? Native American?)," the *O* recipe reads, "mix with another parent (Colombian? Caribbean? German-American? Pakistani Muslim?)
and watch something beautiful happen. Witness these six uncategoriz-
able families who defy stereotyping and show us that the mix is in the
match."[24] People, accessories, families, and city blocks: no matter what
the object, the point is to make the world's wacky wonderful diversity

match. Elsewhere, an O magazine staffer explains, "Mixed-race celebrities are admired for their surfaces, for the promises of difference their features present. . . . For me, being mixed ensures a kind of wakefulness, a birthright invitation to see the world from more than one perspective."[25] Unique beauty (the nose, the coloration, the scar) foretells more than a mirror's happy sigh; it preaches an interior readiness for the new, for the peculiar around the corner that will remind you of the universal already in you.

"The Negro is a sort of seventh son, born with a veil," wrote W. E. B. Du Bois, "gifted with second-sight in this American world."[26] Oprah's advertised genius at therapeutic intervention is not the result of medical or ecclesiastical training but the pedigree of her second-sighted racial position. She began her career as a journalist and an aspiring actress, seeking always to move between audience and story line, between the truth of you and the stories produced by others. Yet Oprah also repeatedly names herself as "black" to accredit herself as America's mediator, transmitter, and healer. She externalizes what Patricia Hill Collins has explained as the ideal dual "otherness" of the black woman when she explains that African American women "as a group experience a world different from that of those who are not Black and female."[27] In her episodes on spiritual transformation and promoting "lifestyle makeovers," Winfrey repeatedly suggests that what we are is an accident, whereas what we become is a choice. The transformation of her diverse sinners depends on a description of self that may be made by the choices to come, not the cultural precursors that may have brought them to where they are now. However, just as she argues we are what we choose, she also ennobles her own history, her own racial and religious premise, as authenticating her message.

"I am every one of [my audience], and they are me," she has said. "That's why we get along so well. I'm vulnerable like them and people say, 'Poor thing. She has big hips, too.' It crosses racial barriers."[28] Winfrey carefully establishes herself as both the paradigm and the exception of her racial lessons. "I transcend race, really."[29] Although she may transcend race in her self-image, in her self-expressions she proclaims her specificity. *Her* race, *her* history, and *her* religious context seep through her enveloping embrace. She wants to be beyond blackness but also points to her blackness as distinguishing her accomplishments. "I'm the first black woman in this country to have a nationally syndicated talk show and it seems to me like that would be worth celebrating."[30] She does not just want an accolade for being successful and black. She wants her success to evoke for people previous icons of blackness. "I stand on solid rock because I come from a great legacy of black people. I was never taught oppression." Elsewhere, she underlines, "We are who we are because someone brave walked before us."[31] Her work surrounds her with white staff unfamiliar with this source of her strength, but that's fine: she has the shoulders of giants to stand upon. "When it's me at a boardroom table surrounded by fifteen white guys, I think of a photo of Katharine Graham in her book *Personal History,*" she told an audience. "It's a picture of her sitting at that table, as head of the *Washington Post,* surrounded by all white guys." Winfrey said she always thinks of herself as "walking into a room bringing with me Sojourner Truth and Harriet Tubman and all the women who never made it into a boardroom."[32]

If you watch or read the products of the Oprah Winfrey empire, you not only know Winfrey is *black* by her own description, but you are also persistently made to believe that her blackness matters. "I was colored, colored, in Mississippi in 1954," Oprah intones to an interviewer. "I was raised with an outhouse, no plumbing. Nobody had any clue that my life could be anything but working in some factory or a cotton field in Mississippi. . . . I feel so strongly that my life is to be used as an example to show people what can be done."[33] Her impoverished black youth, her encounters with prejudice in Milwaukee, Nashville, and Baltimore, her resentment of black nationalism, her comfort with whites, her associations with prominent black leaders, the difficulties of filming black skin, the trouble with black hair, the proportional size of black women, her amusement with white emotional discomfort, her struggle to prove her intelligence, her interest in her slave ancestry—all are mentioned with casual affect and familiar consistency.[34] Winfrey supports an empire of diversity organized by emotional and aesthetic principles of similitude. She names her racial identity as that which collects her in a collective that she wants even as she resists. Winfrey's rhetoric establishes an insider identity position as she sprinkles her talk with prefaces like "black people know all about that," "if you were black, you'd know that," or "black people believe."[35] Such ownership of her racial perspective contrasts with her disavowal of representative sway. In one interview, Winfrey expressed exhaustion with her interpreters. "People feel you have to . . . represent *the race,*" she sighs. "I understand what they're talking about, but you don't have to do what other people want you to do. Blackness is something I just am. I'm black. I'm a woman. I wear a size 10 shoe. It's all the same to me."[36]

Part of her resistance to being named a black leader is that within the black community, her reputation was and is a conflicted one. "When I first started, everything I did was criticized and talked about particularly by black people," she explained. "People would say, 'Oh, she's hugging the white people too much,' or 'She goes to the White people in the audience more' or 'she doesn't have enough Black guests on the show.'"[37] When an interviewer in 1991 asked how "sexism and racism" influenced her career, Winfrey replied:

> I would have to say that I, for the most part, have not been, as far as I know, affected. As a matter of fact, it was because of the riots of the '70s that I think they were looking for minorities. . . . So I was hired as a token, and had to take the heat from my college classmates—I went to an all-black college—with them calling me a token. And I used to say, "Yeah, but I'm a paid token!" I was very defensive about it because I've always had to live with the notion of other black people saying—for any amount of success that you achieve—they say, "Oh, you trying to be white. You are trying to talk white. You are trying to be white," and so forth. Which is such a ridiculous notion to me, since you look in the mirror every morning, and you are black, there is a black face in your reflection.[38]

Alone in front of her mirror, she is black. Read in public through her habits, her talk, and her success as white, Winfrey subtly distances herself from the radicalism of Seventies feminism and Sixties civil rights.[39] She repeatedly admits to loathing Black Power sentiment, especially in the incarnations she witnessed while a student at Tennessee State University. "I refused to conform to the militant thinking at the time. I hated, hated college," she has said. "I felt that most of the kids hated and resented me. They were into black power and anger. I was not."[40] This sort of black distaste followed her, she claimed, throughout her career: "A small but vocal group of black people fear me. Slavery taught us to hate ourselves. I mean, Jane Pauley doesn't have to deal with this. It all comes out of self-hatred. A black person has to ask herself, 'If Oprah Winfrey can make it, what does it say about me?' They no longer have any excuse."[41] Although such sharp descriptions of her black compatriots have lessened in recent years, it did require some healing work to reconcile herself to her image in the black imagination. After conversations with Maya Angelou and Sidney Poitier, she says, "I finally got it. Just because you're a part of my culture doesn't mean you can decide for me. White people don't decide for me. Nobody decides for me. I get to decide for myself. Once I got that, I was free."[42] Free in a relative sense, since her every success, experience, and subplot became a racial story.[43] Nonetheless the freedom she describes here correlates to her own wobbling swagger in the marketplace of self-representation, moving as she does back and forth between a representative black woman and a racially transcendent icon. This code-switching capability models what novelist Zadie Smith has called "the many-colored voice, the multiple sensibility" of the postmodern racial subject.[44]

Winfrey's performance of black accessibility and universality should seem especially familiar to anyone who knows the history of African American Christianity. The history of black preaching has, to some extent, been the history of the consciousness of this abstraction, of inviting spiritual adulation while also defeating it, mocking it, and making ironical the patronizing gaze of white acclaim. Oprah Winfrey bears the historical legacy, the historical presumptions, of this preacher type. "In first grade six white kids were going to beat me up," she related in one episode. "So I told them about Jesus of Nazareth and what happened to people who tried to stone him. The kids called me the Preacher and left me alone after that."[45] Through biographic recollections and spiritual leadership, Winfrey conjures images of the Black Church. When she attempts to explain the virtues of community, she invokes all-day Sunday services and church "mamas" as ideal leaders. When she wants to comfort a despondent guest, she will quote phrases from gospel songs that "her grandmamma used to sing." "I don't know if anybody really skyrockets to success," she ventured during another episode. "I think that success is a process. And I believe that my first Easter speech, at Kosciusko Baptist Church, at the age of three and a half, was the beginning."[46] Winfrey's childhood Sundays were spent shuttling between Sunday school, the Baptist Training Union (BTU), and two church services, a weekly tour recollected with pleasure by the nostalgic Winfrey.[47] Jesus too makes frequent "appearances" on the show, such as when Oprah remarks to a woman ecstatic about receiving a new minivan, "I think she's got Jesus now," or when touched by generous foster parents, she exclaims, "Jesus lives! Jesus lives! Oh God!"[48]

When she says, "Jesus lives!" Winfrey doesn't sound like a soul-salving televangelist. Rather, she deploys "Jesus" as a noun of ecumenical utility; repeating his name confirms her spiritual authenticity while reminding us of her accessibility. Elliot Miller, author of *A Crash Course on the New Age Movement* (1989), claims that her understanding of Jesus mirrors that of her guests: "Jesus is like an ascended master, a God-realized teacher, someone who completely expressed God in their life."[49] This performance of an ecumenical black spirituality and, more specifically, black Christianity is a practice of inclusive exclusion. When Winfrey wields her identity as "black" in front a majority-white audience, she references histories of suffering, endurance, and sagacity that this audience can access no matter their racial positioning. Who among them has not suffered? Who has not endured? But it matters, too, that the audience cannot possess these histories without her channeling of them. She names a blackness that is experientially universal and biographically contingent. "The African American legacy that Oprah Winfrey declares she pursues . . . calls for a 'spiritualized' politics that views individuals' spirituality and morality as a solution to the social or personal problems in which they are trapped," Eva Illouz writes. "Oprah Winfrey's cultural formula offers a model . . . for coping with crisis and psychic pain, and contains the same mix of politics and religiosity that has been the distinctive mark of black social activism."[50] In this description, Illouz follows Winfrey's lead, suggesting that there is an axiomatic relationship between black religion and political action.

This is a familiar caricature, since narratives of the so-called Black Church and its politics, ecstatic preachers, and wise women abound in American culture. This iconography lurks around any account of black religiosity in the United States. Indeed, "the Black Church" is that rare phrase that has been fed into the common lexicon from sites sectarian and scholastic, a cultural referent whose assumed contours are familiar. The Black Church functioned in the narratives of many twentieth-century historians as *the* black institution. Liberationist black scholarship reinforced this cultural importance of the Black Church, casting it as the organizational and inspirational bridge away from slavery, away from economic deprivation, and away from a state of victimization. The Black Church was invoked in part to resist the primitivist consignments of white culture, offering a politically savvy, institutionalized alternative to images of black religion as merely song and dance, just folk wisdom and primitive performances. It was an external structure for a people denied the ability to mold external freedom.

Two problematic ideas persisted within these heroic renditions of the Black Church. First, talk of the Black Church reduced the wide variety of black religious expression to a single assimilated, Christian, institutional body. Just like Oprah, the Black Church becomes then a space into which everyone may funnel his or her specifics, because the Black Church itself is too generic to describe any religious variety. Second, descriptions of the Black Church contributed to tales told by nineteenth-century romantic racialists who attributed to African

Americans an innate religiosity.[51] The Black Church was an institution, but its caricatures abounded with ritual and not ecclesiology. Any reading of Oprah Winfrey as a spiritual leader must include consciousness of this caricature she evokes and invokes. As she notes, "the Church" was a lived religion of her childhood. But any specificity from those denominational or institutional stories is left to the past, and they are carried forward only in images to which her audience can relate: images of her preaching capabilities, hymns sung during difficult times, sagacious women surviving the traumas of imperious men. Instead of political organizing, economic uplift, or educational opportunity, the Church seems to foster as many gender stereotypes as it does disavow primitivist ones. The Church is a repository of survival; it was not an agent of change.

The mammy caricature coordinated with this Black Church historiography, as the romantic racialism of the Black Church purportedly contained generous, smiling church mothers who could comfort anyone through hard times.[52] As late as 1924, a retrospective study of southern plantation life insisted, "There can be no doubt that with the *peculiar African capacity for devotion,* the old mammy dearly loved her charges."[53] Her stereotypical attributes included "her deeply sonorous and effortlessly soothing voice, her infinite patience, her raucous laugh, her self-deprecating wit, her implicit understanding and acceptance of her inferiority and her devotion to whites."[54] Observers regress into descriptions of Oprah as Mammy. "Those who see Winfrey as facilitating such white liberal humanism have charged her with enacting the racially loaded persona of the 'mammy' for white consumption," write Jennifer Harris and Elwood Watson. "As evidence, they point to her on-air behavior: crying with her audience, indoctrinating them into the black vernacular, sharing African American communal knowledge, and . . . ministering to them."[55] This is too easy a facile reduction, since Winfrey's emotional manipulations are those of the manager, producer, and overseer, and not the slave.

The black woman has become a symbol of a double-sided suffering, of suffering experienced and suffering witnessed, with the black woman absorbing into her prodigious bosom the tears of needful whites. The black woman preacher is, in such a context of stereotype, the triumphant sufferer, the woman who has flipped her oppression into professional power. This is no minor revolution, since preaching in African American religion remains overwhelmingly a form of male discourse.[56] This is especially true in the Baptist tradition that nurtured Winfrey. The way the black women entered the ministerial fold was through a turn against an abstract metaphor and toward "a rhetorical emphasis on vivid narratives that reframed core beliefs about the self and the Other around the experience of black women."[57] Free blacks in the North began founding their own churches during the antebellum era, and preaching in the segregated churches was usually reserved for men. In the subsequent stories of African American religion, this male preacher was famously either a builder of institutions (like the nineteenth-century African Methodist Episcopal bishopric) or a marcher for justice (like twentieth-century demonstrators for the Southern Christian Leadership Conference). Placing Winfrey in that story requires rethinking those genealogies, to imagine what other preacher preambles would adduce to her noteworthy ascendance to America's pulpit.

Not all American preachers have been Protestant, but Protestantism inscribed preaching possibility in a way that encouraged its professional expansion in the United States. Stressing that all adherents had direct access to God, Protestants did not require a formally educated and ritually appointed priest as intermediary. This "priesthood of all believers" would contribute mightily to the schismatic compulsion in Protestant history, as every lay believer might, under the right circumstances of personal charisma, theological context, and communal unrest, cajole a new movement or denomination through sermons advocating a new scriptural reading. In African America, these Protestant preachers were by and large men modeling civilized authority to a perceived white gaze. Winfrey would, over the years, invite some occupants of this African American tradition, such as the Reverends Calvin Butts, Jesse Jackson, and Otis Moss Jr., onto her show to speak about issues and concerns in urban America. Studying these Baptist men will reveal little about Winfrey's own preacher preamble in the United States, however. Winfrey devotes her show to her viewing audience. It is through her asides and commentary that her ministry is manifest, not through daily sermons. Hence, calling Winfrey a "preacher" encourages a perusal of like female leaders in a national context in which women seized upon sectarian patterns to construct their own place in a professional role (preacher) and religious movement (Protestantism) that had been the purview of men.

Certain strands of ecclesiastical organization and theological innovation generated more independent religious women than others. Methodist churches in particular allowed a wider swath of lay participation at the pulpit. And it would be this capaciousness of Methodist organization, combined with John Wesley's pursuit of this-worldly perfection

("Be perfect, as your heavenly Father is perfect," Matthew 5:48), that inspired so much schismatic creativity in the nineteenth and early twentieth century. The Holiness crusade, for instance, enjoyed success in any churches—Baptist and Methodist—that held to the Wesleyan teaching on the second blessing of sanctification. If conversion is the first step in a Christian life, then sanctification describes the religious experience that follows. Sanctification is the pursuit of perfection, or the freedom from sin in the present life. Assurance of sanctification may not come immediately. Indeed, it is a divine gift that may require time and experience to recognize. This is a struggling process of renouncing the world in order to root out sin. Sanctification by the Holy Spirit was considered a more important qualification for religious leadership than seminary education was, and many among the ranks of Holiness originators believed that since women helped create the sin that was in the world, they should help to join in the labor to remove it. Precisely because of this theological emphasis on sanctification, the Holiness movement was open to women preachers.[58]

The subsequent Holiness-Pentecostal movement emphasized that sanctification is demonstrated through the gifts of the Holy Spirit, including divine healing and ecstatic forms of communal worship. Pentecostalism might be seen as a description of one subgenre of Holiness, one that is centered on a particular sign of sanctification. Pentecostalism sprang not only from tensions between the established Methodist leaders of the National Holiness Association and their radical, independent Holiness brethren but also from the commitment to Wesleyan perfectionism. This polyglot assemblage resulted in unpredictable changes, as many of the non-Wesleyan participants rallied around the Keswick Convention for the Promotion of Practical Holiness, which argued that power for Christian service was the principal fruit of sanctification and that suppression of sinful desire, not eradication of it, was the best that higher Christian life had to offer. While many Pentecostal interpretations of these gifts existed, one of the most enduring is the Oneness tradition, known widely as the United Pentecostal Church. For these "Jesus only" Pentecostals, the members of the Trinity are only different names for the one true God, who was wholly incarnated in Jesus Christ.[59] Oneness Pentecostals argue that they have cleansed the faith further, ridding Christianity of its vaguely polytheistic references to a Trinity, and placed their faith in a singular expression of deity.

Privileging the necessity of the Spirit, Winfrey's parallel message promotes the unification of self with a clarified comprehension of the divine. For her, *oneness* not only means a focused godhead but also implies a unification of spirit with the world—a palpable lesson in Pentecostal theology. Cleansing the Spirit, sanctifying your individuality, and solidifying your relationship with the Creator describe both the Oprah Winfrey message and the historical message of American Pentecostals. There are differences, too, between this denominational vantage and Winfrey's religious offerings. First, most Pentecostals would be decidedly uncomfortable with Winfrey's Jesus as teacher rather than the singular savior. Second, while Pentecostals promote the primacy of the individual and his or her sanctification, the church remains a denoted community of like-minded believers. Winfrey is not Pentecostal. But this short tour of Holiness-Pentecostal emphasizes the ways she mediates a history of American religion that includes prosperity gospels, fulfilling Spirit, and dreams of perfection. Histories of American Buddhism and American Unitarianism might too produce strong precursors to Winfrey. The point here is to emphasize those traditions—Baptist and Methodist—that encouraged African American women to participate in the U.S. religious public.

Winfrey is, then, a summary everywoman in a context of sectarian difference, someone through whom any number of denominations may be distilled. Remarking upon the relationship between Winfrey and the Holiness-Pentecostal tradition establishes too a way to map Winfrey into a genealogy of preachers. The Holiness-Pentecostal movement and its offshoots (including the Church of the Nazarene and the Salvation Army) have inspired many figures that resonate with Winfrey. Naming these analogies shows three aspects of correlation: first, the success of certain forms of black female preaching among white audiences less disposed to black male preachers; second, the importance of institutional innovation by female preachers seeking independence; and third, the emphasis of mission work by female preachers on reform related to children. Two examples immediately draw attention to these themes.[60] The first, Amanda Berry Smith (1837–1915), was an African American Holiness preacher who enjoyed extensive popularity among white New Yorkers before leaving to work with Methodist missionaries in Liberia. Upon her eventual return to the United States, she founded an orphanage for African American children, the Amanda Smith Industrial School for Girls. The second, Mary Magdalena Lewis Tate (1871–1930), founded the first predominantly black Pentecostal splinter church, the Church of the Living God. Her purported pureness of character brought her the title "Miss Do Right," which led to her followers becoming known as the Do Righters. She became the chief apostle, elder, president, and first chief officer of the Church of the Living God. Tate was southern, whereas Smith worked in the North; Tate dominated her own denomination, whereas Smith always functioned within existent sectarian structures. In their sermons and autobiographies, these women revealed struggles to represent the race and flourish in a hostile Reconstruction America. "It is constructive, then, for us to view the lives of women preachers as alternative living strategies, and the reconstructions of those lives—in the form of life stories—as narrative strategies that reinforce and validate the identity sought in the living script," Elaine J. Lawless has written.[61] As African American women preachers in a postemancipation context, they were especially conscious of their own representative moral purity and fought to protect their reputed private piety from public consumption.

Preserving the public's image of their private character was a primary concern for black female preachers. Contemporaneous white preaching women toyed more with their personal profile, thrilling their public with personal drama as they ascended through propositions of civil piety. Two white peers of Tate and Smith, Evangeline Booth (1865–1950) and Aimee Semple McPherson (1890–1944), possessed more sensational public personae, based less on laborious mission work or the modeling of ideal piety than on stage stunts and revivals that emphasized their ministerial celebrity. The first woman to command the Salvation Army in the United States, Evangeline Booth collected tales of London slums that she deployed as fundraising anecdotes. Her gift for stagecraft and manipulation of human suffering as a sermonic invocation remind us of Winfrey's later use of the afternoon network talk show for melodramatic conversion purposes. As Diane Winston has explained, one of Booth's most significant innovations was to "sanctify commonplaces," from large-scale demonstrations on urban streets to fundraising efforts outside mercantile centers. This self-described campaign to translate sanctification beyond the individual soul and onto the public square was described in the Salvation Army's weekly newspaper in this way:

> The genius of the Army has been from the first that it has secularized religion, or rather that it has religionized secular things. . . . On the one hand it has brought religion out of the clouds into everyday life, and has taught the world that we may and ought to be as religious about our eatings and drinkings and dressing as we are about our prayings. On the other hand it has taught that there is no religion in a place or in an attitude. A house or a store or factory can be just as holy a place as a church; hence we have commonly

preferred to engage a secular place for our meetings . . . our greatest triumphs have been witnessed in the theatres, music halls, rinks, breweries, saloons, stores, and similar places.[62]

It is tempting to suggest that the presence of such powerful women as Evangeline Booth in the Salvation Army necessitated rethinking the normal church sanctuary. To be sure, from the outset the Salvation Army understood itself to be on a mission *to* the needy rather than on a mission to draw the needy to sectarian houses of worship. But with women's slow extraction of themselves from the private sphere of Victorian domestic spaces, it seems reasonable to interpret the gender formation of army leadership as consequential to the reimagining of church as more than a privileged pulpit but also anywhere the minor tasks of life ("eatings and drinkings and dressing") transpired. Women may not yet have been equal before ecclesiastical authorities in most denominations, but they had gained ground in the commercial revolution—their shopping, home decorating, and child rearing here gained messianic urgency as participatory in the formation of holy sites.[63]

As a child, Aimee Semple McPherson attended Methodist church services as well as Salvation Army Sunday school meetings. This Wesleyan, revival backdrop suffused her founding of the International Church of the Foursquare Gospel. McPherson mastered church as spectacle, incorporating into her services dramatic healings, motorcycle riders, and charismatic sermons that invited an audience seeking celebrity encounters as much as faithful conversions. Simmering at the edges of her success were rumors of her own biographical subplots, which suggested that beyond her markedly prim preacher's wardrobe there was a more salacious "Sister Aimee."[64] Visitors claimed her voice was mesmerizing, bringing them into a trance just by listening to it. This voice and her sermonic ability propagated a multimedia empire, including a newspaper *(The Bridal Call)*, a radio station (KFSG), and her own school (LIFE Bible College). McPherson advocated on behalf of women in the ministry, arguing that anyone with a calling should join the effort to cajole souls for Christ. With her savvy media creativity, her mysteriously complicated private life, and fame beyond the average denominational leader, McPherson mapped territory Winfrey would later resettle, consorting as she did with celebrities and cultivating her headquarters, Angelus Temple, near Echo Park in Los Angeles, as a tourist attraction.

With Booth and McPherson, the practice of preaching expanded beyond the church-based podium and into new structures and contexts, blending lines between religion and popular culture, believers and consumers. Not coincidentally, then, they cultivated missions and creeds that might supersede sect and nab a broader contingency of Christian America. The commercialization of Booth's and McPherson's religious personalities correlated to creedal malleability. These were fiercely Christian women, yet this Christianity was not as much a series of codes as it was a differentiating disposition toward the world. New media developments allowed their message to be propagated to far vaster audiences than nineteenth-century denominations had ever imagined, and, in that expanse of potential converts, nouns became more generic and theology became more inclusive. Other white female preachers of the late-nineteenth and twentieth centuries, such as Mary Baker Eddy (1821–1910), founder of the Christian Science movement, and Kathryn Kuhlman (1907–76), Pentecostal faith healer, likewise balanced a distinguishing emphasis (such as an unusual stance toward sickness or a Protestant preaching on miracles) with points of universal access to their message (in Christian Science reading rooms on major urban thoroughfares, revivals held in nondenominational contexts).

To suggest that a balance was created does not mean it was done consciously by the leader in the manner of a business plan, that there is some grand calculus at work by which religious leaders determine how distinctive they can be before they lose an audience share. Such arithmetic may happen, but these actualities are less interesting than the pursuit of equilibrium. Whatever backroom plots transpired at Angelus Temple, Sister Aimee conceived of a middle that compelled the mass. Likewise, I am not compelled to relate a market report on Oprah in which her triumph is framed as the composite result of ruthlessly specific cultural localities. Mention of these comparative preacher women points to patterns of religious productivity, by the intriguing balance established among the religious profiles of charismatic authorities, the ritual processes proposed and staged by those authorities, and their modes of media propagation. If religious figures in modern America seek perpetuation, their expansion must unfold in some combination of entertainment, religious invocation, and multimedia pervasion.

The necessary emphasis for any modern preacher is some naming of the "everyday life" and counsel on its survival. From Amanda Berry Smith's 1893 autobiography to Aimee Semple McPherson's *The Silver Net: Practical Helps to Soul-Winners,* and from *Mother Angelica's Little Book of Life Lessons and Everyday Spirituality* to evangelist Joyce Meyer's *Be Your Best,* the perpetuation of any preacher is practicality, is making otherworldly claims this-worldly for everyone. Joyce Meyer Ministries explicitly offers online "Everyday Answers," which "provides wisdom from God's Word to help deal with life's difficult issues."[65] Joyce Meyer's *Be Your Best* (2008) imitates the style of a magazine ("12 Keys to Looking and Feeling Great!" and "Are You a PEOPLE PLEASER?") and combines Oprah's sort of invocations ("You Can Change Your World!") with Christian insistence. "More than two thousand years ago, Jesus Christ came to earth and started the greatest revolution this world has ever known," she declares. "It's a revolution that takes us outside the four walls of the church and brings us face-to-face with a world that's looking for answers." Joyce dares you to "dream big" and, like Winfrey, combines the pragmatic ("make a list of your dreams and don't limit yourself to a certain number") and the divine imperative ("realize that each effort you make is one step closer to the discipline and dedication required in order to focus your passion for what God's calling you to do").[66] The religious and the commercial intermingle as the product glazes itself with pastel fonts and diverse girl models exhibiting the advocacies.

Each of these nominated comparisons to Winfrey shares some of her institutional ability, her staged therapies, her affection for children and the poor, and her multimedia mastery. Most important, each shares her ongoing battle to represent female piety while, through her very ascent, modeling the difficulty of sustaining those forms. "Women love Oprah because she provides the outlet," explains one reporter, because she "validates ordinary women who are quietly angry and unhappy."[67] By selecting heroines whose professional occupation was primarily preacher, we denote from the selection the difference: Winfrey surpasses any sectarian moniker to serve as a symbol of national normativity. Winfrey's commodification of her preacher queen is the transaction of her ritual communications and the key testimony in her ongoing self-verification as a spiritual salve to American women. For her audience, she not only evokes the Black Church. She is the Black Church.

"I've been black, I've been female all my life," Winfrey remarked. "That's the only thing I know. So I know that experience. I love being a woman, and I love being a black woman."[68] Describing Winfrey as a preacher in a tradition of black women preachers and white women evangelists provokes consideration of not only her race but also her gender affinity, an affinity that creates her audience and her mission. In the world of Harpo, Oprah is noticeably childless. In this, perhaps she also mirrors her preacher predecessors, going without literal childbearing so that she may nurse other mothers and tend their orphans.[69] In

O magazine, the articles posit a female reader, and articles on female anxieties far outweigh those addressing any other topic, including race. "This is a magazine that focuses specifically on the woman," says one *O* magazine editor. "It's about helping her live her best life. It's about giving her the ideas, the inspiration to focus on her life, what's good about it, how to make it even better, how to celebrate her life."[70] The image of the overworked woman permeates its pages: "Many women are doing it all today: earning a paycheck, raising kids, putting food on the table, maintaining a home. And they're just plain exhausted—physically, mentally and emotionally."[71] At the *Oprah* show, women outnumber men in the audience by a ratio of nineteen to one.[72] "Every week," Winfrey describes, "I find my television studio filled with women who tell me they're so concerned with what others think that they've compromised their dreams and completely lost themselves."[73] To this passel of compromised, exhausted women, Winfrey supplies herself as servant. "Women can count on Oprah's show to take seriously issues that affect their daily lives," recounted one reporter. "Not Bosnia, but butter versus margarine in the fitness battle; not long-term environmental crises, but why some women hide their best linen when certain relatives visit."[74] To mention Oprah outside the context of the show and its related productions is often to invoke the domestic, the female, and the emotional. To some extent, Oprah's viewers would not resist this caricature, since the thing about Oprah is that she doesn't make women feel badly about those needs, for flinging their hands in the air over all the undone work. Oprah is a harbor for women tired of performing, ready to be real, or rather ready for her to be real representatively on their behalf.

The magazine is a paean to the marvels and miseries of women. From advertising books about "power babes" and "girl power" to promoting leadership training programs dedicated to getting women into positions of power, the magazine advocates ferocity before the presumptions of women's weakness.[75] "Women aren't supposed to play jazz," intones one article from *O* magazine profiling African American violinist Regina Carter. "Women aren't supposed to play jazz on violins. But one woman has been shattering musical categories since she was a child."[76] The magazine's profiles and interviews seek to motivate your best life, no matter the limits placed by others. "You are built not to shrink down to less but to blossom into more," Winfrey declares. "To be more splendid. To be more extraordinary. To use every moment to fill yourself up."[77] For every inspirational profile of a heroic woman, however, the editorial staff includes a report on women's inability "to be more extraordinary." These articles relate the tensions between female perfection and the pragmatic challenges of time management and competition. Men are of little use to assist with all this anxiety, both because of the ascribed emotional limits of their gender and because Oprah wishes you wouldn't put so much stock in them, anyway. Winfrey advises, "For every one of those moments when you find yourself desperate to join up with someone who doesn't respect or value who you are, remind yourself that man's rejection is often God's protection."[78] The postulated man is needed (indicated by the very first *Oprah* show topic, "How to Marry the Man or Woman of Your Choice") but frustrating, desired but decried. The Oprah woman wishes a lot of the time that she didn't have a man. But the imagined viewer does have one—or at least wants to have one. She needs him, but she doesn't want to need him.

If one thing unites the womanly ministries of Oprah, it is her call to gather mothers into their best spiritual performance. "I always say moms have the toughest job in the world if you're doing it right," Winfrey opines. Even the problems men pose to women can be traced to women in their capacity as mothers. "It is on a mother's back that great nations are built," Winfrey remarks. Men are a "challenge for mothers"; they are "hungering to be heard" by mothers who teach them to talk and teach them to listen. Women hold the destiny of that manhood, of their nation, in their nurturing care. They unite the world through their common mother love. "Mothering" is, according to Winfrey, "the most important spiritual work on earth."[79]

Oprah's Web site connects "O Moms" with one another through message boards from which they can "get parenting solutions, meal ideas and disciplining tips!" The standard Oprah array is thematically oriented toward maternal challenges, including recommended books (*I Was a Really Good Mom before I Had Kids* and *I'd Trade My Husband for a Housekeeper*), confessional opportunity ("Confess Your Mom Moments: Upload Your Confession Video Today!"), endorsed programs ("*In the Motherhood* airs Thursday nights at 8 [7 Central] on ABC"), and role-oriented products ("Mom videos were recorded with Flip Mino HD camcorders").[80] The "mom" is a manic multiplicity in search of resolution. "Let's be honest—you're not just a mother," the Web site describes. "You're also a partner, sister, daughter, entertainer, chef and creative being! And like moms everywhere, you're doing your best to juggle it all. Find out what it really means to be a supermom, and check out our simple stress-relieving exercises to help you live your best life!" The Web site is communal reprieve and one-on-one counselor. You may feel alone, you may feel overwhelmed, and you may feel sometimes inadequate. Oprah's task is to extract from you, to get you to admit the truth that you're fearful of being judged. Oprah conjures a "a judgment-free zone, a sisterhood of motherhood where anything goes."[81]

The products of Oprah frequently cast stay-at-home mothers in a "battle" with working mothers, yet the battle on-air is won: staying at home is favored, if conceded to be most often economically impossible. Oprah frequently seems to suggest she sides with those who stay at home, remarking often that those who are watching are waiting for children to wake from naps, preparing casseroles, and trying to make it to a soccer match. Such comments suggest an audience that regrets not staying at home if they don't and is anxious if they do. No matter which the mother is (working or not), the paradigm of staying home, of being fully present to the craft of child rearing, is excessively praised by Winfrey. "I'm in awe of good mothers," Winfrey marvels, "those heroines all around me who sacrifice daily out of love for their children. . . . I believe the choice to become a mother is the choice to become one of the greatest spiritual teachers there is. . . . I know for sure that few callings are more honorable. To play down mothering as small is to crack the very foundation on which greatness stands. . . . I honor and thank every great spiritual teacher who goes by the name of Mother."[82] Echoing a long history of women religious and religious women, Oprah names the mother as the pivotal sanctuary of the world.

Oprah's care and maternal emphasis reflect the twists of modern feminism, which has become largely identified as a series of personal choices rather than a series of structural concerns. Thus, the epoch of the Equal Rights Amendment was superseded by an epoch of *Sex and the City* feminists, who, to paraphrase a central character, choose their choices: choices in men, reproduction, sex, career, and shoes.[83] Oprah's productions focus on the habits of individual women and the details of their domesticity rather than on the frames of their homes, professional options, and welfare provisions. And so, worries about economic crises become about your household's checkbook and your personal shopping list. Worries about workplace difficulties become discussions of e-mail etiquette and party planning. The lived religion of Oprah focuses on the practices of a humming house, ringed by an excessively laboring woman. This is no easy job. You should mother but not overmother.[84] You should mold but not micromanage. The show constructs replies to the anxieties it fosters. "Mothers need to know that if they can't do it all—or if they don't want to—that doesn't make them failures," one *Oprah* show advises.[85] Consuming Oprah's narratives of mother-hood and domesticity leaves one with the sense that nobody does it well, even as everyone torments herself by imagining that someone else, somewhere, does.

Finding female icons amid this laboring morass is hard but not impossible. While Winfrey regularly celebrates sacrificial moms, she also seeks women of stature to remind those moms what other choices might look like. In 2002, Oprah admiringly interviewed the secretary of state at the time, Condoleezza Rice. "Rice exudes an assuredness underscored by a quiet courage that I know are extensions of two important gifts her parents gave her—a trust in herself and a trust in God," Winfrey summarized in the introduction to their discussion. "In all my years of interviewing, I have never been prouder to spell my name *w-o-m-a-n* than after spending time with Condoleezza Rice." Winfrey admires Rice, who is unmarried, childless, a granddaughter of a sharecropper, a "black woman from segregated Birmingham," for pursuing the "freedom of this country" to excel intellectually and professionally in a field lacking many women, all while maintaining her love of shopping.

Winfrey: What do you like shopping for?

Rice: Clothes—and shoes. Love the shoes![86]

Seven years later, shoes would figure into another *O* interview, with another African American achiever who had eased into the White House:

Winfrey: One of my favorite, favorite moments was during the parade—the two of you getting out of the car and walking, and your arms are linked and your head is sort of on his shoulder. I loved that. But I wondered about the conversation before you got out. Did you just suddenly say, "Look, we're going to walk for a while now"?

Mrs. Obama: We were trying to see if the girls wanted to get out. They were like, "No"—they wanted to stay in the car. . . . But Barack and I felt that walking outside was a natural extension of the campaign: "Okay, we can't come over to you, we can't hug you—can't do that—but we can be out here waving." Of course, then there was a point where we felt like, "Whoa, three blocks is long." My feet started hurting.

Winfrey: How did your feet feel at the seventh ball that night?

Obama: What a good workout, right? I just remembered that even though it was the seventh ball for me, it was the first ball for everyone there. I thought about that during the parade, too. I thought, "I'm going to stand here and cheer for every last person, because this is why they came—to walk in front of the president of the United States."

Winfrey: Weren't you freezing?

Obama: I was a little cube of ice. My coat had layers, but from the legs down, I was cold. I would have loved to be wearing a pair of warm, toasty boots.

Winfrey: But your shoes looked good![87]

Dressed in Easter hues of orange, yellow, and lilac, Michelle Obama and Oprah Winfrey fronted the April 2009 issue of *O, The Oprah Magazine*, together, in Winfrey's first shared cover image. From her very first appearance on the national stage as the feisty candidate's wife, Michelle Obama reflected an Oprah ideal. First, there was her multiplicity: wife, mother, daughter, friend, and lawyer. Second, there was her iconicity: fashion icon, black icon, working mother icon, girl power icon. Third, she shopped and gossiped and joked. She was, in other words, atop everything else, a girlfriend. "She is comfortable in her own skin," an *O* magazine profile hums, "if not always in her shoes, which she feels no compunction about slipping off when the mood strikes. She keeps up with celebrity gossip (Tom and Katie, Brad and Angelina) and enjoys a good margarita (straight up, with salt). Though she moves with the confidence of an athlete, her friend . . . calls her a girl's girl. She has a weakness for handbags and manicures. She's the rare woman in American politics who likes to wear a dress."[88] Just like you, Michelle likes to talk tabloids, she likes to talk to her girls, and she has "weaknesses" for handbags, manicures, and shoes that hurt. Be not afraid, America: despite her disciplined education, her professional achievements, her easy beauty, her athlete's confidence, her "best friend" husband, and her bodacious biceps, she is one of us.[89]

She is, almost, except she is successful. Oprah consistently names Michelle Obama as like us but different, different because she doesn't need Oprah. "She is not likened to anybody," Winfrey will remark on one episode of the *Oprah* show, dismissing comparisons to Eleanor Roosevelt with a harrumph. "If I had a list of all the women I've ever known, or sort of known, or heard about, I could not come up with a single one more perfect to fill the role of First Lady than Michelle Obama," writes Winfrey.[90] Unlike so many mothers, Michelle knows to take care of herself through fitness, friends, and laughter.[91] "I marveled at how she managed her home, her family, her career, and still found time for herself," wrote Winfrey. "She was waking up at 4:30 A.M. to make sure she had time to work out. She realized even then that if she didn't take care of herself, she'd run out of juice to take care of everything else." As if describing a divine among us, Winfrey notes Obama's gait, her conversational style, her smile, her hand gestures, her mother's touch, her Target shopping strategy, and her taste in belts. Everything in Michelle, of Michelle, and accessorizing Michelle matters because Michelle has made it work. She matches. "*She's* her best self—regardless of what she's wearing or doing," Winfrey explained. "And watching her be her best makes us want to be better. . . . Authentic power. It happens when purpose aligns with personality to serve the greater good."[92]

Oprah isn't alone in what some termed the "O-phoria" surrounding President Obama and "the world's most visible African-American woman."[93] Indeed, exhilaration surrounding the First Couple mirrored aspects of Winfrey's success, including consumer influence and iconic acclaim. Like Oprah, Michelle Obama had an "effect" named after her, the "Michelle Effect," which referred to her influence on the fashion runways and, in particular, her preferred "one-zip" dress.[94] "What can the First Lady accomplish when she accompanies her husband on his first trip to Europe? She can play a role in the re-branding of America," anticipated one reporter prior to their first state tour of Europe. "Michelle Obama embodies a new American brand—diversity and accomplishment."[95] Newspaper accounts suggested that the Obamas would usher in a new Camelot. "The Obamas are launching an early '60s sitcom before our eyes," one observer described. "The First Family . . . may represent a big social shift, but their retro, TV Land ordinariness helped get American comfortable with Dad."[96]

The retro may be seen beyond Michelle's initial hair flip or Barack's old school cool. The structures of Michelle's transformation over the course of the campaign—called by some her "momification"—suggested a makeover, albeit of a back-to-the-future sort. Michelle Obama, Chicago working mother and senator's spouse, became, by the time of the inauguration, solely the "Mom-in-Chief," with plans for a kitchen garden, working with military families, and hopes for two well-raised girls. "Only 10 months ago, Mrs. Obama was described as an angry black woman by some conservatives and as a liability to her husband," reported one journalist. "Now, she is widely admired for her warmth, and her vibrant and accessible manner, and her race seems almost an afterthought to many Americans."[97] In this, the momification of Michelle is also her Oprahfication.[98] *Oprahfication* here means more than the confessional skill frequently cited in the term's invocation.[99] It means the makeover that happens when individuals agree to subject their private selves to public display. This is a makeover that includes not only testimonies of self but also the addition of external accessories and demonstrations of internal resolve. Michelle Obama experienced Oprahfication not only in her public display of self-care but also in her related relinquishing of political input.[100] "It's never been her style to weigh in at his policymaking table," a *People* magazine reporter explains. "The last thing he consulted her on? Spring break, she says."[101] Journalists suggested that after some embarrassing moments early in the campaign "her strategists worked in the final months of the campaign to soften her image." Now, she would talk "less about Princeton and Harvard and more about how she tried to keep her daughters grounded amid the ever-more-intense flare."[102]

In the ecstasy of the election, reports sought to find optimistic indications of Michelle's previous insouciant spirit still shining. "I personally hope she will let . . . that true, colorful personality seep through," *Newsweek* commentator Allison Samuels remarked, adding that there were some "good hints she might." What are those hints? "Her daring election-night red-speckled dress, designed by Narciso Rodriguez, was hardly a cautious choice," Samuels swooned. "It wasn't altogether flattering, but it showed that Michelle is searching for her own style."[103] A postinauguration profile in *People* magazine offered a similar invocation of style as stand-in for individual character. "For her first big dinner, the Governors' Ball, she mixed three different china patterns for the dinner service and let slip to reporters that she already plans to design an Obama china for the White House before she leaves." An interview with Ann Stock, social secretary from the Clinton White House, adds this compliment for her dishware aspirations: "What she's doing is very imaginative."[104] The selection of dishware does, indeed, pose a sort of change. Symbolism ought never be undersold as mere accessory, and, as we have seen, the mix-and-match of china patterns may echo the racial pastiche the Obamas brought with them in their persons to the White House. Yet Michelle herself has become, has accepted, her status as accessory to the event—as the brand that comforts us against the political pins and international arrows of Barack's outrageous fortune.

Women and femininity in Oprah's empire are, therefore, served up to be sacrificed. Like the preacher who honors them, they are bound up in costumes and codes that they construct and in traditions—denominational, racial, gendered—built long ago. Liberation from shoe compliments and inspirational axioms seems impossible insofar as they are declared motivational to female excellence. "The sentimental bargain of femininity is, after all, that the emotional service economy serves both intimates and the woman herself, who receives her own value back not only in the labor of recognition she performs but in the sensual spectacle of its impacts," Lauren Berlant has written. "It is the project of femininity—whatever place in the wide variety of kinds of life women take up—to be proximate to this story of emotional centrality." We need our women to be as they are, or the world—the world Oprah describes as in the arms of mothers—will sag. Berlant continues: "The circularity of the feminine project will not escape you, therefore: it is a perfect form, a sphere infused with activities of ongoing circuits of attachment that can at the same time look like and feel like zero."[105]

The products of Oprah add up to the stature of strong numbers, pulling women from feeling like zero to feeling like her, the all-inclusive O. Late in Winfrey's *A&E Biography*, a clip from *The Oprah Winfrey Show* shows an African American woman named Joanie Jacks, sitting in the studio audience, telling a story. The subject was, unsurprisingly, shoes.[106] At a charity auction, Oprah sold her once-worn shoes and clothing:

> *Jacks*: I came to Oprah's charity sale, and I didn't have that much money, because I didn't have a job. And one of the least things—you know, one of the little bitty pieces—was a pair of black shoes. I wear a seven, and she wears another size.
>
> *Winfrey*: Ten. [*Audience laughter.*]
>
> *Jacks*: And so I bought the shoes, and I really loved them. And I kept them in my bedroom, and when I got really, really depressed and I couldn't find anybody to talk to, I took the shoes out and [*stops, overwhelmed*]
> . . .
>
> *Winfrey*: Stood in my shoes. She would stand in my shoes. To make herself feel better, she would stand in my shoes. And now she says she doesn't have to stand in the shoes as much, because she's standing on her own. Isn't that the best story you've ever heard?

To make herself feel better at size 7 she would stand in Winfrey's size-10 shoes. To make herself feel better, she made herself feel like a woman she has seen on television, a wealthy woman with no need for those particular shoes. This is how Joanie Jacks made her life better, through daily doses of reminder, through daily pretenses of walking in Oprah's shoes.

After your momentary glee (the pleasure of the show, that momentary satisfaction over a perfectly produced poignancy), you realize that what she wants you to believe is the same story she tells, always: the dreaming big, in big magic shoes. Emphasizing purchase, practice, and the repeated invocation of Winfrey's presence, the process by which Joanie

Jacks came to "feel better" feels very much like an advertisement. We're happy for the woman and glad for her good tidings, but we are left with the itching uncertainty that we don't feel very good about all this commodity fetishism. Economic ethicist Deirdre McCloskey beckons us to get over it already, since "coming to terms with the moral ambiguities of materialism is the life of *any* bourgeois person."[107] Yet those moral ambiguities seem the most tormenting to the women in Oprah's pews and to their daughters: be perfect but have fun; be yourself but look great while doing so. Or, as one *New York Times* article reported from Newton North High School in Massachusetts, "It's out of style to admit it, but it is more important to be hot than smart." Girls at this high school underline this message, describing how looking "effortlessly hot" has become requisite for being the "amazing girl" everyone wants to be. "If you are free to be everything," the reporter summarizes their postfeminist condition, "you are also expected to be everything."[108] Oprah replies to this expectation with herself, shoehorning her everything into the space between yourself and your freedoms. Just when you thought it was too much to be, too much to expect, too much to imagine, there she is, cajoling you once again from her electronic bully pulpit to overcome and prevail.

CHAPTER 5

Reading Religiously

The Reformations of Oprah's Book Club

The book club was back, and Oprah was happy. She hummed gospel tunes, she distributed carefully packaged print material, and she redressed her audience to clothe them for receipt of this, her old mission made new:

> Winfrey: *[Singing]* "Oh, happy day." Hey, everybody. It's a happy day for me. Because in case you haven't heard, the book club is back, and I am on a mission. My mission is to make this the biggest book club in the world and get people reading again—not just reading, but reading great books.

On June 18, 2003, Oprah Winfrey announced the return of Oprah's Book Club, which had run originally from September 1996 until April 2002. "Oprah did the literary equivalent of inventing penicillin," the vice president of Scribner remarked. "Honestly, how many people would have read so many of these wonderful books without her?"[1] The end of her first club devastated viewers and the American book industry; since its conclusion, several factions of her audience lobbied for its revival, and bookstores claimed a downturn in sales.[2] Such market demand made it perhaps inevitable that the club would rise again. The hotly anticipated episode that resuscitated her reading reign (titled appropriately, "The Return") opened with the familiar ritual cadence of surprise plots, as Oprah "hit the highways of Chicago in search of new book club members" in the "Book Club mobile." She stunned preselected readers with her arrival at their doorsteps and cubicles, appearing without notice to their awe:

Winfrey: Hey, come to the door!

Woman #4: Oh, my God!

Winfrey: Hi, ladybug house.

Woman #4: Oh, my God!

Winfrey: How are you?

Woman #4: Oh, my God!

Winfrey was as excited as her chosen viewers, doling out books wrapped to hide their eventual reveal, returning finally, breathlessly, to her studio for the announcement: "Whoo-hoo! Whoo-hoo! Hello! Hello! Whoo-hoo! Beautiful. Hi. How much fun is that? How much fun is that? Hey! Great! Hey! That's so much fun." The studio was filled with readers from across the country to help unwrap the selection, and Winfrey spotlighted some new book club members to build anticipation for the revival, simultaneously reminding the world of the particular thrall of her Nielsen share. We learn of their diversity ("We've got everybody. We've got the top book lovers in Los Angeles. We've got everybody from a mother of three who could not sleep when the book club closed, to a man—and that's news in itself—a *man* in a book club—to a woman who schleps her books around from country to country"); we learn of their devotion ("I read in the bathroom and steal time whenever I can"); and we learn just how distraught they were when Oprah concluded her first club:

> Well, a part of me did die. I—my whole life revolved around the Oprah Book Club. I would make appointments and revolve my whole life around that particular show. So I—when you sat there and said, "This is the end of the Oprah Book Club as we know it," I just sat there with my mouth gaping open. The color just drained from my face, and immediately after, my phone was ringing. I had friends and relatives calling me, saying, "Are you OK? Are you going to survive?" So I did. And I'm here. And I'm thrilled that it's back.

"The Return" represents the club's one-year absence as a death, an unbearable silence, a something that nothing else could fill. Its return would fill that void. The unwrapping resurrection was nothing less than orgiastic in its count-off climax:

Winfrey: Audience, OK—audience, everybody, New York, LA, Chicago, Roz, everybody, look under your chairs, grab your top-secret wrapped book. Does everybody have their books? Everybody have their books? OK. OK. OK. And now on the count—ready, New York? Ready, Los Angeles? Atlanta? On the count of three. On the count of three. All together now, one, two, three. Open your books! Open your books. The book selection, *East of Eden*. *East of Eden* by John Steinbeck. Yea! *East of Eden* by John Steinbeck. Whoo! John Steinbeck, wherever he is today in the spirit world, is very happy about this. I tell you all.

One, two, three, and here it is, another book, another gift, another promise for a moment of conversation, community, and confession. Wherever he is, Steinbeck's spirit is glad. *East of Eden! East of Eden!* Each of the preceding forty-eight announcements had an equal exclamatory volume to their holler *(Vinegar Hill! Vinegar Hill! Sula! Sula!);* each one was received with the squeals of a Favorite Things seasonal episode or the unveiling of a makeover triumph. After the distribution (wrapping paper drunkenly strewn everywhere, gasping gals clutching Steinbeck to their chests), the summer was set.

Before viewers and readers retreat to read, however, the episode has a few more stops to make. Because no one is fully recast for the reading experience Oprah prescribes: "Audience! Audience! You're all going home with our brand-new book club gear. Models, bring out the goods!" For those audience members timing the show, they know there is still more to be seen, still more to be given. "When we come back, we've scoured the stores for the best summer looks in bathing suits for every body," Winfrey transitions to commercial. "Gotta look cute when you're reading." If you haven't thought before about how you look when you read, Winfrey speaks to this issue after a break:

> *Winfrey*: And now that you have this new summer book to read—it is perfect for summer, I'm telling you; it's perfect—you need some cute things to wear while you're flipping the pages. That is the truth. Because I have figured out this. Like, if you wake up in the morning and you are—just throw on your sweats and you never, like, even put on any makeup, not even a lipstick, or something during the day, you feel like a schlub all day long. And so I have—you know, I'm Oprah Winfrey. I'm Oprah Winfrey. I have to dress every day. And so on the weekends, I've been thinking. "Oh, I don't have to dress"—but just the other day I said, "I am going to put on at least some lipstick."
>
> *Stacy London* (host of *What Not to Wear*): Amen!

Truth and *cute* are strong words for Winfrey, pulled together from spheres (spiritual and sartorial) that are, for her, overlapping categories of appraisal. Just like the honest friend who will tell you if that skirt bunches at your hips, just like the shrewd sister who catches you at your self-deceiving lies, Oprah is here to tell you: you don't want to be a schlub. Winfrey underlines: "We want to make sure that while you sit by the pool reading *East of Eden—East of Eden*—that's our book club selection—that you have the best bathing suit for your body type." These are codependent, interacting aspects of female expression: the lipstick and the schlub, the bathing suit and book, whispering around it all, *"East of Eden—East of Eden."* Not even she, not even Oprah Winfrey ("I'm Oprah Winfrey. I'm Oprah Winfrey"), can withstand a day away from costume without feeling less than herself. Have a little self-loving dignity, and, please, put on makeup, lipstick, something. There has never been a better time. "Amen."

> *London*: Just a few things to start. Oprah, this has never been a better season for being a girl.
> *Winfrey*: Really?
> *London*: A woman. OK.
> *Winfrey*: A woman. OK.

There are so many reasons why this is the best season, not the least of which is *East of Eden (East of Eden!)* and Oprah Winfrey ("I'm Oprah Winfrey"):

> *London*: But this little juicy denim jacket, throw your blue denim away! It is about pink!
> *Winfrey*: Really? It's about pink!
> *London*: It is about pink.
> *Winfrey*: Pink is the new denim!

The goal is to hit the extreme truth of now ("Pink is the new denim!"), to know what is right, what is fashionable, while staying true to the bare-bottom truth of you:

> *Suze Yalof Schwartz* (*Glamour* magazine): We're having—this is great if you have a larger rear, you can cover it up. This one's great by La Blanca, because it's a halter top, so it lifts up your breasts and it makes them a little bit more ample.
> *Winfrey*: It does.

The end of the episode ties the multiple elements of "The Return" into an advertisement for the whole. There are no haunting one-liners from *East of Eden* tempting viewers to text, just a cover pressed into the camera ("one more look at *East of Eden*") and a reminder for purchase, for re-creating every little piece of the one-hour pleasure now concluded:

> *Winfrey*: OK. Our new book—new book club book is *East of Eden,* by John Steinbeck, and I hope you go right out and get yourself a copy. It is a guaranteed great summer read. If you want to officially join our book club, log on to Oprah.com to get all the details. You never know, our Book Club mobile might show up in your town. I have special thanks to DaimlerChrysler for our Book Club mobile and to Acclaim Sign Company in Batavia, Illinois, for customizing our Book Club mobile and making it one of a kind. Happy re— You know, I love that little Chrysler truck. Ever since Celine Dion had her baby in the Chrysler . . . Let me get a Chrysler truck. Thank you so much. Thanks, everybody.

The half-said enjoinder to read ("Happy re—") is interrupted by the remembrance of purchase enjoyment ("I love that little Chrysler truck"). Reading here does and will matter, but it matters in its collaborative role with other things, things that interrupt, always; things with other gerunds, with other practice imperatives.

In the final moments, as the credits roll, the list of practices might be made from the previously heard commandments: Need to buy a book, need to join a club, need to get the details, need to prepare for the mobile's surprise appearance, need to consider daily lipstick ("at least some lipstick"), need a swimsuit to flatter my shape ("There are pear shapes, and there are apple shapes, right?"), need to get a truck, need a little jiggle in my wiggle ("A little jiggle never hurt nobody"), need to need, need to know, need to be, need her, need her, need her. The voice persists as the summary need well beyond the moment of book distribution, of swimsuit makeover, of sated good-bye. The book club is back. Now Oprah's elected words are ours, are mine, again.

Oprah Winfrey's relationship to reading is perhaps her most publicized practice. Books litter her empire as they litter her past; because her past was filled with books, so will her world, now, be made of them. "I've loved—and I mean *loved*—books ever since I can remember," Winfrey explains as often as she can. "I learned to read when I was 3 years old, on my grandmother's farm in Mississippi, and from that point on, I could usually be found curled up in a corner reading happily while other kids played outdoors. Both then and now, my books are my friends."[3] Winfrey's production is her emboss. Her taste, wisdom, advice, biography, and presence are her product. Books and reading in the empire of

Harpo are not made by her but rather are cast by her in practices (how we select, handle, arrange, and display books) and situations (how we experience reading alone, how we share reading together, how we use reading to make our best lives). In the history of Harpo, Inc., the arrival of reading recommendations cajoled multimedia expansion, with text begetting text:

> *Winfrey*: For the first time, you can now go to Oprah.com and officially join our book club. That's what I want you all to do. Go to Oprah.com. It's absolutely free. And when you sign up, here's what you get: a state-of-the-art online study guide to keep you on track with our books; book experts to answer all of your questions. We're going to hook you all up with fellow readers all over the world or even in your own neighborhood, Naperville. And every week—every week I'll be e-mailing you—I will actually be doing it myself. I know how to do that. I'm very techno savvy now. And we'll be reading the book together, 'cause I'm gonna start reading it again tomorrow.[4]

With this announcement, Winfrey institutionalized her literary management of American literacy to capitalize upon multiple media support networks.[5] Through her strategic use of regular e-mails Winfrey literally entered her readers' homes, offering a posture of privacy for lesson plans to guide their individual journey through books she recommended.[6] This is all "absolutely free." As one academic observer of Oprah's Book Club remarked, Winfrey "has no official relationship with the publishers or book distributors, and she makes no money by endorsing the books."[7] To be sure, the first clause of this statement is, apparently, true. Yet the second ("she makes no money by endorsing the books") is a dodgier claim to corroborate. To imagine that recommendations of books are not enterprises steeped in purchase, in self-care that encourages more purchase, and in life revolutions that encourage more consumption of her is to miss the magisterial glory of the package.

Reading, like religion, does not need to lose its preciousness the minute it gains profitability. In Winfrey's world of books and reading, there is no division between the camp of literature, books, and reading and that of sentiment, product, and revelatory believing. They commingle, they dwell, and together, with symphonic interpretive and exhibitionist effect, they sell. Over the course of this chapter, I will traverse several aspects of Oprah's Book Club: her descriptions and deployment of books throughout her empire; the nature and reception of her book club selections; the framing of book club authors; the historical and religious forerunners to her club; and the ritual and relational strategies of the televised club meetings. Throughout this perusal of her club and its tentacular reach, certain themes will reappear. Note, for example, the anxieties expressed by, about, and on behalf of the masses, the middle-brow, and the popular; note the promotion of lay interpretation along-side manifestations of charismatic dogma; note the increasing emphasis on personal experience as an inspiration for belief; finally, note the persistent attempts to substantiate a collective moral culture over and against an encroaching, defamed world. In short, note how the making of Oprah's Book Club shares aspects with the continuing dissemina-tions of the Protestant Reformation.[8]

Like the reformers who preceded her, Oprah is rhetorically adamant about the disintegration of authority and passionate about the possibil-ity of getting her books—her idea of The Book—into the hands of all believers. At the most basic level, her relationship to books and read-ings can be seen in the multiple ways she distributes individual titles. On her show, she recommends books; on her Web site, she cross-lists those recommendations with the episodes in which they are mentioned. Every edition of O, The Oprah Magazine includes the "Reading Room," which selects nonfiction and fiction highlights from publisher's recent releases. A comparison of these two locations (the show and the maga-zine) exhibits two different sorts of recommendation. In July 2002, for example, twenty books were advertised on The Oprah Winfrey Show, either as centerpiece exhibits (the episode "Cooking with Art Smith" showed Oprah and Art Smith preparing recipes from his Back to the Table: The Reunion of Food and Family) or as résumé endorsements (the episode "How's Your Heart?" included advice from Drs. Mehmet Oz and Judith Reichman, whose books Healing from the Heart and Relax, This Won't Hurt: Painless Answers to Women's Most Pressing Health Questions were cited as components of the vitae that brought them to Oprah's couch). The July 2002 issue of O, The Oprah Magazine recommended half as many books but included with each of the recom-mendations longer blurbs of description than were presented with the televised bibliographic citations of Smith, Oz, or Reichman. In addition to five or six longer pieces discussing single works of fiction or nonfic-tion or both, the "Reading Room" includes a monthly sidebar, "BibliO," with three or four shorter profiles in "from our shelf to yours," like this one from that same month:

> Set in Chicago, Lucky in the Corner (Houghton Mifflin), by Carol Anshaw, explores with sharp humor and perception the mixed-up world of 21-year-old

Fern, whose lesbian mother, cross-dressing uncle, and best friend Tracy take turns vexing, consoling, challenging, and confiding in her. Only when Fern loses her lifelong pet, Lucky, does she find balance—Lucky's dying "made Fern see the line between life and death as not all that hard and fast"—and fresh appreciation of these significant, vitally offbeat relationships.[9]

With a plurality of "vitally offbeat" characters providing gerunds of counsel (*vexing, consoling, challenging,* and *confiding*), Fern lives in the city (Chicago) with the pet (dog Lucky). Every invocation references the editorial O (Oprah lives in and loves Chicago; Oprah lives with and loves dogs). The blurb possesses fortune-cookie happiness, reminding the casual reader that even if they don't have time for Anshaw's prose, they have time, always, to remember how the kooky people in their lives sustain their survival.

The magazine details subplots and literary creativity, whereas the show largely endorses celebrity revelation, domestic advice, and nonfiction reportage. So when the magazine recommends memoirs such as the South African novelist J. M. Coetzee's *Youth,* the show recommends actor Michael J. Fox's *Lucky Man;* when the magazine suggests Alice Sebold's fictional study of murder and the afterlife, *The Lovely Bones,* the show suggests Dominick Dunne's true-crime reportage in *A Season in Purgatory;* if the magazine endorses Pulitzer Prize–winning novelist Richard Russo's *The Whore's Child and Other Stories* (including spare, poetic stories of marital woe and erotic fantasy run amuck), the show will commend Hilda Hutcherson's chatty *What Your Mother Never Told You about Sex.* The magazine seeks the tiny graceful detail while the *Oprah* show explodes it into tabloid stereotype. Whether you are watching the show or reading the magazine, the practice imperative *(read!)* remains the same.

There is no solo signature scripture in the empire of O. Rather, the *idea* of a book is scriptural. Nothing stops an Oprah conversation more than the invocation of a book, either in its literary effects or in its material manifestation. The book's the thing. If the topics of texts differ between show and magazine, their management and molding are, by editorial and production staff, largely the same. Typical of Winfrey's usage is the monthly "Reading Room" subsection "Books That Made a Difference," which includes five books selected by a spotlighted author or celebrity. This person opens usually with a personal narrative relating how he or she was "turned on" to reading as a lifelong pleasure by a teacher, relative, friend, or coworker. Everyone is encouraged to foster a personal collection (buy these books, read and reread them, underline and redistribute to friends), in part as an imitation of the famous ("if Natalie Portman likes Amos Oz, maybe I will, too!") and in part as a bibliophilic voyeurism.[10] The magazine transforms books into objects worthy of the smoldering, cinematic frames of celebrity. "You still get a jolt of pleasure when you think about the Jane Austen novel that clued you in on sexual politics, or the story by Gabriel García Márquez that gorgeously blurred the line between reality and illusion," O magazine editors remind readers. "You still leaf through those dog-eared volumes because they speak to the private you, the one who understands that life, in all its rapturous, sorrowful variety, can be contained within a page, a paragraph, a sentence, even a single, perfect word."[11]

Books are decoration. "Both Eve and Ron have beautiful books—hers about fashion, his about art—and Mallery has stacked them on the tables," reports an O decorator.[12] Books are inspiration. "Few pleasures are as enduring as a great book—the kind that transports or transforms us, makes us cry on airplanes, or laugh out loud, even when we're alone."[13] Books decorate and they transform, and so they are, therefore, "enchanted" objects altering minds and spaces.[14] They possess irreducible magic. "I can't throw books out. I can give them away . . . but I can't put them in the trash," Winfrey remarks. "Throwing a book in the trash is like throwing away a person."[15] To give the gift of a book, then, is a supreme sort of gift, the passing of a powerful amulet with unpredictable consequences. And like any gift worth giving (like the gifts, material and maternal, that her viewers give to their children and husbands) these are gifts that take time to winnow, including working through tall piles of possible options by the exhausted Oprah. "I've been all year trying to figure out what is going to be the summer book, reading, reading, reading, till I was exhausted reading," Winfrey related before distributing *The Poisonwood Bible*.[16] The gift of a book is the gift of reverie and magic, a rare pause in the normal proceedings of daily life. Books are worth the work of their acquiring; they are worthy of Winfrey's sacrifices.

Books beget other gifts, adding physical richness and commiserating relationships to our lives.[17] "Reading—not occasionally, not only on vacation but every day—gives me nourishment and enlarges my life in mysterious and essential ways," the novelist Mona Simpson explains.[18] The section "O to go" in each magazine includes tear-out postcards, bookmarks, and table place cards. These magazine takeaways include quotations from Dickens, Woolf, Bachelard, and Descartes, among others, cutting lines from texts like teaser lines in a movie preview or product slogans from ad copy. Table place cards with quotations on epicurean matters "remind you what an amazing party is all about"; book plates mark singular volumes as your possessions; and gift cards are supplied to "tuck . . . inside the sweater you made for your favorite aunt, the baseball tickets you bought for your nephew, the peach pie you baked for the whole family." Lacquered with the O-approved wisdom of authorial voices, these monthly party favors from O magazine mark objects as "literary" and encourage consumption that is literarily marked. Books decorate you, they decorate your home, and the idea of books inspires more books and more decoration:

> *Winfrey*: Now [when] you join the book club on Oprah.com, you'll have exclusive access to our brand-new book club boutique. We've got the cutest stuff there. We've got T-shirts and hats, like Roz was wearing, totes. It's what you wear when you're reading this summer. And the best news is that when you buy the totes or the—the hats or anything on Oprah.com, all of the profits from our boutique go straight to our Angel Network, every single dime, I guarantee it.[19]

Again, the redressing of the audience members is not solely to emboss them with Winfrey's signature O. Rather, it is also to ready them for "reading time," which is, for Oprah, "a ritual." Another columnist appoints reading sacred time. "By the end of my day, I yearn for a different kind of time—reading time," Pamela Erens writes. "I wonder if there isn't something in the nature of reading itself that requires a ritual of withdrawal such as the one I perform each night. Any truly literary work . . . demands surrender."[20]

To create the circumstances of surrender, Winfrey prescribes countless practices.[21] The Winfrey read is a situational read; according to her repeated recommendations, the revolutionary power of reading is maximized if done in the right place, in the right clothes, with the right pillows. "I know all you busy moms especially owe yourself a few afternoons to get lost in a great book," Winfrey proclaims. "Just you, a porch if you have one, a book, maybe an iced tea, a little lemonade on the side."[22] This emphasis on luxurious practice is consistent throughout Oprah's realm, as she frequently offers images of herself in comfortable contexts for her readers to enjoy vicariously and to emulate faithfully. In a column about her faith in miracles she writes that a "miracle" is "having pomegranate, kiwi, and mango on a pretty tray for breakfast." Here, the practice of savored beauty makes a minor moment a miraculous occurrence. For her consumer, then, Oprah encourages daily practices that create comfortable, sometimes decadent, circumstances. Consider the following description from Oprah's monthly "What I Know for Sure" column in O magazine: "In the evenings right before sleep I don't read or watch anything—including late-night news—that would add anxiety. . . . I also keep a gratitude journal and, at the end of a workday, I 'come down' by reading a great novel or just sitting with myself to come back to my center—it's what I call going mindless." Notice that here, books are seen as a relaxant. "Great novels" can make one "mindless" as they take a busy woman back to her "center."

The first book club was taped in locations meant to echo the appointed abundance of these private reading practices. There, preselected women (and some men) gathered with Winfrey and the author in a willfully casual atmosphere, such as a living room filled with pillows and sofas or a dining room table strewn with passable dishes. "Most early Book Clubs included comments about the food, the chef, and the restaurant or other venue where the meeting was held," Cecilia Farr has explained. "*The Deep End of the Ocean* Book Club was held at Oprah's house over wild mushroom ravioli and crème brulée with fresh raspberries and caramel shortbread cookies," whereas "the *Stones from the River* meeting, held in a public library in Riverside, Illinois, featured the seared yellow-tailed tuna."[23] Candles, food, and luxuriant clothing simulated the sense that this was an elect moment, a performance of exclusive colloquialism. Although the meetings frequently took place in one of Winfrey's opulent homes, the setting was established to suggest that this could be any living room or den or dining room.[24] The primary trope was the conversation in the context of refined cutlery, delicious food, comfortable chairs, and guests with makeovers. Both the discourse and the decorations indicated that the participants were in earnest, providing the dramatization of a significant event requisite for ritual action. One could certainly host a book club among austere Shaker furnishings or in an unfinished suburban basement, but the first Winfrey book club modeled a decorous importance.[25] Through the constructed comfort of the conversational situation, Winfrey created a ceremonial space, an arena for earnest discussion and sacred disclosure. The ritual care of the early book club context suggests the prescriptive impulse. Later book club gatherings took place in settings resonant with the selected book. For example, those who discussed *Where the Heart Is* met at a Wal-Mart. Once she found it difficult to name additional contemporary authors to celebrate, Winfrey turned to "classic" authors, finding there forests of options to peruse and repackage. Now, in this incarnation of Oprah's Book Club, the trip might include a visit to the place where the book itself was written to highlight the quotidian contexts that might inspire greatness.

Making a space for ritual reading and restful coming down is essential for the imagined audience of Winfrey's productions. "Wouldn't it be lovely to have a place with no phone, no pressure, no people?" The editors of O reply to their own postulate, "No problem. Simply stake out a corner of your home or garden, and make it a zone of your own."[26] Your life (the copy implies) is chaos, strewn with plastic toys and unopened bills and "to do" lists that may never get done. You need a pause from that tugging and donating, "a break from the frantic, noisy, overpopulated world," a place where you have "permission to write, read, rest, draw, paint, do yoga, listen to music, sit and stare—anything that evokes the deepest, most peaceful part of you." The best part—the "fun" part—of making this sanctuary is "picking the delicious stuff to surround you."[27] Build your retreat through a cordoned space by "feathering a personal nest."[28] Pillows, bath oils, and scented candles establish the perimeter and the saturating sense of difference. This place (bed, table, corner, bunker) is not *theirs;* it is *yours.* And so, this is no time to be cheap: "Spoil yourself with sensuous little things: a perfect celadon bowl, a print you love, an alabaster Buddha . . . a warm throw or an enveloping quilt is a must."[29] Previous chapters described how Oprah's viewership exists perpetually in a state of crisis over what is left undone. Commanded to be perfect, compromised by their every choice, these women deserve something that is under their control, something that heralds their private glory.

As with her every prescription, Winfrey preaches only what she practices. The cover of "The Books Issue" of O at Home advertises a view of OPRAH'S PRIVATE LIBRARY: AN ALL-ACCESS GUIDE TO HER FAVORITE ROOM.[30] Inside the editorial voice does not linger long on the mystical promise of separate space. Rather, it emphasizes the construction of that space, of how viewers may model the invention of a library. For example, readers are offered "an anatomy of Oprah's bookshelves," supplying a map of where Oprah's Book Club selections sit on her cream shelving and where one can find first-edition biographies, Paul Laurence Dunbar's poetry, and Pulitzer Prize winners.[31] In case this "anatomy" is not enough of a how-to manual, the same issue provides, in a separate story, a two-page guide to bookshelf arrangement, revealing the "formula for creating photo shoot-ready shelves." For the article, stylist Heather Chontos supplied tips for turning "an otherwise utilitarian stash into an intriguing display," and library consultant Nick Harvill "weighed in to ensure that pretty didn't totally trump practical." Harvill's advice was matter-of-fact: "A library should reflect your interests. And it should definitely look like it gets used." How to effect this used appearance? The counsel is crystalline: arrange your books by height (an "interspersing horizontal stack breaks up monotonous rows"); incorporate vases and other interesting objects (but "avoid clutter: one item . . . per section prevents a curio-cabinet effect"); display "gorgeous interiors" by propping some books open; create a sequestered spot for paperbacks ("instead of banishing embarrassing reads—those Harlequin romances, perhaps?—hide them behind a framed picture"); and place heavier volumes in the middle bottom of your shelving. Finally, don't limit yourself to books, since other forms of print deserve their due: "*Make magazines part of the collection:* Periodicals most certainly belong in your library. Bind the keepers (covering a year's worth of O *at Home* starts at about $25) for future reference. Stash the current rotation in holders like these Dransfield & Ross driftwood versions ($48 each; at Gracious Home, 800-338-7809)."[32]

Later in the same issue of O *at Home,* regular Winfrey adviser Martha Beck declares, "The cause of almost all decorating paralysis can be summed up in one little word: fear." After the explanatory work of Heather Chontos and Nick Harvill, no reader need fear, again, the galling problem of how to arrange his or her books so they look pretty (but practical), used (but intriguing), and enjoyed (but carefully positioned, arranged, propped, and banished). The advertisement of binding for magazines only underlines what is conveyed by the entire enterprise, namely, that such construction does not come without necessary, product-perpetuating cost. Such book beauty requires many layers of human enterprise: as a reader, as a collector of quirky (but not too curio) objects, as a decorator, and as a buyer of books, of binding, of shelving, of obscuring frames and driftwood holders. Everything can be had for a price. The price of individual books may go to publishers, but the value of a book's place in the home, and in the psyche of the reader, is purveyed by Winfrey. Her gift is not the trip to Barnes and Noble but a lifetime of reminder that you loved yourself well enough to go.

Readers are encouraged in their decorations to cultivate quirky instincts and personal taste; however, the point of origin for this material exposition is not immaterial. Oprah's Book Club has its own visual culture, marking each book, and each author, with insignia, demonstrating the bandying dynamic between product placement and soulful selection, between publishing house and Harpo, Inc. Every volume selected for the club undergoes a new printing, with the same cover as designated by the publisher save for the addition of the usually yellow and orange O crowning the book, along with its author, as a member of Oprah's Book Club.[33] The "Oprah seal" or "O logo" would become a beacon to some and kryptonite to others. "Friends of mine confessed to some hesitation, even squeamishness, about the Oprah's Book Club seal," Margo Jefferson, a compatriot of Winfrey and a book club commentator, "but they have never let it get in the way of giving a book that interested them a chance."[34] When novelist Jonathan Franzen became the only author nominated to Oprah's Book Club to reject the nomination, he cited the O emblem as central to his dismissal of Winfrey's invitation. To a radio interviewer, Franzen said, "I see this as my book, my creation, and I didn't want that logo of corporate ownership on it."[35] In a *New York Times* article addressing Franzen's dismissal of Oprah's emboss, novelist Rick Moody countered that such branding was inescapable:

> Mr. Moody said he would happily appear on her show, if asked. "If you want to sell 700,000 copies," he said, "then you have to play ball with the 700,000-copy vehicles, and then you are in Oprah-land." He said it was hypocritical to object to Ms. Winfrey's logo. "I am published by the AOL Time Warner empire," he said. "If you are being published by one of the big houses, you can't object that you are not commercial in some way: what book doesn't have the publisher's logo on the spine?" Jonathan Galassi, Mr. Franzen's editor at Farrar, Straus & Giroux, concurred. "The logo never bothered me, but it is not my book," he said. "The jacket itself is advertising."[36]

Galassi and Moody infer that Franzen's radical rebuff of Winfrey's embrace lacked coherence, since nobody selling a book can claim to have evaded corporate complicity. Such a defense of the O seal is just another log on the commercial fire. Of course, the Franzen imbroglio wasn't about the sticker as much as it was about the corporate rabbit hole he believed it initiated. To mark a book with the O is to incorporate that book, and that author, into the system of disseminations and products circled by the same O, ringed and wrung by Winfrey for purposes beyond the control of any solo actor.

Oprah is here cast as the middlebrow, and Franzen, postulating himself as "solidly in the high-art literary tradition," was cast as the "highbrow."[37] "To the 'taste' class, the popular Oprah represents the Dark Other against which it defines itself," wrote journalist Charles Freund.[38] Still, though, Winfrey monitors her own taste class, obscuring romance novels and illuminating classic authors. Winfrey's particular bourgeois embarrasses some, even as this bourgeois—this notion of the middle class—supplies the audience for so much fiction. Moreover, it also provides subjects of so many of those same novels (e.g., the Lambert clan from Franzen's *The Corrections*).[39] Obscured by such labeling (middlebrow, highbrow, bourgeois, high-art) is the contested content of the selected novels themselves, the question of their quality and position within the range of available literature published. "Most commentators have confidently placed Oprah's club in the great tradition of middlebrow uplift pioneered by the BOMC and Mid-Century Club, but it actually represents this later stage of bundling readers into pre-existing niche demographics," wrote one journalist. "The Oprah club is now its own recognizable market brand—and its very titles serve as shorthand for commonly recognized genre conventions."[40] This rendering lacks the subtlety of Winfrey's shifty taste. From 1996 to 1999, her book club endorsed works that were, by some measures, more typically "popular" contemporary novels (Jacqueline Mitchard, *The Deep End of the Ocean;* Wally Lamb, *She's Come Undone;* Anna Quindlen, *Black and Blue*) than they were "literary" (Toni Morrison, *Song of Solomon;* Ernest Gaines's *A Lesson before Dying;* Jane Hamilton, *The Book of Ruth*). "In total," writes one observer, "out of thirty selections, approximately six were literary from 1996 to 2000." Beginning in 2000, the balance shifted dramatically toward the so-called literary, adding to the list works by Isabel Allende, Joyce Carol Oates, and Barbara Kingsolver.[41] The climax in this shifting fictional landscape was the Jonathan Franzen debacle. Shortly after Winfrey retracted her offer to host Franzen, she ended her book club in April 2002, amid claims that she had just gotten too tired from all the hunting for the "perfect" book. Ending the book club reminded viewers that this brand was a woman, a woman who claimed she was tired of the shopping. The onset of this exhaustion at the end of an episode in which the book bit back reminded everyone, from authors to publishers, from viewers to producers, that this logo lived.

When Winfrey returned, she briefly rid herself of living authors, delighting instead in the product that couldn't talk. Now, she could make whatever montage she wanted and pick whatever she wanted: nobody could rebut from the grave. Her naming of the "classic" as "hers," her insertion of that text into her corporate product of self, emphasized the emboss of the always-triumphant O. As one observer remarked, the next incarnation of the book club only underlined how well Winfrey "manages literature's subversive potential and instead emphasizes ideas supportive of the American Dream and consumer capitalism."[42] The product plugs multiplied in this new reading ritual, in part to ease readers into difficult books, and in part because Winfrey could, now, give up the ghost. Pleasing the taste classes meant nothing to her anymore. Now, she could call upon women to "look cute while reading," to propagate, simultaneously, her beloved books and her beloved bodily accoutrements. Subtracting the author meant a reification of Her.

Winfrey has said she is drawn to novels that feature "voices of young girls, women in struggle, who ultimately have to triumph."[43] Indeed, the majority of Oprah's Book Club picks share a common narrative trajectory: a woman, usually of eccentric yet compelling character, experiences an enormous trauma (or has a persistent dilemma, such as obesity or a cruel mother). The remainder of the plot follows the character as she manages the psychological, material, or social aftereffects of this trauma. Usually, the stories conclude on a neutral note, with the central character wiser for her experiences, though on the whole not entirely happy with the way her life has evolved. "Oprah's Book Club selections tell a story—her own story—over and over again in different ways with different characters and different situations."[44] This telling, like the confessions of the show itself, conspires to inspire the downtrodden. "Oprah's selections have purveyed much the same message that O herself (in both television and periodical guises) continues to hammer away at," a *Slate* commentator offered. "Bad things happen, women suffer, and one day, further along, once you undertake that perilous journey from bitterness to forgiveness, you will be vouchsafed the reason for your tenure on earth."[45] This is a rebuttal to a long history of beaten women, turning instead to beaten women beating back: "Oprah's book selections radicalize the 'feminine' character of the novel, but with one important twist. The plot of all these stories never revolves around 'finding' love; instead, the woman protagonist almost always already belongs to a dense network of commitments and social relations."[46] Rather than rely on a resuscitating Prince Charming, Oprah's books transform the Harlequin into the heroine, charging the leading character with their own makeover and mission of self-discovery.

Winfrey believes this paradigmatic plotline will not only resonate with her viewers but also express a universal truth revolving back into her more explicitly spiritual work. In any given book club episode, such a restatement of her defining "truth" may be articulated by Winfrey, or it could be summarized by the author (or even a precocious participant). When asked to summarize his six-hundred-page novel, Rohinton Mistry

offered this to O viewers: "*A Fine Balance* is a story about four characters who against tremendous odds, endure life, survive, not only endure
but manage to find happiness in it and come together as a family."[47]
Here, Mistry defines a sprawling, Dickensian rendering of 1970s Bom-
bay as fable of talk show redemption. Suffering and adversity abound,
as they do in real life, and yet are bound up by patience, optimism, and
goodwill. Although his novel possesses labyrinthine complexity, Mistry and the *Oprah* viewing audience emerge from the episode with a
satisfying summary of man's universal plot. Speaking of *We Were the
Mulvaneys*, Winfrey remarked, "It is more than a novel. It is about
life." The life translated on book club episodes is inevitably a careful
redaction of accessibility, a tightened slogan often not entirely representative of contradictions related within the chosen novels. The novel
doesn't exist for its own sake; it exists to connect and redact reader's
experiences with their complexity, their suffering. When she announced
her first book club pick in 1996, Winfrey personalized the inaugural
choice, explaining that she "was so moved" when she read the story,
that it fulfilled her aim to feature books that "people can feel some
sort of emotional attachment to. I always feel right, right will follow."
The *Newsweek* article that reported this statement commercialized this
imperative: "If that doesn't sound especially profound, rest assured that
to every publisher in America, it [sounded] like Shakespeare."[48]Students
of American culture will recognize in this terming of profundity the
deep background of U.S. popular literature, women's fiction, and popular American religion. "In the book club's content and methods, I saw
a revitalization of the feminized literacy that had been so appealing to
earlier generations of women," writes Sarah Robbins of Oprah's club.
"Framing her book discussions in highly sentimental terms, and asking
her club members to construct stories about their own reading experiences as life guiding, Winfrey's original club affiliated itself with the
gendered tradition of social literacy that had been central to the domestic literacy narrative from the early nineteenth century onward."[49] This
domestic literacy narrative included books that ranged from romances
to religious fiction, novels about family life and novels about pastoral
struggle. These novels—authored by nineteenth-century women such
as Harriet Beecher Stowe, Susan Warner, and Maria Cummins—have
been cast as sweeping historical narratives of American culture. In *The
Feminization of American Culture*, Ann Douglas cites such domestic fiction and its readership as complicit in the commercialization of
literature.[50] Douglas describes the literary history of the nineteenth

century as a steady process in which women wrote stories of female trial and romantic resolution; women began to consume those sagas en masse; and those sentimentalized, feminized women began to dominate the churches. Formatted by their fictions and funneling their energies into moral reform, women defined new modes of theology (evangelical, sentimental, anti-intellectual) and new modes of culture (consumer, kitsch, mass-market) that would dominate the twentieth century. Thus, the "feminization of American culture" was the triumph of domestic literary production and consumption over and against a "manly" literary posture of restraint and rationalism. This arc suggested that "the removal of religion to the interior precincts of feeling and belief tended over time to reduce the specificity of religious conviction and religious difference to politically weightless matters of affect."[51]

Much of Douglas's narrative has been edited and curtailed by countering histories that suggest women's role in the churches, their consumption of sentimental fiction, and the countervailing actions of church authorities were more complicated than Douglas suggests.[52] Yet the image of "feminization" held sway long before Douglas historicized it, especially within early-twentieth-century Protestant circles as the fear of the feminizing menace emboldened evangelical preachers and Protestant leaders to rally institutional growth and print cultures around the fear of women's affect (and effects). A "muscular" Christianity arose to supply modern men with manly means to renegotiate a public sphere that increasingly included women's presence at the polls, in the office, and behind the pulpit. The texts that emerged from this spiral of anxiety played with the divide between the secular and the religious. "Rules for evaluating evangelical texts differed from the standards of secular literature," Candy Gunther Brown has written. "New publications gained entrance to the canon if they shared certain marks of membership, in other words, if they reinforced the same values as texts previously recognized as canonical."[53] If in the nineteenth-century religious texts were harder to distinguish from "secular" ones because of the pervasive Protestant consensus, the twentieth century produced a clearly delineated sequestering of "religious" fictions to feed those memberships that wanted material unscathed by secular worldliness.

These works were, in some ways, respondent to the imagined feminization of a culture after industrialization. For example, in Harold Bell Wright's *The Calling of Dan Matthews* (1909), the title character leaves the ministry to become a mine developer. "A fine, manly man, Matthews finds the effeminate role of minister chafes him," literary historian

Erin A. Smith writes. "If Wright's ministry of print is descended from female sentimental fiction writers, he is at pains to distinguish himself from them here, dismissing as trivial all of the sacred, domestic rituals they invested with transcendent importance."[54] Wright's profligate print ministry differentiated itself from female sentimental fiction in its rejection of domestic pieties and ministerial leadership, yet colluded with emergent lines of demarcation on the literary scene. Wright's "blatant" commercialism and his "evangelical fervor" put him "at odds with elite literary culture" that developed around "modernist" authors at the time of his greatest productivity. "If I entered a library of the man of scholarly-intellectual type I should not expect to find my books upon his shelves," Wright explained in 1921. "But it gives me great joy to find them, as I often do, upon the desk of a superintendent of a great power company." Desiring the applicability of a middlebrow man over and above literary consequence, Wright eschews the latter, believing the former a more pious cause: "As God is my Judge, I have never claimed . . . so much as a single literary pin-feather."[55] In a twentieth-century landscape of decreased religious authority, religious fiction asserted itself as scriptural commentary and as a counter to the new scriptures some were making of works by Joyce, Yeats, and Eliot.

Oprah's Book Club borrows from aspects of both "religious" publication and the "secular" author, for she encourages the usability of fiction while also lionizing the writer as a sacred figure. Book club episodes often begin with an author montage, including seminal moments in his or her development. Rather than pose the writer as an exiled, idiosyncratic, and elite hero, the author is transformed into a chummy mystic, a possible comrade who shares the same familial challenges, wardrobe struggles, and self-doubts as Oprah's viewers, albeit with an overdeveloped gift with words. A common visual thread in these montages is the solitary walk, with the author traversing his or her backyard, urban neighborhood, or scenic vista while gazing into the distance. "This could be you," suggests the teleplay, as viewers recall the reflective stroll as one of Winfrey's most popular prescriptions. Joel Pfister explains through the example of Eugene O'Neill how literary modernists were conscious advocates of their own visual culture, deploying the "faraway interior look" and "brooding" profile to effect the depth of a "romantic-psychological self."[56] Authors in Winfrey's multimedia exposition model modernist depth in their ruminative introduction and yet are expected to join the fray as soon as the club discussion begins. In response to being asked how she felt "about Winfrey's approach to fiction as something that really happens," Christina Schwartz, author of *Drowning Ruth*, answered, "Well, to be honest, that's not my approach to fiction. First, they do this little author profile before the show about the book. And they definitely had specific issues that they wanted me to talk about that were not the ones I thought the book was really about. But it's their show and they know what makes good television. So I think that how you approach a book is sort of a matter of personal opinion."[57]

The author is brought to Winfrey's size; if the book and its creator will not yield to the incorporations of Harpo, then they will not be allowed into Winfrey's world. "Oprah's readers," book club author Jacquelyn Mitchard has remarked, "are loyal to Oprah," not to the writers she selects.[58] Thus, the books selected must amplify and resonate "with many of her show's existing themes and narrative formats, especially the theme of suffering biographies."[59] For the program featuring Anita Shreve's novel *The Pilot's Wife* (May 6, 1999), the show included a discussion with several women who, like the pilot's wife, found that their husbands had other families. In a later interview, Shreve recalled, "By the time I was out there, it was, who needs the author?"[60] This is not to say that Winfrey doesn't hallow authors; indeed, she lavishes them with celebrating copy. The "O Contributors" pages of *O, The Oprah Magazine* luxuriates in authors, not only selling the article they wrote within that particular issue, but also framing their investigation or commentary in personal growth. "I've learned more about day-to-day courage from writing this piece than from anything I've ever written about before," reports Ronna Lichtenberg. "Writing is my form of celebration and prayer," reports Diane Ackerman. "Writing for me is always about untangling an argument with myself," explains Jill Bialosky.[61] Authors are photographed with their children for these introductions, narrating the chaos of their lives around the inspired, and inspirational, work of writing itself. These profiles in "O Contributors" provide more than personal history for the reader's admiration; they exhibit writers as products. With larger head shots and more biographical copy than shown in parallel publications, *O* writers experience the makeover treatment and concentrated emphasis of later objects in the publication.

All books and all authors are portholes to Winfrey's other prescriptions and her other products. When Ken Follett's *The Pillars of the Earth* was a book club selection, Follett found himself in the tag line for episodes beyond the book club. In "Behind the Scenes with Bob Greene, Kevin Everett, and More" (June 2, 2008), Follett and Winfrey are shown "after the show" sharing "a laugh," to include an authorial profile in the montage of backstage familiarity and hilarity. On "World Record Holders" (January 30, 2008), Winfrey showcases "the grandma with the world's smallest waist, the world's fastest clapper, and the jump-roping dog!" In addition, "Ken Follett, author of *The Pillars of the Earth*, is here!" Follett's presence on such an episode makes an Oprah sort of sense, since "Oprah's Book Club selection *The Pillars of the Earth* broke a few of its own" records. "Not only is it the longest book she's ever chosen—at 973 pages—it's also the fastest-selling book in Oprah's Book Club history." Even the turn to classic texts did not diminish Winfrey's tie-in talent. With fewer female writers and more muddied plotlines, Winfrey still easily spun something pithy from quagmires of romantic, political, familial, and social experience. The description of *Anna Karenina* on Oprah.com hailed the novel as "an extremely sexy and engrossing read" that tells "the tale of one of the most enthralling love affairs in the history of literature—it truly was the 'Harlequin Romance' of its day."[62] Elsewhere, the editorial voice of Harpo explains, "At the heart of [*As I Lay Dying*] beats a family's response to the loss of the most important person in their lives. They laugh, they curse, they fight, they bleed, they break, they love, they endure—just like we do."[63]

The spiritual hums around the corners of every book club promotion. On September 2004, Winfrey finished her discussion of Tolstoy's *Anna Karenina* by announcing that her next selection would be *The Good Earth*, by Pearl S. Buck. Winfrey began her description of *The Good Earth* by referring to the novel's reputation as a "sweeping saga that's been called 'a universal tale of the destiny of man.'" *The Good Earth*, Winfrey tells readers, is "juicy as all get out!"[64] Set during an unspecified period in the nineteenth or early twentieth century, *The Good Earth* focuses exclusively on Chinese characters (and, in particular, Chinese peasant life), rendering their lives in minute detail.[65] As with all Oprah picks, Winfrey finds a way to connect plot points from distant fictional shores to the experiences of women and men today. "Do you find it interesting how even today, when a spouse decides to fool around, they go through much of the 'makeover process' Wang Lung went through—cutting off his traditional hair, getting new clothes, avoiding garlic and bathing with soap every day," Winfrey writes in her e-mail newsletter to the book club. "The absolute nerve!"[66] Winfrey plucks from Buck's story a feminist observation. "Pearl Buck's China is a severe culture where women, even beloved wives and daughters, are called slaves and considered bad luck. But even the women who seem to silently accept their position in society have their moments of quiet defiance. It is O-lan's strength, determination, and resourcefulness that sustain the family."[67] Quiet defiance and individual determination are attributes that transcend literary locality.

Winfrey's framing of her heroines coordinates with spiritual emphases throughout her empire and with religious cultures throughout her nation's past. That Winfrey reclaimed Pearl Buck with such feminist intonations, for example, reflects Buck's own social and religious position in the midcentury American landscape. As Harold R. Isaacs wrote in 1958, "It can almost be said that for a whole generation of Americans she 'created' the Chinese, in the same sense that Dickens 'created' for so many of us the people who lived in the slums of Victorian England."[68] Raised in China by missionary parents, Buck derived this "creation" from a paradigm of religious criticism. In a 1949 *New York Times Magazine* article, Buck wrote that she preferred the Chinese creation myth, based on yin and yang, male and female, over the Judeo-Christian myth of Adam's rib, calling the latter an "almost insuperable" obstacle in the path of women's advancement in the West. Buck went so far as to declare the idea "that Chinese women have been much suppressed" an "American myth," contrasting what she saw as Chinese women's efforts to attain independence from men in the late 1940s with American women's concentration on marriage and domestic life. Her efforts to break from a preconceived Western model of women's experience in China foreshadowed recent scholarship in Chinese women's history, much of which has emphasized women's agency and even power rather than simply oppression.[69] By focusing on women's lives, Buck concluded that the United States was not the center of a "free world." In so doing, she challenged the foundations of cold war ideology and promoted an idea of universal female suffrage that Winfrey would have applauded.[70]

Buck sustained such a critique not merely as a feminist or an anti-imperial antagonist but also as a heavy-handed critic of the missionary experience. "Missionary, missions!" she exploded in front of one American audience. "[It is a] name that I for one have come to hate."[71] Indeed, historian Grant Wacker has described Pearl Buck as a signal figure in the "process by which millions of Americans came to doubt the morality of exporting Christianity to a non-Christian culture."[72] Dismissing supernaturalism and Eucharistic mystery, Buck endorsed instead the "figure" of Jesus Christ. Wacker writes, "That figure, that ideal, symbolized 'men's dreams of simplest and most beautiful goodness,' the highest values of the universal human imagination. If to traditional Christians Buck's Christ figure represented a pastiche of watered-down Buddhism,

Transcendentalism, and Positive Thinking, to Buck the Christ figure served as a great purifying, unifying wave overwhelming all the discordant eddies of daily life. It betokened inner serenity, harmony with the environment, and concern for the suffering of others."[73] Like many of her late-Victorian comrades, Buck retreated from the preformatted, hierarchical theology that had defined their Protestant childhoods. Freed from "narrow-minded, creed-driven ideologues," these women and men turned toward spirituality that retained Christian iconicity (Jesus) and value (concern for suffering) but embraced a cosmopolitan buffet.[74]

Moving into the story of Pearl Buck demonstrates how Oprah's products are not merely hers; they possess their own preface, their own histories, and their own religious identities. And while not every author selected by Oprah coordinates so perfectly with her agenda and emphases, many do. Agitating for gender equality, promoting universal figures of spiritual wellness, and drafting tales of long-ago triumph by besieged heroines, Buck was an Oprah sort of woman. Through interviews with living authors, Winfrey seeks ways to commiserate with their pasts and to find connections to her broader program. The book club stages contexts of raised mutual consciousness rotating around established *Oprah* show revelatory patterns. The point, then, is not to share a close reading of impenetrable texts. Rather, close readings of texts (from *The Good Earth* to Eckhart Tolle's *A New Earth*) return women to an Oprah way of life. Sociologist Elizabeth Long observes, "Reading thus requires . . . an infrastructure as social base, in much the same way as modern transportation requires a physical infrastructure of highways, airports, and fuel supplies."[75] *Oprah* infrastructures resonate with a swath of women's conversations in the contemporary period as well as precedents from their national and international pasts.

Thus the context of Oprah's Book Club is broader than just that of contemporary reading and contemporary women; it connects to figures and commentaries that organized other fights for popular dissent and spiritual debate. The history of such "textual communities" is an extensive one, reaching as far back as the twelfth century.[76] The scholarship on this form of sociability emphasizes its ability to "sustain collective memory, generate knowledge, and challenge tradition" in addition to its capacity (in a parlance inappropriate to the late medieval period, yet popular in the contemporary scholarly idiom) to "empower."[77] Eventually, this empowerment took the form of writing as reply to what was read. The religious history of this process is a reforming one. The Bible, now accessible through translation into the vernacular, became a site of debate and creativity. As Natalie Zemon Davis has argued, most modern reading groups were probably "secret Protestant assemblies."[78] The history of Christianity has been a history of excitable dissent, encouraged at its productive margins by the meeting of small groups to discuss new gospels, new teachings, and new readings of old proverbs. From the Puritan dissenter Anne Hutchinson to the Mormon fundamentalist Warren Jeffs, in the American context the question for church authorities has been how to police these borders, how to keep local scriptural discussions from impinging on ecclesiastical authority. "America, like nineteenth-century Europe, has had its theoreticians of dissent, but in far greater abundance has it had its practitioners," Edwin Gaustad has written. "Dissenters against the structure and authority of ecclesiasticism, dissenters against the rigidity or folly or sterility of religious ideas, dissenters against the hopes and the messianic pretensions of the social order."[79]

Even as recently as the mid-1990s, for example, the Church of Latter-day Saints combated the "Mormon dissidents" who were "preoccupied with Armageddon" and gathering in small study groups of "superpatriots" and "survivalists." The Mormon apostle Boyd K. Packer warned against the formation of these communities. "Do not be deceived by them—those deceivers," Packer preached. "If there is to be any gathering, it will be announced by those who have been regularly ordained and who are known to the Church to have authority. Come away from any others. Follow your leaders who have been duly ordained and have been publicly sustained, and you will not be led astray."[80] Splinter factions threaten schism. Church authorities rebut these infringements with reassertions of authority ("those who have been regularly ordained") and transparency ("it will be announced," "publicly sustained"). Huddled around books and people, dissident textual communities encouraged renewals of orthodox piety.

During the late nineteenth century, fears of divisive textual communities competed with anxieties about urban immigrant plurality. The Gilded Age of industrialization and modernization provoked fears among many business and religious leaders that the public had grown secularized and undignified. These fears led to an epoch of conscientious cultural invention, when "educators . . . conceptualized literary culture as a foundation of American citizenship and too for Americanization."[81] Partly in reply to the aftertaste of splinters around the time of the Civil War, groups goading devotion to a coherent culture arose in an effort to educate and organize atomized urban areas and provincial rural outposts. Included in this set of civilizing reforms were the "club" movement and the Chautauqua circuit. The so-called literary club movement reflected patterns established by other reform movements (such as efforts agitating for temperance and suffrage) and club cultures that littered the organizational landscape.[82] Before the mid-nineteenth century, most women's associations were either auxiliaries of men's groups or church-sponsored aid societies. Although women played a determining role in those early national women's groups, men controlled the elected and appointed positions of leadership. The turn from those adjunct women's organizations to women's "clubs" was a move by women to create separate gender-exclusive collectives in order to encourage women's education and community service, as well as to foster culture through fundraising efforts on behalf of new libraries, libraries in the public schools, and the distribution of books to poorer communities. Later, Oprah Winfrey would propagate a similar cultural prescription, as her book club "helped spur a boom in book groups organized in suburban living rooms and big city libraries" and motivated "the creation of citywide reading programs."[83] Winfrey and the club women shared a sense of responsibility to the fostering and expansion of a literate public.

The late-nineteenth-century club members who sought to prescribe culture were middle-aged, wealthy white women. "This kind of homogeneity may have made it easier for women to speak in their book clubs," and it also may have encouraged the diminishment of what one clubwoman called a "tedious selfhood" limited to purely "self-inclusive" thinking about subjects "such as dress, family, neighbors, or the fads of the day."[84] A parallel movement among similarly well-off African American women grew, forming, among other national bodies, the National Association of Colored Women (NACW) in 1896. These groups prescribed the same sorts of literacy and educational ventures while also becoming an organizational launching pad for intellectual replies to lynching and other assaults, spiritual and domestic, of the Jim Crow South.[85] These clubs were selective and elite, developing book discussions in parlors while also promoting carefully mapped civic reform efforts.

Somewhat more rugged were the activities of the Chautauqua Institution, founded in 1874 by Lewis Miller, an Akron, Ohio, inventor and manufacturer, and by John Heyl Vincent, a Methodist minister. In an optimistic phrasing Winfrey might admire, Chautauqua was founded on the belief that everyone "has a right to be all that he can be—know all that he can know." This was a religious venture in ritual criticism, completed by Methodists who were discomforted by typical camp meeting revivalism. Chautauqua was, then, a conscious rejection of the "anxious bench" enthusiasms described in chapter 3. Miller and Vincent believed that revival meetings made for "passive" spectators and more "histrionic and sensationalistic" preachers, creating, as one observer claimed, "the decline of the sermon from the vernacular to the vulgar." The Chautauqua camp, as well as its eventual yearlong courses and rural circuit tours, was meant to be nothing like a camp meeting "in the familiar evangelical sense, but [one that] would devote itself to Bible study, teacher-training classes, musical entertainment, lecturers, and recreation as well as devotional exercises." Lectures such as "Pie, People and Politics" or "How to Master One's Self" were standard fare.[86] This was religion for broad spectatorship, intended less to convert the unchurched than to expand religious appreciation among the presumptively churched. "At Chautauqua, Christ and his gospel have constituted the center of all teaching from the first day until the present," John Vincent wrote in the early years.[87]

The religious agenda of Chautauqua was backdrop and Christian coloration, infusing the proceedings with the sacred separation of religious space. "The evangelical religious agenda of Chautauqua distinguished it to some extent from public pursuits," Jeanne Kilde writes. "The grounds of religious camp meetings had long been considered qualitatively different from the sinful 'outside' world, and, although Chautauqua was not precisely a camp meeting, it was located on a former camp-meeting site." Like the camp meeting sites of the early national period, the Chautauqua camp formed a "new field of activity" for women where they behaved differently from how they might have in their normal domestic, reform, and church geographies. Lacking the "prior, traditional meanings" assigned to sacred or secular spaces, Chautauqua offered "alternative gender performance" by allowing women to pursue vigorously "personal and political interests—interests that tested and negotiated the constraints of prescribed gender roles."[88] The self-reliant economy of camp life encouraged respectable women, relieved of their usual domestic duties, to rough it in the forest. Many factors contributed to the eventual decline of Chautauqua, including the proliferation of clubs (resultant in part from the club movement), a market flooded with "secular" entertainments, and the saturation of radio in the rural markets where Chautauqua once thrived. "The Chautauqua assembly has passed, leaving in its place recreational centers or religious conferences," one historian relates. "The circuit Chautauqua, having made its last stand in a few widely scattered rural towns, apparently has no offspring."[89]

The citation of Chautauqua in a chapter on Oprah's Book Club suggests that it may, indeed, have some offspring, albeit now televised and deloused of the itinerant's wear and tear. What is particularly compelling about the Chautauqua example as a comparative moment in U.S. education and entertainment is the melding of commercial appeal, religious themes, and mobile, relatable education. A 2009 revival of Chautauqua-style performance on Broadway concluded, "Does the number belong to rarefied art or debased commerce? By the end of this illuminating show, the question itself seems entirely wrong."[90] The Chautauqua circuit was a commercialized, touring version of the campground in upstate New York. As an imported middlebrow culture, the circuit "brought performance to those who would otherwise not see it." This wasn't merely because rural locales lacked cosmopolitan encounter but also because many Protestant American audiences rejected theater and actors as disreputable. They could, however, embrace "readers, elocutionists, and others who spoke the drama aloud in public without 'painting' themselves . . . since most middle-class families habitually read aloud at home, readings by authors and elocutionists . . . represented nothing less than the professional extension of a favorite family activity."[91] Any discussion of reading history in the United States, then, must examine the relationship between publicized reading habits (like those of the literacy clubs and Chautauqua elocutionists) and the privatized, often devotional ones. In her description of early-twentieth-century Lutheran family devotions, Betty DeBerg writes that women's societies prescribed pious time for parents and children. She elaborates:

> Breakfast time, the evening meal, or before retiring at night might be a good time for Bible stories, prayers, and songs. Older children were encouraged to read the Bible aloud or perhaps responsively, so that all the family could participate in worship. Reciting sentence-length prayers, memorizing hymns, reading chapters from a devotional book, and studying the lives of Christian heroes and famous missionaries were all appropriate activities for family worship. Lutheran organizations for women . . . published prayer books for children, devotional pamphlets, inspirational articles, and reading lists of useful religious books for mothers.[92]

DeBerg's ideal Lutheran family modeled a Christian tranquility as well as Protestant domestic piety, including the exchange and interpretation of scripture, as well as additional commentaries on that scripture that makes its applications explicit for children, for mothers, and for busy fathers. Home devotions translated scriptural injunctions into daily habits of domestic piety.

Scholars of Oprah's Book Club have leaned away from these explicitly religious instances of nineteenth- and twentieth-century literacy practices, choosing instead to focus on the Book-of-the-Month Club, the Literary Guild, and the Mid-Century and Reader's Subscription book clubs as predecessors to Winfrey's reading prescription. Editorial observers breathlessly proclaimed that Oprah's Book Club was "one of the biggest boons to reading and book sales since the creation of the Book-of-the-Month Club more than 75 years ago."[93] To be sure, these organized attempts to get America reading offer useful comparative vantage, particularly as they too put people in contact with books they may otherwise have never read and as they applied innovative uses of new media (such as direct-mail marketing) to press the masses back into the literate fold.[94] "Resisting the rampant materialism of prosperous economic times and restoring or igniting a sense of culture were the underlying aims of the mail-order club for most of those involved," writes Cecilia Konchar Farr, "though the primary purpose was always to select a few good books, make them readily accessible, and sell them cheap to whoever would buy them."[95] Functioning as a discretionary sieve on behalf of her audience, Winfrey, like the editorial overseers of the Book-of-the-Month Club (and the Religious Book Club, which arose subsequently to parallel it), distills what texts were beneficial and what was beneficial from these texts. "Oprah's Book Club invites readers to share Oprah's life—in a small and controlled fashion—by reading books along with her. It is virtual community at its finest."[96] The Religious Book Club, for example, sought to find books "in which moral and spiritual ideals find effective expression."[97] This mission was met most successfully in their work to connect readers "affectively with characters, authors, and judges in ways that seemed intimate and personal."[98] This personalism was most obvious in Religious Book Club lesson plans pertaining to biographies of saints and religious leaders from the past. Robert Norwood's *The Heresy of Antioch,* for example, presented the life of the Apostle Paul. The RBC's *Bulletin* wrote, "The Great Apostle is portrayed, not as a theologian, but as a great human."[99] Making the text accessible would be a hallmark of popularization ventures from literacy clubs to Winfrey's sofa interventions.

Moving from the women's clubs to Chautauqua, from literacy clubs to religious book clubs, demonstrates the strands of organization and textual election that preceded Oprah's Book Club particular. The Oprah club distinguishes itself, however, with the centrality of its first-name purveyor. Preexisting American book clubs may have encouraged fellowship and self-improvement, but Winfrey made the reading of all those stories into a sweeping summation of *her* story. The personal touch begins with Winfrey's signature O on the cover of every volume and feeds into every aspect of the discussion. This is no neat narcissism: her personalization exists to encourage yours. Book club episodes open with a voice-over by Winfrey citing the astonishing number of letters received from viewers about the chosen book. Alongside this excited citation, Winfrey usually proclaims the universal appeal of that text, the message that spawned such epistolary abundance. From the cadre of letter writers, Winfrey then elaborately selects an appropriate cohort of participants. For instance, in the discussion of *Cane River*, a multigenerational story of slavery in Louisiana, Winfrey picked four perfectly diverse women: Danielle, an African American kindergarten teacher, wife of a white man, and granddaughter of a "proud Creole woman"; Jeanne, a white single mother who read the book in the wake of her mother's cancer diagnosis; Stephanie, an African American still struggling with the darkness of her skin; and Tracey, a white high school teacher who recently discovered her family had owned slaves. Again, although her cast possesses an apparent diversity, their shared emotive response to the text binds them in experiential similarity. Thus, Jeanne and Stephanie, though racially and economically different, will find their universal humanity through their common response to *Cane River*.[100] This "cultural politics of progressive multiculturalism" forms the central argument to every scholar's (and publisher's and editor's) "almost exclusively laudatory" praise of Oprah's Book Club.[101] "Noting that anxieties about mass culture have historically targeted cultural forms produced for and enjoyed by subordinate social groups (i.e., women, the working class, people of color), scholarly analysts are inclined to represent Winfrey's 'literacy initiative' as a democratic corrective to high cultural elitism," Janice Peck explains further.[102] Such elision of difference is a classic attribute of ritual. "Rituals create a setting in which persons can appear, by appearing in their culture, by devising a reality in which they may stand as a part," writes anthropologist Barbara G. Myerhoff. "In their rituals, we see persons dramatizing self and culture at once, each made by the other."[103] As Jeanne and Stephanie share their biographical compatibility with *Cane River*, they will find that the details of their stories are secondary to their driving passion for the book and, indeed, their lives. *Cane River* and the other books of

Oprah's Book Club provide a temporary reality, a space for conversation and connection among disparate characters.

Within the ritual of a book club conversation, typical television rules apply: commercial breaks cordon topic distinctions, any major conflict is edited to the second half so as to tempt viewers to keep watching through the full hour, and Winfrey neatens any internal messiness with her editorial inserts. The ritual impulse of these dialogues. Like religious rituals held in sanctuaries, the book club encourages the renewal of identity. Throughout the book club conversations, Winfrey's driving want is to create connection: between the participants and the authors, among the participants, and between herself and her viewing audience. For Winfrey, such "connection" ("Make the Connection") is made through recognition. If participants identify affinities with the characters and can articulate how their own identity is mirrored in or contradicted by their interpretations of the novel, then connection is inaugurated. Identification with the sacral center allows participants to achieve individual reformation. Viewers and book club guests achieve such ritual success through several rhetorical tropes, including the establishment of relational affiliation, the proclamation of thematic universality, the description of a codified moral, the assessment of character, and communal catharsis. Although each of these tropes will be assessed individually, in enactment they overlap, roping readers into a compelling claim of future revolution.

As demonstrated by the sort of book club guests whom Winfrey selects to join the "intimate" conversation, the best club members are those with clear analogical links to the plot of the novel. Book club episodes frequently open with Winfrey proclaiming, "For every woman who's ever been [fill in blank], this show is for you." The blank could refer to women who have been divorced or have discovered family secrets or experienced shocking tragedy, debilitating illness, or personal betrayal. Regardless the textual specific, the point of the proclamation is the declaration of relational affinity. "The majority of our e-mails," announced Winfrey at the opening of the *Icy Sparks* discussion, "were from thousands of you who identified with the story of a girl just trying to fit in, like Kerry Strano, our fourth and final guest, who grew up biracial in a predominantly white English community." Even though *Icy Sparks* focuses on a girl with Tourette's syndrome, Winfrey translates that uncommon disorder into common experience. Everyone has access to the experience of "trying to fit in," even if it is not accompanied by debilitating muscular spasms.[104] Introducing the guests for the book club episode addressing *Fall on Your Knees,* Winfrey describes each through her kinship with the text:

> For Lynne Sherman, this book was a window to exploring her family's secrets, including, she says, the sexual abuse that Lynne hadn't ever discussed with her other siblings. Chaka Reed related to the sacrifices that the siblings made for each other in the novel. And she and her sister adopted their young brother when her mother abandoned them. And Audrey Sytes was struck by the memories that we leave for our children, she says, and how harmful some of those may be. Sue Johnston is another survivor of sexual abuse who says this book helped her see abusers in a different light. And Brenda Zufria is an educator in the prevention of sexual abuse of children.[105]

Again, the fee for book club admission is the women's self-described affinity with the text that they offer through their letters. Through this prefatory profile, Winfrey not only details the participants as products but also piques her audience's interest, teasing the upcoming discussion with voyeuristic disclosure. The viewers know that these aren't mere tidbits; these are previews of the confessionals to come. Sue Johnston is not only a survivor. She is a survivor who will speak, bringing to painful light her abuse in the pillowed bower of Oprah's Book Club.

The book club, Ted Striphas has argued, offers "a set of symbolic and material resources with which feminist cultural producers might begin piecing together a feminist aesthetics." In the book club, he continues, "women were encouraged to use books and book reading as vehicles both to step outside of and to interrogate critically values and routines."[106] Evangelical Protestant Bible ministries have sought to encourage similarly relational reading by their faithful. In her study of contemporary evangelical readers, Amy Johnson Frykholm suggests that this utilitarian usage of scripture is a regular practice among Christians, what she calls the "life application method." In accordance with previous Calvinist models of scriptural connection, members of a Bible study group read the Bible in order to apply it immediately to daily life. In this context, scripture buttresses its readers against the assault of the world. "The purpose of the Bible study then is not to explore the Bible," Frykholm explains, "not to contemplate the various meanings or to look into the historical context of the message . . . rather, the purpose is to focus the reading through the lens of one's own life and then determine how the reading can be directly and somewhat immediately applied." The goal of this sort of scriptural study is a "take-home message," not theological development or historical debate.[107] Like pull-out postcards from the magazine or O-marked key chains, the right scriptural interpretation can travel with the reader-believer wherever he or she may need instantaneous spiritual affirmation for continuance in the hard big world.

As the conversation proceeds, Winfrey prods the relational touchstones of her participants, seeking the same take-home slogans and axioms for daily survival. "I want to ask this question: What in the book most related to you?" Winfrey repeatedly asks. "When did you think, 'This is my story'?" No matter the geographic or historical context of the novel, book club guests arrive armed to respond in detail to this ritual question. Viewers are drawn into the lives of the reader-guests as they offer details to fill the discussion and legitimize their reading of the text. Quickly, the subject of the discussion turns from the novel to the guests, to the novelistic retellings of their life stories.[108] "For many of us, it was just a story, but for these women, it was all too real," Winfrey announces at the beginning of a segment. "Most of us only read that story. They lived it."[109] This identification with the book club text was and is, as Trysh Travis has written, not "an end in itself." Instead, "it was the first step toward a richer connection of the self to the world."[110] Winfrey underlines this transition to the "real world" with montages and testimonials from women who may or may not have read the novel but certainly have access to its plot. "Next, how perfectly normal women just lost their minds during divorce," she warns. "Next, why, if you're harboring a family secret of your own and you're watching this, you need to get it out in the open."[111] These segments involving "real-life women" are inserted to heighten the drama of the episode, to transfer from two-dimensional fiction into three-dimensional contemporary dilemmas. Fictional women provide portholes to real women, to deeper interpretations of this televised, but purportedly more authentic, reality.

Scholars of readers' reception have described this sort of textual explorer as the "resisting reader," the woman who brings a social identity to her encounter with a text.[112] Winfrey's premise is that real women will feel more comfortable speaking about that identity if they have a communal preexistent vocabulary from which to borrow. The sanctioned, embossed ritual text provides an alternate language for self-description, providing a degree of linguistic (and, therefore, emotional) removal from their own reality. Through a conversational affinity with the text, a book club participant can achieve therapeutic levels of disclosure. And, as in an evangelical confession, the witness will benefit as much as the testifier from the ritual release of the biographic. Among the largely praising commentaries on Oprah's Book Club, Winfrey's turn to the relentless memoir receives the greatest criticism. Writing in the *New York Times Magazine*, observer D. T. Max worries, "There's something odd about Winfrey's insistence on treating novels as springboards for self-reflection. Aren't novels about stepping outside one's experience?"[113] Others are even more prescriptively condemnatory. "Winfrey's autobiographically candid reactions to the books were among the lower orders of reader response," Kathleen Rooney decides. "Her insistence on real autobiography as a lens to focus on fiction indicated her own questionable, immature, and possibly even unhealthy attitude toward literature, and in turn cultivated a similarly shallow, narcissistic approach to fiction on the part of her audience."[114] In defense of the biographic particular as a site of reading exchange, the book club novelist Anna Quindlen had this to say: "An Oprah discussion of *Anna Karenina . . .* would likely go to the question of whether it is right or wise to leave your marriage for romantic love. I can understand the criticism but I think any mechanism that leads hundreds of thousands of people to read a literary novel is on its face a good thing. I think there are almost no negatives connected with the book club."[115]

While useful for establishing relational affinity, the particulars of the selected novel's plot and prose are unnecessary for book club viewing. The invited book club guests read favorite quotations, and frequently moments from the text are debated, but the driving editorial thrust of the episode is beyond the book. "Truly great books bring out thoughts that go far beyond just the work itself," Winfrey explained in her analysis of *A Fine Balance*.[116] Oprah's Book Club episodes are, by Winfrey's constant contrivance, not about the book; they are about what people do with books. Across her empire, this message is repeated. In *O at Home* a profile of a Philadelphia book club advocates on behalf of this connective reading process: "As much as I loved *What Is the What* [by Dave Eggers], I love more how it sparks Allyson, an ob-gyn, to tell us about her recent trip to Nigeria, the third time she has used her vacation to volunteer there, delivering babies and treating dozens of patients who walk days to get to her. . . . Every meeting comes to this—to moments drawn from our lives more than the book."[117] Small groups oriented around the promotion of Christian piety also emphasize study of "lives" more than they do The Book. Early-twentieth-century evangelical Protestants, for example, formed Bible classes for young adults across the country in what was called the Adult Bible Class movement. By 1922, the International Sunday School Association conservatively estimated that five million women and men were members of nearly fifty thousand

Bible classes.[118] "Friendship saturated the devotional culture of these turn of the century Bible classes," writes Christopher Cantwell. "Both the word itself as well as themes of interpersonal intimacy filled Bible class newsletters, promotional material, service programs and correspondence."[119] Interpersonal, faithful fellowship inspired the gatherings; knowing the Bible well was a mere collateral effect of such Bible study.

On the ground, making such a sharp distinction between knowing the text and knowing one another through talking about the text may be too neat. Yet it is telling that Winfrey began *O, The Oprah Magazine* with aspirations of reprinting fiction. The first few issues of *O* reprinted excerpts from books, lesson plans for your book club, and new short fiction by contemporary writers. However, this excerpting and instruction quickly gave way to blurbs and books reviews. This subtraction of fictional texts from her magazine copy might be explained as a reply to consumer attention span or the result of the market share for a magazine.[120] Televised book club conversations succeed when they are accessible to as many people in the audience as possible, even those who have never read the selected book. The turn to the first-person reader response is not only the pursuit of a recognizable modern celebration of the individuated revelation but also an easier product to market. So long as the magazine sells descriptions of books, so long as the show sells montages of experiences with books, books themselves remain a fantasy for consumption, not a tiresome task to complete. And Oprah women already have too many tasks to finish, too many parts to perfect.

In the effort to serve the mass market of network television, Winfrey emphasizes the universal impetus of a given text, gearing discussion toward abstracted versions of character dilemmas rather than textual specifics. "Now this book gives you a sense from the inside and out of what it is like to have Tourette's or any other affliction that makes you feel different," Winfrey remarked in the *Icy Sparks* discussion. The *Icy Sparks* episode provided a thumbnail discussion of Tourette's and its limited treatments, and it spotlighted viewers who had family members with this diagnosis. But a large portion of the conversation focused on communal cruelty toward difference and on the importance of compassionate parenting that breeds children amenable and empathetic to others. "I just love a book that enthralls you and also teaches, and that is exactly what many took away from this experience," explained Winfrey during the discussion of *Cane River.* "One universal theme that particularly inspired our readers is how the women in the book, with such limited choices, aspired to do so much for the coming generations." The universal themes in book club books often focus on honesty, quality child rearing, and the courage that creates individual redemption.

One way Winfrey emphasizes the universal themes within book club novels is by acknowledging fictional settings. Social issues are highlighted yet are conclusively subsumed within the overarching therapeutic impetus of the episode. "I'm telling you the book isn't about slavery," Winfrey explained during the discussion of *Cane River.* "It's about what these women did after they were freed and, you know, one of the things that amazes me is that people are able to, after such degradation, after suffering like that, to be able to love again, to be able to step out of that and say, 'I will now build a family of my own.' That is—to me, is just the most extraordinary thing." The praise embedded within Winfrey's commentary would be evident to any *Oprah* viewer. Regardless his or her race or genealogy or access to the social circumstances of *Cane River,* any *Oprah* viewer with an experience of "degradation" can take something uplifting from this assertion. In other *Oprah* episodes, "learning to love again" and personal regeneration have been central pedagogical themes. Now, in *Cane River,* they are modeled and reasserted. The viewers may have never been to Louisiana, but if they know "degradation," they, too, can access the message of that episode. A white woman who has never left Winnetka, Illinois, can therefore find as much purpose and meaning in *Cane River* as a black woman from Biloxi. The social realities profiled in the selected novels are sidebars to the moral intention of the text.

Winfrey names the moral intention. Oprah's Book Club discussions are discussions, with shared conversational space for all the participants. Nevertheless, Winfrey is the organizing principle. It is her careful ministry that orders and guides enlightenment. Whether in the editing room or in her bracketing summations, Winfrey steers the moral of the story. Every book club episode revolves around an ethical theme or message, a message that is the truth taken from some disarming plot. Winfrey does not act without endorsement, however; the author often provides a validating synopsis of the message. "And you have to get to the bottom before you can turn around and start up again," explained Elizabeth Berg when responding to a panelist's question about the "real truth" of her novel *Open House.*[121] However, Oprah also frequently announces the sermonic center of the episode, as she did in the book club meeting for *Drowning Ruth:* "The secret holds so much power for you, and when you let it out into the light, you see that was all your big fear." The moral can also emerge in dialogue with a book club guest.

In her analysis of *Icy Sparks,* Paula, a selected book club participant, remarked, "And I think that—that the saving grace in the book—and I find it to be so in my extended family also—is that unconditional love is what will conquer Tourette's." Winfrey didn't miss a beat: "Everything. It can—conquers almost everything." Whether through dialogue or pointed pronouncement, the primary message is inevitably one that endorses Winfrey's overarching therapeutic intent. In the discussion of *Drowning Ruth,* Patrick, another book club guest, articulated Winfrey's ambition:

> Well, one thing that this book helped me to do is see secrets from different people's lives. And that's why it really just drew home with me is because in my particular situation I had always realized it from just my viewpoint and how it affected me, which is very selfish. But this book opened my eyes to how it affected other people. . . . If books are gonna be this good, then I—then I want to read them because—because they—great literature is very powerful and it has the power to affect us all in different ways. And—and it's wonderful.

Winfrey immediately validated Patrick's insight: "That's what I think, Patrick. Literature is powerful. It has the ability to change people's—the way they—the way we think." Regardless of the moral specificity—or ambiguity—of a given novel, Winfrey frames the discussion around the reader's consolidated clarity. In the world of Winfrey, reading is a critical practice of "making the connection," of "behaving" to success.

Oprah Winfrey's moral message isn't merely proffered in affirming maxims. Indeed, Winfrey communicates as much in her condemnations as in her enthusiasms. Every episode of Oprah's Book Club includes an indignant Winfrey. "The only thing I didn't believe is that she went to Tiffany's and then gave that bracelet away," Winfrey remarked about Amanda, the consumerist divorcée from Elizabeth Berg's *Open House.* "I do not believe she gave that bracelet away to a homeless woman." Regardless of the protestations of other club participants or the author herself, Winfrey persisted in her opinion. Interestingly, Winfrey's disbelief is not couched in textual discontinuity. Never does Winfrey suggest that the text fails to support whatever she rejects; rather, it is the idea of the action or character that frustrates her. For example, the character of Amanda in *Drowning Ruth* receives harsh criticism because of her secrecy. "She's the one I had some issues with," Winfrey announced. "I'm not so sure we love Amanda." Amanda's inability to tell the truth placed her in the lowest echelons of Winfrey's estimation: "I think she had no integrity." Because she could not "live in integrity," Winfrey disdained her. Christina Schwarz, the author, is taken aback and defends her character from such assassination, noting Amanda's upbringing and context as rationale for her impotence. Winfrey refuses to compromise her position:

> *Schwarz*: You really didn't like her.
>
> *Winfrey*: No, I did not like her.

The irony of Winfrey's dismissal is that her overarching intent for the club is to counteract such reductive assessments of others. "That's what I love about a book," Winfrey proclaimed during the discussion of *Drowning Ruth*. "It just opens up all those doors." Winfrey consistently argues that books can act as lessons in compassion, yet her own moral compass remains apparently unaltered by her readings. Although she suggests that she has seen new worlds and accumulated new ideas through reading, Winfrey never admits to a personal recalibration through reading. In this public ritual, reading is always confirmation of what she already knew and what others need to learn. Winfrey summarizes this conflict with a host's glee. "I love this," she says. "It's like these people are real."

Kathy, from *The House of Sand and Fog*, also garnered little empathy from Winfrey: "You know, I have some issues with her." Interestingly, although the character of the colonel from Dubus's novel caused Winfrey's club participants more trouble, she forgave him his transgressions. "I was sympathetic to his culture and him trying to come here to build a better life," she said. But Kathy received tougher treatment. "Why didn't she open her damn mail? That's what I want to know," Winfrey exclaimed. "She is one of those people who sits around and doesn't open their mail because they're trying to hide from their bills. Why didn't she open her mail?"[122] Here, the viewer experiences the symphonic assimilation of Oprah's varied therapies. Not only is she responding to the novel in a conversational dialect; she is also signaling her audience that the more banal topics of other episodes can be brought to bear on the elegant abstractions of fiction. Any viewer of the *Oprah* show is familiar with Winfrey's parade of financial counselors and their repeated admonitions to the indebted and those "hiding from bills." Winfrey's degradation of a fictional character reiterates a broader programming ambition. For her, any sympathy is diminished by personal irresponsibility and delusion. The bounds of kindness extend only as far as you adhere to her prescriptions. What Kathy really needed was a daily dose of Oprah.

All of this conversation and correction, assessment and moral summation, climaxes in the lightbulb or aha moments. Oprah Winfrey's
purpose is to provoke such moments, which she defines in the following
explanation:

> Well, over the years, I know you've heard me talk a lot about lightbulb
> moments, and thousands of you have written to us after experiencing little
> epiphanies of your own. That's what a lightbulb moment is. In the magazine,
> I call it "aha moments," that moment when you go, "Aha," while watching
> the show. I have them all the time. Lightbulb, aha moments, happen when
> you hear something that suddenly clicks for you. What's exciting about a
> lightbulb moment . . . —or one of those aha moments—is that you feel in
> that moment you know you discovered something new and important that
> can change your life. What's really outstanding about those moments is usu-
> ally when you hear something like that, it's—it's—it's reminding you of what
> you already know. That's what the aha is, 'cause it feels like, "I knew this;
> I just didn't know the words to put it," you know? That's what it is. That's
> what's fabulous about it.[123]

As examined earlier, lightbulb moments, those "little epiphanies" that
"change your life," are the transaction of Winfrey ritual. Whether
called "born again" experiences or "nirvana" or "aha" moments, these
instances are conjured through the televised narratives of book club participants. The entire trajectory of the *Oprah* show episodes is designed
to quicken the occurrence of such instances. "Today's show is going to
break your heart and heal it again," Winfrey announced at the beginning
of her *We Were the Mulvaneys* discussion. "Break your heart and heal
it again."[124] Meetings of the televised Oprah's Book Club follow this
plot, moving from depressive opening confessionals through communal
contemplations of character to collective comprehension of the selected
sermonic focus. Lightbulb moments bring closure to the last portion of
the ritual event. Patty Jan, management consultant and mother of two,
had this lightbulb moment while reading *A Fine Balance*:

> I picked up this book to read, and I—I was going through a really hard time.
> I'd lost my job and—and things were out of control, so a really good friend
> recommended the book for me to read. I was in awe of how beautifully it
> was written. But I didn't get it. And one day I—I just sort of realized through
> my actions and—and the book came back to me that what had happened to
> me was a change that was thrust into my life, and I had to embrace it in order
> to move on, and that is the fundamental message in this book.[125]

Winfrey cajoles these confessions, only then to conclude the book
club episode by sharing with the question, "What did it take for you

to get over [fill in blank]?" Again, the blank may refer to a divorce or a death, a familial sorrow or a career disappointment. With this quizzical encouragement, book club participants happily contribute their lightbulb breakthroughs. The message is here summarized and underlined, with Winfrey framing these disparate tales of triumph with her own pedagogical ambition. "Well, you know what we have to teach our daughters? Is to give up the fantasy," she decides at the end of one club meeting. Translating the therapeutic purpose of the text into action is a critical conclusive trope of Oprah's Book Club. "I celebrate and honor you for the women that you've become, for taking your pain and taking what was a very difficult time and turning it into triumph for your children and for your lives," Winfrey pronounced at the close of her discussion of *Open House*. "Here's to you all, and here's to Elizabeth Berg. Here's to books."

The realist revelation of Oprah's Book Club episodes mirrors the sort of conclusions of her chosen novels. "I'm always accused of not having happy endings," Winfrey remarked. "I look for whatever is realistic, whatever is meaningful, whatever is going to take me to the next level with these characters. I don't look for necessarily a happy ending." The conclusions of book club participants are personally uplifting and relentlessly pragmatic. Participants agree on the universality of suffering, of secrecy, of generational disappointment. They persist despite these downtrodden sentiments because of the opportunities for connection and the possibility of the lightbulb. Or, in the words of *Fall on Your Knees* author Ann-Marie MacDonald, participants endure in the pursuit of "fairly happy" endings: "Some people ask me, or they—they ask each other, is it a happy ending? And there is a kind of desire to be reassured that it's going to be okay, and I think that what unfolds over the course of the book is that the truth is told. The story comes out. The secrets come out. Something is released. And something else can rest in peace. You know, when the past is resting in peace and we can go forward with the story, and that's fairly happy."[126] And so the story moves forward in a never-ending cycle of truth and mishap, seeking resolution even as it seems so often to recede. Readers circumambulate to resolve; viewers resolve to crumble again into Oprah's arms.

Anthropologists have suggested that ritual itself necessitates a cycle; every ritual acknowledges the passage from one stage to another, a transition from one level of awareness to another. Such a description of ritual mirrors Oprah's Book Club, with participants and other readers achieving temporary relief through the confession of personal trial and the connection with characters and other readers experiencing corresponding troubles. Through ceremonial observances, "a constant flow of indulgences is spread through society, with others who are present constantly reminding the individual that he must keep himself together as a well demeaned person and affirm the sacred quality of these others," explained Erving Goffman.[127] Or, to follow Winfrey's own summation during the 2002 conclusion of the first incarnation of her book club: "A great book makes us look closer in the mirror. A great book tells the truth of our own experiences. And sometimes a great book offers nothing short of salvation."[128]

Such talk elicits harsh reply from book club witnesses. "I have always found there to be something cloying about Oprah's Book Club," Scott Stossel wrote, "though my objection is less to the books she chooses than to the way she approaches them: there is something so relentlessly *therapeutic,* so consciously *self-improving,* about the book club that it seems antithetical to discussion of serious literature. Literature should disturb the mind and derange the senses; it can be palliative, but it is not meant to be the easy, soothing one that Oprah would make it."[129] Naming what literature should and should not do is resonant with the aspirations of Winfrey's nineteenth-century club movement forebears who thought they could assign what might properly "disturb" or "derange" in order to civilize the masses. Denis Donoghue, critical of such a limited view of what literature, and reading, should be, argues, "When we read a work of literature as a symbolic action, we purge the political, but we also purge the metaphysical, the religious, the economic, the historical, or any other ideological discourse."[130] If we side with Stossel and worry about bleak consequences of "easy" reads and "soothing" fellowship, then we miss discourses named by Donoghue, places of conversation not necessarily encompassed by some impossibly "pure" concept of literary consumption. Furthermore, we also slip into two traps familiar to our survey of Oprah: first, the desire for a "secular" opinion, deduced independently from an individual's rationality; second, the belief that talk of liberation engenders liberation. Neither the history of reading nor the history of liberation demonstrates Stossel's doomsday account.

Winfrey's possible transformations do not, however, mitigate the imperial nature of her process. The plotline is not to direct viewers away from her but inevitably, unstoppably, back to her. The brilliance of this book club isn't that of the college classroom or the psychoanalyst's office; optimistically, in the therapeutic and collegiate contexts, the subject seeks eventual graduation.[131] The book club needs viewers to remain in arrested development, needing always more of the specific Oprah supplies. The strongest similarity is to the ministry, which through its technology of care and intimacy of commandment cajoles the reader to return to the ideal exegete, to the ministerial someone who really knows.

"That's why I love books," Winfrey announced in the very first book club episode. "You read about somebody else's life, but it makes you think about your own."[132] In its exuberant endorsement of print culture, in its celebration of a self independent of institutional knowledge, in its viral use of new media, and in its relentless pursuit of the "good news" given through narrative forms, the book club replays the sorts of cultural contingencies and transformative imperatives reverberating since sixteenth-century protests against Catholic indulgences. Any explanatory tale of the post-Reformation "reading public" must include the appearance of the printing press, the rise of the nation-state, and the development of a commercial sphere that was complicit (and concomitant) in the nation-state's conception. Among the many ways this confluence of commodity, therapeutic gatherings, and celebrated texts has been portrayed, the most religiously obvious is that of the ongoing process by which the laity is lifted to interpretive authority. Reading, once akin to monastic prayer, became the layperson's labor, an externalized quest for the right way to know the Word.[133] This is never an unmitigated process; within denominational confines, this reading is, and has always been, managed and monitored. Yet the Reformation and its subsequent reverberations were propelled by the drive to achieve more independence from posited structures of dogma and creed, even as new creeds and new dogmas were made to instantiate that freedom. That Oprah is the one handing out the books, as well as the one reminding her fellow readers what to believe, is not so much hypocrisy as it is a most recognizable process of modern commercial reformation.

Oprah transforms this commercial practice into ritual enterprise. Although rituals can be tedious and indifferent, routine and vacant, they can also provide the framework for spiritual uplift. The question for cultural critics is whether Oprah's progress is a sort of progress to endorse or decry. Because it is clear that there is only one way to read books with Oprah: the way she does. Reading books as Oprah does is to read with the problems of the reader being negotiated alongside the problems of the characters. This is not peculiar to Oprah as we all read texts in part to find comfort, commonality, and resolution through the fictions of others. Yet reading "the Oprah way" is to read only with the intent to solve the *reader's* dilemmas; in the empire of Oprah, the reader is always her. "Oprah's Book Club maintains a paradox in which reading, figured as an act of self-definition, turns nonetheless on the defining stamp of one reader, Oprah herself," Yung-Hsing Wu has written.[134] The solipsism of the reader is emphasized over the aesthetic of the text or the potential social critiques offered within the texts. In Oprah's Book Club, social change and literary eloquence are appendages to the primary duty of any text: to make the reader feel better. Like all ritual enactments, reading with Winfrey is rarely a one-time revelation. Inevitably, the predictable exhilaration of episodic television and canny ritual tactics inspires return participants to consume and to exhort this satisfying return. In the discussion of *Drowning Ruth,* Oprah named her vision: "It is just remarkable to me . . . how a work of fiction can touch and, really, begin to help heal the lives of readers in ways that a lot of self-help books and therapy and conversations cannot. Our lesson from *Drowning Ruth,* for a lot of people, is this: that if you are harboring any kind of family secret, y'all need to let it out; let it go. Maybe this Thanksgiving is a good time. Just everybody around the table talk about their feelings. See how that dinner goes." One ritual is never enough; every ritual feeds into another. It is this infinite reproduction that makes the book club not only good ritual but also good television.

CHAPTER 6

Missionary Gift

The Globalization of Inspiration

Since the first deported Africans arrived enslaved on New World shores, African Americans hatched plans to return to their native homes and tribal communities. An optimistic sense of individual transformation drove these "back to Africa" colonization efforts. Their African American and Anglo-American organizers believed that through removal from their enslaved geography they could rid themselves of the brutalizing consequences of that past while also establishing new all-black nations. Like these repatriating dreamers, Oprah Winfrey perceived in Africa the possibility of a fresh start for eventual race redemption. In South Africa, she claimed to have found needy students who wanted something more than iPods. These students desired something only she could provide: a perfectly produced individual reformation. The plotline was clear. She would return to the continent of her ancestors to establish her own mission field, a place where personal electronics would be secondary to uniforms, textbooks, and self-esteem. Her postulated Africa did not have a political past or interventionist precedents. It hosted no messianic rivals. Most of all, this designated mission field lacked her.

In the realm of missionary labor, *exploitation* is perhaps a relative term, since whatever transaction occurs is premised on inequality. For scholars of religion, a missionary is defined as an individual participating in a ministry commissioned by a religious organization to propagate its faith or carry on humanitarian work. Missionaries usually regulate their enterprise through a careful course of sermons and services given to convert the nonbeliever or to quicken the diminished faith of any denomination. Throughout American history, missionary activity has been predominantly Christian, and missionaries have labored to assimilate non-Christians to their worldview both at home and abroad. They have been a critical component of settlement and colonialism, providing social networks for America's physical and cultural expansion, thereby linking national growth and spiritual development as interlocking processes. There have been as many ways of being missionaries as there have been missionaries and as many sorts of missions as there have been designated mission wards. The interdisciplinary field of missiology developed in part to delineate between practices of Christianity that are requisite to be Christian and those that might be adjusted to the cultural locality of the mission field and particular denominational expectations. Mission science is an effort to decide the terms of conversion from where people were spiritually before to where the missionaries want them to move immediately.

Highlighting the processes of missionary work demonstrates the strategic schematics of conversion. If inculcating catechismal lessons and cajoling the memorization of creeds are the tedium of mission labor, then its magic is found in the transition from one position to another. The dark subject—native, indigenous, unchurched—is brought to the missionary's cosmopolitan, civilized, and converted light. In the late twentieth and early twenty-first centuries, corporate outsourcing and off-shoring of professional services have formed a new sort of foreign mission, unfolding development projects as accessories to corporations' exported industries.

Harpo, Inc., tracks this pattern of globalization, superseding the provincial borders of Winfrey's native nation-state, foisting the O brand as a circulating object of the new international economy. This occurs as a virtual globalization through the international broadcast of the daily television show and a literal globalization through her philanthropic outposts. This creation of satellite operations echoes not only the contemporary globalization of American brands abroad but also the globalization of U.S. religions, especially the "enchanted internationalism" of contemporary evangelicalism.[1] Evangelical church growth and international missionary operations develop from unabashedly merchandizing metaphors, promising transformation, emancipation, and revitalized selves through the acceptance of a converting product.[2] Like the modernity in which they are complicit, these evangelicals promise a new economy belief premised on a renovation of the old.

Nothing is cleanly operative in their or Winfrey's missionary maneuver. Alongside headlines about globalizing industry, Winfrey's documentation of the Oprah Winfrey Leadership Academy for Girls—on a prime-time special, her daily television show, her Web site, and in multiple issues of O, The Oprah Magazine and O at Home—supplies transparency to the oft-privatized American activity of gift giving. This outsourcing has precedent that isn't merely economic. It is no coincidence that this woman, an African American woman, has found her purpose, her "life's work," in such a colonizing return to an ancestral site. It is also unsurprising that her focus is on the promise of young women to embolden the future of the race. African American activism—especially that organized by Christian institutions—has always emphasized conversion and missionary growth, refiguring the native convert not only as a new Christian but also as a new member of the black bourgeoisie.[3] "The present-day problem in missions is to reach the great central power in society, the mothers and home," announced the black missionary Mrs. Moses Smith at an ecumenical conference of 1900. "Only a woman can break the Bread of life to women. Logically, it follows that the agency through which this can be done is the most far-reaching and certain force the Church has for the redemption of the race."[4] Smith names women as essential agents of that "most far-reaching and certain" network, missions. Missionary success and devoted missionary women have a longstanding complicity, because gender formats the shape and content of missions while missions in turn also reinstate gender norms of the domesticating religions. Black Christian women joined missionary endeavors to upend images of the primitive while also prescribing a womanly refinement bent on upright domesticity.

Winfrey is, in her language, "on a mission" to connect people to the practice of giving. Winfrey gives gifts (of information, of object, of inspiration) as a way to propel more missions. "I am proud of how we evolved from a TV show to an hour filled with purpose and intention," Winfrey explains in an interview honoring her twentieth season. "The show is a force for good. Good information. Good entertainment. Goodwill."[5] This goodwill is used to propel makeovers, legitimatize female consumption, and foster a universalizing discourse of spirit that will connect the diversity of her audience under a common banner of reformative ambition. Everything in Oprah's world is connected to everything else, with the dreams of new businesses and better marriages linked explicitly to the self-care of better desserts and detergents. In the discursive landscape of Harpo, Inc., a "mission" is a category that connects the giving of an under-the-seat present ("everybody in the audience is getting a computer!") with her giving of grand philanthropic games ("everybody in the audience is going to give back!"). Everything in Harpo is ringed with the truth of earnest Spirit, no matter its commodity function. The mission isn't the mandate; your heart is.

Changing the hearts of others to see the light of her abundance has been a central trope of Winfrey's storybook celebrity. Throughout her public career, Africa has always been on her mind. In April 2002, South Africa was the site of the first international edition of O, The Oprah Magazine. Cathleen Black, chief executive of Hearst Magazines, said of the choice of South Africa for the first overseas edition of O, "It seemed like a natural for Oprah to do this in a country where opportunities for women are just beginning."[6] The donations to South Africa did not conclude with this print culture intervention. She would hold three ChristmasKindness parties in 2002 for nearly fifty thousand children from Soweto, Durban, and Umtata. These gift-filled tent revivals caused her to connect, finally, to her ultimate mission. "I realized in those moments why I was born, why I am not married and do not have children of my own. These are my children. I made a decision to be a voice for those children, to empower them, to help educate them, so the spirit that burns alive inside each of them does not die."[7] Indeed, Winfrey would subsequently claim a genetic tie to the Zulu people as further endorsement of her righteous role in that nation's development. Like previous African American sojourners to Africa, Winfrey cast herself as a part of a diaspora of blackness that needed, inevitably and inexorably, to return home to Africa in service of those not as lucky as her. The descendant of slaves was now returning to her continental origin to compel the unconverted.

The Angel Network also contributed to the renovation of the Seven Fountains Primary School, a school in KwaZulu-Natal. "When Oprah first visited, the school was in a building with no heat, limited running water and electricity, four toilets, dirt floors, no playground and broken windows," intones the writers of the "O Philanthropy" Web text. "Despite these conditions, close to 1,000 eager children attended school." Proceeding through documentary photographs, Web surfers learn that "before the school's makeover, the children were often forced to learn in overcrowded classrooms . . . some students used cement blocks as desks . . . some worked outside on chairs, having no desk at all." According to the Web site, the trouble with the school is material, not spiritual. These students and their teachers have everything they need but the goods. In partnership with the KwaZulu-Natal Department of Education, Oprah's Angel Network funded the construction of a new facility at a cost of less than two million dollars in American money. "We spent the same amount of money that the government spends on all the schools. That's what we wanted to say—with this kind of budget, this is what you can do," Oprah explained triumphantly.[8] Beauty isn't a matter of money, Oprah intones; beauty is a matter of care.

And nobody offers care like Oprah. A scan of the marketed philanthropies of Winfrey and Harpo, Inc., leaves the viewer overwhelmed by the parties and prayers prescribed for women's possible improvement. "In postmodern colonialism, control of land or political organization or nation-states is less important than over consciousness and consumption," legal scholar Susan S. Silbey explains.[9] The O insignia is embroidered on every African action, every photograph documenting the Oprah Winfrey Leadership Academy for Girls, and every girl's backpack, threading Winfrey's company with her charismatic touch, her before-and-after transformational promise. The O ornaments inorganic products with the organic biographical experience of Oprah. Winfrey counters any academy doubters with her own biography. "My own success has come from a strong background in reading and learning," she declares. "The greatest gift you can give is the gift of learning."[10] The crown jewel in her philanthropy is, therefore, the leadership academy itself. "We are going to change the face of Africa," Oprah explains in her voice-over on her prime-time special *Building the Dream*. "All dreams start from the core," and Africa, she says, is "the root" of her. From three thousand applicants she selected fewer than three hundred students to open this boarding school for grades seven through twelve, located in Henly-on-Klip, about forty miles outside Johannesburg. Set on twenty-two acres and spread over twenty-eight buildings, the complex exports the Winfrey urban aesthetic to a pastoral fantasy. The academy features oversized rooms done in beiges and browns with a yoga studio, a beauty salon, indoor and outdoor theaters, hundreds of pieces of original tribal art, and sidewalks speckled with colorful tiles. "This is a school for leaders," Oprah says. "This is a school for powerful girls who will use their power in service to their nation and to our world."[11]

Using funds from the Oprah Winfrey Leadership Academy Foundation, teams of educators, architects, interior designers, artists, bricklayers, and painters created what Oprah calls "an atmosphere of possibility."[12] Despite the strong talk of leadership and nation, the focus of her advance exhibition is the reprinting of product and object, and not people or pedagogy. John Lardas Modern describes this phenomenon among antebellum evangelical missionaries, writing, "In their 'system-atizing mania,' antebellum evangelicals sought to create, maintain, and manage the conditions of circulation." Like the early-nineteenth-century missionaries as described by Modern, Harpo, Inc., produces a "proce-dural logic of stagecraft" by which the "spiritual good of the masses" is advertised.[13] Glossy images of the academy's production illustrate the grandeur of the effort. Illustration and exhibition have long been com-ponents of the missionary home tour, calling new believers to the cloth and the foreign pulpit. In the materials promoting the academy, much is made of Winfrey's academy's aesthetics over and above its curriculum or its guiding instructions to its new residents.

Harpo, Inc., emphasizes Winfrey's role as a designer more than any other aspect of her discretion. "Beautiful environments inspire beauty in you," Winfrey suggests. "I said, from the start, I am creating everything in this school that I would have wanted for myself—so the girls will have the absolute best that my imagination can offer."[14] Her Web site, magazine, television programming, and carefully managed publicity unrelated to Harpo repeat her controlling hand in every design decision. "Every single thing that you see here was chosen by me for you because I care so much about you," she tells the girls as they tour their new school.[15] "Every tile, every doorknob, has been Oprah's specific choice," explains her Web site. "Oprah made decisions that ranged from the buildings' softly curving contours to the school's classic yet kicky uniforms and included the fine-art and crafts pieces . . . as well as the lighting fixtures, bathroom tiles, linens, rugs, chairs, and hardware," writes a Harpo reporter.[16] Viewers are led to believe that no aspect of the academy's production escaped the sieve of Oprah's civilizing taste. "'Some cups feel better in your hand than others. . . . I love *this* one for them,' [Oprah] says, holding it. She chooses white plates, and flatware with a thinner, more feminine handle. 'They're little girls,' she reminds us."[17] No part of the building process was beneath her discrimination. "Oprah sent the original brick samples back three times because they were, well, simply not the color she had in mind," reported an *O at Home* journalist. "They were too institutional-looking," Oprah observed, ultimately selecting a "honey-colored brick that turns a gorgeous gold at sunset and works well as part of the multilayered surfaces of stone, ceramics, and etched glass that make all 26 academic buildings on the 22-acre campus look solid and sound yet [are] colorful and approachable."[18] This is no corporate campus from a multiple-choice design scheme. This is personal, loving, and particular. This is *Oprah* love, selected by her for her sweetest subjects.

Viewers can also partake of these Santa Claus pleasures. The online Oprah Winfrey Leadership Academy Foundation Registry allows fans to contribute to building the dream. The registry displays three categories of potential purchase: "Girls' Life" (for $100, "girls will feel proud to wear the complete Leadership Academy uniform a blazer, skirt, shirt, socks and shoes"); "Classroom" (for $150, "give the gift of knowledge with a year's worth of textbooks for math, English, science, history, and other courses"); and "Wellness and Creativity" (for $20, "nurture the girls' visual arts talent and creative expression"). More expansive donors could support an entire year of a girl's education for $15,000. An online "shopping basket" and range of purchase options allow the donors to feel as if they are contributing building blocks to the school. However, this is a mock exercise. Purchasers are warned: "Donations do not go directly to girls but to The Oprah Winfrey Leadership Academy Foundation that operates the Oprah Winfrey Leadership Academy for Girls–South Africa. Your donation selection is subject to change. It will, however, go toward the Foundation's efforts where needed most."[19] The shoppers' dollhouse fantasy is strictly virtual. In the real exchange of dollars and goods, Oprah is Oz.

Flashbacks in her prime-time special *Building a Dream* emphasize the material contrast between academy students' point of origin and their newfound Oprah bounty. Their preexisting poverty is conveyed through vivid portholes. See the tiny one room for a four-member family; wince at the sight of a single narrow bed for two children and three adults; observe the cluttered outhouse to which girls must walk for nighttime constitutionals. These details are not disconnected from the broader image empire of O. Frequent consumers of Oprah experience the echo of other episodes devoted to thread counts, organization strategies, and scatological self-observation. Watch enough Oprah and you know there is no such thing as healthy clutter or happy crowding. Oprah's American audience luxuriates daily within the digestive, nocturnal, sartorial, and psychological practices Oprah prescribes. However, the African girls have no such purchase prospects. "At home I sleep on the floor and it's really, really painful especially when it's cold," described one student. "But in the dorm we sleep on the bed and the bed is so very, very soft." These girls are not just lacking objects. They lack Oprah goods, which are, by their very source, prescriptions for not only a stylish self but also a holistic salve of self. "You girls are worth it," Oprah remarks as she gestures to a gymnasium that has, for a day, been transformed into a shopping spree.[20] The academy is a forty-million-dollar exhibition of accessories.

Such material redressing is no surprise to the *Oprah* viewer; Winfrey has made herself famous through her benevolent peddling of dreams and goods. But at the level of international patronage, the cleansing and remaking of native subjects carries a dubious legacy. Missionary photographs from the nineteenth and early twentieth centuries illustrate the Christian pride taken at the exchange of indigenous garb for three-piece suits. Whether the indigenous under consideration are the Sioux of the American plains or the Kru of Liberia, the converted minority stares back at us from history, made proper by a colonial etiquette and the Sears, Roebuck and Company catalog. "There is no wrong question," Oprah declares at the outset of the opening night feast. "Place the napkin in your lap, and use the fork on your left."[21] The similarities between Oprah Winfrey's African adventures and the history of Protestant missions are no mere Emily Post parallels. She repeats the same comparative processes and gendered patterns as her Protestant predecessors.

Missionary work has always been the purview of American women. When the first five representatives of the American Board of Commissioners for Foreign Missions (ABCFM) departed for India in 1812, three were accompanied by their wives. This incorporation of women—albeit as assistant, not yet free-standing missionaries—was a domestic turn for American missions, which had, in the seventeenth and eighteenth centuries, been dominated by famously antiestablishment men. Yet women won the missionary demographic day. In 1861, a group of women founded the Women's Union Missionary Society, an independent, interdenominational mission board run by women for the purpose of sending single women out as missionaries. By the late nineteenth century, women emerged from the confines of their marital status to become full-blown Christian laborers.[22] Certain social facts may be culled from the last century and a half of missionary labor: women made the most effective missionaries; educational institutions anchored mission success; and the conversion of women and children prefaced the mass conversion of nations.

As nineteenth-century women's groups founded their own journals to disseminate missionary intelligence to their constituencies, a common missiology emerged known as "Woman's Work for Woman." The proponents of this theory assumed that non-Christian religions led to the degradation of women, while Christianity provided not only salvation but also civilization, the nineteenth-century term for social liberation. "The emphasis on social change toward western norms, couched in the language of helping to bring about God's kingdom on earth, made

'Woman's Work for Woman' a partner with the myths of western supe-
riority so prominent during the late nineteenth century," writes Dana
Robert.[23] Civilizing and evangelizing were one and the same for missionary women in their advocacy of sewing practices, sanitation techniques, and childcare tactics within the confines of prayer meetings and
Bible studies: "A mission theory based on the Christian home made little
practical distinction between spiritual and physical needs, or between
mind and body."[24]

Simmering within this practical application of spiritual transformation were very real divides of race. Missionary labor was, in the case
of Africa, always linked to racial reconciliation. In the first half of the
nineteenth century, Protestant missionaries to Africa were energized in
part by the possibility of black repatriation. According to its supporters,
resettlement in Africa served, in the words of the Presbyterian General
Assembly of 1832, two important aims: "to provide the people of colour
an opportunity to escape from the oppression which they suffer in this
country . . . and for the introduction of Christianity and civilization into
that benighted continent."[25] Black and white missionaries alike imagined the salvation of Africa as advancement for free blacks in the United
States who might arrive, en masse, to the converted shores of Ethiopia,
Liberia, and the Congo. Fantasies of nations without racism flourished.

No matter the racial composition of the missionary relationship,
however, it was predicated on a fundamental difference between the
proselytizers (white or black) and the proselytes.[26] This difference was
an inequality. "The prejudice that assumed the necessity of transforming
proselyte populations in the first place belied the inclusive promise of
evangelical Christianity," writes Derek Chang. By naming "uplift" as the
initiating premise, missionaries presupposed an uneven exchange.[27] For
Oprah, the nature of the generous act presupposes an insufficiency. But
she would be the last proselytizer to suggest that the proselytized are
spiritually lacking. Indeed, as she repeats in her multimedia promotions,
these girls give to her as much as she gives to them. From her reading of
their "wise" faces and "brave" souls, Oprah translates spiritual content
equal to any American acolyte. "For Oprah, it is not the native child
who is a degenerate," explains Zine Magubane. "Rather, it is the system, produced largely by adult white men, that is itself degenerate and
operates to produce and reproduce the image of the Black woman and
child as hopelessly degraded."[28] For Oprah, the postcolonial colonizer,
the only fair inequality to posit—the only reason to justify her philanthropic presence—is material inequality. These girls may have wisdom

greater than any faraway bureaucrat or invading missionary. But they don't have yellow tiles or Body Shop soaps to line their cluttered outhouses. And this donation is where Oprah's mission begins.

"For better or worse, for centuries America has been invested with symbolic, even religious, meaning and significance within the human geography of the world," asserts David Chidester.[29] From Coca-Cola to Microsoft, our exports are not mere product placement but teleological declaration. Now, instead of cardboard boxes bearing Nikes, we have Oprah Winfrey's cursive O labeling T-shirts and book bags, lampshades and pencils, for the distribution to hungry daughters-to-be, 'round the world. The commodity deserves sacred regard, Oprah suggests, because of her divine care in its selection and because of her omnipotent certitude that through this abundance the girls will know her love. This prescriptive practice reverberates throughout her empire. The products selected for Winfrey's monthly "favorite things" catalog, "the O List" ("a few things Oprah thinks are great"), connect spiritual meaning with the application of a joyful consumption. Pertinent for this examination of her missionary endeavors is that these products, advertised monthly in her magazine, rarely come from locations outside the United States. "The O List" produces an O American aesthetic that is less indigenous eclectic than ornate *Town & Country* classic.

Editors sequester the objects modeling Winfrey's taste for postcolonial celebration—those imported through the global boutique network of fair-trade ethnicity—on their own pages, proximate yet separate from the "the O List." Such style exclusives mirror descriptions deployed by all women's style magazines for spotlighted accessories, elevating a surprising combination of aspect and object to the embossed heights of signifying glamour. The O version of these features capitalizes on the female stories underlying geopolitical complexity. "The O Bracelet," for example, was "designed specifically for O magazine and handbeaded by women in Rwanda and Zambia." The premise of the purchase is outlined with blended psychological panache: "Let's just assume (A) you know that women in Africa face a pileup of hardships—serial rape, AIDS, illiteracy, hunger, poverty, genocide. (B) You care and would like to help, although *how on earth* is the daunting question. (C) If we changed the subject to jewelry—hey, catch that sudden glint of spirit, the lift of pleasure? Without doubt, tiny bits of shimmer and color release slaphappy chemicals in the brain. (Science will prove it; you watch.)" The practice of purchase advocated by Winfrey achieves here climactic global effect, beginning with an abstract political worry (what to do about serial rape and genocide), transitioning to a helpless flail in searching for a specific action *(how on earth),* and ending with a quick distraction by something pretty. Uncomfortable feminists, be at peace (the narrative proceeds). We aren't girls who just want to have bauble fun. We are girls distracted by a slaphappy spiritual glint around which anyone could rally. The article hawks, "So may we twist your arm into slipping on one of these bracelets?"[30]

Careful economic practice suffuses the advertising annotation. "One hundred percent of the profits on these bracelets go to the women, who are employed full-time for the duration of the project." This woman's work was designed by Mary Fisher, "the well-heeled suburban mother from a prominent family who stunned the country in 1992 by announcing at the Republican Convention that she was HIV-positive." Mary's story proceeds predictably apace: her ex-husband, who infected her, died, but Mary "hit life running," spending time in Africa working with AIDS victims who are "blown away to meet a white woman with the disease, much less one sitting on the ground next to them, talking frankly and trading crafts skills. In Rwanda they call her *Mirarukundo*—'full of love.'" In Africa, Mary connected with the head of Fair Winds Trading, Willa Shalit. Willa, who, we're told, is "called *Uwacu,* meaning 'ours,'" provided the market for the product. "To complete the circle," the article concludes, "there's you: We hope that wearing an O magazine bracelet will make you feel good—and that you'll feel even better knowing how it's improved the life of the woman who made it for you. Call it an ethical luxury. A conscientious indulgence. If nothing else, it's a really good buy."[31]

Globalization is frequently sighted by scholars and activists as a homogenizing force, exporting a singular global culture of McDonald's and Starbucks to make the world in a largely American image. Critics of this view of homogenization reply that the incursion of multinational corporations creates it own polarizing effects, in which local cultures counteract. Interconnectivity does not, they argue, force uniformity. It is more popular, then, to speak of the hybridizing consequences of globalization, in which syncretic forms emerge from collaboration.[32] "The O Bracelet" translates these debates in multiple ways, simultaneously selling a universal brand in its O form and name, collaborating with multiple agencies and individuals, and bracing any nervous critics of the assault of polarization with the chummy insert of native naming practices. Mary is "full of love" and Willa is "ours": these women are the global economy of Oprah. "Nothing, arguably, is as important today in the political economy of development as an adequate recognition of political, economic and social participation and leadership of women," writes Amartya Sen.[33] The narrative of triumphant women overcoming disappointing men (men, say, who infect them with AIDS), befriending other women (sister to sister, hands across an ocean), to "hit life running" as leaders of a new globalized economy of female empowerment and missionary purpose, suffuses Oprah's propositional empire. Every fissure is sealed with squatting talk about crafts, and every confusion is alleviated by purchase. The moral is assured as the advertisement-as-article concludes: "If nothing else, it's a really good buy."

This "nothing" is noticeable for its dance with the Africa it seeks to represent. Every aspect of the O bracelet, save for the mechanical labor of the beading, is managed by Americans, even as it is an object draped with the virtue of an organic Africa. In order to preserve that Africa, the Africa of Winfrey's ancestry, the Africa that is the home of these beautiful girls, one must buy these bracelets exclusively at Macy's. This is not the first time an Africa has been packaged and programmed for an American audience. In their efforts to assay the meaning of Paul Simon's Grammy-winning multiplatinum album *Graceland* (1986), ethnomusicologists have sought to discern the appropriating quotient of Simon's African infusion.[34] Through his use of melodies, instruments, and singers and other musicians native to cultures that were not his own, did Simon engage in a "benign, perhaps even beneficial act of hybridization"? Or was this "exoticism for the sake of novelty"?[35] White South Africans celebrated the album, writing that Simon "has filtered the [South African] sound with his own style, lyrics and Western influence to concoct a colorful collage which, while retaining its Afro elements, makes them less raw, more flowy, more gentle. And most pleasant!" By contrast, the African National Congress leader Walter Sisulu called on South African artists not to "become the old spit in Paul Simon's mouth, something that he has swallowed and is now reproducing according to his own taste." If *Graceland* alerted white South Africa to the profitable sublime of black South African expression, then it also encouraged the appropriation of black music by white South Africa "as a means of establishing a White African (as opposed to colonial) identity."[36] Jacqueline Warwick speaks plainly of the discomforting tug of *Graceland*: "Surely we should also be concerned with the consequences *within Western society* of representing a relationship in which a famous American male can insert himself as a soloist over the music of 'township' bands."[37] Because Simon accounted repeatedly for the Senegalese and South African inspirations upon which he drew, *Graceland* cannot be understood as a naive aestheticism. Simon and Winfrey share a seemingly resolute amenability to the contradictions of their composite signs, propagating into the marketplace products that promote Africa, promote themselves, and promote the production of themselves (as artists, as cosmopolitans, as donators, as spiritual servants) as comfortably African.

These goods are presumptively positive products, offering contracts to local labor and educative products to faraway shopping malls. It was surprising, therefore, that the American obsession with possessions is what forced Oprah from inner-city Chicago to the Gauteng Province. "I became so frustrated with visiting inner-city schools [in the United States]," Winfrey told one reporter. "The sense that you need to learn just isn't there. [In America] if you ask the kids what they want or need, they will say an iPod or some sneakers."[38] She, like so many before her, found the perceived asceticism of her chosen natives appealing because it contrasted with the excesses of her resident nation. But who is to blame for this American excess, for the materialism of her deplored inner-city students seeking iPods and sneakers? Any answer to that question must include a citation of the ultimate gift giver, the one with the Pontiacs and holiday Favorite Things bonanzas. Winfrey's endless donations are labeled liberatory, and indeed they may be so. But encoded within this uplift from shanty to starry schoolhouse is a soteriology worth noting. In 1832, Sarah Lyman, missionary wife to the Sandwich Islands, explained that the best way to get any message across was not to force it in antagonistic dialogue but to present it in preexisting institutional contexts, adding that, believing as they did, "the way to convert a nation was to give them the Bible in their own language and that the easiest way of getting it into circulation, was to introduce it into the schools."[39] Getting the Bible or the O in through the school is one way to convert a country to a more modern clarity.

Giving a gift—in the form of money, institutions, or military occupation—is one thing Americans do best. We are now so committed to an ideology of gifting that it seems impossible to conceive of a world outside such objecthood, to imagine what could be worrisome about the export of an O. From paparazzi photographs to magazine advertisements, the main impression of America abroad is that we are a nation of appearance, not substance. For Winfrey, a spiritual message is sealed within this shiny wrapping: the right goods can make a right person, constructing an exterior that the interior can later fulfill. Sociologist Nick Stevenson places this in the context of what he defines as cultural citizenship.

"Cultural citizenship," he says, "can be said to have been fulfilled to the extent to which society makes commonly available the semiotic material cultures necessary in order to make social life meaningful, critique practices of domination, and to allow for the recognition of difference under conditions of tolerance and mutual respect."[40] Does Winfrey's philanthropy produce such reciprocal exchange, elaborating tolerance and mutual respect through the postulation of a global culture?

Oprah's every philanthropic encouragement resolves with the basic act of purchase, of choice, of careful selection. "Remember, every little bit helps, so whether you buy someone lunch or buy them a car, you are changing lives," her Web site cajoles. Recommendations for individual service are oriented entirely around expenditure; "buy" is the persistent imperative. "Buy lunch for a homeless person," suggests Oprah. "Buy a board game for a local children's hospital; buy school supplies for a needy school; buy pet food and supplies for the animals at the pound; donate iPods for soldiers serving in Iraq; buy a new wardrobe for kids in need." Service and social life, politics and economic realities: all are obscured beneath the impermeable power of purchase. "Any emancipatory movement that tries to fashion a new, coherent identity," writes one transnational observer, "carries with it its own repressive agenda."[41] Even in the exhilarating high of new accessories and personal missions there are ties that prevent us from perpetual revolution.

No one perhaps knows this better than Oprah herself, who in the months leading up to the January 2007 academy opening revealed some anxieties about her philanthropic ventures:

> Shortly after I arrived in Chicago, I started a mentorship program for teenage girls living in the Cabrini-Green housing projects. I was able to work with them only once a week, which wasn't enough time to instill values in girls whose upbringing wasn't aligned with my teachings. I had to end the program. Months later I came up with the misguided idea of moving families out of the projects and into new homes. Trying to show people how to build successful lives was overwhelming—I had taken for granted that they understood what it means to go to work, be on time, and make sure their children go to school and do their homework. So I failed with that idea, but I learned something invaluable: In order to make meaningful changes, you have to transform the way people think.[42]

Once she had learned that the family makeover was a "misguided" strategy, she turned to the practices of transformation. Not before further mistakes, however. In another column, she relates a similarly failed enterprise, describing how in 2002 she "adopted" ten children, ages seven to fourteen, who had no parents or family. She enrolled them in a private boarding school and hired caretakers to track their progress. Her surprise visit to these children was again narrated in her monthly claim "What I Know for Sure":

> I walked in and surprised them—they had no idea I was coming . . . when I sat them down in the living room for a conversation, everyone's cell phone kept going off—the latest "razor" phone that costs about $500. And the inner spark I was used to seeing in their eyes was gone, replaced by their delight in their rooms full of things. Most of the girls had long, braided hair extensions flowing down their backs—too much hair under baseball caps shading their eyes. No one felt comfortable to speak. And they could barely look me in the eye. I think they felt embarrassed. They could talk about what they owned—the latest portable PlayStations, iPods, and sneakers—but they couldn't speak of what they'd done.[43]

Winfrey describes a painful scene of the arrival of the benefactor and the flaccidity of her beneficiaries. Characteristic Oprah sins pockmark the description: lack of focus, failure to supply eye contact, physical appearance blocking the emergence of a "true" interactive self. Hair is a prominent theme in Oprah adjudications; indeed, a component of her applicant terms for the leadership academy is hairstyle. "Her requirements are stringent," wrote an O magazine reporter: "no pregnancies, no drugs or alcohol; hair must be short or neatly braided."[44]

What, then, does Oprah conclude from this encounter? As with the Cabrini-Green families, she comes to understand something troublesome about all this giving. "I knew immediately that I'd given them too much, without instilling values to accompany the gifts," she wrote. "What I now know for sure is that a gift isn't a gift unless it has meaning. Just giving things to people, especially children, creates the expectation of more things."[45] And yet, it seems she is unable to stop herself, compulsively shopping for her South African venture. Citing her own childhood poverty in segregated Mississippi, Winfrey argues against advisers who encouraged a more pared-down leadership academy. She resists such counsel, posing it as ascetic condescension to the equally deserving. "Planners advised that these African children were not accustomed to much. . . . Oprah was told that the simplest environment would be a luxury to them, that they would need only basics," explains a January 2007 article in O, The Oprah Magazine. "She sent the plans back." A Newsweek journalist offered Oprah's elaborated version of this exchange: "From the very beginning, the developers sent me plans for the school that resembled a chicken coop," she says. "It was clear that the attitude was 'These are poor African girls. Why spend all this on them?' It was unbelievably upsetting."[46] The *Newsweek* reporter quoted a South African government official explaining that the government had retracted its support of the project because "the academy was too elitist and lavish for such a poor country."[47] Although the government of South Africa may have resisted Winfrey's excesses, the people of South Africa have not. Since the arrival of Winfrey, her entourage, and her school, reportage of her ventures has been celebratory. She has become a hero to the public and a heroine to African women.

In part, Oprah has been embraced by the populace precisely because she is, in her passionate institutionalizations, counterinstitutional. Oprah's response to the government's description of the academy was typically self-assured: "I understand that many in the school system and out feel that I'm going overboard, and that's fine." For Oprah, circumstances are simultaneously determining and inconsequential. Oprah declares that her costly wraps and gargantuan spectacle are precisely what, after so many years of suffering, her subjects deserve. Yet her own biography contradicts the aspirations she has for her students. No fairy godmother interceded in her oppression, molestation, or teenage pregnancy. She seeks to give her African daughters the advantages—dolled up, dressed to the nines—that she lacked. She seeks to be the gift around which their changes will, inevitably and prescriptively, revolve.

Conclusion

Shanell: Oprah for me is God.

Bebe: No, no, no, no, you can't say that. I'm a spiritual person.

Shanell: No, no, no, Oprah is responsible literally for me originally when I lost over sixty pounds of my weight.

Bebe: You were that big?

Shanell: I was 217 . . . I was 42 inches around. And it is literally because of her show, and her inspiration, that I lost all of that weight.[1]

In some circles of the American academy, some circles of religious America, and some circles of bourgeois America, the discussion between Bebe and Shanell, contestants on the 2009 season of Logo Network's *RuPaul's Drag Race,* might cause a minor bit of stomach churning. The reasons for the indigestion are multiple, but one of them might be called the intensity of their shallowness. Is weight loss guidance reason enough to name your inspiration a god? When everything is sacred—later Shanell also refers to the singer Cher as "a god"—how can anything be? The relentless personalism of these two drag queens would seem by such a critical gaze an aggrandizing celebration of one sort of self at the expense of a nation. Once upon a time, the story goes, this was a nation of self-critical arbiters. Now we know more about waist size than we do about scripture or about creeds. It was somehow better then, and it is definitely shallower now, shallow with an intensity that breeds reality programming, Second Life online identities, and the career of *American Idol* host Ryan Seacrest.

"Nostalgia is best defined as a yearning for that which we know we have destroyed," David Blight has said.[2] Nostalgia is probably something much crueler: it is that which we believe someone else has destroyed, leaving us alone with ourselves and alone with these corrupted queens. Tales of recent religious history have struggled to decide where we are, now, whether it is a time of bleak solipsism or potlatch jubilee. For critical observers both inside and outside academia, the verdict seems to lead more toward the dour. "The very texture of modern life is inflected by loneliness," one observer suggests.[3] Facing the loneliness of a perceived loss, of a dissipated critical world, scholars often consign the body-obsessed pop idols to the spittoon of cultural embarrassment.[4] Yes, these people exist, but let us not let them say too much on our behalf.

But they speak. They plead. They name her, Oprah Winfrey, as Their God. What would he, Shanell, be without her? What meaning carries that lost weight? Scholars remain irresolute on the matter, as they cannot seem to decide whether to affirm or decry the agency of the consumer or the dreams of self-actualization. Susan Douglas, for example, has pursued the ways that a certain form of narcissism emerged in the Eighties—the era of Oprah's ascent. She describes how this discourse encouraged women to break away from Seventies feminism, to "forget the political" and "get back to the personal." In this environment, one body part became the symbol of this newly liberated woman. Namely, "the perfectly sculpted, dimple-free upper thigh and buttock." It was the Eighties, Douglas reports, that gave us "perfect thighs" as an achievement and a product, one that exhibited just what women had made of themselves. The idealized "buns of steel" bore no marks of age, instead showcasing how the thigh-sculpting ladies were able to be "both competitive workaholics *and* sex objects, to be active workers in control of their bodies *and* passive ornaments for the pleasure of men, to be hard-as-nails superwomen *and* vulnerable, unthreatening teenage beach bunnies."[5]

Into this pursuit of cellulite-free legs, Oprah Winfrey's productions insert an additional imperative: as you shape, be sure, too, that you feel better. "Psychological tests show that our sense of who we are is deeply connected to how satisfied we are with our bodies and that women are, in general, most dissatisfied with their hips, thighs, and buttocks," O magazine guest writer Veronica Chambers attests. "In other words, if we don't like our bottoms, we're not likely to accept ourselves." Alongside that encouragement of self-acceptance is a quartet of modeling shots offering "how to get firmed, toned, and profoundly uplifted" through squats, lunges, and leg lifts.[6] Atop Douglas's profile of thighs befitting a supermom, a super sex kitten, and a super aerobics instructor, Winfrey says, sure, sure, sure, but I just want you to feel good. Do you? Don't you? If not, why?

Against the protests of her many admirers, then, and against the easy subjugations of her cultural critics, we conclude with a worry over the reproduction not of an Oprah transformation but of an Oprah trap. Watching the *Oprah* show presses viewers into an inspirational overdrive, in which at every turn they are encouraged to take care of themselves, nurture themselves, and sculpt their best lives in an immediate inspirational Now. What does it mean to need to feel good, now? Yoga teacher and performance artist Robyn Okrant began a blog in 2008 devoted to living life according to Oprah Winfrey's recommendation. "I wonder," she asked at the outset, "will I find bliss if I commit wholeheartedly to her lifestyle suggestions? Would the costs of living as Oprah prescribes . . . be worth the results?"[7] Okrant received abundant media attention because she seemed to embody the curiosity of an audience outside Winfrey's sway, showing the world the interior world of O consumption. Okrant delivered daily blog entries with self-critical delight. "With some of the things, like the clothes, in the beginning I was like, 'How dare she tell me what to wear! I'm an individual!' But recently, when I went shopping with my mom, I was really excited to fulfill some of the rules. I felt kind of proud of myself. It takes a huge amount of pressure off to be handed a spiritual path." Okrant quickly journeys from resistance to submission to relief, finding a "spiritual path" that guides her through a morass of clothing options and liberates her from the oppressively high standard placed by the modern possibility of an original individuality. Now that she is part of a path, though, she can't help but succumb to some of the shared malaise of her new community. A *New York Times* reporter explains, "A self-described tank-tops-and-jeans girl, Ms. Okrant has become hyperconscious about her appearance." Her husband, Jim Stevens, remarked, "I hear her comparing herself to something she saw on television, commenting on the way a piece of clothing fit or didn't fit." Elsewhere, he emphasizes the daily self-scrutiny: "We have a daily conversation about the way she looks now that wasn't there before." Winfrey had, Ms. Okrant admitted, gotten into her head, and "that self-consciousness, it doesn't just turn off." The gift exchange is painful, but she can't decide if it's fair or not. Letting Oprah think for her is, after all, a bit of a relief: "I haven't had to decide what book to read, what exercise to do, what movie to see, in a long time."[8] The great thing about an Oprah trap is at least it gives a girl a break.

In the introduction, I argued that Oprah is a way to survive the secular. The secular is not an absence of religion; rather, the secular is religion's kaleidoscopic buffet. Religion is so much of a choice, and life seems so much of a choice, who can possibly know what next, where next, or how next to do, to see, or to be? "In my 15 years or so of dealing with people and their dysfunctions, day in and day out," says Winfrey, "I've learned that the word that most defines this decade, even this century, is disconnect."[9] Psychologists John T. Cacioppo and William Patrick agree, writing, "As individuals, and as a society, we have everything to gain, and everything to lose, in how well or how poorly we manage our need for human connection."[10] In the loneliness of daily disconnection and the paralysis of abundance, Oprah pervades with selective, incorporated, reliable, ritual regularity. She soothes as she sifts. "What this magazine does," she explains, "is reconnect people to what deserves priority and to bring meaning to their lives."[11] So, see *that* movie. Buy *that* car. Transform into *this* sort of woman. And feel good about every little piece. As Aaron Curtis has written about Robyn Okrant, this is a *practice*, since individual women choose not only to "relinquish" their "power of choice" but also to commit "to a faithfully neutral obedience." Curtis points out, however, that in being so very submissively "orthodox," Okrant commits an Oprah heresy. Oprah never says you have to do anything. What you do, as well as who you follow, is your choice.[12] She never claims to have the answer; what she has is *her* answer. Your job is to connect your best you with the life you deserve to have.

Because of this "flexodoxy," Winfrey is frequently collected with other easygoing spiritual purveyors, sequestered in one section of the local bookstore and one paragraph of textbooks on American religion. Our attention in religious history remains arrested by sectarian religions, those "real" religions of tax-free status and worship halls, even as believers insistently testify to their proudly hodgepodge identities. Dismissed from the ranks of serious scholarship as spiritual ephemera and from the ranks of serious society as women's notions, the dominating corporations of popular culture expand their realms of moral arbitration and ritual regulation without serious explanation from the academic ranks. And so, we wake up to warnings; for instance, "If you don't brand yourself," readers of the *New York Times* were recently warned, "Google will brand you."[13] While we're being branded, religious studies scholars huddle at the level of the adherents and congratulate them for their stalwart stay in whatever creative configuration they compose. Scholars of American religion will need to add to their survey more than the blaring data of tax-exempt religiosity if ever they hope to explain the totality of religion in modernity.

This is, however, more than a historiographic itch. Studying Oprah suggests more than historical revisions for an exclusive enclave of admirable cultural observers. The haunting figure of the disconnected individual and her reduced waist leads us beyond religious studies and into the very problem of modern subjectivity. Whatever neoliberalism is or isn't, whatever postmodernity has or has not provided, whatever capitalism will or will not become, we must agree that one of the great success stories of Oprah's years has been the complete conversion—the conversion of a nation—to consumption as the adjudicating determinant of our relative freedom. The results of that consumption have acquired an axiomatic valence, for the makeover has become mandatory. Even at the beginning of a global economic crisis, Oprah held one of her Favorite Things episodes and CNN reporters breathlessly detailed Michelle Obama's wardrobe for her 2009 European tour. Ridding ourselves of our national affluenza will take more than foreclosures and depleted retirement funds.[14] It will require new formats to make practicable new instantiations of the social self. For now, however, we are, from all available evidence, trapped in makeover dreams.

Why, then, if it is so expensive and harrowing, do we watch it? "Watching Oprah does fill you with hope. It also plunges you into despair. She has become something like America itself."[15] In America we find Oprah; in Oprah we find America. This is hope wrapped in despair wrapped in hope wrapped in despair. And "it is this plot, the plot of optimism for the iconic *thing*," writes Lauren Berlant, that "must go in for radical surgery."[16] The procedure will not be easy, since we are, by now, prepared only for that optimism. We know well enough how to play to happiness, yet we are less generous, less capable, and less creative when it comes to despair. "Americans know from an early age how they're supposed to look when happy and what they're supposed to do or buy to be happy," Philip Slater writes. "But for some reason their fantasies are unrealizable and leave them disappointed and embittered."[17]

That "for some reason" is, as we have seen, in no small way due to our obsession with the ritual return to change, with our national belief that change itself—born again, away from fatherlands, father figures, mother churches, mother countries, and any and all family ties—is the American calling.[18] This is the change we can believe in, the one we chant and emboss in our first person. I know I can change, I believe we can change, I know it, I know it, I know it. We believe this in order to dream a dream of individuation, the dream that apart from it all, from the oppressing them and the mean-spirited they, we may find our own volition, our own better way. We conceive of ourselves as better off when composed of bullet-points on a social networking site than we ever were when bound to a past, to a history, to anything that limits the sovereignty we won, the sovereignty we self-supply. This, then, is our calling not merely to change as the grand individual *I* but also as our magisterial, civilizational deflation as an *Us*. "Her inability to understand how someone as wealthy and powerful as she is can feel so overwhelmed, helpless and in peril captures, in miniature, the nation's free-floating angst," writes one recent commentator.[19] Her taste is her product, but her failure is her profit, since her incapability (she's "just like us!") is what makes her not merely tolerable but inspirational. She too stands up, in her big, magical shoes, day after day. And she does it saying the same thing, squealing the same O. The question is not why we watch her but how she does it, how she can bear to stand, considering the cost of the footwear and the promised connection it never sustains.

Still, the search for "the why" is compelling. As I have written on Oprah's empire—on the rituals of her book club and her makeover shows, on her preacher precedents in U.S. religious history, on the sort of spirituality she inscribes on her Soul Series and in her Change Your Life TV—I have repeatedly heard two replies. The first is from academic colleagues, curious about my topical choice: so, this is your first book, they squint, pressing me—implicitly and directly—to explain just how a scholar of American religious history has come to a contemporary subject from that most profane place, talk show TV. The second reply has been equally confounded, although narrower in its stare. It has come from audience members, always women, wondering what I am doing to this woman, to *their* Oprah. I am not alone in this experience; any time an article on Oprah appears in any magazine, readers respond in her defense. No matter the content of the motivating piece, viewers feel compelled to underline the reality of an Oprah experience, to remind us, as one wrote, "I feel empowered and inspired when I view Oprah's show."[20] One viewer posts to a message board, "I am never 'taken in' by Oprah, and instead when I do watch I am usually glad she is using her influence for essentially Good Things. I don't get why some people seem so angry at her. If you don't like her, don't watch her show."[21] I have encountered less outrage than these replies may infer, but no less passion, as listeners request that I relinquish all critical posturing and agnostic safe havens and give it to them, for real. "But how do you *feel* about her?" has been the repeated refrain. Do you like her? And if not, if you don't like her, how can you not? How can you try to take from me the one thing, the one thing that helps me, hugs me, returns to me, and *sees* me?

My reply to these two inquiries has been the same: I am studying what we're watching and what it consistently conveys.[22] For the field of religious studies, such critical attention is one way we sidestep the pieties of our objects in order to discern patterns in those traditions, sects, scriptures, and rites that correlate to other cultural objects. I conduct this particular act of scrutiny because it tells us about how religious forms are configured by and through the modern moment. From this investigation, I have found that whatever distinguishing marks we make between commodities and religion, they are, for all practical purposes, arbitrary. Our consumption and our religiosity can be described only in their infectious, ritual commingling, both in their distribution and in their consumption. *Oprah: The Gospel of an Icon* demonstrates this through one product, a product that possesses acclaimed omnipotence and proclaimed omniscience. To study *any* product is to study an icon that will and does tell us, over and over again, not only to buy it but also to believe it and to believe in it. The subject is worthy of many books—from books speaking to the differences between cotton swabs and Angelina Jolie, from Ford sedans to Cheerios, the iconic brand subjects are infinite. Yet any descriptive iconic survey will return to the same point, to the inseparability of consumer choice and religious option in the modern period.

Dissatisfaction with such a reply abounds. Fine, fine, fine, the listener responds, I can believe that, I suppose. But still, they wonder, *why?* Why do we buy this thing and not that one, and why do we believe this idea and not that one? Why is Oprah the product being purchased, rather than anything else? Why do we need her so much? This book names what we're watching, but only intimates, through its emphasis on its religious invocations, the why.

Epilogue

Political Spirituality, or the Oprahfication of Obama

First, you need a name. Not just any name. An unusual name: a biblical misspelling, maybe, or an invocation of some distant land. No matter what, the name needs an O. The O will come in handy when you need to summon a common sphere, encourage chanting, or design an expansive logo. Never deny the utility of its replication, never avoid its allusion, and never miss an opportunity for its branding.[1] An O is a space anyone can fill with anything.

Second, you need a life. Not just any life. A life that is ready to be a story, prepared for metaphor, assembled in advance by memoir, by professional mode or by fictional expectation. If Aaron Sorkin or Alice Walker is not available for its incantation, you must be prepared to tell your story yourself again and again, mentioning its familiar bits like tired icebreakers to loosen the uncomfortable, the unfamiliar, and the closet racists. It helps if you can redistribute your tale by media cultures, through Web sites, television specials, and periodicals. The more you say it, the more it will become the new normal. Advertise your chronological or genealogical messiness: the hardscrabble youth, the absent parent, the nonnuclear family, the experiments with drugs, the cultural patois that produced your singular self. Tell the story as if it is utterly improbable that it happened, even as you knew, you knew from the beginning, that you were destined. Your small, sweeping, rural, urban, abusive, tender, confusing, and familiar tale of ascent is what they have been waiting to hear. The American Dream is no conjure. It is you.[2]

Third, you will need a crew. Not many people, just enough to create a familiar inner circle of stand-up, saucy influences. A truth-telling African American female intimate is a must. So is a tall, experienced white man. Whereas the white guy can be crass, even obnoxious, the woman must learn when to be silent, to relax her hair, and to look fantastic, always. Keeping great people nearby is important, because you will often feel alone. Being alone is strange, since it is your burden to be that which nobody can dislike, which everyone wants to be near. Prepare yourself: this is an exhausting sort of friendliness. Rick Warren and Gene Robinson must feel comfortable next to you. Starlets and statesmen must respect you. Bill Cosby must like you. White women need to feel safe with you. Homosexuals must love you, even as you sometimes co-opt their affections and ignore their causes. Resist the temptation to call old friends who may infect you with toxic associations. Celebrate mothers and family but steer clear of feminists and fathers. Mourn the loss of midcentury America, even if it was the America that segregated you. Assign a family life you never had; endorse the nuclear your childhood biography belies. Eschew race reification but cultivate black institutions early. Their loyalty will supersede your betrayals. Develop an iconography of African American bookshelf notables. Connect personally with Africa. Connect with Peoria. Connect with the Bronx. Vacation on the Pacific Rim but live in Chicago. *Be* Chicago. Attend Jeremiah Wright's church. Use the music of U2 and Stevie Wonder and any high-spirited, progressive-friendly country you can find. Get a dog.[3]

Fourth, you will need a style. This developed manner will help you endure some hard knocks. Inevitably, some people will call you the Antichrist. Others will call you a sellout. Some will call you a cult leader. Take these assaults with nonchalance. Make criticism about you seem silly, cynical, even bigoted. Through it all, master the encompassing hold, the sense that you are accessible to everyone. Yet retain an incommensurable mystery. Keep people guessing: Does she mean it? What does he really believe? Some will regard this as an admirable capaciousness, while others will see it as a shallow equanimity. No matter. You will counter those claims with discipline, with consistency, with extraordinary prescience.[4] You will confound expectations over and over again. Your mistakes will be translated as incidentally brilliant. You will possess a preternatural ability to give people what they want, to know what they need, to sell what they will buy. Prepare yourself for the resultant sale of yourself. You have to get over any anxieties about your own assimilation, incorporation, and amalgamation. Be the commodity. Put your O everywhere. Your iconography is how they brace against the disappointments of your humanity.

Fifth, you will need to be ambivalent. You have always been neither here nor there, neither us nor them, and neither of nor outside. You have always been able to see from many perspectives, to appeal to many sorts of people, to believe many different things. You do so even as you are fiercely moral, upstanding, and almost pious. You are, as everyone knows, a Protestant. But you dabble in everything, never shying away from the Koran or kabbalah, Jewish professors or Eastern spiritual advisers.[5] You will entertain anything that might embolden your O. You are the ambiguity of your epoch, the middle that makes the mass, the crossroads of a country that excited your youth, raped your ancestral continent, and claps now for your beautiful children. You are a global distribution suffused with spiritual truth. You are motivated with missionary zeal to convert everyone, unrelentingly, to change. You make them believe their best lives are yet to come. You make it impossible to look away, to hate, to dissent, or to change the channel. You make us feel good, finally. You are our redemption.[6] You are our favorite smile. And you are our satisfaction at the possibility of a Spirit that made it all so.

As I wrote those words in the days before the inauguration of Barack Hussein Obama, the world seemed to be in a state of perpetual postcoital sighing.[7] After a two-year bated breath, a nation of new believers could, finally, exhale: We did it, they hummed; it has happened. Hope lives. Diversity thrives. America *is.*

Historians make lousy politicians, and religionists make even dodgier prophets, but from the minute Barack Obama took a Springfield, Illinois, stage and said, "I am as you are," it seemed more plausible than not that he could run the game. Those resistant to his possible victory were in part protective of his symbolic meaning. Yet the statement "no one will ever elect a black man president in America" was made often by observers who would, absolutely, vote for a black president. "I'll admit that when Obama first entered this race, my jaded friends and I rolled our eyes," reported one writer in the *Washington Post,* explaining that they reflexively "doubted the humanity of the people he needed to convince in order to win."[8]

The nation waited nervously, watching the romantic comedy play out. Typical intervening problems ensued, including appearances of several stock archetypes. There was the shadowy figure from the past, offering information to threaten the relationship; the dorky but superprepared gal competitor, reminding the audience that in love, good people get hurt; the disturbingly uninformed but superhot girl, reminding the audience that looks can be deceiving; and the grumpy old wiseacre man, the one with the story of torturous times and more socioeconomic sway. In the end, he's the one who contorted the most and did, with his old heroism and aching body, hit home a taste or two of guilt. But those are the breaks. Love isn't love if it hasn't met reasonable alternatives and turned them down; if it hasn't heard some tough things and moved beyond; if it hasn't seen the darker side of human sadness and felt redeemed. Any good requited love story requires the looming sense of its own implausibility in order for the release, for that final embrace to feel so won. They did it, you smile in the dark theater; they beat them all. Yes, we can. Yes, we can. Yes, we can.

Rimming the route to Oz was our Glinda, the divine Miss O. She was there, if occasionally hidden from view. Sometimes she preached before a podium, proud. Other times, she joined the masses, with tears streaming down her face. Her varied positions reflected her own multivalent occupations, as she simultaneously played cheerleading promoter, platinum donor, and average voter. She repeatedly refused credit for his success, saying that it wasn't anything she had done. His Spirit had permeated the masses, she said, and this spirit reminded people not only of who he was but also of what they could be.

The relationship between Oprah Winfrey and Barack Obama is not only the relationship between plug and product, between the endorser and the endorsed. It is more: it is a correlation between two products that format themselves in strikingly similar ways. Oprahfication describes a type of commodification in which the personal is commercialized and spiritualized through confessions, conversions, and popular showcases of pluralism. Any subject, once Oprahfied, does not talk about structures and systems. Instead, he or she tells stories and solicits yours and, from those particulars, distills generic slogans of change, of spirit, of the now. Describing Obama as "Oprahfied" emphasizes that the nation was readied, in part, for receipt of him by her.

Despite Winfrey's domineering symbolic heft on behalf of and in service to her nation, the presidency has never been seriously considered by her. When an interviewer asked Oprah in 1997 if she'd consider a run for the presidency, her reply was, "Television is more powerful than politics."[9] Embattled Illinois governor Rod Blagojevich, desperate for any distraction from his prosecutor's glare, considered offering Barack Obama's vacated Senate seat to Oprah. "She was obviously someone with a much broader bully pulpit than other senators," he told *Good Morning America*.[10]

In reply to these needful compliments, she flicked away political life like a minor orbiting moon of a distant planet. What she did was more potent than elected office, she said. She had more freedom and more regular access to regular folks than any DC insider. Yet this disinclination toward electoral politics should not suggest that she is apolitical. As demonstrated by the work of Janice Peck, Winfrey's project possesses political consequences and political descriptions even as it evades political issues. Since the switch to Change Your Life TV, Winfrey has avoided debates on abortion and gay marriage, choosing instead to spotlight the difficulties facing young mothers and the happy lives of "out" fashion designers. Her 2001 episode on war encapsulates her emphasis. "As we all face here the possibility of war and question whether it is a choice we should make here at our crossroads in humanity, it is important, I think, to realize and to remember what the real face of war is," she announces before a montage of children in war-torn countries. "What it looks like, what it feels like, and what it does to humanity."[11] Never a politico like her talk show predecessor (and personal hero) Phil Donahue, Oprah finds her strongest sway by the hearth and in the home. Donahue was to liberalism what Oprah is to neoliberalism, with his assembling of debates and her assembling of affects. Directing readers, consumers, and voters to focus upon the domestic and the sentimental is an emphasis with a long political genealogy. The Oprah difference is to remind any viewer—Democrat or Republican—that priority one is care not of politics, not of other people, but of *you*. Care of nation will radiate from that self-nursing.

Her Change Your Life TV ferried politics from legislative bickering to pastel portraits. In the 2000 and 2004 elections, she interviewed each of the major party candidates separately and evenly. Prior to those elections, she had not interviewed candidates because she felt she could not discern their truth. "I've interviewed thousands of people over the years, but until today I've stayed away from politicians, really for one main reason: I—I—I never felt like I could have a real, real honest conversation with—there's this—kind of this wall that exists between the people and the authentic part of the candidate."[12] Now, in the twenty-first century, after Change Your Life TV, she could sit there with them, face to face. After all, through her self-produced spiritualization and subsequent multimedia expansion, she had become any president's equal. The only question left was to wonder on whose side she stood. People suspected from her pet issues that she is a Democrat; people guessed from her income bracket she is a Republican. But no one knew for sure what her electoral preferences are. Then, in 2004, she saw Barack Obama give his address at the Democratic Convention, and she said to herself, "I think this is the One."[13] In 2008, she broke her voting silence and committed to limited campaign appearances and major fundraising efforts on his behalf. Her repeated rationale for her entrance into this election was how perfectly Obama meshed with her ideal of the singular self. "I don't consider myself political, and I seldom interview politicians," she would repeat. "So when I decided to talk with [Obama], people around me were like, 'What's happened to you?' I said, 'I think this is beyond and above politics.' It feels like something new."[14] Obama was a candidate she believed transcended the pettiness of a two-party system to meet her in her undivided O.

Voting viewers predicted hers would be an influential endorsement. "I think Oprah is John the Baptist, leading the way for Obama to win," observed one Iowa caucus voter.[15] On the other hand, some media reports suggested that this endorsement cost Winfrey some Nielsen points, that she had expended her most valuable gift, her opinionated neutrality. Whatever costs there were, none diluted her own sense of product clarity. The endorsement of him, against all Nielsen tugs, proved again that the product was not the manipulation of market researchers but was hers and hers alone. Obama was, like the items on "The O List," another thing that Oprah thought was just great. That greatness has no podiums or positions. Like a purse, an ice cream flavor, or an Oprah's Book Club selection, Oprah's presidential nominee was an extension of her partiality as her brand. It also turned out that, as with most everything else, her taste was her nation's preference.[16] He won.

Now Oprah and Obama are names locked into documentary fusion. Forever, they will be the double Os in the textbook, famous for what they are and for what they have done with the telling of who they are. "What Obama did, he's run as an American who is black, not as the black American," Colin Powell observed. "There's a difference. . . . He ran honestly on the basis of who he is and what he is and his background, which is a fascinating background, but he didn't run just to appeal to black people or to say a black person could do it. He's running as an American."[17] This is an elision of the truth, since Obama ran as a conscious color palette, as a man whose conjure of his colors has defined his manhood and cosmopolitan citizenship, shaping and naming and infusing his every motion. To Oprah, he would say, "I had to reconcile that I could be proud of my African American heritage and not be limited by it," and she would reply, "That's now my favorite Barack Obama quote!"[18] In the naming of no limits, in the making of self black but not broken, not bitter, not sad, and not trapped, Obama became, as political scientist Ross K. Baker would remark, "the post-polarization candidate," just as "Oprah is a post-polarization celebrity."[19] They find themselves, united, in a compromised civility that their corporate merger supplies.

The question of this book has been to describe just what this merger is. In a lecture at the New York Public Library, novelist Zadie Smith spoke about the voice she grew up with in the London district of Willesden and the voice she "added" when she went to Cambridge. For a while, and sometimes still, she has slipped back and forth between her dialects. But now she says, "This voice I picked up along the way is no longer an exotic garment I put on like a college gown whenever I choose—now it is my only voice, whether I want it or not. I regret it; I should have kept both voices alive in my mouth." Smith admires the way Barack Obama has had "more than one voice" and the way he has used this plurality to posit himself as a Dream City, a collective space for people from nowhere to find themselves, finally, somewhere cool, somewhere that celebrates who they are now rather than who they were from wherever weird place they came. "Throughout his campaign," Smith continued, "Obama was careful always to say 'we.' He was noticeably wary of 'I.' By speaking so, he wasn't simply avoiding a singularity he didn't feel, he was also drawing us in with him. He had the audacity to suggest that, even if you can't see it stamped on their faces, most people come from Dream City, too. Most of us have complicated back stories, messy histories, multiple narratives."[20]

The key pronoun is the repeated *we*. This collective supplies a seeming contrast between Oprah and Obama, since Winfrey rarely speaks of a "we," instead reiterating the authority of her "I." This is because Oprah believes that her "I" represents the "we." Oprah is, in this way, more exterior than Obama in her incorporations. She knows that what she is building is a consensus invented through her taste, a postulated "we" designed expressly for *us* by *her*. Obama, on the other hand, seeks to name common values that are not personal—even as his life story exhibits them, even as it is his particular "I" that he advocated in his election. He names the "we" but steers away from his "I." "We're not as divided as our politics would indicate," he says. "You meet with the average person—I don't care if they're Republican, Democrat, conservative, liberal—they don't think in labels, they're not particularly ideological, everybody is sort of a mix of what you might consider some liberal ideas, what you might consider some conservative ideas. But there is a set of common values that everybody buys into: Everybody thinks you should have to work hard for what you get, everybody believes that things like equal opportunity should be real, not just a slogan."[21]

. What are those common values? Smith's praise of Obama's Dream City invites real questions about the connection between campaigning and governing, between advertisement and application. Estimations of Obama's policies are still to come. What is pressing for this work is the problem of the common, for an *I* or a *we* posited to be you and me. It seems that the representative value of Oprah Winfrey and Barack Obama is in part their ability to name a collective that seems permeable and plural while also restricting it, bounding it by values and rules that won them their place in the pantheon of American ascent and assimilation.

The lessons become clearer. How now to Oprahfy yourself? Make your past, your peculiarity, your irreconcilability into a garnish for your J. Crew cardigan. Take the hard stories from before and capture them in an amulet that you string about your neck and color-code with the outfit assembled for your long day. Toss the sari over your shoulder to reveal the navy knit sheath beneath. Fling a father's abandonment onto a bookshelf smartly arranged to exhibit the bibliographic array. Nab the childhood abuse and smack it into a sound-bite submission. This isn't Victorian curio containment, nor is it ribald plurality. This is collage collected carefully by scrapbook handbooks that tell you which wardrobe item to keep (the always classic Oxford shirt) and what to relinquish (Mama's unloving gaze), which memory to encapsulate and which to let go. This is how you, too, can become an icon.

This is not a new dream. Obama is, as many have said before, a familiar sort of savior, offering a recognizable call for national, personal, and spiritual change. We have tried before to release ourselves from precedent, and we have tried through many men to redeem ourselves.[22] We have also tried in our rituals, our theologies, our purchases, and our makeovers to rid the world of ethnic rumbling and to sleek our motley collectives into productive social calm. What makes Obama different is that he is so very good at it, at the talk and the modeling, the dreamscape and the productivity, that he convinces us, better than anyone before, that we should feel good about the costs of his incorporations. Feel good because we do, in the final hour, want to feel what he proposed. We want to be inspired. We want to feel good. We want to know change over and against the messes that we know we can never contain and will never stop making. At the appointed hour, the television is on, and we wait, humming and hoping for the same spirit, again. Only time will tell just what we lost when we threw ourselves, so eagerly, into him, into her, into the stores and wars and speeches and serials that form the flames of this, our modern revival.

Notes

INTRODUCTION

1. "Doing the television show is easy. I just go on and be Oprah." Oprah Winfrey, quoted in Terry Lawson, "The Long Road to 'Beloved,'" *Detroit Free Press* (October 11, 1998), 1E. "There [is] no authentic Winfrey; there [is] the image of Winfrey's authenticity." Jane Shattuc, *The Talking Cure: TV Talk Shows and Women* (New York: Routledge, 1997), 57.

2. "Listing of Full Trademarks," www.oprah.com/article/oprahdotcom/trademark.

3. This "megatextual structure" of the show is the focus of Eva Illouz's *Oprah Winfrey and the Glamour of Misery* (New York: Columbia University Press, 2003). Like *The Glamour of Misery, Oprah: The Gospel of an Icon* focuses on the textual productions of Winfrey's empire to discern "cultural forms" from her televised processes of recovery. Illouz emphasizes psychological transactions and audience reception to incisive effect in the analysis of viewer identity formation: "Oprah addresses those arenas that are most ridden with uncertainties and offers powerful symbolic tools and rituals to alleviate those uncertainties. She stages in an unsurpassed way the profound disarray in which the late modern self is caught and offers resources to cope with it" (115). Illouz's culling of Oprah's "sources and resources" as well as her perception of Winfrey's "commercial ubiquity" influenced this research (178–205, 221).

4. Oprah Winfrey, quoted in Barb Galbincea, "Oprah's Surprise at Tri-C Fund-Raiser, Winfrey Stuns Crowd with Pledge to Match about $600,000," *Plain Dealer Reporter* (November 9, 2002), 1A.

5. For renditions of this transitional moment, see Cecilia Konchar Farr, *Reading Oprah: How Oprah's Book Club Changed the Way America Reads* (New York: State University of New York Press, 2005), 29–30; Illouz, *Oprah Winfrey and the Glamour of Misery,* 125; and Janice Peck, *The Age of Oprah: Cultural Icon for the Neoliberal Era* (Boulder, CO: Paradigm Publishers, 2008), 4–6, 39. For characterizations of this moment in talk show television, see Vicki Abt and Leonard Mustazza, *Coming after Oprah: Cultural Fallout in the Age of the TV Talk Show* (Bowling Green, OH: Bowling Green State University Popular Press, 1997); Linda Grindstaff, *The Money Shot: Trash, Class and the Making of TV Talk Shows* (Chicago: University of Chicago Press, 2002), 21–24; and Horace Newcomb, ed., "Talk Shows in the United States," in *Encyclopedia of Television* (New York: Firzroy Dearborn, 2004), 2260–62. For Oprah's particular position within this context, see Jane Shattuc, "The 'Oprahfication' of America? Identity Politics and Public Sphere Debate," in *The Talking Cure,* 85–110.

6. On the overarching therapeutic bent of the talk show genre, see Kathleen S. Lowney, *Baring Our Souls: TV Talk Shows and the Religion of Recovery* (New York: Aldine de Gruyter, 1999); Julie Engel Manga, *Talking Trash: The Cultural Politics of Daytime TV Talk Shows* (New York: New York University Press, 2003); and Joanna Thornborrow, "'Has It Ever Happened to You?' Talk Show Stories as Mediated Performance," in *Television Talk Shows: Discourse, Performance, Spectacle,* ed. Andrew Tolson (Mahwah, NJ: Lawrence Erlbaum Associates, 2001).

7. Kathryn Straach, "Oprah Can Play in Amarillo until the Cows Come Home," *Dallas Morning News* (January 18, 1998), 6G; Paul Katel, "Winfrey Wins Burger War in Texas," *USA Today* (February 27, 1998), 3A; "Oprah Says Amarillo Experience 'a Blessing,'" Associated Press, Amarillo, Texas (March 2, 1998). "Rarely mentioned is the fact that the lawsuit was essentially one megacorporation suing another megacorporation, a war between corporate business giants each attempting to protect their bottom lines," writes Jennifer Richardson in "Phenomenon on Trial: Reading Rhetoric at *Texas Beef v. Oprah Winfrey,*" in *The Oprah Phenomenon,* ed. Jennifer Harris and Elwood Watson (Lexington: University Press of Kentucky, 2007), 181.

8. Quoted in Bill Adler, *The Uncommon Wisdom of Oprah Winfrey: A Portrait in Her Own Words* (New York: Carol Publishing Group, 1996), 76.

9. J. Randy Taraborrelli, "The Change That Has Made Oprah So Happy," *Redbook* 189:1 (May 1997), 94; Caroline Jeffs, "Oprah Comes to Greencastle," *DePauw University Wire* (September 19, 1997); Dana Kennedy, "Oprah: Act Two," *Entertainment Weekly* (September 9, 1994), 20.

10. Wendy Parkins, "Oprah Winfrey's Change Your Life TV and the Spiritual Everyday," *Continuum: Journal of Media and Cultural Studies* 15:2 (July 2001), 145–57. The relationship between Oprah and the late-twentieth-century political economy has been mapped by Peck in *The Age of Oprah.* "Winfrey's journey to a position of singular cultural authority has to do with the fit between the neoliberal strategy of governing and her configuration of self, illness, and technology of healing" (39). Peck's excoriation of the particulars of Winfrey's deployment of suffering and racial politics devastates any liberationist interpretation of the Oprah project: "Her enterprise can be understood as an ensemble

of ideological practices that help legitimize a world of growing inequality and shrinking possibilities by promoting and embodying a configuration of self compatible with that world" (217).

11. Quoted in Jessica Madore Fitch, "The Rich List: Oprah Winfrey, 46," *Chicago Sun-Times* (October 29, 2000), 6.

12. Quoted in Latonya Taylor, "The Church of O," *Christianity Today* 46:4 (April 1, 2002). For more on the religious structures of talk show transformation, see Lowney, *Baring Our Souls.*

13. Oprah Winfrey, "What I Know for Sure," *O, The Oprah Magazine* 10:11 (November 2009), 236.

14. "Perhaps no other corporate entity was better positioned than Winfrey to capitalize on this spiritualization of the brand. . . . Winfrey's image makeover in the 1990s was not simply a personal endeavor but a financial one; her ascent to the position of 'prophet' paralleled a meteoric rise in her profits during the same period." Peck, *The Age of Oprah,* 190. "The spiritual concerns that began to shape *The Oprah Winfrey Show* in 1994 not only enhanced Brand Oprah, but also served to unify the proliferating extensions of the brand." Trysh Travis, "'It Will Change the World If Everybody Reads This Book': New Thought Religion in Oprah's Book Club," in *Religion and Politics in the Contemporary United States,* ed. R. Marie Griffith and Melani McAlister (Baltimore: Johns Hopkins University Press, 2008), 502.

15. The sweeping process of contemporary mass marketing has been explored by George Ritzer, *The McDonaldization of Society* (Newbury Park, CA: Pine Forge Press, 1993). See also Mark Alfino, John S. Caputo, and Robin Wynyard, eds., *McDonaldization Revisited: Critical Essays on Consumer Culture* (Westport, CT: Praeger, 1998). David Chidester has studied the religious aspects of this globalized marketing; see "The Church of Baseball, the Fetish of Coca-Cola, and the Potlatch of Rock 'n' Roll: Theoretical Models for the Study of Religion in American Popular Culture," *Journal of the American Academy of Religion* 64:4 (Winter 1996), 743–765, the ideas of which are expanded in David Chidester, *Authentic Fakes: Religion and American Popular Culture* (Berkeley: University of California Press, 2005), introduction, chapter 1, and chapter 2, 1–51. On the Oprah Winfrey Network, see Robert Kolker, "Can Oprah Escape *Oprah?*" *New York* (March 29, 2010): 26–31.

16. Alex Kuczynski, "Winfrey Breaks New Ground with Magazine," *New York Times* (April 3, 2000), C15. Says one Harpo insider: "She owns the show; she owns the production company; she owns the studio; and now she owns a major part of the distributor." Quoted in Paul Noglows, "Oprah: The Year of Living Dangerously," *Working Woman* (May 1994), 52. When Oprah negotiated the contract for 1999–2000, she was granted options to purchase five hundred thousand shares of King World stock at an exercise price of $39.31. Winfrey already had options to buy 1.55 million shares. The deal made Winfrey the largest holder of King World shares, and she now owns as much as 5 percent of the company. Martin Peers, "Update: Oprah Speculation Dents King World Stock," *Daily Variety* (September 3, 1997), 1.

17. Oprah Winfrey, "What I Know for Sure," *O, The Oprah Magazine* 4:7 (July 2003), 186.

18. J. Heath Atchley has described the secular as something like this, as a "kind of silence—the inability to speak, the lack of a promise of revelation." He defines secular in this way so as to move "the secular from merely a condition to a concept that produces thought, that is, becomes part of a philosophical practice . . . imagine a philosophical sense of the secular as neither a triumph (we have overcome the irrationality of religion) nor a lament (we have lost the meaningfulness the religion once gave) but an opportunity." Atchley, "The Silence of the Secular," *Literature & Theology* 21:1 (March 2007), 67.

19. Lynette Clemetson, "Women of the New Century: It Is Constant Work," *Newsweek* (January 8, 2001), 44.

20. "Leave it to Winfrey to have a trademark on the letter that's the symbol for the element of oxygen; it's as if she owned the very air we breathe." Nancy Franklin, "Oprah's World," *New Yorker* 84:6 (March 24, 2008). "Oprah Winfrey is way past merely rich and famous. She's more on the order of, oh, say, ubiquitous. Or peripatetic. Or mega." Stephen Rebello, "Brand Oprah: Connecting with 20 Million 'Customers' a Day," SuccessMagazine.com (May 1998).

21. John Lardas Modern has named secularism as a form of common sense: "I use the analytical category of secularism to encompass a field of tropes, styles, and sensibilities that not only generated a particular distinction between the religious and the secular but also made this distinction a matter of common sense." Modern, "Evangelical Secularism and the Measure of Leviathan," *Church History* 77:4 (December 2008), 806 fn. 21. He attributes this to particular processes of religious media: "Evangelical media practices have instantiated secularism as a matter of common sense" (870). Earlier, Clifford Geertz sought to divide common sense from religion and each of those from the secular. "The religious perspective differs from the common-sensical in that, as already pointed out, it moves beyond the realities of everyday life to wider ones which correct and complete them. . . . It is this sense of the 'really real' upon which the religious perspective rests and which the symbolic activities of religion as a cultural system are devoted to producing, intensifying, and, so far as possible, rendering inviolable by the discordant revelations of secular experience." Geertz, "Religion as a Cultural System," *The Interpretation of Cultures: Selected Essays* (New York: Basic Books, 1973), 112. See also Clifford Geertz, "Common Sense as a Cultural System," in *Local Knowledge* (New York: Basic Books, 1983), 73–93. Geertz's dichotomy is shown to be overly determined when pursuing the "really real" products of these "discordant revelations."

22. Akhil Gupta and James Ferguson, "Beyond 'Culture': Space, Identity, and the Politics of Difference," in *Culture Power, Place: Explorations in Critical Anthropology*, ed. Akhil Gupta and James Ferguson (Durham, NC: Duke University Press, 1997), 37.

23. S. Paige Baty, *American Monroe: The Making of a Body Politic* (Berkeley: University of California Press, 1995); Erika Lee Doss, *Elvis Culture: Fans, Faith, and Image* (Lawrence: University Press of Kansas, 2004); Wayne Koestenbaum, *Jackie under My Skin: Interpreting an Icon* (New York: Plume, 1996); Robert Miklitsch, *From Hegel to Madonna: Towards a General Economy of "Commodity Fetishism"* (Albany: State University of New York Press, 1998); Stephen

Prothero, *American Jesus: How the Son of God Became a National Icon* (New York: Farrar, Straus and Giroux, 2004); Gilbert B. Rodman, *Elvis after Elvis: The Posthumous Career of a Living Legend* (New York: Routledge, 1996). With his posthumous following, Graceland pilgrimage site, and impersonators, Elvis supplies the strongest parallel to an Oprah. While he (and his estate) did much to foster his mythology and inscribe his iconography, they did not seek to solve the problems of those who cathected his icon.

24. Debates over who could be Oprah's inheritor only serve to show how particular is her position. "Replacing Oprah," *Showbiz Tonight*, CNN (November 19, 2008). The strongest nominee is Tyra Banks, a candidate who shares some of Oprah's business savvy and down-home sauce but none of Winfrey's epic public suffering. Lynn Hirschberg, "Banksable," *New York Times Magazine* (June 1, 2008); Adrienne P. Samuels, "Tyra Banks: The Frugal Stylista," *Ebony* 64:2 (December 2008), 76. Other options have emerged, including most recently a profile that nominated actress Gwyneth Paltrow as a successor, because of her nascent interest in "lifestyle" advocacy. Bob Morris, "Martha, Oprah . . . Gwyneth?" *New York Times* (February 21, 2009).

25. Famous industrial founders (Andrew Carnegie, J. Pierpont Morgan, Leland Stanford, John D. Rockefeller) dominated the nineteenth-century economic landscape and the twentieth (Michael Eisner, Steve Forbes, Bill Gates, Rupert Murdoch, Sumner Redstone). By the late twentieth century, the pursuit of starry outside management was typical practice, if heavily criticized within academic business circles. Rakesh Khurana, *Searching for a Corporate Savior: The Irrational Quest for Charismatic CEOs* (Princeton, NJ: Princeton University Press, 2004).

26. Ken Lawrence, *The World according to Oprah: An Unauthorized Portrait in Her Own Words* (Kansas City, MO: Andrews McMeel Publishing, 2005), 16.

27. "Whatever religion 'is,' its definition seems to be thought to lie with others—with courts and practitioners—and not with the academic field charged with its study." Jonathan Z. Smith, "God Save This Honourable Court: Religion and Civic Discourse," in *Relating Religion: Essays in the Study of Religion* (Chicago: University of Chicago Press, 2004), 375. Thus, Oprah is not a "religion," because she does not pass the 14-point test supplied by the U.S. Internal Revenue Service, which seeks to identify groups that exist (in their words) "exclusively" for "religious" purposes. This is the line demarcating between those bodies that earn 501(c)(3) status and those which are considered "for profit." This book will show some parallels between that 14-point test and Winfrey's labors (including her possession of "a recognized creed and form of worship," "formal code of doctrine and discipline," "membership not associated with any other church or denomination," "ordained ministers selected after completing prescribed studies," "a literature of its own," and "regular religious services") to demonstrate how the legal definition of a "church" is not a description exclusive to a non-profit institution.

28. R. Danielle Egan and Stephen D. Papson, "'You Either Get It or You Don't': Conversion Experiences and *The Dr. Phil Show*," *Journal of Religion and Popular Culture* 10 (Summer 2005), 38.

29. For a lucid defense of spirituality against its condemnatory conflation with the market, see Leigh Eric Schmidt, *Restless Souls: The Making of American Spirituality* (San Francisco: HarperSanFrancisco, 2005), 282–90.

30. Works that organize their tables of contents by this trio include Eric Michael Mazur and Kate McCarthy, eds., *God in the Details: American Religion in Popular Culture* (New York: Routledge, 2001); Bruce David Forbes and Jeffrey H. Mahan, eds., *Religion and Popular Culture in America* (Berkeley: University of California Press, 2000); and C.K. Robertson, ed., *Religion as Entertainment* (New York: Peter Lang, 2002). To note the persistence of this drab categorical trio in these volumes is not to besmirch their contents; rather, it is to prod a shared intellectual concern about the "religion in" and "religion as" formulations, redacting religion as an isolated ingredient rather than a pervasive discursive formation. Moreover, it is to disassemble the unifying clarity of the category of religion in an effort to reduce its bounded framing in analysis of pop cultural objects. David Chidester has led the way in naming this trio as an academic habit and has supplied significant scholarship addressing the messiness of the third, namely, on the religious aspects of popular cultural production: "What counts as religion is the focus of the problem of authenticity in religion and American popular culture" (Chidester, *Authentic Fakes*, 9). For a model of the sort of cultural studies I encourage, see Susan L. Mizruchi, ed., *Religion and Cultural Studies* (Princeton, NJ: Princeton University Press, 2001).

31. "Commercial aspects of religion are traceable in any century," writes R. Laurence Moore, in *Selling God: American Religion in the Marketplace of Culture* (New York: Oxford University Press, 1994), 7. In addition to Moore's *Selling God*, Leigh Eric Schmidt's *Consumer Rites: The Buying and Selling of American Holidays* (Princeton, NJ: Princeton University Press, 1995) supplies a stunning cultural appraisal of a cyclical genre of contestation between ideas about religion and practices of consumption. The reference to pigeon sellers invokes Matthew 21:12, a source for much of the Christian anxiety about popular culture and its detrimental effects to the clarity of "Christian" spaces over and against worldly spaces.

32. Fred Goodman, "Madonna and Oprah," *Working Woman* (December 1991), 53.

33. Tom Gliatto et al., "So, Where's the Beef?" *People* 49:6 (February 16, 1998), 170.

34. Clemetson, "Women of the New Century," 44; Oprah Winfrey, "What I Know for Sure," *O, The Oprah Magazine* 9:8 (August 2008), 224.

35. Here I am suggesting that Oprah is a formation of the secular in the vein described by Talal Asad, in *Formations of the Secular: Christianity, Islam, Modernity* (Stanford, CA: Stanford University Press, 2003). Jeffrey J. Kripal's *Esalen: America and the Religion of No Religion* (Chicago: University of Chicago Press, 2007) offers a strong model of such an analysis.

36. Gil Anidjar, "Secularism," *Critical Inquiry* 31:1 (Autumn 2006): 52–77; John Lardas Modern, "Ghosts of Sing Sing, or the Metaphysics of Secularism," *Journal of the American Academy of Religion* 75:3 (September 2007): 615–50.

37. This is a phenomenon that Stanley Fish has labeled "boutique multiculturalism": "Boutique multiculturalists will always stop short of approving

other cultures at a point where some value at their center generates an act that offends against the canons of civilized decency as they have been either declared or assumed." Fish, "Boutique Multiculturalism, or Why Liberals Are Incapable of Thinking about Hate Speech," *Critical Inquiry* 23 (Winter 1997), 378.

38. Tracy Fessenden, *Culture and Redemption: Religion, the Secular, and American Literature* (Princeton, NJ: Princeton University Press, 2007), 4.

39. "Interview: Oprah Winfrey," Academy of Achievement (February 21, 1991), www.achievement.org/autodoc/page/winoint-1.

40. "Through the power of media," the Oprah.com authors describe, "Oprah Winfrey has created an unparalleled connection with people around the world. As supervising producer and host of the top-rated, award-winning *The Oprah Winfrey Show*, she has entertained, enlightened and uplifted millions of viewers for the past two decades. Her accomplishments as a global media leader and philanthropist have established her as one of the most respected and admired public figures today." In the case of her celebrated work, the reader can continue to track just how "unparalleled" Oprah is by scrolling "through photos and videos in Oprah's interactive biography," supplying as it does thumbnail sketches of her as (their categories) television pioneer, magazine founder and editorial director, producer/actress, online leader, philanthropist, television programming creator, and satellite radio programmer. www.oprah.com/article/pressroom/oprahsbio/20080602_orig_oprahsbio (accessed on February 4, 2009).

Also, another section is devoted to "honorary achievements," and here one is reminded that she was named (for instance) one of the hundred most influential people in the world by *Time* magazine in 1998, 2004, 2005, 2006, and 2007; received the 2007 Elie Wiesel Foundation for Humanity Humanitarian Award and the 2004 Global Humanitarian Action Award from the United Nations Association; received the 50th Anniversary Gold Medal from the National Book Foundation (1999) and the Association of American Publishers Honors Award (2003) and was named a Library Lion by the New York Public Library (2006); and garnered the National Freedom Award from the National Civil Rights Museum and earned a spot in the Hall of Fame for the National Association for the Advancement of Colored People, both in 2005. From her media origins, she has achieved recognition through the International Emmy Founders Award (2005), the Distinguished Service Award from the National Association of Broadcasters (2004), the Bob Hope Humanitarian Award at the 54th Annual Primetime Emmy Awards (2002), and the National Academy of Television Arts and Sciences Lifetime Achievement Award (1998), the last leading her to remove herself from Emmy consideration after winning more than forty Daytime Emmy Awards. This isn't to speak of the minor annual accolades from *TV Guide, Forbes, Newsweek, Ebony, Essence,* and so forth, naming her the most significant person in the multiple hues (television personality, philanthropic donor, celebrity, African American, woman, working woman, greatest human being alive) by which she has made her acclaim. www.oprah.com/article/pressroom/oprahsbio/20080602_orig_oprahsbio/9.

41. Theodor Adorno, *The Culture Industry* (London: Routledge, 1991), 93.

42. "In short, I would like . . . to search instead for instances of discursive production (which also administer silences, to be sure), of the production of

power (which sometimes have the function of prohibiting), of the propagation of knowledge (which often cause mistaken beliefs or systematic misconceptions to circulate)." Michel Foucault, *The History of Sexuality,* vol. 1: *An Introduction* (New York: Vintage Books, 1990), 12.

43. I borrow this application of Borges from Smith, "Bible and Religion," in *Relating Religion,* 209. See also Jonathan Z. Smith, "Map Is Not Territory," in *Map Is Not Territory: Studies in the History of Religions* (Chicago: University of Chicago Press, 1978), 289–310.

44. On agency and its relationship to the history of Protestantism, see Webb Keane, *Christian Moderns: Freedom and Fetish in the Mission Encounter* (Berkeley: University of California Press, 2007), 51–58, 193–96.

45. Thomas A. Tweed, *Crossing and Dwelling: A Theory of Religion* (Cambridge, MA: Harvard University Press, 2006).

1. PRACTICING PURCHASE

1. Joel Pfister, "Getting Personal and Getting Personnel: U.S. Capitalism as a System of Emotional Reproduction," *American Quarterly* 60:4 (December 2008), 1141.

2. "It is no accident that, when [tastes] have to be justified, they are asserted purely negatively, by the refusal of other tastes. In matters of taste, more than anything else, all determination is negation." Pierre Bourdieu, *Distinction: A Social Critique of the Judgement of Taste* (London: Routledge and Kegan Paul, 1984), 56.

3. "What is perhaps most undeniably proof of Oprah's extraordinary symbolic and economic power is the fact that she is able to re-brand a wide variety of products," write Eitan Wilf and Eva Illouz. "Oprah thus managed to recruit consumers into a continuous relationship that in turn made her into a successful brand." Eitan Wilf and Eva Illouz, "Dynamic Branding: The Case of Oprah Winfrey," *Women & Performance: a journal of feminist theory* 18:1 (March 2008), 73, 80.

4. Max Weber, *The Protestant Ethic and the Spirit of Capitalism* (London: Routledge, 1992), 177.

5. Ibid., 170.

6. Nicole Woolsey Biggart, *Charismatic Capitalism: Direct Selling Organizations in America* (Chicago: University of Chicago Press, 1990); Jean Comaroff, *Millennial Capitalism and the Culture of Neoliberalism* (Durham, NC: Duke University Press, 2001), 2.

7. Oprah Winfrey, "What I Know for Sure," *O, The Oprah Magazine* 6:12 (December 2005), 332.

8. Stephanie Clifford, "Infomercials Find Their Way to Television's Prime Time," *New York Times* (January 26, 2009); David Lieberman, "Pop Culture Pulls in Major Bucks," *USA Today* (April 16, 2008), 4B; Stephanie Clifford, "Product Placements Acquire a Life of Their Own on Shows," *New York Times* (July 14, 2008), C1.

9. *The Oprah Winfrey Show 20th Anniversary Collection,* disc 2, Harpo, Inc. (2005).

10. Sharon Salzberg, "Choosing Faith over Fear," *O, The Oprah Magazine* 3:1 (January 2002), 28.

11. From a voiceover on *The Oprah Winfrey Show 20th Anniversary Collection,* disc 2.

12. "Appreciating Your Life," *The Oprah Winfrey Show* (November 21, 2001). An intriguing contrast might be drawn between Winfrey's injunctions to purchase and the recent renewal of plenary indulgences in the Roman Catholic Church. Paul Vitello, "For Catholics, a Door to Absolution Is Reopened," *New York Times* (February 10, 2009).

13. Michel de Certeau, *The Practice of Everyday Life* (Berkeley: University of California Press, 1984), xiv.

14. Oprah Winfrey, "What I Know for Sure," *O, The Oprah Magazine* 6:5 (May 2005), 400.

15. Lynette Clemetson, "Oprah on Oprah," *Newsweek* 137:2 (January 8, 2001), 38–44.

16. Judith Shulevitz, "The Stories of O," *Time* 155:16 (April 24, 2000), 76.

17. Jennifer Weiner, "Another Winner for Winfrey?" *Philadelphia Inquirer* (April 16, 2000), D1.

18. Many definitions of religion focus on its role in the making of calendars and apportioning of time; likewise, such organizing thought constitutes a significant portion of religious engagement. Intriguing from the American perspective is the role entrepreneurial Mormons have played in the production of not merely their own sacred calendars but also commercial calendars for the monitoring of family time, working time, and spiritual time. The Franklin Covey Web site (www.franklinplanner.com/fc/company_information) explains the multipronged corporate gathering that occurred when Covey, a devout Mormon, joined with Franklin planners:

> In 1984, the first Franklin Day Planner was produced, followed by a popular time management workshop. New designs and formats are created continually, and the FranklinCovey Planning System is now used by more than 15 million people worldwide. In 1989, *The 7 Habits of Highly Effective People* by Stephen R. Covey was published, and training and consulting based on its concepts were developed. The book has become one of the top-selling business books of all time. Franklin Quest and Covey Leadership Center announced their intent to merge January 22, 1997. The new company, FranklinCovey, was finalized on May 30 of that year.

On the Latter-Day Saints origins of these corporate time management prescriptions, see Del Jones, "Covey Takes a Lesson from Himself, Releases '8th Habit,'" *USA Today* (November 8, 2004).

19. "July Calendar," *O, The Oprah Magazine* 3:7 (July 2002), 31.

20. "June Calendar," *O, The Oprah Magazine* 3:6 (June 2002), 35.

21. Oprah Winfrey, "The O List," *O, The Oprah Magazine* 4:8 (August 2003), 87; "The O List," *O, The Oprah Magazine* 5:11 (November 2004), 105.

22. "The impulse was not to copy, but to partake—of power and of the glory, strength, and beauty that were believed to inhere in those who stood at the peak of society," Richard Bushman has written of nineteenth-century consumers. "At its best . . . emulation meant acquiring a refinement of spirit, a sensitivity to

beauty, a regard for the feelings of others, a wish to please, all long associated with aristocracy at its best." Bushman, *The Refinement of America: Persons, Houses, Cities* (New York: Vintage Books, 1992), 406.

23. Oprah Winfrey, "The O List," *O, The Oprah Magazine* 2:7 (July 2001), 107; "The O List," *O, The Oprah Magazine* 4:11 (November 2003), 119; "The O List," *O, The Oprah Magazine* 10:1 (January 2009), 66.

24. Oprah Winfrey, "The O List," *O, The Oprah Magazine* 9:7 (July 2008), 76; "The O List," *O, The Oprah Magazine* 4:5 (May 2003), 118; "The O List," *O, The Oprah Magazine* 5:7 (July 2004), 73; "The O List," *O, The Oprah Magazine* 4:7 (July 2003), 79; "The O List," *O, The Oprah Magazine* 4:8 (August 2003), 85, 87; "The O List," *O, The Oprah Magazine* 5:11 (November 2004), 106.

25. Oprah Winfrey, "The O List," *O, The Oprah Magazine* 7:3 (March 2006), 107; "The O List," *O, The Oprah Magazine* 3:3 (March 2002), 95; "The O List," *O, The Oprah Magazine* 4:7 (July 2003), 77; "The O List," *O, The Oprah Magazine* 2:7 (July 2001), 106; "The O List," *O, The Oprah Magazine* 2:11 (November 2001), 121.

26. "September Calendar," *O, The Oprah Magazine* 3:9 (September 2002), 59.

27. Oprah Winfrey, "The O List," *O, The Oprah Magazine* 3:8 (August 2002), 95.

28. Oprah Winfrey, "The O List," *O, The Oprah Magazine* 3:1 (January 2002), 69.

29. "October Calendar," *O, The Oprah Magazine* 3:10 (October 2002), 43.

30. Table of contents, *Cosmopolitan* 246:1 (January 2009), 5, 8.

31. "Contents," *Redbook* 212:1 (January 2009), 3.

32. "Contents," *Good Housekeeping* 248:1 (January 2009), 3–4, 7.

33. "Contents," *Real Simple* (January 2009), 11–12.

34. "Features" and "Departments," *Town & Country* (January 2009), 9, 10.

35. An editorial describes the difference between the two in religious vocabulary. "Martha Stewart has a cult, with rituals and fetishes—applying the sprinkles to a frosted cupcake one by one with tweezers, that sort of thing. Oprah presides over something grander and more significant. It's more like a church." Eugene Robinson, "Church of Oprah," *Washington Post* (May 10, 2005), A21. For Robinson, the difference between a cult and a church is the difference between being forced into absurdity and being inspired toward a higher calling. "The Church of Oprah," he writes, "is the church of possibility."

36. Contents, *Martha Stewart Living* (January 2009), 7–8.

37. Charlotte Brunsdon, "Feminism, Postfeminism, Martha, Martha, and Nigella," *Cinema Journal* 44:2 (Winter 2005), 110–11. See also Christopher Brown, *Martha Inc.: The Incredible Story of Martha Stewart Living Omnimedia* (New York: Wiley, 2002).

38. Sarah A. Leavitt, *From Catharine Beecher to Martha Stewart: A Cultural History of Domestic Advice* (Chapel Hill: University of North Carolina at Chapel Hill, 2002).

39. Nancy Haught, "Martha Stewart and Oprah Winfrey," *The Oregonian* (June 15, 2003), L01.

40. Clemetson, "Oprah on Oprah." See also Nancy Franklin, "Talk of the Town: Where's the Oprah in O?" *New Yorker* (May 8, 2000), 56.

41. "7 Boyfriend Looks to Follow," *Cosmopolitan* 246:1 (January 2009), 51; "Look What We Found at . . . L.L. Bean," *Redbook* 212:1 (January 2009), 41; "Sweater Coats," *Good Housekeeping* 248:1 (January 2009), 69; "55 Must-Haves," *Town & Country* (January 2009), 112; "Fit Your Figure," *Real Simple* (January 2009), 96–101; "In the Skein of Things," *Martha Stewart Living* (January 2009), 58.

42. Jennifer Scanlon, *Inarticulate Longings: The Ladies' Home Journal, Gender, and the Promises of Consumer Culture* (New York: Routledge, 1995), 5.

43. "The Height Report," *O, The Oprah Magazine* 10:1 (January 2009), 72.

44. Lizabeth Cohen, *A Consumers' Republic: The Politics of Mass Consumption in Postwar America* (New York: Vintage Books, 2003), 9–10.

45. Bill Brown, *A Sense of Things: The Object Matter of American Literature* (Chicago: University of Chicago Press, 2003), 117.

46. Cohen, *A Consumers' Republic*, 9. "Now that no one buys our vote, the public has long since cast off its cares: the people that once bestowed commons, consulships, legions, and all else, now meddles no more and longs eagerly for just two things—Bread and Circuses!" Juvenal, quoted in Patrick Brantlinger, *Bread and Circuses: Theories of Mass Culture as Social Decay* (Ithaca, NY: Cornell University Press, 1983), 22.

47. Cohen, *A Consumers' Republic*, 403.

48. Brown, *A Sense of Things*, 5.

49. Gary Cross, *An All-Consuming Century: Why Commercialism Won in Modern America* (New York: Columbia University Press, 2000), 236.

50. Jackson Lears, *Fables of Abundance: A Cultural History of Advertising in America* (New York: Basic Books, 1994), 74, 66, 71–72. See also Raymond Williams, "Advertising: The Magic System," in *Culture and Materialism: Selected Essays* (London: Verso, 2005), 190.

51. Quoted in Amy Welborn, "The Feel-Good Spirituality of Oprah," *Our Sunday Visitor*, January 13, 2001.

52. Bill Brown, "Thing Theory," *Critical Inquiry* 28:1 (Autumn 2001), 5.

53. Adam Gopnik, "Display Cases," *New Yorker* (April 26/May 3, 1999), 178, 179.

54. Alan Trachtenberg, *The Incorporation of America: Culture and Society in the Gilded Age* (New York: Hill and Wang, 1982), 135.

55. Valerie Monroe, "Shopping for All the Right Reasons," *O, The Oprah Magazine* 5:9 (September 2004), 278.

56. Brooke Kosofsky Glassberg, "How Greene Is My Tote Bag," *O, The Oprah Magazine* 9:7 (July 2008), 215; Barry Yeoman, "The Good Shopper," *O, The Oprah Magazine* 7:9 (September 2006), 329.

57. "The Savvy Shopper," *O, The Oprah Magazine* 5:9 (September 2004), 165, 166, 168.

58. "Only the Best," *The Oprah Winfrey Show* (February 12, 2003).

59. Patricia Volk, "Cheap Thrills," *O, The Oprah Magazine* 2:11 (December 2001), 77, 78.

60. Oprah Winfrey, "What I Know for Sure," *O, The Oprah Magazine* 5:9 (September 2004), 334.

61. "Smart Shopping 2006," *O, The Oprah Magazine* 7:9 (September 2006), 317. Roberta Sassatelli has observed, "If the consumer society is that in which daily needs are satisfied in a capitalist way through the acquisition of commodities, it is also that in which each consumer has to constantly engage in re-evaluating these objects beyond their price." Sassatelli, *Consumer Culture: History, Theory and Politics* (London: Sage Publications, 2007), 5.

62. "The Oprah Store," *O, The Oprah Magazine* 9:4 (April 2008), 124.

63. Kevin Pang, "Taking Home Oprah: Joining the Pilgrimage to Winfrey's Wonder Emporium," *Chicago Tribune* (May 20, 2008), section 5, 7.

64. Quotations from the "Oprah Store Tour," at http://oprahstore.oprah.com/t-oprah_store_tour.aspx.

65. "The Oprah Store," *O, The Oprah Magazine* 9:4 (April 2008), 124.

66. Pang, "Taking Home Oprah," section 5, 1.

67. Gretchen Morgenson, ed., *Forbes Great Minds of Business* (New York: Wiley, 1997), 128.

68. T. Scott Boatright, "Girls, Dolls Awaken American History," *Ruston Daily Leader* (Ruston, LA) (February 9, 2009).

69. Daniel Miller, *The Comfort of Things* (Cambridge: Polity Press, 2008), 204. To prepare this description, I consulted the November 2008 mail-order American Girl catalog, as well as the Web site www.americangirl.com/.

70. Carolina Acosta-Alzuru and Elizabeth P. Lester Roushanzamir, "'Everything We Do Is a Celebration of You!' Pleasant Company Constructs American Girlhood," *Communication Review* 6:45–69 (2003), 54.

71. Ibid., 58.

72. www.americangirl.com/stores/experience_shopping.php.

73. Bill Glauber, "From Dollhouse to Doghouse: American Girl Founder's Makeover of Upstate N.Y. Town Rankles Some Locals," *Milwaukee Journal Sentinel* (July 23, 2007).

74. Susan Stewart, *On Longing: Narratives of the Miniature, the Gigantic, the Souvenir, the Collection* (Durham, NC: Duke University Press, 1993), 158.

75. A.O. Scott, "A Girl's Life," *New York Times* (June 29, 2008).

76. Kenneth J. Gergen, *The Saturated Self: Dilemmas of Identity in Contemporary Life* (New York: Basic Books, 1991), 212.

77. For an account of the back story to *The Secret,* see Allen Salkin, "Shaking Riches out of the Cosmos," *New York Times* (February 25, 2007).

78. Catherine Albanese, "From New Thought to New Vision: The Shamanic Paradigm in Contemporary Spirituality," in *Communication and Change In American Religious History,* ed. Leonard Sweet (Grand Rapids, MI: William B. Eerdmans Publishing Company, 1993), 335–54; Charles Braden, *Spirits in Rebellion: The Rise and Development of New Thought* (Dallas: Southern Methodist University Press, 1963); Heather Curtis, *Faith in the Great Physician: Suffering and Divine Healing in American Culture, 1860–1900* (Baltimore, MD: Johns Hopkins University Press, 2007); Marie Griffith, *Born Again Bodies: Flesh and Spirit in American Christianity* (Berkeley: University of California Press, 2004), chapters 2 and 3; Beryl Satter, *Each Mind a Kingdom: American Women, Sexual Purity, and the New Thought Movement, 1875–1920* (Berkeley: University of California Press, 1999).

79. Rhonda Byrne, *The Secret* (New York: Atria Books, 2006), 139.

80. Ibid., 139, 99, 157.

81. "The Secret," *The Oprah Winfrey Show* (February 8, 2007).

82. Ibid.

83. Oprah Winfrey, "What I Know for Sure," O, *The Oprah Magazine* 9:3 (March 2008), 292.

84. Byrne, *The Secret*, 150.

85. "The Secret," *The Oprah Winfrey Show* (February 8, 2007).

86. "One Week Later: The Reaction to *The Secret*," *The Oprah Winfrey Show* (February 16, 2007).

87. Ibid.

88. Barbara Ehrenreich, "The Power of Negative Thinking," *New York Times* (September 24, 2008).

89. Bruce Barron, *The Health and Wealth Gospel: What's Going on Today in a Movement That Has Shaped the Faith of Millions* (Downers Grove, IL: InterVarsity Press, 1987), 62–63; quoted in Simon Coleman, *The Globalisation of Charismatic Christianity: Spreading the Gospel of Prosperity* (Cambridge: Cambridge University Press, 2000), 41.

90. Jonathan L. Walton, *Watch This! The Ethics and Aesthetics of Black Televangelism* (New York: New York University Press, 2009), xi.

91. David Van Biema and Mark Thompson, "Going after the Money Ministries," *Time* 170:22 (November 26, 2007).

92. Coleman, *The Globalisation of Charismatic Christianity*, 33; Simon Coleman, "America Loves Sweden: Prosperity Theology and the Cultures of Capitalism," in *Religion and the Transformations of Capitalism*, ed. Richard H. Roberts (London: Routledge, 1995), 161–79; Rosalind Hackett, "The Gospel of Prosperity in West Africa," *Religion and the Transformations of Capitalism*, ed. Roberts, 199–214; David Hollinger, "Enjoying God Forever: An Historical/Sociological Profile of the Health and Wealth Gospel in the USA," in *Religion and Power, Decline and Growth: Sociological Analyses of Religion in Britain, Poland, and the Americas*, ed. Peter Gee and John Fulton (Twickenham: British Sociological Association, Sociology of Religion Study Group, 1991), 53–66.

93. David Van Biema and Jeff Chu, "Does God Want You to Be Rich?" *Time* 168:12 (September 18, 2006), 48.

94. T.D. Jakes, *The Great Investment: Faith, Family, and Finance* (New York: G.P. Putnam's Sons, 2000), 14; T.D. Jakes, *Can You Stand to Be Blessed? Insights to Help You Survive the Peaks and Valleys* (Shippensburg, PA: Treasure House, 1994), 49; both quoted in Walton, *Watch This!* 109.

95. David Van Biema, "America's Best: Spirit Raiser—Preacher," *Time* 158:11 (September 17, 2001), 52 ff.

96. David Van Biema, "Maybe We Should Blame God for the Subprime Mess," Time.com (October 3, 2008).

97. Van Biema and Chu, "Does God Want You to Be Rich?" 48.

98. Marla Frederick-McGlathery, "But, It's Bible: African American Women and Television Preachers," in *Women and Religion in the African Diaspora: Knowledge, Power and Performance*, ed. R. Marie Griffith and Barbara Dianne Savage (Baltimore: Johns Hopkins University Press, 2006), 286.

99. Jean Chatzky, "The Great American Debt Diet: Before and After," O, *The Oprah Magazine* 7:10 (October 2006), 105.

100. "The Debt Diet, Step by Step," O, *The Oprah Magazine* 7:10 (October 2006), 110.

101. Chatzky, "The Great American Debt Diet," 106.

102. Julie Morgenstern, "You've Got . . . Clutter," O, *The Oprah Magazine* 5:4 (April 2004), 84.

103. "Oprah's Favorite Things," *The Oprah Winfrey Show* (November 17, 2000); "Oprah Says She Can't Bear to Waste Anything," *Jet* (November 30, 1998).

104. Oprah Winfrey, "What I Know for Sure," O, *The Oprah Magazine* 8:5 (May 2007), 378.

105. On this episode, see Rod Dreher, "Islam according to Oprah," *National Review* (October 8, 2001). For other episodes relating religious practice, see in particular her coverage of polygamy and Mormon fundamentalism: "Polygamy in America: Lisa Ling Reports," *The Oprah Winfrey Show* (October 26, 2007); and "Forced to Marry at 14: Lisa Ling's Special Report," *The Oprah Winfrey Show* (May 14, 2008). In April 2009, Oprah herself would go into a "fundamentalist compound," pursuing her own brand of exploitative exploration. Fatemeh Fakhraie, "Oprah Talks Down to Fundamentalist Mormon Girls," ReligionDispatches.org (April 3, 2009).

106. For a survey of the changing relationship between ethnic identity formation and participation in consumer culture, see Marilyn Halter, *Shopping for Identity: The Marketing of Ethnicity* (New York: Schocken Books, 2000).

2. CELEBRITY SPIRIT

1. Janice Peck, *The Age of Oprah: Cultural Icon for the Neoliberal Era* (Boulder, CO: Paradigm Publishers, 2008), chapter 4.

2. Margaret Lamberts Bendroth and Virginia Lieson Brereton, eds., *Women and Twentieth-Century Protestantism* (Urbana: University of Illinois Press, 2002); R. Marie Griffith, *God's Daughters: Evangelical Women and the Power of Submission* (Berkeley: University of California Press, 2000); Julie Ingersoll, *Evangelical Christian Women: War Stories in the Gender Battles* (New York: New York University Press, 2003).

3. Wade Clark Roof, *Spiritual Marketplace: Baby Boomers and the Remaking of American Religion* (Princeton, NJ: Princeton University Press, 2001).

4. See Catherine L. Albanese, *Nature Religion in America: From the Algonkian Indians to the New Age* (Chicago: University of Chicago Press, 1991); Wouter J. Hanegraaff, *New Age Religion and Western Culture: Esotericism in the Mirror of Secular Thought* (Albany: State University of New York Press, 1998); Paul Heelas, *The New Age Movement: The Celebration of the Self and the Sacralization of Modernity* (Cambridge, MA: Blackwell Publishing, 1996); and Sarah M. Pike, *New Age and Neopagan Religions in America* (New York: Columbia University Press, 2006).

5. In a *Chicago Sun-Times* article, cultural critic Richard Roeper writes of this phenomenon: "A front-page article in USA Today this week detailed Oprah's effect on the marketplace. Just a few examples: After Bill Cosby's Little

Bill children's books were featured on the show in December, 1.5 million copies were sold in just three weeks. Sales of a particular line of pajama soared 200 percent after getting the Oprah seal of approval. Michael Bolton sold 250,000 copies of his latest CD after appearing on 'Oprah,' and Yanni sold 200,000 copies of his CD, 'Reflections of Passion,' after performing two songs on the show." Richard Roeper, "Oprah's Sheep Ready to Follow Every Whim," *Chicago Sun-Times* (January 22, 1998), 11.

6. "Best Life Week: Finding Your Spiritual Path," *The Oprah Winfrey Show* (January 7, 2009).

7. Ibid.

8. For previous reflections on the spiritual content of Oprah's empire, see Eva Illouz, *Oprah Winfrey and the Glamour of Misery* (New York: Columbia University Press, 2003), 43–46, 149–52, 230–35; Kathleen S. Lowney, *Baring Our Souls: TV Talk Shows and the Religion of Recovery* (New York: Aldine de Gruyter, 1999), 19–21, 89–107; Denise Martin, "Oprah Winfrey and Spirituality," in *The Oprah Phenomenon*, ed. Jennifer Harris and Elwood Watson (Lexington: University Press of Kentucky, 2007), 147–64; Maria McGrath, "Spiritual Talk: The Oprah Winfrey Show and the Popularization of the New Age," in *The Oprah Phenomenon*, ed. Harris and Watson, 125–46; and Peck, *The Age of Oprah*, 104–11, 208–10.

9. "We live in an age consumed by worship of the psyche . . . we share a belief that feelings are sacred and salvation lies in self-esteem, that happiness is the ultimate goal and psychological healing the means. Today Americans turn to psychological cures as reflexively as they once turned to God." Eva S. Moskowitz, *In Therapy We Trust: America's Obsession with Self-Fulfillment* (Baltimore: Johns Hopkins University Press, 2001), 1. The therapeutic aspect of talk show television—as well as the therapeutic aspect of twentieth-century American religion—has been well addressed. See Frank Furedi, *Therapy Culture: Cultivating Vulnerability in an Uncertain Age* (London: Routledge, 2004); Wendy Kaminer, *I'm Dysfunctional, You're Dysfunctional: The Recovery Movement and Other Self-Help Fashions* (New York: Madison Wesley Press, 1992); T. J. Jackson Lears, "From Salvation to Self-Realization: Advertising and the Therapeutic Roots of the Consumer Culture, 1880–1930," in *The Culture of Consumption*, ed. Richard Wightman Fox and T. J. Jackson Lears (New York: Pantheon Books, 1983); Chana Ullman, *The Transformed Self: The Psychology of Religious Conversion* (New York: Plenum Press, 1989); and Mimi White, *Tele-Advising: Therapeutic Discourse in American Television* (Chapel Hill: University of North Carolina Press, 1992).

10. She repeatedly disavows naming herself as a therapist. "I'm not a therapist," she responds to one reader's question, "so I can't tell you how to treat your depression." Expertise is important to Oprah. Her expertise is her biographical experience; it is not medical counsel regarding mental illness. Winfrey, "Battling Depression," *O, The Oprah Magazine* 6:4 (April 2005), 194.

11. Such a claim has evidence, since talk of wellness, feeling good, and knowing happiness pervades these productions. Eva Illouz, *Saving the Modern Soul: Therapy, Emotions, and the Culture of Self-Help* (Berkeley: University of California Press, 2008).

12. Aimee Lee Ball, "Journey to the Center of Yourself," O, *The Oprah Magazine* 8:6 (June 2007), 198.

13. Lisa Granatstein, "Spiritual Awakening," *Mediaweek* 10:14 (April 3, 2000), 74.

14. Christopher G. White, *Unsettled Minds: Psychology and the American Search for Spiritual Assurance, 1830–1940* (Berkeley: University of California Press, 2009), 7.

15. William James, *The Varieties of Religious Experience: A Study in Human Nature: Being the Gifford Lectures on Natural Religion Delivered at Edinburgh in 1901–1902* (New York: Longmans, Green, 1902).

16. "The Spiritual Connection," O, *The Oprah Magazine* 9:5 (May 2008), 278.

17. In 1975, the World Council of Churches declared its formal opposition to any "conscious or unconscious attempts to create a new religion composed of elements taken from different religions." Amanda Porterfield, *The Transformation of American Religion: The Story of a Late Twentieth-Century Awakening* (New York: Oxford University Press, 2001), 40.

18. Martha Sherrill, "Welcome to the Banquet," O, *The Oprah Magazine* 9:5 (May 2008), 280.

19. The notable exceptions to this scholarly lacuna have sought to connect discourses and practices of spirituality with the capaciousness of a disestablished nation and its politically and intellectually liberal propellers. Porterfield, *The Transformation of American Religion;* Leigh Eric Schmidt, *Restless Souls: The Making of American Spirituality* (San Francisco: HarperSanFrancisco, 2005); Wade Clark Roof, *A Generation of Seekers: The Spiritual Journeys of the Baby Boom Generation* (San Francisco: Harper, 1993); Robert Wuthnow, *After Heaven: Spirituality in America since the 1950s* (Berkeley: University of California Press, 1998).

20. Tony Walter and Grace Davie, "The Religiosity of Women in the Modern West," *British Journal of Sociology* 49:4 (1998), 656.

21. The O in O, *The Oprah Magazine* stands, according to one reporter, "for Oprah—heartfelt, improving and mysteriously able to transform the commercial exploitation of bathos into a unique blend of self-help spirituality, pop feminism and Benjamin Franklin optimism." Judith Shulevitz, "The Stories of O," *Time* 155:16 (April 24, 2000), 76.

22. Oprah Winfrey, "Oprah Goes Colonial," O, *The Oprah Magazine* 5:6 (June 2004), 60.

23. Sherrill, "Welcome to the Banquet," 281.

24. Catherine Albanese, *A Republic of Mind and Spirit: A Cultural History of American Metaphysical Religion* (New Haven, CT: Yale University Press, 2007), 515.

25. Lee Siegel, "Thank You for Sharing: The Strange Genius of Oprah," *New Republic* 234:21–22 (June 5 and 12, 2006), 19.

26. Schmidt, *Restless Souls,* 21.

27. Phillip Charles Lucas, "New Age Spirituality," in *Contemporary American Religion,* vol. 2, ed. Wade Clark Roof (New York: Macmillan Reference USA, 2000), 488–91; Ann Taves, *Fits, Trances, and Visions: Experiencing Religion*

and Explaining Experience from Wesley to James (Princeton, NJ: Princeton University Press, 1999), chapter 5.

28. Quoted in Ofhir Avtalion, Letter to the Editor, *New York Times* (November 8, 1998).

29. This summary of the e-mail newsletter offers examples from the following: "Empower Yourself, Awakening Joy and More!" *Spirit Newsletter* (September 8, 2008); "Your First Lesson in Spirituality 1010, Resolution Solutions and More!" *Spirit Newsletter* (December 15, 2008); "Find Your Purpose, Maintain a Spiritual Connection and More!" *Spirit Newsletter* (April 6, 2009); "Get Inspired, Cure Your Self-Consciousness and More!" *Spirit Newsletter* (April 13, 2009); "Boost Your Spirits, Rediscover Happiness and More!" *Spirit Newsletter* (April 20, 2009).

30. On the episode titled "Balance Your Energy, Balance Your Life" (March 11, 2003), Winfrey iterated these dual messages, commanding that women work harder to work less. It's not that you need more time, she said; it's that you need more energy. If you manage your energy, she claimed, you'll manage your time. This just happened to advocate on behalf of a new book by Jim Loehr and Tony Schwartz, *The Power of Full Engagement: Managing Energy, Not Time, Is the Key to High Performance and Personal Renewal* (New York: Free Press, 2003):

> Winfrey: OK, so the book is challenging an assumption that most of us make about how to manage our busy lives. The authors say that we are too obsessed with trying to find more time in the day. Aren't you? Everybody's always looking for time. Oh, you are so wrong. You need to shift that paradigm. Multitasking ourselves, we are, to death, when what really matters is not managing your time; it's managing your energy. Did you know that? OK, this is going to change your life today.

31. "Shhhhh . . . ," *O, The Oprah Magazine* 3:10 (October 2002), 175.

32. www.oprah.com/article/spirit/inspiration/ss_insp_med_lybloprah.

33. "Best Life Week: Finding Your Spiritual Path," *The Oprah Winfrey Show* (January 7, 2009).

34. Ken Lawrence, *The World according to Oprah: An Unauthorized Portrait in Her Own Words* (Kansas City, MO: Andrews McMeel Publishing, 2005), 106.

35. Oprah Winfrey, "What I Know for Sure," *O, The Oprah Magazine* 6:3 (March 2005), 266.

36. "It's a Miracle," *The Oprah Winfrey Show* (March 28, 2001); Rosemary Mahoney, "Looking for a Miracle," *O, The Oprah Magazine* 4:4 (April 2003), 212–13; www.oprah.com/contributor/spirit/mariannewilliamson.

37. Oprah Winfrey, "What I Know for Sure," *O, The Oprah Magazine* 3:7 (July 2002), 196.

38. Aimee Lee Ball, "Losing Weight: The Mind Game," *O, The Oprah Magazine* 7:12 (December 2006), 200; Katherine Russell Rich, "In a Single Stroke," *O, The Oprah Magazine* 3:10 (October 2002), 214.

39. Lynette Clemetson, "Oprah on Oprah," *Newsweek* 137:2 (January 8, 2001), 38–44.

40. Wendy Kaminer, "Why We Love Gurus," *Newsweek* 130:16 (October 20, 1997), 60.

41. Jeff MacGregor, "Inner Peace, Empowerment and Host Worship," *New York Times* (October 25, 1998).

42. "*The Secret*," *The Oprah Winfrey Show* (February 8, 2007); Clemetson, "Oprah on Oprah."

43. Lisa Granatstein, "Oprah Chats about This and That . . . ," *Mediaweek* (April 3, 2000), 75.

44. Lynette Clemetson, "It Is Constant Work," *Newsweek* (January 8, 2001), 44.

45. David Denby, "Fallen Idols," *New Yorker* (October 22, 2007), 110.

46. Chris Rojek, *Celebrity* (London: Reaktion, 2001), 90.

47. Denby, "Fallen Idols," 112.

48. Graeme Turner, *Understanding Celebrity* (London: Sage Publications, 2004), 23–25. Neal Gabler elaborates: "The spirituality, the alternative reality, the easy transcendence, the celebrity homilies, the gospels inspired by celebrities' deaths, the icons on their way to apotheosis—all these edged entertainment, as incarnated by celebrities, ever closer to theology, in a way, turning the tables. If religion had become entertainment, entertainment was now becoming a religion." Gabler, *Life the Movie: How Entertainment Conquered Reality* (New York: Knopf, 1998), 174.

49. "Stars—They're Just Like Us!" *US Weekly* (December 1, 2008), 37–38; Richard Schickel, *Intimate Strangers: The Culture of Celebrity in America* (Chicago: Ivan R. Dee, 2000); P. David Marshall, *Celebrity and Power: Fame in Contemporary Culture* (Minneapolis: University of Minnesota Press, 1997).

50. On the democratic turn in celebrity culture, see Thomas de Zengotita, "Attack of the Superzeroes," *Harper's Magazine* (December 2004), 35–42.

51. Granatstein, "Oprah Chats about This and That . . . ," 75.

52. Daniel Herwitz, *The Star as Icon: Celebrity in the Age of Mass Consumption* (New York: Columbia University Press, 2008), 133.

53. Peter Brown, "The Rise and Function of the Holy Man in Late Antiquity," *Journal of Roman Studies* 61 (1971), 91.

54. Kathryn Lofton, "The Preacher Paradigm: Biographical Promotions and the Modern-Made Evangelist," *Religion and American Culture: A Journal of Interpretation* 16:1 (Winter 2006), 105.

55. Oprah Winfrey, "My Confession," *O, The Oprah Magazine* 10:1 (January 2009), 150, 151.

56. Kinney Littlefield, "Oprah Winfrey Is Tired and Tearful but Still Enjoying Her TV Power," *Pittsburgh Post-Gazette* (May 19, 1997), D2.

57. Oprah Winfrey, *Journey to Beloved* (New York: Hyperion, 1998), 18–19.

58. Allison Samuels, "Something Wasn't Wright, So Oprah Left His Church," *Newsweek* (May 12, 2008), 8.

59. "One Week Later: The Huge Reaction to *The Secret*," *The Oprah Winfrey Show* (February 16, 2007).

60. Jill Smolowe, "O on the Go," *People* 56:3 (July 16, 2001), 50.

61. Winfrey, *Journey to Beloved*, 30.

62. Eric Deggans and Babita Persaud, "Fans Awe-Struck by Oprah," *St. Petersburg Times* (June 22, 2003).

63. Clemetson, "Oprah on Oprah."

64. Siegel, "Thank You for Sharing," 22.

65. "Oprah Talks to Hugh Jackman," *O, The Oprah Magazine* 7:6 (June 2006), 270.

66. "Oprah Talks to Eckhart Tolle," *O, The Oprah Magazine* 9:5 (May 2008), 344.

67. "Jim Carrey," *The Oprah Winfrey Show* (November 28, 2001).

68. "A New Side of Madonna," *The Oprah Winfrey Show* (September 16, 2003).

69. www.oprah.com/slideshow/relationships/sex/slideshow1_ss_sex_release sexpot/5.

70. Timothy Miller, *America's Alternative Religions* (Albany: State University of New York Press, 1995); Len Oakes, *Prophetic Charisma: The Psychology of Revolutionary Religious Personalities* (Syracuse, NY: Syracuse University Press, 1997); Anthony Storr, *Feet of Clay: A Study of Gurus, Saints, Sinners, and Madmen* (New York: Free Press, 1996).

71. Clemetson, "Oprah on Oprah."

72. "For the society around him, the holy man is the one man who can stand outside the ties of family, and of economic interest," Peter Brown has written. "He was thought of as a man who owed nothing to society." Brown, "The Rise and Function of the Holy Man in Late Antiquity," 91–92.

73. Amy Welborn, "The Feel-Good Spirituality of Oprah," *Our Sunday Visitor* (January 13, 2001), www.osv.com.

74. Carolyn Barnett, "False Teachings of Marianne Williamson and Oprah Winfrey," purchased by the author from eBay (June 14, 2008).

75. David J. Stewart, "Oprah Winfrey EXPOSED!" mailed unsolicited to the author.

76. Carrington Steele, *Don't Drink the Kool-Aid* (pamphlet published by Carrington Steele, 2008), 5. To see the video Steele produced, go to his personal Web site: www.carringtonsteele.citymax.com/page/page/5663569.htm.

77. Latonya Taylor, "The Church of O," *Christianity Today* 46:4 (April 1, 2002), 38.

78. Quentin J. Schultze, *Televangelism and American Culture: The Business of Popular Religion* (Grand Rapids, MI: Baker Book House, 1991), chapters 3 and 4, 69–124.

79. Kris Axtman, "The Rise of the American Megachurch," *Christian Science Monitor* (December 30, 2003), 1. For profiles of contemporary megachurches and their leadership, see Frances Fitzgerald, "Come One, Come All," *New Yorker* (December 3, 2007), 46–56; Jonathan Mahler, "The Soul of the New Exurb," *New York Times Magazine* (March 27, 2005); David Van Biema, "The Global Ambition of Rick Warren," *Time* (August 18, 2008), 37–42; and Molly Worthen, "Who Would Jesus Smack Down?" *New York Times Magazine* (January 11, 2009).

80. Jonathan L. Walton, *Watch This! The Ethics and Aesthetics of Black Televangelism* (New York: New York University Press, 2009), 110.

81. Tyler Wigg-Stevenson, "Jesus Is Not a Brand," *Christianity Today* (January 2, 2009), www.christianitytoday.com/ct/2009/january/10.20.html.

82. Candy Gunther Brown, *The Word in the World: Evangelical Writing, Publishing, and Reading in America, 1789–1880* (Chapel Hill: University of North Carolina Press, 2004), 7. See also John Lardas Modern, "Evangelical Secularism and the Measure of Leviathan," *Church History* 77:4 (December 2008), 824.

83. www.lakewood.cc/MINISTRIES/Pages/index.aspx. See also Robert Wuthnow, *Sharing the Journey: Support Groups and America's New Quest for Community* (New York: Free Press, 1994).

84. Lisa Russell and Cindy Dampier, "Oprah Winfrey," *People Weekly* 51:10 (March 15–22, 1999), 143.

85. Clemetson, "Oprah on Oprah."

86. Nate Berkus, "What Nate's Giving His Friends," O, *The Oprah Magazine* 7:12 (December 2006), 227.

87. "Recession-Proof Your Family with Suze Orman," *The Oprah Winfrey Show* (September 23, 2008).

88. Table of contents, "5th Anniversary Special," O, *The Oprah Magazine* 6:5 (May 2005), 3.

89. Valerie Frankel, "Soul Mates: A Primer," O, *The Oprah Magazine* 3:4 (April 2002), 75–76.

90. "Oprah Talks to Pema Chödrön," O, *The Oprah Magazine* 9:2 (February 2008), 196; "Oprah Talks to a Phenomenal Man: Archbishop Desmond Tutu," O, *The Oprah Magazine* 6:2 (February 2005), 182; "Oprah Talks to the Dalai Lama," O, *The Oprah Magazine* 2:8 (August 2001), 120.

91. Pike, *New Age and Neopagan Religions in America*, 23.

92. Lucas, "New Age Spirituality."

93. Oprah Winfrey, "What I Know for Sure," O, *The Oprah Magazine* 9:7 (July 2008), 236.

94. Oprah Winfrey, "What I Know for Sure," O, *The Oprah Magazine* 7:4 (April 2006), 322.

95. Wade Clark Roof, "American Spirituality," *Religion and American Culture* 9 (Summer 1999), 137.

96. Clemetson, "Oprah on Oprah."

97. Katherine Russell, "Throw Yourself a Line," O, *The Oprah Magazine* 5:7 (July 2004), 154–155.

98. Jenna Wortham, "With Oprah Onboard, Twitter Grows," *New York Times* (April 18, 2009).

3. DIVERTING CONVERSIONS

1. "Princess for a Day," *The Oprah Winfrey Show* (February 17, 2003). Official tapes and transcripts for *The Oprah Winfrey Show* are available through Burrell's Transcripts. When I began watching the Oprah show in 1998, customers would call Burrell's directly and a tape or printed transcript would be sent. Eventually, Winfrey's Web site overtook the business of purchase and, soon, PDF download. Over the course of these ten years, the transcripts available

from previous seasons have become more and more limited, so that currently only a small fraction of transcripts from the last three seasons are available for purchase. http://oprahstore.oprah.com/c-89-oprah-show-transcripts.aspx.

2. The *Oprah* show toys here with the nostalgic parallel to *Queen for a Day*, a televised game show that began its nine-year run as the number-one daytime show in 1955. Each day, the show selected five women from the studio audience who would then tell their most sorrowful tale to Jack Bailey, the host. Novelist Denise Giardina remembers watching these confessions as a child: "The women, dressed plainly and often weeping, poured out their sorrows before the whole world, and the studio audience judged by their applause which woman was to be pitied most." Through readings on an applause meter, the audience picked the most pitiable. Draped with a robe and capped with a crown, the woman might weep or wave as Bailey proclaimed, "I now pronounce you . . . Queen for a Day!" Mary Ann Watson, *Defining Visions: Television and the American Experience in the 20th Century* (Malden, MA: Blackwell, 2008), 208–9.

3. Daniel Dayan and Elihu Katz, *Media Events: The Live Broadcasting of History* (Cambridge, MA: Harvard University Press, 1992), 27; Milly Buonanno, *The Age of Television: Experiences and Theories* (Chicago: University of Chicago Press for Intellect Books, 2007), 46.

4. Claude Lévi-Strauss, *The Naked Man,* trans. John and Doreen Weightman (New York: Harper and Row, 1981), 672.

5. J. C. Heestermann, *The Inner Conflict of Tradition: Essays in Indian Ritual, Kingship and Society* (Chicago: University of Chicago Press, 1985), 3. Neil Postman echoes this sentiment in his description of the medium of television: "How television stages the world becomes the model for how the world is properly to be staged." Postman, *Amusing Ourselves to Death: Public Discourse in the Age of Show Business* (New York: Viking, 1985), 92.

6. Marcel Mauss, *The Gift* (Glencoe, IL: Free Press, 1954).

7. Maria Heim, *Theories of the Gift in South Asia* (New York: Routledge, 2004), xviii. Heim points out that South Asian theorists do not share this reading, insisting instead that *dāna* is asymmetrical and unreciprocated.

8. Eva Illouz, *Oprah Winfrey and the Glamour of Misery* (New York: Columbia University Press, 2003), chapter 6.

9. Mary Elizabeth Williams, "In Oprah We Trust," *TV Guide* (October 10, 2004), 34; Sholnn Freeman, "Oprah's GM Giveaway Was Stroke of Luck for Agency, Audience," *Wall Street Journal* (September 14, 2004), B1, B14.

10. Kelly Williams, "Drive, She Said," *People* 62:13 (September 27, 2004), 93–94. "Giving a present or doing a favor demonstrates trust in another," writers Peter M. Blau. "The other's reciprocation validates this trust as justified." Blau, *Exchange and Power in Social Life* (New Brunswick, NJ: Transaction Publishers, 1996), 107.

11. "Oprah Winfrey Reveals the Real Reason Why She Stayed on TV," *Jet* 93:1 (November 24, 1997), 58.

12. In 2009 on Highway 57 outside Chicago, a billboard could be seen invoking the name "Oprah" as such a generic invocation of request. "Oprah" here replaces "God" as a noun of desiring address for a nonprofit that provides

facial reconstructions for children without medical care. "Oprah, 3 Million Children with Clefts Need Our Help. We Need Yours. SmileTrain."

13. The category of evangelical disclosure I borrow from Patricia Joyner Priest, *Public Intimacies: Talk Show Participants and Tell-All TV* (Cresskill, NJ: Hampton Press, 1995), 57.

14. Oprah Winfrey, "What I Know for Sure," *O, The Oprah Magazine* 3:7 (July 2002), 196.

15. "Tatum O'Neal's Hollywood Nightmare," *The Oprah Winfrey Show* (October 12, 2004).

16. "The performance of the confession on national television underlines the existence of that social order, and the host—a foot squarely placed in both public and private domains—often articulates and reiterates it even as he or she solicits and receives the deeply personal disclosure." Louann Haarman, "Performing Talk," in *Television Talk Shows: Discourse, Performance, Spectacle,* ed. Andrew Tolson (Mahwah, NJ: Lawrence Erlbaum Associates, 2001), 53.

17. As if to underline the corporate point, in April 2009 an insurance company, Mutual of Omaha, sued Oprah Winfrey and her production company over use of the phrase "aha moment." Even ejaculations of enlightenment may be trademarked. Timberly Ross, "Aha Moment: Mutual of Omaha Sues Oprah over the Use of Catchphrase in an Advertising Campaign," Associated Press (April 24, 2009).

18. Octavia Butler, "Eye Witness," *O, The Oprah Magazine* 3:5 (May 2002), 80.

19. "Edwidge Danticat's Aha! Moment," *O, The Oprah Magazine* 3:12 (December 2002), 53; "Dorothy Allison's Aha! Moment," *O, The Oprah Magazine* 3:11 (November 2002), 111.

20. Tyler Perry, "The End of Fury," *O, The Oprah Magazine* 7:3 (March 2006), 215; Donald Trump, "The Amaze-able," *O, The Oprah Magazine* 7:3 (March 2006), 221.

21. Michael Cunningham, "The Pivotal Moment," *O, The Oprah Magazine* 5:1 (January 2004), 152

22. Judith Shulevitz, "The Stories of O," *Time* 155:16 (April 24, 2000), 76.

23. Susan Wise Bauer, *The Art of the Public Grovel: Sexual Sin and Public Confession in America* (Princeton, NJ: Princeton University Press, 2008), 2, 3.

24. Martha Beck, "Spilling the Beans," *O, The Oprah Magazine* 3:6 (June 2002), 185.

25. Mark Leyner, "Spilling the Beans," *O, The Oprah Magazine* 3:6 (June 2002), 191.

26. "Calling All Dreamers," *O, The Oprah Magazine* 3:9 (September 2002), 55.

27. After "finding a comfortable position in a chair" and clearing your mind, you should let your "thoughts and emotions flow freely . . . be risky. Be daring. Be you." To women "struggling to get started," journalist Michele Weldon offers the following advice: "When the fear of writing is upon you, write anyway; move beyond the superficial; quiet down; check out the flip side; and reread your work." *The Oprah Winfrey Show* (July 14, 2004). www.oprah.com/tows/pastshows/tows_2002/tows_past_20020624_b.jhtml.

28. www.oprah.com/journal/journal_howto.jhtml.

29. Harry S. Stout, *The New England Soul: Preaching and Religious Culture in Colonial New England* (New York: Oxford University Press, 1986), 39. For a thorough engagement with eighteenth-century journaling practices among American Christians, see Catherine Brekus, "Writing as a Protestant Practice: Devotional Diaries in Early New England," in *Practicing Protestants: Histories of Christian Life in America, 1630–1965,* ed. Laurie F. Maffly-Kipp, Leigh E. Schmidt, and Mark Valeri (Baltimore: Johns Hopkins University Press, 2006), 19–34.

30. Gregory S. Jackson, *The Word and Its Witness: The Spiritualization of American Realism* (Chicago: University of Chicago Press, 2009), 108.

31. An interesting contrast here might be drawn between the management of such a murder by Oprah Winfrey as opposed to Jerry Springer. For Winfrey, individual tragedy supplies the first line of a daily sermon; for Springer, individual tragedy offers the first step in a social sacrifice, about which the most grotesque of rejoinders may be expelled for viewers' mocking pleasure. Greg Myers, "'I'm Out of It, You Guys Argue': Making an Issue of It on the Jerry Springer Show," in *Television Talk Shows,* ed. Tolson, 173–92.

32. On Winfrey's first-person confessional text, see Kirk T. Hughes, "Ethics in the First Person: New American Confessions by Carver, Wojnarowicz, and Winfrey," Ph.D. dissertation, University of Pennsylvania (1997). On Oprah's positioning of herself as the role model in the *Oprah* show performance ecology, see Elizabeth Montgomery, "Talkshow Performance Practices and the Display of Identity," Ph.D. dissertation, Northwestern University (1997).

33. Jill Nelson, "Oprah Winfrey—for the Daytime Queen, Vulnerability Wins Out," *Washington Post* (July 19, 1987), Y7.

34. Lee Siegel, "Thank You for Sharing: The Strange Genius of Oprah," *New Republic* 234:21–22 (June 5 and 12, 2006), 21.

35. "Whether it's conscious or not," one reporter remarks, "it is this wash-rinse-repeat cycle of publicly confronting her problems, seeming to overcome them, then getting felled by them once again that is key to her enduring popularity." Maureen Callahan, "Bloated, Depressed—as O Goes, So Goes the Nation," *New York Post* (January 24, 2009).

36. Charles A. Johnson, *The Frontier Camp Meeting* (Dallas, TX: Southern Methodist University Press, 1955), 132–42.

37. Charles G. Finney, *Charles G. Finney: An Autobiography* (1876; Old Tappan, NJ: Fleming H. Revell Company, 1908), 289. Narratives of the Rochester campaign can be found in Charles E. Hambrick-Stowe, "The Anxious Seat," in *Charles G. Finney and the Spirit of American Evangelicalism* (Grand Rapids, MI: William B. Eerdmans Publishing Company, 1996), 101–30; and Paul E. Johnson, *A Shopkeeper's Millennium: Society and Revivals in Rochester, New York, 1815–1837* (New York: Hill and Wang, 1978), 96–102.

38. For a perspective on the coercive elements of antebellum preaching, see Donald G. Mathews, "The Second Great Awakening as an Organizing Process, 1780–1830: An Hypothesis," *American Quarterly* 21 (Spring 1969), 23–43; and Leonard I. Sweet, "The View of Man Inherent in New Measures Revivalism," *Church History* 45:2 (June 1976), 206. For a more liberatory social

interpretation of revivalism, see Nathan Hatch, *The Democratization of American Christianity* (New Haven, CT: Yale University Press, 1991).

39. Sweet, "The View of Man Inherent in New Measures Revivalism," 217.

40. Charles Finney, "Measures to Promote Revivals," in *Lectures on Revivals of Religion by Charles Grandison Finney,* ed. William G. McLoughlin (Cambridge, MA: Belknap Press of Harvard University Press, 1960), 267.

41. James M. Davis, *A Plea for "New Measures" in the Promotion of Revivals; or, A Reply to Dr. Nevin Against the "Anxious Bench"* (Pittsburgh: printed by A. Jaynes, 1844), 29.

42. Theodore W. Jennings, "On Ritual Knowledge," *Journal of Religion* 62:2 (April 1982), 111, 112–13.

43. When on hiatus (June, July, August) or in transition (May, September), the show offers fewer new episodes, even as the topical variety is maintained through carefully arranged repeats. This level of variety has been standard since 2002, a fact substantiated by eleven years of content analysis, transcription records, and cross-referencing episodes with the monthly magazine (since 2000) and Web site (since 1999).

44. Other scholars have gestured to this parallel between evangelical confession tactics and Winfrey's interviewing strategy. See Haarman, "Performing Talk," 53; Kathleen S. Lowney, *Baring Our Souls: TV Talk Shows and the Religion of Recovery* (New York: Aldine de Gruyter, 1999), 18; Sujata Moorti, "Cathartic Confessions or Emancipatory Texts? Rape Narratives on *The Oprah Winfrey Show*," *Social Text* 16:4 (Winter 1998), 86–87; and Janice Peck, "Talk about Racism: Framing a Popular Discourse of Race on Oprah Winfrey," *Cultural Critique* 27 (Spring 1994), 94–95.

45. "James Frey and the *Million Little Pieces* Controversy," *The Oprah Winfrey Show* (January 26, 2006). The original Oprah's Book Club episode, "The Man Who Kept Oprah Awake at Night: *A Million Little Pieces,*" aired on October 26, 2005.

46. John W. Nevin, *The Anxious Bench* (Chambersburg, PA: printed at the Office of *The Weekly Messenger,* 1843), 39.

47. Katherine Zoepf, "Saudi Women Find an Unlikely Role Model: Oprah," *New York Times* (September 19, 2008).

48. Robin Givhan, "We Share Your Loss, and Your Gain," *Washington Post* (December 14, 2008). For a full accounting of Winfrey's weight loss journey, see Ella Howard, "From Fasting toward Self-Acceptance: Oprah Winfrey and Weight Loss in American Culture," in *The Oprah Phenomenon,* ed. Jennifer Harris and Elwood Watson (Lexington: University Press of Kentucky, 2007), 101–23.

49. Brenda Weber, "Beauty, Desire, and Anxiety: The Economy of Sameness in ABC's Extreme Makeover," *Genders* 41 (2005), www.genders.org/g41/g41_weber.html.

50. Robert A. Orsi, *Thank You, St. Jude: Women's Devotion to the Patron Saint of Hopeless Causes* (New Haven, CT: Yale University Press, 1998), 67.

51. Marie Griffith, *Born Again Bodies: Flesh and Spirit in American Christianity* (Berkeley: University of California Press, 2004), 241, 240.

52. Michelle M. Lelwica, "Losing Their Way to Salvation: Women, Weight Loss, and the Salvation Myth of Culture Lite," in *Religion and Popular Culture*

in America, ed. Bruce David Forbes and Jeffrey H. Mahan (Berkeley: University of California Press, 2005), 174–94.

53. Transcripts of "Oprah's Confessions," www.oprah.com/media/2008 1124_sas_tease; and "Oprah's Weight Gain Confession," www.oprah.com/media/20081030_tows_confession.

54. "Incredible Weight-Loss Stories," *The Oprah Winfrey Show* (February 10, 2003).

55. Lise Funderburg, "The 90-Day Challenge," *O, The Oprah Magazine* 3:10 (October 2002), 187.

56. For one example among many, see ibid., 183.

57. www.oprah.com/slideshow/relationships/sex/slideshow1_ss_sex_release sexpot/1.

58. Martha Beck, "Makeover Madness," *O, The Oprah Magazine* 6:4 (April 2005), 176.

59. "How to Look (at Least) 10 Years Younger," *O, The Oprah Magazine* 7:3 (March 2006), 244–45.

60. Martha Beck, "Growing Wings," *O, The Oprah Magazine* 5:1 (January 2004), 171.

61. "Fresh Starts," *O, The Oprah Magazine* 10:1 (January 2009), 135.

62. "Step Out of Your Box," *The Oprah Winfrey Show* (November 15, 2002).

63. Sara Reistad-Long, "How to Multi-Task without Losing Your Mind," *O, The Oprah Magazine* 8:8 (August 2007), 141–42.

64. Martha Beck, "Balance," *O, The Oprah Magazine* 4:4 (April 2003), 194.

65. Kathleen Norris, "The Weary Woman's Manifesto," *O, The Oprah Magazine* 4:7 (July 2003), 145.

66. Martha Beck, "You Have the Right to Remain Silent," *O, The Oprah Magazine* 5:12 (December 2004), 87–89; Karen Schoemer, "You, Unplugged—Try It," *O, The Oprah Magazine* 5:8 (August 2004), 60; Sharon Salzberg, "The Cure for Craziness," *O, The Oprah Magazine* 5:6 (June 2004), 67–68.

67. Martha Beck, "I'm Reacting as Fast as I Can!" *O, The Oprah Magazine* 3:4 (April 2002), 58–60.

68. Oprah Winfrey, "What I Know for Sure," *O, The Oprah Magazine* 5:7 (July 2004), 190.

69. Martha Beck, "Wait! Stop! It's All Too Much!" *O, The Oprah Magazine* 8:11 (November 2007), 97–100; Judith Newman, "Things That Make You Go 'Ahhh,'" *O, The Oprah Magazine* 3:10 (October 2002), 250–52; "Tickets to Fun," *O, The Oprah Magazine* 3:5 (May 2002).

70. "The O List," *O, The Oprah Magazine* 6:3 (March 2005), 101; "Modern Times," *O, The Oprah Magazine* 5:4 (April 2004), 238; "Watches," *O, The Oprah Magazine* 7:9 (September 2006), 348; "Play Time," *O, The Oprah Magazine* 10:2 (February 2008), 213.

71. "Watches," *O, The Oprah Magazine,* 349; "A Rich Harvest," *O, The Oprah Magazine* 9:11 (November 2008), 97.

72. "July Calendar," *O, The Oprah Magazine* 3:7 (July 2002), 30–31.

73. In his seventeenth-century work of biblical counseling, *The Christian Directory* (1673), Richard Baxter describes the melancholic Christian in a way that is reminiscent of the resultant Oprah consumer, flitting from one

timed task to another, all under the guise of spiritual betterment: "He is endless in his scruples: afraid lest he sin in every word he speaketh, and in every thought, and every look, and every meal he eateth, and all the clothes he weareth: and if he think to amend them, he is still scrupling his supposed amendments: he dare neither travel, nor stay at home, neither speak, nor be silent; but he is scrupling all; as if he were wholly composed of self-perplexing scruples." Richard Baxter, *The Practical Works of Richard Baxter* (London: George Virtue, 1838), 262.

74. "The Best Is Yet To Come," *The Oprah Winfrey Show* (December 13, 2001). See also Holly Brubach, "You Don't Need More Willpower . . . ," *O, The Oprah Magazine* 10:1 (January 2009), 138.

75. Ronna Lichtenberg, "Me, Inc. Revisited," *O, The Oprah Magazine* 3:4 (April 2002), 117.

76. "Transformation," *O, The Oprah Magazine* 5:1 (January 2004), 139.

77. Lichtenberg, "Me, Inc. Revisited," 115.

78. Jill Smolowe, "O on the Go," *People* 56:3 (July 16, 2001), 50.

79. "How'd She Do It?" *O, The Oprah Magazine* 3:9 (September 2002), 240–47.

80. "Lifestyle Makeovers: Uncovering Your Shadow Beliefs," *The Oprah Winfrey Show* (November 6, 2000).

81. Siobhan B. Somerville, "Queer," in *Keywords for American Cultural Studies*, ed. Bruce Burgett and Glenn Hendler (New York: New York University Press, 2007), 187.

82. Mark Jordan, "Touching and Acting, *or* the Closet of Abjection," *Journal of the History of Sexuality* 10:2 (April 2001), 182–83.

83. Debbie Epstein and Deborah Lynn Steinberg, "Love's Labours: Playing It Straight on the *Oprah Winfrey Show*," in *Border Patrols: Policing the Boundaries of Heterosexuality,* ed. Deborah Lynn Steinberg, Debbie Epstein, and Richard Johnson (London: Cassell, 1997), 35. For more on the stylistics of televised gay identities, see Chris Strayer and Tom Waugh, "Queer TV Style," *GLQ* 11:1 (2005), 95–117.

84. Winifred Gallagher, "Six Ways to Right a Wrong," *O, The Oprah Magazine* 3:6 (June 2002), 195.

85. Scott Herring, *Queering the Underworld: Slumming, Literature, and the Undoing of Lesbian and Gay History* (Chicago: University of Chicago Press, 2007), 204, 205.

86. "When I Knew I Was Gay," *The Oprah Winfrey Show* (November 17, 2005).

87. "Evangelist Ted Haggard, His Wife, and the Gay Sex Scandal," *The Oprah Winfrey Show* (January 28, 2009).

88. Erving Goffman, *Asylums* (Chicago: Aldine, 1962), 115.

89. "Wives Confess They Are Gay," *The Oprah Winfrey Show* (October 2, 2006).

90. "Lifestyle Makeovers: Uncovering Your Shadow Beliefs," *The Oprah Winfrey Show.*

91. Aimee Lee Ball, "When Gay Men Happen to Straight Women," *O, The Oprah Magazine* 5:12 (December 2004), 259. For a description of the inverse

exchange (lesbian women, straight men), see Mary A. Fischer, "She's So Fine!" *O, The Oprah Magazine* 10:4 (April 2009), 170.

92. George W.S. Trow, *Within the Context of No Context* (New York: Atlantic Monthly Press, 1980), 45.

93. Guy DeBord, *The Society of the Spectacle* (New York: Zone Books, 1994).

94. Signal works in this historiography include Linda Grindstaff, *The Money Shot: Trash, Class and the Making of TV Talk Shows* (Chicago: University of Chicago Press, 2002); John Dovey, *Freakshow: First Person Media and Factual Television* (London: Pluto Press, 2002); and Joshua Gamson, *Freaks Talk Back: Tabloid Talk Shows and Sexual Nonconformity* (Chicago: University of Chicago Press, 1998). For more on therapeutic culture, see Frank Furedi, *Therapy Culture: Cultivating Vulnerability in an Uncertain Age* (London: Routledge, 2004); Wendy Kaminer, *I'm Dysfunctional, You're Dysfunctional: The Recovery Movement and Other Self-Help Fashions* (New York: Madison Wesley Press, 1992); T.J. Jackson Lears, "From Salvation to Self-Realization: Advertising and the Therapeutic Roots of the Consumer Culture, 1880–1930," in *The Culture of Consumption*, ed. Richard Wightman Fox and T.J. Jackson Lears (New York: Pantheon Books, 1983); Chana Ullman, *The Transformed Self: The Psychology of Religious Conversion* (New York: Plenum Press, 1989); and Mimi White, *Tele-Advising: Therapeutic Discourse in American Television* (Chapel Hill: University of North Carolina Press, 1992).

95. Siegel, "Thank You for Sharing," 21.

96. Richard Sennett, *The Fall of Public Man* (New York: Alfred A. Knopf, 1977), 269.

97. Stewart M. Hoover, *Religion in the Media Age* (London: Routledge, 2006), 289.

98. Joanna Thornborrow, "'Has It Ever Happened to You?' Talk Show Stories as Mediated Performance," in *Television Talk Shows*, ed. Tolson, 133; Vicki Abt and Leonard Mustazza, *Coming after Oprah: Cultural Fallout in the Age of the TV Talk Show* (Bowling Green, OH: Bowling Green State University Popular Press, 1997), 98.

99. *The Oprah Winfrey Show 20th Anniversary Collection*, disc 4, Harpo, Inc. (2005).

100. Beck, "Spilling the Beans," 185.

101. Smolowe, "O on the Go," 50.

4. PREACHER QUEEN

1. Robert D. McFadden, "In a Stadium of Heroes, Prayers for the Fallen and Solace for Those Left Behind," *New York Times* (September 24, 2001), B7.

2. www.oprah.com/tows/pfa/pfa_oprah.jhtml.

3. Bernard M. Timberg, *Television Talk: A History of the TV Talk Show* (Austin: University of Texas Press, 2002), 139.

4. If Winfrey is the ideal American assembler, Chicago may be the ideal assembled urbanity. As scholars of religion have written, Chicago "anchors and radiates influence into the Midwest" as the climax in that region's Rust Belt

postindustrial accomplishments. Chicago represents the region of the Midwest in all its caricatures while also standing as its avant-garde edge. Midwestern identity is double-sided: on the one hand, the heartland is framed from the outside as a vastness, someplace "lost in the middle . . . not clearly formed" and indistinct. Likewise, the Midwest is the country's "representative and steady essence" that offers a "microcosm" of American normalcy. The myth of the Midwest is, then, that "the region is bland but virtuous, and that its identity is weak, though tough to define precisely because it actually is the nation's Heartland, the real America." Philip Barlow and Becky Cantonwine, "Introduction: Not Oz," in *Religion and Public Life in the Midwest: America's Common Denominator*, ed. Philip Barlow and Marks Silk (Lanham, MD: Rowman and Littlefield, 2004), 15, 12, 13. In this, Chicago stands, possessing "a Protestant commercial, manufacturing, benevolent, and opinion-shaping establishment" while also having a Catholic majority. Increasingly, though, religious markers may be superseded by racial ones. "I don't think Chicago is Catholic anymore," someone else remarked. "I think the ambience of the city is black right now." John B. Jentz and Irene Hansen, eds., *Rethinking the History of Religion in Chicago: A Symposium* (Chicago: Newberry Library, 1986), 5, 8, 12, 14.

5. Charles Carroll Bonney, "Genesis of the World's Religious Congresses," *New Church Review* 1 (January 1894), 82–83, 87–89.

6. John Gmeiner, "Religious Union of the Human Race," in *The Dawn of Religious Pluralism: Voices from the World's Parliament of Religions, 1893*, ed. Richard Hughes Seager, (La Salle, IL: Open Court, 1993), 165.

7. John Henry Barrows summarized the speeches emphasizing reunion in his "Hopes for the Religious Union of the Whole Human Family," in *The World's Parliament of Religions: An Illustrated and Popular Story of the World's First Parliament of Religions, Held in Chicago in Connection with the Columbian Exposition of 1893*, ed. John Henry Barrows (Chicago: Parliament, 1893), 242–47.

8. Richard Hughes Seager, *The World's Parliament of Religions: The East/West Encounter, Chicago, 1893* (Bloomington: Indiana University Press, 1995); Richard Hughes Seager, "Pluralism and the American Mainstream: The View from the World's Parliament of Religions," in *A Museum of Faiths: Histories and Legacies of the 1893 World's Parliament of Religions*, ed. Eric J. Ziolkowski (Atlanta, GA: Scholar's Press, 1993), 191–218.

9. First, several participants from the East, such as Narasima Charya and Virchand Gandhi, agreed with the possibility of spiritual unification, yet clearly stated that Christian missionary work contradicted such aspiration. Thus, the colonial habits of the host country were made obvious, both in the boutique "exhibitions" of foreign religious ritual and the ongoing missionary endeavors of many participating Christian parliamentarians. Second, the entire event was determined by Christian ritual and nationalist plot lines. The opening ceremony began with the Lord's Prayer (subsequently defined as the "Universal Prayer"), and two weeks of meetings were concluded with the entire parliament singing "America the Beautiful." Several prominent speakers, including the American Buddhist sympathizer Paul Carus, openly acknowledged that the "universal religion" at the heart of the parliament's dream was merely a "broad Christianity."

10. Lee Siegel, "Thank You for Sharing: The Strange Genius of Oprah," *New Republic* 234:21–22 (June 5 and 12, 2006)," 20, 21. In this, Winfrey inverts a typical discursive move of talk show discussions, since "daytime talk show members often attempt to close down discussion by asserting that by nature of their oppression—race, gender, or class standing—they are a priori morally right." Jane Shattuc, *The Talking Cure: TV Talk Shows and Women* (New York: Routledge, 1997), 99.

11. Amy Welborn, "The Feel-Good Spirituality of Oprah," *Our Sunday Visitor* (January 13, 2001).

12. Arlene Dávila, *Latinos, Inc.: The Marketing and Making of a People* (Berkeley: University of California Press, 2001), 11.

13. Aimee Lee Ball, "Journey to the Center of Yourself," *O, The Oprah Magazine* 8:6 (June 2007), 197.

14. *O, The Oprah Magazine* leans on the side of *Redbook*, as exemplified in a December 2006 spread on "one dress, three ways." *O, The Oprah Magazine* 7:12 (December 2006), 154.

15. The fashion label the United Colors of Benetton forms an intriguing comparison to *O, The Oprah Magazine* and its fashion multiculturalism. On the Benetton case, see Henry A. Giroux, "Consuming Social Change: The 'United Colors of Benetton'," *Cultural Critique* 26 (Winter 1993–94), 5–32; Ann Tyler, "It's a Nice World after All: The Vision of 'Difference' in Colors," *Design Issues* 12:3 (Autumn 1996), 60–76.

16. "Suits: The Female of the Species," *O, The Oprah Magazine* 7:10 (October 2006), 322, 324, 325, 327.

17. Barbara Maria Stafford, *Echo Objects: The Cognitive Work of Images* (Chicago: University of Chicago, 2009), 163; Sophie Thomas, *Romanticism and Visuality: Fragments, History, Spectacle* (New York: Routledge, 2007), 120.

18. Oprah Winfrey, "What I Know for Sure," *O, The Oprah Magazine* 4:3 (March 2003), 244.

19. "The Bold and the Beautiful," *O, The Oprah Magazine* 3:8 (August 2002), 153, 157.

20. Sharon Heijin Lee, "Lessons from 'Around the World with Oprah': Neoliberalism, Race, and the (Geo)politics of Beauty," *Women & Performance: a journal of feminist theory* 18:1 (March 2008), 25–41.

21. Quoted in Jessica Grose, "Life in the Time of Oprah," *New York Times* (August 17, 2008).

22. "Have Style, Will Travel," *O, The Oprah Magazine* 9:7 (July 2008), 190.

23. Rey Chow, *The Protestant Ethnic and the Spirit of Catholicism* (New York: Columbia University Press, 2002), 51.

24. "Harmonic Convergences," *O, The Oprah Magazine* 7:4 (April 2006), 273–75.

25. Lise Funderburg, "Our Town," *O, The Oprah Magazine* 7:4 (April 2006), 279.

26. W.E.B. Du Bois, *The Souls of Black Folk* (New York: Alfred A. Knopf, 1993), 8. This "double-voiced" identity is explored in Timberg, *Television Talk*, 139. For further evaluations of this discourse of blackness, see Ewan Allinson, "'It's a Black Thing': Hearing How Whites Can't," *Cultural Studies* 2 (October

1988), 438–56; and Herman Gray, *Watching Race: Television and the Struggle for "Blackness"* (Minneapolis: University of Minnesota Press, 1995).

27. Patricia Hill Collins, "Defining Black Feminist Thought," in *The Second Wave: A Reader in Feminist Theory,* ed. Linda J. Nicholson (New York: Routledge, 1997), 246. Winfrey's 2005 "Legends Ball" was a celebration of her sorts of black women, the icons that created the premise for her transcendence. Laurie Winer, "The Legends Who Lunch: A Weekend of Glory at Promised Land," *O, The Oprah Magazine* 6:8 (August 2005), 174–91.

28. Ken Lawrence, *The World according to Oprah: An Unauthorized Portrait in Her Own Words* (Kansas City, MO: Andrews McMeel Publishing, 2005), 28.

29. Quoted in Janice Peck, *The Age of Oprah: Cultural Icon for the Neoliberal Era* (Boulder, CO: Paradigm Publishers, 2008), 152.

30. Jill Nelson, "Oprah Winfrey—for the Daytime Queen, Vulnerability Wins Out," *Washington Post* (July 19, 1987), Y7.

31. Lawrence, *The World according to Oprah,* 119; Oprah Winfrey, "Oprah Goes Colonial," *O, The Oprah Magazine* 5:6 (June 2004), 60.

32. Mike Hofman, "Oprah Gets Psyched," *Inc.* 23:12 (September 2001), 158.

33. Kinney Littlefield, "Oprah Winfrey Is Tired and Tearful but Still Enjoying Her TV Power," *Pittsburgh Post-Gazette* (May 19, 1997), D2.

34. It is perhaps not incidental that in a major attempt to speak to a specific aspect of the black experience, she failed. I refer to the making of the film *Beloved,* about which she remarked, "I will never do another film about slavery. I won't try to touch race again in this form, because people just aren't ready to hear it." Lawrence, *The World according to Oprah,* 43.

35. Oprah's racial subjectivity was put to the test in Henry Louis Gates Jr.'s 2006 PBS special *African-American Lives,* in which he used genetic technology to trace the racial roots of black celebrities. www.pbs.org/wnet/aalives/. Proven to be indeed an African American (albeit with Caucasian genetic coding, too), she is able to invoke her identity with scientifically proven emboss, so she can remark that something "in the Negro culture . . . means you're a hot mama." "Lifestyle Makeovers: Uncovering Your Shadow Beliefs," *The Oprah Winfrey Show* (November 6, 2000).

36. Alan Richman, "Oprah," *People Weekly* 27:2 (January 12, 1987), 48, quoted in Eva Illouz, *Oprah Winfrey and the Glamour of Misery* (New York: Columbia University Press, 2003), 23.

37. Laura Randolph, "Oprah! The Most Powerful Woman in Entertainment Talks about Her Fame, Her Father, and Her Future in TV," *Ebony* (July 1995), 23.

38. "Interview: Oprah Winfrey," Academy of Achievement (February 21, 1991), www.achievement.org/autodoc/page/winoint-1. For an intriguing account of black women's impressions of Winfrey, see Katrina Bell McDonald, "Embracing Oprah Winfrey," in *Embracing Sisterhood: Class, Identity, and Contemporary Black Women* (Lanham, MD: Rowman and Littlefield Publishers, 2006), chapter 6, 160–74.

39. Quentin Fottrell, "The Cult of Oprah Inc.," *Irish Times Weekend Magazine* (August 5, 2000), 61; quoted in Peck, *The Age of Oprah,* 152.

40. Anne Saidman, *Oprah Winfrey: Media Success Story* (Minneapolis: Lerner Publications Company, 1990), 17.

41. George Mair, *Oprah Winfrey: The Real Story* (Secaucus, NJ: Birch Lane Press, 1994), 183. For an overview of Winfrey's first-person reflections about race and the problem with Black History Month, see Oprah Winfrey, *Journey to Beloved* (New York: Hyperion, 1998), 22–27.

42. Laura Randolph, "Oprah! The Most Powerful Woman in Entertainment Talks about Her Fame, Her Father and Her Future in TV," *Ebony* (July 1995), 23; Audrey Edwards, "The O Factor," *Essence* (October 2003), 180.

43. Subsequent to her childhood, the most notorious public incidence of racism in her life involved shopping. In 2005, Winfrey was denied access to a Hermès store in Paris. Both the store and Winfrey disclaimed that the incident transpired, even though it was widely reported that race had been the impetus for her stalled appearance in front of a store door. Yet "Winfrey's inability to 'buy' her way out of racial attacks via her celebrity or financial clout has not excluded her from criticism about the status of her racial identification." Jennifer Harris and Elwood Watson, "Introduction: Oprah Winfrey as Subject and Spectacle," in *The Oprah Phenomenon*, ed. Jennifer Harris and Elwood Watson (Lexington: University Press of Kentucky, 2007), 15.

44. Zadie Smith, "Speaking in Tongues," *New York Review of Books* 56:3 (February 26, 2009).

45. Norman King, *Everybody Loves Oprah!* (New York: William Morrow, 1988), 31.

46. "Interview: Oprah Winfrey," Academy of Achievement.

47. Timberg, *Television Talk*, 139.

48. "More Extraordinary Families," *The Oprah Winfrey Show* (March 10, 2003). Winfrey even switches to a southern dialect, especially when reflecting on her race, her church, and Jesus, literally performing a public double consciousness. On this code switching, see Shattuc, *The Talking Cure*, 106–7.

49. Latonya Taylor, "The Church of O," *Christianity Today* (April 1, 2002), 38.

50. Illouz, *Oprah Winfrey and the Glamour of Misery*, 191.

51. "The sentimentalist conception of blacks as naturally religious or the image of blacks as a release from the constraints of bourgeois morality contained no mechanism for dealing with real blacks seeking jobs and living space in the adjoining neighborhood." Curtis J. Evans, *The Burden of Black Religion* (New York: Oxford University Press, 2008), 277.

52. For an example of the relationship between the Church and the spiritual mammy, see Micki McElya, *Clinging to Mammy: The Faithful Slave in Twentieth-Century America* (Cambridge, MA: Harvard University Press, 2007), 69.

53. Quoted in Kimberly Wallace-Sanders, *Mammy: A Century of Race, Gender, and Southern Memory* (Ann Arbor: University of Michigan Press, 2008), 8.

54. Ibid., 2.

55. Harris and Watson, "Introduction," 11. Mammy as icon "was not meant to accurately reflect the black woman's feelings about mothering; rather, it was generated out of a white desire for affirmation." Tarshia L. Stanley, "The Specter

of Oprah Winfrey: Critical Black Female Spectatorship," in *The Oprah Phenomenon,* ed. Harris and Watson, 40. See also George Frederickson, *The Black Image in the White Mind: The Debate on Afro-American Character and Destiny, 1817–1914* (Middletown, CT: Wesleyan University Press, 1971); and Laurie L. Haag, "Oprah Winfrey: The Construction of Intimacy in the Talk Show Setting," *Journal of Popular Culture* 26 (1993), 115–21.

56. Cheryl Townsend Gilkes, *"If It Wasn't for the Women . . .": Black Women's Experience and Womanist Culture in Church and Community* (Maryknoll, NY: Orbis Books, 2001), 129.

57. Roxanne Mountford, *The Gendered Pulpit: Preaching in American Protestant Spaces* (Carbondale: Southern Illinois University Press, 2003), 102. For more on the role of black preaching in the United States, see Wallace Best, "The Spirit of the Holy Ghost Is a Male Spirit: African American Preaching Women and the Paradoxes of Gender," in *Women and Religion in the African Diaspora: Knowledge, Power, and Performance,* ed. R. Marie Griffith and Barbara Dianne Savage (Baltimore: Johns Hopkins University Press, 2006), 101–27; Marla Frederick-McGlathery, "But, It's Bible: African American Women and Television Preachers," in *Women and Religion in the African Diaspora,* ed. Griffith and Savage, 266–92; Cleophus J. Larue, *The Heart of Black Preaching* (Louisville, KY: Westminster John Knox Press, 2000); Richard Lischer, *The Preacher King: Martin Luther King, Jr. and the Word That Moved America* (New York: Oxford University Press, 1995); Henry H. Mitchell, *Black Preaching* (Philadelphia: Lippincott, 1970); and Henry H. Mitchell, *Black Preaching: The Recovery of a Powerful Art* (Nashville, TN: Abingdon, 1991).

58. On women in the Holiness tradition, see Heather Curtis, *Faith in the Great Physician: Suffering and Divine Healing in American Culture, 1860–1900* (Baltimore, MD: Johns Hopkins University Press, 2007); and Susan Hill Lindley, *"You Have Stept Out of Your Place": A History of Women and Religion in America* (Louisville, KY: Westminster John Knox Press, 1996).

59. Grant Wacker, "Pentecostalism," in *Encyclopedia of the American Religious Experience,* ed. Charles H. Lippy and Peter Williams (New York: Scribner, 1988), 933.

60. Several of the preacher analogies drawn here were made too in Kelly Willis Mendiola, "The Hand of a Woman: Four Holiness-Pentecostal Evangelists and American Culture, 1840–1930," Ph.D. dissertation, University of Texas at Austin (2002).

61. Elaine J. Lawless, "Not So Different a Story After All: Pentecostal Women in the Pulpit," in *Women's Leadership in Marginal Religions: Explorations outside the Mainstream,* ed. Catherine Wessinger (Urbana: University of Illinois Press, 1993), 45.

62. Quoted in Diane Winston, "All the World's a Stage: The Performed Religion of the Salvation Army, 1880–1920," in *Practicing Religion in the Age of the Media: Explorations in Media, Religion, and Culture,* ed. Stewart M. Hoover and Lynn Schofield Clark (New York: Columbia University Press, 2002), 115.

63. For a more tempered view of women's role in the Salvation Army, see Andrew Mark Eason, *Women in God's Army: Gender and Equality in the Early*

Salvation Army (Waterloo, Ontario: published by Wilfrid Laurier University Press for the Canadian Corporation for Studies in Religion, 2003).

64. The best description of McPherson's preaching technique and entertainment contexts can be found in Matthew Avery Sutton, *Aimee Semple McPherson and the Resurrection of Christian America* (Cambridge, MA: Harvard University Press, 2007).

65. www.joycemeyer.org/OurMinistries/EverydayAnswers/.

66. Joyce Meyer, *Be Your Best* (New York: FaithWords, 2008), cover, 44, 39.

67. Debra Dickerson, "A Woman's Woman," *U.S. News & World Report* 123:12 (September 29, 1997), 10.

68. "Interview: Oprah Winfrey," Academy of Achievement.

69. The scholar of religion Mary Farrell Bednarowski has proposed that women have achieved leadership positions in religions that possessed "a view of marriage that did not stress the married state and motherhood as the proper sphere for woman and her only means of fulfillment." Bednarowski, "Outside the Mainstream: Women's Religion and Women Religious Leaders in Nineteenth-Century America," *Journal of the American Academy of Religion* 48:2 (June 1980), 209.

70. Quoted in Jennifer Weiner, "Another Winner for Winfrey?" *Philadelphia Inquirer* (April 16, 2000), D1.

71. Audrey Edwards, "Why You Don't Want to Have Sex," *O, The Oprah Magazine* 1:2 (July–August 2000), 181.

72. On the question of women and the *Oprah* show, see Gloria-Jean Mascariotte, "C'mon Girl: Oprah Winfrey and the Discourse of Feminine Talk," *Genders* 11 (Fall 1999), 81–110; and Corinne Squire, "Empowering Women? The Oprah Winfrey Show," *Feminism and Psychology* 41:1 (1994), 63–79.

73. Oprah Winfrey, "What I Know for Sure," *O, The Oprah Magazine* 4:2 (February 2003), 194.

74. Dickerson, "A Woman's Woman," 10.

75. "Reading Room," *O, The Oprah Magazine* 9:2 (February 2008), 135; "Reading Room," *O, The Oprah Magazine* 8:8 (August 2007), 151; "Women Rule!" *O, The Oprah Magazine* 9:4 (April 2008), 73.

76. Susan Chumsky, "Got the World on a String," *O, The Oprah Magazine* 3:4 (April 2002), 93.

77. Oprah Winfrey, "What I Know for Sure," *O, The Oprah Magazine* 4:2 (February 2003), 194.

78. Oprah Winfrey, "What I Know for Sure," *O, The Oprah Magazine* 3:3 (March 2002), 216.

79. "Secret Lives of Moms," *The Oprah Winfrey Show* (April 6, 2009); "Moms around the World," *The Oprah Winfrey Show* (October 23, 2006); Oprah Winfrey, "What I Know for Sure," *O, The Oprah Magazine* 6:6 (June 2005), 252; Oprah Winfrey, "The O Interview: Oprah Talks to a Mother of 9," *O, The Oprah Magazine* 4:5 (May 2003), 232.

80. Like all of Winfrey's confessions, the mom confessions posted here wander from the spiritual to the scatological. For additional "confessions" of mothers, see "Mothers around the World," *The Oprah Winfrey Show* (October 23, 2006). Vicki Glembocki, a mom of two, says she had a "pee incident" recently

during a seven-hour drive with her kids. "I looked in the back, and the kids were sleeping, which was literally a miracle from God, but the problem was I had to pee," she says. "So I'm thinking, 'If I stop at a rest area, they're totally going to wake up, and I do not want them to wake up.' So I reached into the diaper bag, I pulled out a diaper and I peed into it." "Secret Lives of Moms," *The Oprah Winfrey Show* (April 6, 2009).

81. Web site descriptions located at www.oprah.com/article/relationships/parenting/pkgomoms/20090406-orig-omoms-advice-mom; descriptions of "feeling" from "Secret Lives of Moms," *The Oprah Winfrey Show* (April 6, 2009).

82. Oprah Winfrey, "What I Know for Sure," O, *The Oprah Magazine* 4:5 (May 2003), 290.

83. Lisa Belkin, "The Opt-Out Revolution," *New York Times Magazine* (October 26, 2003); Vicki Glembocki, "Now What? The Existential Crisis of the Stay-at-Home Mom," *Philadelphia Magazine* (October 2008), 72. On *Sex and the City* feminism, see Kim Akass and Janet McCabe, eds., *Reading "Sex and the City"* (London: I.B. Tauris, 2004).

84. Amanda Robb, "Look! Up in the Sky! It's a Bird! It's a Plane! It's . . . Supermom!" O, *The Oprah Magazine* 9:7 (July 2008), 210. Overparenting has its own literature of advice. Starting around 1920 the child-care literature raised a "new and frightening" specter: "the dangerous mother." This idea was popularized through the writings of John B. Watson, whose best-selling *Psychological Care of Infant and Child* described the "danger of too much mother love." "Invalidism," he warns, is on the rise in most American homes, because children are being "over-coddled." John B. Watson, *Psychological Care of Infant and Child* (New York: W.W. Norton, 1928), 80, quoted in Maxine L. Margolis, *True to Her Nature: Changing Advice to American Women* (Prospect Heights, IL: Waveland Press, 2000), 33–34. "A major tenet of the Watsonian school of child rearing was scheduling," explains one historian. "Children were to be kept on a rigid schedule for feeding, sleeping, toilet training, and nearly all other activities; any deviation from routine was viewed as harmful." Margolis, *True to Her Nature*, 35. These schedules were developed in part to train good habits and multiple skills but also to protect children from the dangerous freedom of spare time. In recent years, such habits of scheduling have led to criticism. "Children are protected to the point of fetishization," one blogger has written. Deborah Needleman, "A Garden of Politics and Possibility," *New York Times* (March 21, 2009). "In middle-class America the mother not only tends to be the exclusive daytime adult contact of the child, but also has a mission to create a near-perfect being," Philip Slater explains. "This means that every maternal quirk, every maternal hang-up, and every maternal deprivation is experienced by the child as heavily amplified noise from which there is no escape." Slater, *The Pursuit of Loneliness* (Boston: Beacon Press, 1990), 73. Thus, the process of child rearing becomes "a dauntingly complex enterprise," Caitlin Flanagan has commented. "The curious thing about this labor-intensive variety of parenting is that it has arisen now, when parents—and specifically mothers—have less time to devote to their children than ever before." Parents thus become "co-presidents of an industrious little corporation." Flanagan, "The Wifely Duty," *Atlantic Monthly* (January–February 2003), 178, 181. On

the phenomenon of overparenting, see Joan Acocella, "The Child Trap," *New Yorker* (November 17, 2008), 100–105; Jill Lepore, "Baby Food," *New Yorker* (January 19, 2009); and Judith Warner, "Camp Codependence," *New York Times* (July 31, 2008).

85. "Secret Lives of Moms," *The Oprah Winfrey Show*.

86. Oprah Winfrey, "The O Interview: Condoleezza Rice," *O, The Oprah Magazine* 3:2 (February 2002), 120, 180, 179. Rice illustrates an article from a later issue in which O reported that the "most financially successful women in America are also the least likely to have children." Karen Durbin, "A Pregnant Pause," *O, The Oprah Magazine* 3:4 (April 2002), 189.

87. "The O Interview: Oprah Talks to Michelle Obama," *O, The Oprah Magazine* 10:4 (April 2009), 143.

88. Holly Yeager, "The Heart and Mind of Michelle Obama," *O, The Oprah Magazine* 8:11 (November 2007), 338.

89. "Michelle Obama: The Right to Bare Arms," *The Week* 9:404 (March 20, 2009), 19.

90. Oprah Winfrey, "What I Know for Sure," *O, The Oprah Magazine* 10:4 (April 2009), 196. Tina Brown has even suggested that Michelle is the "New Oprah" for these reasons. Tina Brown, "Is Michelle the New Oprah?" TheDaily Beast.com (April 2, 2009).

91. Winfrey, "The O Interview: Oprah Talks to a Mother of 9," 287–88.

92. Oprah Winfrey, "What I Know for Sure," *O, The Oprah Magazine* 10:4 (April 2009), 196.

93. Allison Samuels, "What Michelle Means to Us," *Newsweek* (December 1, 2008), 29.

94. Noam Friedlander, "'Michelle Obama Effect' Hits New York Fashion Week," *Telegraph* (February 16, 2009).

95. Bill Schneider, "Mrs. Obama Heads to Europe," CNN.com (March 30, 2009).

96. James Poniewozik, "Tuned In: Meet the Obamas," *Time* (December 1, 2008), 24.

97. Rachel L. Swarns, "First Lady in Control of Building Her Image," *New York Times* (April 24, 2009).

98. "The Oprah-fication of Michelle Obama," *New York Times* (August 26, 2008).

99. For the standard description of Oprahfication, see Jane Shattuc, "The Oprahfication of America: Talk Shows and the Public Sphere," in *Television, History, and American Culture: Feminist Critical Essays,* ed. Mary Beth Haralovich and Lauren Rabinovitz (Durham, NC: Duke University Press, 1999), 168–80.

100. "Michelle Obama began the campaign as a bold, outspoken woman with a career of her own, and she was called a hard-ass. Now, as she prepares to move into the White House, she appears poised to recede into a fifties-era role of 'mom-in-chief.' It will be heartbreaking if, in an effort to avoid the kind of criticism that followed Hillary Clinton, the First Lady is reduced to a lightweight." Amanda Fortini, "The National Interest: The 'Bitch' and the 'Ditz,'" *New York* (November 24, 2008), 34. See also Rachel L. Swarns, "From Home and Away, Advice for a First Lady," *New York Times* (November 24, 2008).

101. Sandra Sobieraj Westfall, "Michelle Obama: We're Home," *People* 71:9 (March 9, 2009), 114.

102. Peter Slevin, "Mrs. Obama Goes to Washington," *Princeton Alumni Weekly* 109:10 (March 18, 2009), 22.

103. Samuels, "What Michelle Means to Us," 30.

104. Quoted in Westfall, "Michelle Obama: We're Home," 117.

105. Lauren Berlant, *The Female Complaint: The Unfinished Business of Sentimentality in American Culture* (Durham, NC: Duke University Press, 2008), 20.

106. The only moment in which shoes became a theorized object on the *Oprah* show was introduced by Diane Keaton:

Winfrey: Uh, your favorite accessory? Good, good question for you.

Keaton: Oh, no question, no, uh, no, uh, shoes.

Winfrey: Really?

Keaton: Shoes. *[Camera zooms in to her black stilettos with ankle ties]*

Winfrey: No question.

Keaton: And you know why, right, right?

Winfrey: Why? *[Crowd laughing]*

Keaton: Well, I think they're penis substitutes, right. *[Crowd laughing]* I'm sorry, that's, that's bad. I know.

Winfrey: Are they really?

Keaton: Well, they are. You were like, you know you're interested in that, obviously.

Winfrey: I've never heard that in my whole forty-three-year-old life. I've never—has anybody ever heard that shoes were a penis substitute?

Keaton: I'm wrong, right? Okay.

Winfrey: Never heard that in my whole life, but I will be talking about it some more.

The promise to talk about it some more was never kept, leaving the symbolism of the shoes untied. *The Oprah Winfrey Show 20th Anniversary Collection*, disc 4, Harpo, Inc. (2005).

107. Deirdre N. McCloskey, *The Bourgeois Virtues: Ethics for an Age of Commerce* (Chicago: University of Chicago Press, 2006), 81.

108. Sara Rimer, "For Girls, It's Be Yourself, and Be Perfect, Too," *New York Times* (April 1, 2007). According to a *Newsweek* study, by the time a currently ten-year-old girl is fifty, she'll have spent nearly three hundred thousand dollars on just her hair and face. Jessica Bennett, "Tales of a Modern Diva," *Newsweek* (April 6, 2009), 42. Another poll found that 25 percent of young women questioned would rather win first prize on *America's Next Top Model* than the Nobel Peace Prize. Half said they'd marry an ugly man if he were rich. From "Bad Week for . . . ," *The Week* (April 3, 2009), 4.

5. READING RELIGIOUSLY

1. Pat Eisemann, Scribner vice president and director of publicity, quoted in Karen Valby, "Final Chapter," *Entertainment Weekly* 649:67 (April 19, 2002), 67.

2. "In April 2005, Word of Mouth, a group of 158 authors, penned an open letter to Oprah Winfrey begging her to reinstate her original book club's focus on contemporary fiction. . . . The Word of Mouth writers lamented that sales of contemporary fiction had plummeted since the dissolution of the original book club. Without Winfrey's direction, the writers' group insisted, 'the American literary landscape is in distress. . . . Readers have trouble finding contemporary books they'll like. They, the readers, need you. And we, the writers, need you. . . . Oprah Winfrey, we wish you'd come back.'" Janice Peck, *The Age of Oprah: Cultural Icon for the Neoliberal Era* (Boulder, CO: Paradigm Publishers, 2008), 175.

3. Oprah Winfrey, "Come On In!" *O at Home* 5:3 (Fall 2008), 11.

4. "The Return," *The Oprah Winfrey Show* (June 18, 2003).

5. Sarah Robbins, "Making Corrections to Oprah's Book Club: Reclaiming Literary Power for Gendered Literacy Management," in *The Oprah Phenomenon,* ed. Jennifer Harris and Elwood Watson (Lexington: University Press of Kentucky, 2007), 250.

6. Yung-Hsing Wu, "The Romance of Reading Like Oprah," in *The Oprah Affect: Critical Essays on Oprah's Book Club* (Albany: State University of New York Press, 2008), 77. For more on contemporary book clubs and the reading group discussion guides sold by publishers, see William McGinley and Katanna Conley, "Literary Retailing and the (Re)making of Popular Reading," *Journal of Popular Culture* 35:2 (Fall 2001), 207–20.

7. Kathryn McClymond, "The Gospel according to Oprah: A Canon for Contemporary Living," in *Religion as Entertainment,* ed. C.K. Robertson (New York: Peter Lang, 2002), 175.

8. These patterns map most nearly to the Pietistic wing of the Reformation. On varieties of the Reformation, see Hans H. Hillerbrand, ed., *The Protestant Reformation* (New York: Harper Perennial, 1968).

9. Lisa Shea, "BibliO: From Our Shelf to Yours," *O, The Oprah Magazine* (July 2002), 124.

10. "Books That Made a Difference to Natalie Portman," *O, The Oprah Magazine* 9:3 (March 2008), 186.

11. "Reading Room," *O, The Oprah Magazine* 5:7 (July 2004), 115.

12. Penelope Green, "Can This Room Be Saved?" *O, The Oprah Magazine* 3:12 (December 2002), 214. Elsewhere in Winfrey's print culture, objects related to reading are sold as decoration. Next to an image of books serving as free-floating shelves (for vases, for keys), the copy reads, "The transformation of vintage hardcovers gives new meaning to the word *bookshelf* ($40 each, curiosityshoppeonline.com)." "Look What We Found: A Clever Cover Model," *O at Home* 5:3 (Fall 2008), 20. Later in the same issue, the magazine instructs the reader to "banish blah, institutional gray-metal bookends, and support your reading habit in high style with these ten terrific thrillers." The "thrillers" are "snappy" bookends, including zebras ($375 apiece), pyramids made of reclaimed teak ($250), little Rosie the Riveter figures made of resin and stone ($36), and replicas of Oxford University's Radcliffe Camera Library ($525). "Snappy Endings," *O at Home* 5:3 (Fall 2008), 46–47.

13. "Reading Rooms," *O at Home* 5:3 (Fall 2008), 87. "25 of our favorite decorators, landscape architects, and artists tell us which titles helped them

think, see, and dream. (A few may surprise you.)" "The Most Inspiring Design Books of All Time," *O at Home* 5:3 (Fall 2008), 32–34.

14. Trysh Travis, "'It Will Change the World If Everybody Reads This Book': New Thought Religion in Oprah's Book Club," in *Religion and Politics in the Contemporary United States,* ed. R. Marie Griffith and Melani McAlister (Baltimore: Johns Hopkins University Press, 2008), 493.

15. "An Instant Classic: Oprah's Private Library," *O at Home* 5:3 (Fall 2008), 95.

16. "Oprah's Book Club: *While I Was Gone,*" *The Oprah Winfrey Show* (June 23, 2000). Indeed, the shopper's "exhaustion" led to the cancellation of the first incarnation of her book club. Kathy Rooney reports that after one schoolteacher begs Winfrey to continue her club, Winfrey replies with laughter that "she does not want to have to read and select classic novels on the basis of their potential for an accompanying dinner." Kathy Rooney, "Oprah Learns Her Lesson," *The Nation* (May 20, 2002), 56.

17. "We celebrate how books enrich our lives, and homes, by leading us to the perfect paint color, taking us inside favorite writers' houses, and giving us reason to serve up food and friendship." "Reading Rooms," *O at Home,* 87.

18. Mona Simpson, "Books That Made a Difference: Beautiful Minds," *O, The Oprah Magazine* 3:5 (May 2002), 181.

19. "The Return," *The Oprah Winfrey Show.*

20. Pamela Erens, "She's Gotta Read It," *O, The Oprah Magazine* 2:11 (December 2001), 83, 84.

21. "From the beginning, Oprah's Book Club sanctioned particular reading practices." Roberta F. Hammett and Audrey Dentith, "Some Lessons before Dying: Gender, Morality, and the Missing Critical Discourse in Oprah's Book Club," in *The Oprah Phenomenon,* ed. Harris and Watson, 210.

22. "Writers on Writing," *The Oprah Winfrey Show* (June 20, 2001).

23. Cecilia Konchar Farr, *Reading Oprah: How Oprah's Book Club Changed the Way America Reads* (Albany: State University of New York Press, 2005), 81. These meals became such celebrated moments on the show's calendar that there was a behind-the-scenes episode about Winfrey's Book Club dinner parties (December 3, 1996).

24. "Several book club episodes have occurred at Winfrey's Chicago home; there guests are not only treated to the experience of hobnobbing with authors but treated as friends whom Oprah has invited for a casual but elegant dinner." Wu, "The Romance of Reading Like Oprah," 77.

25. On ritual as the dramatization of a significant event, see Gregor T. Goethals, *The TV Ritual: Worship at the Video Altar* (Boston: Beacon Press, 1981). On ritual as repeated action distinguished in its formality and sincerity, see Roy Rappaport, *Ecology, Meaning, and Religion* (Berkeley, CA: North Atlantic, 1979).

26. "Shhhhh . . . ," *O, The Oprah Magazine* 3:10 (October 2002), 175.

27. Ibid., 176.

28. Winifred Gallagher, "What Makes a Home," *O, The Oprah Magazine* 3:12 (December 2002), 204.

29. "Shhhhh . . . ," 178.

30. *O at Home* 5:3 (Fall 2008), cover. This was not the first time Oprah's private interior made her magazine's exterior; the Spring 2008 issue introduced readers to Oprah's California Teahouse ("Oprah's Retreat: WHERE SHE GOES TO GET AWAY FROM IT ALL").

31. "An Anatomy of Oprah's Bookshelves," *O at Home* 5:3 (Fall 2008), 92–93.

32. Melinda Page, "Why This Works," *O at Home* 5:3 (Fall 2008), 58–59.

33. These coronations mirror those described in chapter 3. For a description of authors' lives before and after the book club nomination, including a sidebar describing the ways authors spent the money from this "royalty flush," see Paula Chin and Christina Cheakalos, "Touched by an Oprah," *People* 52:24 (December 20, 1999), 112–22.

34. Margo Jefferson, "There Goes the Neighborhood," *New York Times* (November 25, 2001).

35. Steven Zeitchik, "Oprah Author Disinvited from Show," *Publishers Weekly* (October 29, 2001), 14.

36. David D. Kirkpatrick, "'Oprah' Gaffe by Franzen Draws Ire and Sales," *New York Times* (October 29, 2001), E1.

37. Jeff Giles, "Errors and 'Corrections,'" *Newsweek* (November 5, 2001), 68. The "middlebrow" has many definitions. "Liking the book better than the movie is a middlebrow rite of passage." Willing Davidson, "Great Book, Bad Movie: How Hollywood Ruins Novels," *Slate* (February 17, 2009).

38. "The whole point of the development of a self-aware 'high art' tradition, over the past 200 years, was disdain for this very audience. . . . The whole point of creating highbrow cultural institutions—from PBS to your local cultural center—was to enable persons of 'taste' to segregate themselves from everyone else. . . . In fact, the first people to complain about the Oprah sticker were customers at the little bookstores where Franzen did readings. It threatened their 'taste' status. Franzen blew everybody's cultural cover." Charles Paul Freund, "Franzen's Folly: The Novelist vs. High Art's Dark Other," *Reason* 33:8 (January 2002). Margo Jefferson agrees: The Franzen controversy was "a fable about the literary class system today." Jefferson, "There Goes the Neighborhood."

39. Scott Stossel makes this point in his appraisal of the Franzen debacle in "Elitism for Everyone," TheAtlantic.com (November 29, 2001). Elsewhere, in a similar vein, Laura Miller writes, "America's book culture too often seems composed of two resentful camps, hunkered down in their foxholes, lobbing the occasional grenade at each other and nursing their grievances. One side sees itself as scorned by a snotty self-styled elite and the other sees itself as keepers of the literary flame, neglected by a vulgarian mainstream that would rather wallow in mediocrity and dreck. Each side remains exquisitely sensitive to perceived rejection from the other, and the fact that one is often characterized as female and the other as male resonates with the edgy relations between the sexes." Miller, "Book Lovers' Quarrel," Salon.com (April 18, 2001).

40. Chris Lehmann, "Oprah's Book Fatigue: How Fiction's Best Friend Ran Out of Stuff to Read," *Slate* online (April 10, 2002).

41. "The shift toward the literary in 2000 introduced eruptions in the show's discourse." Malin Pereira, "Oprah's Book Club and the American Dream," in *The Oprah Phenomenon*, ed. Harris and Watson, 196.

42. Ibid., 201. See also Debbie Epstein and Deborah Lynn Steinberg, "American Dreamin': Discoursing Liberally on *The Oprah Winfrey Show*," *Women's Studies International Forum* 21:1 (1998), 77–94.

43. Bob Minzesheimer, "Winfrey's Book Talk Wins Publishing Gold," *USA Today* (November 17, 1999), 1D.

44. Hammett and Dentith, "Some Lessons before Dying," 217. Compare the plot of these novels to the "chick-lit category" of contemporary fiction, described as "girl meets guy; girl gets guy but first she has to discuss him endlessly with her gal friends and perhaps Mother, who is typically a dragon or an ex-model or both." Cathy Horyn, "And the Plot Thinned . . . ," *New York Times* (July 24, 2008).

45. Lehmann, "Oprah's Book Fatigue."

46. Illouz, *Oprah Winfrey and the Glamour of Misery*, 104. "All the women in these novels are primarily defined as mothers, sisters, daughters, or wives, and not, as in the classical romance formula, as (actual or potential) lovers" (105).

47. "Oprah's Book Club: *A Fine Balance*," *The Oprah Winfrey Show* (January 24, 2002).

48. "The Book Club, according to Oprah," *Newsweek* (October 10, 1996), 83.

49. Robbins, "Making Corrections to Oprah's Book Club," 244.

50. "In her now-classic *The Feminization of American Culture*, Ann Douglas argues that disestablishment, and the attendant hope eclipse of the moral authority of Calvinist elite, marked a disastrous loss of 'intellectual rigor and imaginative precision,' with the result that religion came to be dangerously sentimentalized, relegated to a mawkish, 'feminized' sphere where faith was demoted to 'feeling' and accorded cultural representation precisely in exchange for its refusal to interfere in political life." Tracy Fessenden, *Culture and Redemption: Religion, the Secular, and American Literature* (Princeton, NJ: Princeton University Press, 2007), 60; quoting Ann Douglas, *The Feminization of American Culture* (New York: Anchor Press, 1988), 5.

51. Fessenden, *Culture and Redemption*, 60–61.

52. "When critics dismiss sentimental fiction because it is out of touch with reality, they do so because the reality they perceive is organized according to a different set of conventions for constituting experience. For while the attack on sentimental fiction claims for itself freedom from the distorting effects of a naïve religious perspective, the real naïveté is to think that that attack is launched from no perspective whatsoever, or that its perspective is disintegrated and not culture-bound in the way the sentimental novelists were." Jane Tompkins, *Sensational Designs: The Cultural Work of American Fiction, 1790–1860* (New York: Oxford University Press, 1985), 159–60.

53. Candy Gunther Brown, *Word in the World: Evangelical Writing, Publishing, and Reading in America, 1789–1880* (Chapel Hill: University of North Carolina Press, 2004), 7.

54. Erin A. Smith, "Melodrama, Popular Religion, and Literary Value: The Case of Harold Bell Wright," *American Literary History* 17:2 (Summer 2005), 220.

55. Wright quoted ibid., 226, 222.

56. Joel Pfister, *Staging Depth: Eugene O'Neill and The Politics of Psychological Discourse* (Chapel Hill: University of North Carolina Press, 1995), 9, 10. "Since the rise of romanticism," writes Eli Zaretsky, "the artist has symbolized the free individual who brought to society not the performance of an assigned function but his or her own self." Zaretsky, *Capitalism, Family, and Personal Life* (New York: Harper and Row, 1976), 92.

57. Kathleen Rooney, *Reading with Oprah: The Book Club That Changed America* (Fayetteville: University of Arkansas Press, 2005), 140.

58. Malcolm Jones, "The Hard Sell," *Newsweek* 138:9 (August 27, 2001), 52–54.

59. Illouz, *Oprah Winfrey and the Glamour of Misery*, 103; R. Mark Hall, "The 'Oprahfication' of Literacy: Reading 'Oprah's Book Club,'" *College English* 65:6 (July 2003), 646–67.

60. Quoted in David D. Kirkpatrick, "Oprah Will Curtail 'Book Club' Picks, and Authors Weep," *New York Times* (April 6, 2002), A1.

61. "O Contributors," *O, The Oprah Magazine* 3:10 (October 2002), 24; "O Contributors," *O, The Oprah Magazine* 3:8 (August 2002), 22; "O Contributors," *O, The Oprah Magazine* 3:7 (July 2002), 14.

62. "Your Guide to Leo Tolstoy's *Anna Karenina*: About the Book," Oprah.com, www.oprah.com/article/oprahsbookclub/annakarenina/anna_book_about/2.

63. "Your Guide to *As I Lay Dying*," Oprah.com, www.oprah.com/article/oprahsbookclub/asilaydying/ilay_about/2.

64. "Ashley Judd/Oprah's Book Club," *The Oprah Winfrey Show* (April 27, 2000); Wu, "The Romance of Reading Like Oprah," 77.

65. Buck's narrative was typical of prewar depictions of Asia. See Christina Klein, *Cold War Orientalism: Asia in the Middlebrow Imagination, 1945–1961* (Berkeley: University of California Press, 2003); and Karen J. Leong, *The China Mystique: Pearl S. Buck, Anna May Wong, Mayling Soong, and the Transformation of American Orientalism* (Berkeley: University of California Press, 2005).

66. Oprah Winfrey, "Defining Moments in *The Good Earth*," *OprahNewsletter* (October 26, 2004).

67. Oprah Winfrey, "Beauty and Sacrifice in *The Good Earth*," *OprahNewsletter* (October 1, 2004).

68. Quoted in Robert Shaffer, "Women and International Relations: Pearl S. Buck's Critique of the Cold War," *Journal of Women's History* 11:3 (Autumn 1999), 151.

69. Pearl S. Buck, "Our Dangerous Myths about China," *New York Times Magazine* (October 23, 1949); reprinted in Pearl S. Buck, *China as I See It* (New York: John Day Co., 1970), 252–64, quotation on 262. See also Ann Waltner, "Recent Scholarship on Chinese Women," *Signs* 21 (Winter 1996), 410–28; Jinhua Emma Teng, "The Construction of the 'Traditional Chinese Woman' in the Western Academy," *Signs* 22 (Autumn 1996), 115–51; and Dorothy Ko, *Teachers of the Inner Chambers: Women and Culture in Seventeenth-Century China* (Stanford, CA: Stanford University Press, 1994).

70. Shaffer, "Women and International Relations," 161.

71. Pearl S. Buck, "And Yet—Jesus Christ," *Far Horizons* (January 1932), 10; quoted in Grant Wacker, "Pearl S. Buck and the Waning of the Missionary Impulse," *Church History* 72:4 (December 2003), 861.

72. Wacker, "Pearl S. Buck and the Waning of the Missionary Impulse," 856.

73. Ibid., 860–61.

74. Ibid., 870.

75. Elizabeth Long, *Book Clubs: Women and the Uses of Reading in Everyday Life* (Chicago: University of Chicago Press, 2003), 10.

76. Laurel Amtower, *Engaging Words: The Culture of Reading in the Later Middle Ages* (New York: St. Martin's Press, 2000); Brian Stock, *The Implications of Literacy: Written Language and Models of Interpretation in the Eleventh and Twelfth Centuries* (Princeton, NJ: Princeton University Press, 1983).

77. Long, *Book Clubs,* 32.

78. Ibid., 32. Long quoting Natalie Zemon Davis, "Printing and the People," in *Society and Culture in Early Modern France: Eight Essays* (Stanford, CA: Stanford University Press, 1975), 214.

79. Edwin Scott Gaustad, *Dissent in American Religion* (1973; Chicago: University of Chicago Press, 2006), 6.

80. "Mormon Church Purges Survivalism," United Press International (November 30, 1992); Boyd K. Packer, "'To Be Learned Is Good If . . . ,'" *Ensign* (November 1992), 71; "Ultraconservative Mormons Say Church Is Purging Them," Associated Press (November 30, 1992).

81. Long, *Book Clubs,* 37. For more on the effort to collect, exhibit, teach, and engender an American "culture" in the late nineteenth century, see Lawrence Levine, *Highbrow/Lowbrow: The Emergence of Cultural Hierarchy in America* (Cambridge, MA: Harvard University Press, 1988); and Paul J. DiMaggio, "Cultural Entrepreneurship in Nineteenth-Century Boston," in *Nonprofit Enterprise in the Arts: Studies in Mission and Constraint,* ed. Paul J. DiMaggio (New York: Oxford University Press, 1987), 41–62.

82. On the combined efforts of reform by club groups, see Maureen A. Flanagan, "Gender and Urban Political Reform: The City Club and the Woman's City Club of Chicago in the Progressive Era," *American Historical Review* 95:4 (October 1990), 1032–50; and Linda J. Rynbrandt, "The 'Ladies of the Club' and Caroline Bartlett Crane: Affiliation and Alienation in Progressive Social Reform," *Gender and Society* 11:2 (April 1997), 200–214.

83. David D. Kirkpatrick, "To the Dismay of Publishers, Oprah Winfrey Ends Her Book Club," *New York Times* (April 5, 2002); Kirkpatrick, "Oprah Will Curtail 'Book Club' Picks, and Authors Weep."

84. "Tedious selfhood" is found in Martha E. White, "The Work of the Woman's Club," *Atlantic Monthly* 93:559 (1903), 620; "self-inclusive" is found in Julia Ward Howe, "How Can Women Best Associate?" in *Papers and Letters Presented at the First Woman's Congress of the Association for the Advancement of Woman, 1873* (New York: Association for the Advancement of Woman, 1874), 6, quoted in Long, *Book Clubs,* 49.

85. Ann Gere, *Intimate Practices: Literacy and Cultural Work in U.S. Women's Clubs, 1880–1920* (Urbana: University of Illinois Press, 1997); Anne Ruggles Gere and Sarah R. Robbins, "Gendered Literacy in Black and White:

Turn-of-the-Century African-American and European-American Club Women's Printed Texts," *Signs* 21:3 (Spring 1996), 643–78.

86. Charlotte M. Canning, *The Most American Thing in America: Circuit Chautauqua as Performance* (Iowa City: University of Iowa Press, 2005), 6, 14. "To the vulgar" is from Richard Hofstadter, *Anti-Intellectualism in American Life* (New York: Vintage Books, 1963), 112; "familiar evangelical sense" is from Theodore Morrison, *Chautauqua: A Center for Education, Religion, and Arts in America* (Chicago: University of Chicago Press, 1974), 31; both quoted in Canning.

87. John H. Vincent, "The Hall of the Christ at Chautauqua," *Biblical World* 6:6 (December 1895), 530–531.

88. Jeanne Halgren Kilde, "The 'Predominance of the Feminine' at Chautauqua: Rethinking the Gender-Space Relationship in Victorian America," *Signs* 24:2 (1999), 461, 455–56, 465, 470.

89. R. B. Tozier, "A Short Life-History of the Chautauqua," *American Journal of Sociology* 40:1 (July 1934), 73.

90. Jason Zinoman, "Theater Review: *Chautauqua!* Recalling When Entertainment Joined Education," *New York Times* (March 1, 2009).

91. Charlotte Canning, "The Platform versus the Stage: The Circuit Chautauqua's Antitheatrical Theatre," *Theatre Journal* 50 (1998), 303, 309, 312. The last passage quotes from John Gentile, *Cast of One: One-Person Shows from the Chautauqua Platform to the Broadway Stage* (Urbana: University of Illinois Press, 1989), 8.

92. Betty DeBerg, "Lutheran Family Devotions," in *Religions of the United States in Practice*, vol. 2, ed. Colleen McDannell (Princeton, NJ: Princeton University Press, 2001), 25–26.

93. Kirkpatrick, "Oprah Will Curtail 'Book Club' Picks, and Authors Weep."

94. Started in 1926 by the New York entrepreneur Harry Scherman, the Book-of-the-Month Club targeted "a well-heeled audience already cognizant of literature," an audience initially gleaned from the New York Social Register and college alumni lists. Joan Shelley Rubin, "Self, Culture, and Self-Culture in Modern America: The Early History of the Book-of-the-Month Club," *Journal of American History* 71:4 (March 1985), 789; Janice Radway, *A Feeling for Books: The Book-of-the-Month Club* (Chapel Hill: University of North Carolina Press, 1997), 295.

95. Farr, *Reading Oprah*, 34.

96. McClymond, "The Gospel according to Oprah," 179.

97. Erin A. Smith, "The Religious Book Club: Print Culture, Consumerism, and the Spiritual Life of American Protestants between the Wars," in *Religion and the Culture of Print in Modern America*, ed. Charles L. Cohen and Paul S. Boyer (Madison: University of Wisconsin Press, 2008), 218.

98. Ibid., 228.

99. Ibid., 230.

100. "Oprah's Book Club: *Cane River*," *The Oprah Winfrey Show* (September 24, 2001).

101. Travis, "'It Will Change the World If Everybody Reads This Book,'" 491. For one among many admiring appraisals, see Robert McHenry, "All Hail Oprah's Book Club," *Chronicle of Higher Education* (May 10, 2002), B17.

102. Peck, *The Age of Oprah,* 180.

103. Barbara G. Myerhoff, "A Death in Due Time: Construction of Self and Culture in Ritual Drama," in *Rite, Drama, Festival, Spectacle: Rehearsals Toward a Theory of Cultural Performance,* ed. John MacAloon (Philadelphia: Institute for the Study of Human Issues, 1984), 156.

104. "Oprah's Book Club: *Icy Sparks,*" *The Oprah Winfrey Show* (May 16, 2001).

105. "Oprah's Book Club: *Fall on Your Knees,*" *The Oprah Winfrey Show* (April 5, 2002).

106. Ted Striphas, "A Dialectic with the Everyday: Communication and Cultural Politics on Oprah Winfrey's Book Club," *Critical Studies in Mass Communication* 20:3 (September 2003), 297, 298.

107. Amy Johnson Frykholm, *Rapture Culture:* Left Behind *in Evangelical America* (New York: Oxford University Press, 2004), 115, quoted in Erin A. Smith, "'What Would Jesus Do?' The Social Gospel and the Literary Marketplace," *Book History* 10 (2007), 206–7. For more on evangelical reading clubs, see Lynn Neal, "The Discipline of Fun," in *Romancing God: Evangelical Women and Inspirational Fiction* (Chapel Hill: University of North Carolina at Chapel Hill Press, 2006), chapter 2, 43–72. On the role of small groups in American religion, see Robert Wuthnow, *I Come Away Stronger: How Small Groups Are Shaping American Religion* (Grand Rapids, MI: William B. Eerdmans Publishing Company, 2001).

108. Sociologist Long has observed that little time is spent on the book itself. "The book functioned, then, as a launching pad to somewhere else." Long, *Book Clubs,* 203.

109. "Oprah's Book Club: *We Were the Mulvaneys,*" *The Oprah Winfrey Show* (March 8, 2001); "Oprah's Book Club: *Drowning Ruth,*" *The Oprah Winfrey Show* (November 16, 2000).

110. Travis, "'It Will Change the World If Everybody Reads This Book,'" 506.

111. "Oprah's Book Club: *Drowning Ruth,*" *The Oprah Winfrey Show.*

112. Judith Fetterley, *The Resisting Reader: A Feminist Approach to American Fiction* (Bloomington: Indiana University Press, 1978). See also the essays by Patrocinio P. Schweickart, Susan Schibanoff, and Elizabeth A. Flynn in *Gender and Reading: Essays on Readers, Texts and Contexts,* ed. Elizabeth A. Flynn and Patrocinio P. Schweickart (Baltimore: Johns Hopkins University Press, 1986), 31–62, 83–106, and 267–88, respectively.

113. D.T. Max, "The Oprah Effect," *New York Times Magazine* (December 26, 1999), 36.

114. Rooney, *Reading with Oprah,* 158.

115. Ibid., 144.

116. "Oprah's Book Club: *A Fine Balance,*" *The Oprah Winfrey Show* (January 24, 2002).

117. Lise Funderburg, "A Novel Affair," *O at Home* 5:3 (Fall 2008), 130.

118. Raymond A. Smith, "The Adult Bible Class Movement," B.D. thesis, University of Chicago (1922), 27.

119. Christopher Cantwell, "'Once a Member, Always a Member': Feeling, Faith, and Friendship in the Adult Bible Class Movement," paper presented at the Annual Meeting of the American Historical Association (January 4, 2009).

120. See, for example, the July–August 2000 issue, which included then–First Lady Hillary Clinton's thoughts on Henri J.M. Nouwen's *The Return of the Prodigal Son* and an excerpt from that book, as well as a short story by Elizabeth Strout, "Basket of Trips."

121. "Oprah's Book Club: *Open House,*" *The Oprah Winfrey Show* (September 27, 2000).

122. "Oprah's Book Club: *The House of Sand and Fog,*" *The Oprah Winfrey Show* (January 24, 2001).

123. "Gary Zukav's Light Bulb Moments," *The Oprah Winfrey Show* (October 13, 2000).

124. "Oprah's Book Club: *We Were the Mulvaneys,*" *The Oprah Winfrey Show.*

125. "Oprah's Book Club: *A Fine Balance,*" *The Oprah Winfrey Show* (January 24, 2002).

126. "Oprah's Book Club: *Fall on Your Knees,*" *The Oprah Winfrey Show.*

127. Erving Goffman, *Interaction Ritual: Essays on Face-to-Face Behavior* (New York: Doubleday, 1967), 91.

128. "Oprah's Book Club: *Sula,*" *The Oprah Winfrey Show* (May 2, 2002).

129. Stossel, "Elitism for Everyone."

130. Denis Donoghue, *The Practice of Reading* (New Haven, CT: Yale University Press, 1998), 63, 64.

131. "Oprah's Book Club is not a college English major's course syllabus; it is a guide for making sense of life—specifically a woman's life—in modern America." McClymond, "The Gospel according to Oprah," 184.

132. "Oprah's Book Club: *The Deep End of the Ocean,*" *The Oprah Winfrey Show* (October 18, 1996).

133. James Simpson, *Burning to Read: English Fundamentalism and Its Reformation Opponents* (Cambridge, MA: Belknap Press, 2007); Brian Stock, *Implications of Literacy: Written Language and Models of Interpretation in the Eleventh and Twelfth Centuries* (Princeton, NJ: Princeton University Press, 1983).

134. Wu, "The Romance of Reading Like Oprah," 81.

6. MISSIONARY GIFT

1. On "enchanted internationalism," see Melani McAlister, "What Is Your Heart For? Affect and Internationalism in the Evangelical Public Sphere," *American Literary History* 20:4 (2008), 870–95. On religions and globalization, see José Casanova, "Religion, the New Millennium, and Globalization," *Sociology of Religion* 62:4 (Winter 2001), 415–41.

2. David N. Dixon, "Aid Workers or Evangelists, Charity or Conspiracy: Framing of Missionary Activity as a Function of International Political Alliances," *Journal of Media and Religion* 4:1 (February 2005), 13–25. For a critical

reading of the relationship between evangelicalism and "cowboy capitalism," see William E. Connolly, "The Evangelical-Capitalist Resonance Machine," *Political Theory* 33:6 (December 2005), 869–86.

3. Julius Bailey, *Around the Family Altar: Domesticity in the African Methodist Episcopal Church, 1865–1900* (Gainesville: University Press of Florida, 2005).

4. Quoted Patricia R. Hill, *The World Their Household: The American Woman's Foreign Mission Movement and Cultural Transformation, 1870–1920* (Ann Arbor: University of Michigan Press, 1985), 115.

5. Lisa Kogan, "Q & O," *O, The Oprah Magazine* 6:10 (October 2005), 279.

6. Quoted in David Carr, "O Magazine Expands to South Africa," *New York Times* (April 8, 2002).

7. Quoted in Craig Kielburger et al., *The World Needs Your Kid: Raising Children Who Care and Contribute* (Vancouver, Canada: Greystone Books, 2010), 167.

8. www.oprah.com/spirit/Seven-Fountains_2.

9. Susan S. Silbey, "'Let Them Eat Cake': Globalization, Postmodern Colonialism, and the Possibilities of Justice," 1996 Presidential Address, *Law & Society Review* 31:2 (1997), 219.

10. Pamela Gien, "Building a Dream," *O, The Oprah Magazine* 8:1 (January 2007), 156.

11. *Building a Dream: The Oprah Winfrey Leadership Academy*, DVD, Harpo, Inc. (2007).

12. Suzanne Slesin, "Live and Learn," *O at Home* 4:2 (Summer 2007), 88.

13. John Lardas Modern, "Evangelical Secularism and the Measure of Leviathan," *Church History* 77:4 (December 2008), 845, 846.

14. Quoted in Gien, "Building a Dream," 158, 156.

15. *Building a Dream*, DVD.

16. Slesin, "Live and Learn," 88.

17. Quoted in Gien, "Building a Dream, 158.

18. Slesin, "Live and Learn," 88.

19. The Oprah Winfrey Leadership Academy Foundation Registry, http://oprahwinfreyleadershipacademy.o-philanthropy.org.

20. *Building a Dream*, DVD.

21. Ibid.

22. Dana L. Robert, "Evangelist or Homemaker? Mission Strategies of Early Nineteenth-Century Missionary Wives in Burma and Hawaii," in *North American Foreign Missions, 1810–1914*, ed. Wilbert R. Shenk (Grand Rapids, MI: William B. Eerdmans Publishing Company, 2004), 116.

23. Dana L. Robert, *American Women in Mission: A Social History of Their Thought and Practice* (Macon, GA: Macon University Press, 1997), 136.

24. Ibid., 70.

25. Arthur Judson Brown, *One Hundred Years: A History of the Foreign Missionary Work of the Presbyterian Church in the U.S.A.* (New York: Revell, 1936), 196.

26. Derek Chang, "'Marked in Body, Mind, and Spirit': Home Missionaries and the Remaking of Race and Nation," in *Race, Nation, and Religion in the*

Americas, ed. Henry Goldschmidt and Elizabeth McAlister (New York: Oxford University Press, 2004), 137.

27. Ibid., 139.

28. Zine Magubane, "The (Product) Red Man's Burden: Charity, Celebrity, and the Contradictions of Coevalness," *Journal of Pan African Studies* 2:6 (2008), 102.8.

29. David Chidester, *Authentic Fakes: Religion and American Popular Culture* (Berkeley: University of California Press, 2005), 223.

30. "The O Bracelet," *O, The Oprah Magazine* 8:5 (May 2007), 152.

31. Ibid.

32. This emphasis on homogenization, polarization, and hybridization can be found in Robert Holton, "Globalization's Cultural Consequences," *Annals of the American Academy of Political and Social Science* 570 (July 2000), 140–52.

33. Amartya Sen, *Development as Freedom* (New York: Anchor Press, 1999), 203.

34. Paul Simon is a Winfrey familiar, having penned the soundtrack for her tenth season, "10 Years (*Oprah Winfrey Show* 10 Year Anniversary Theme)," singing in the lugubrious opener, "You are moving on a crowded street/Through various shades of people/In the summer's harshest heat/A story in your eye." Likewise, Paul Simon was also the subject of "the worst spat" of Oprah and Gayle's friendship, which occurred during their 2006 cross-country trip. While driving across the Great Plains, Oprah and Gayle began discussing the meaning of "Graceland," a Paul Simon song that Oprah says is one of her all-time favorites:

"Was he talking about Elvis Presley's Graceland when he did that?" Gayle said.

"He was talking about going to Graceland," Oprah said. "Yes."

"I thought he was talking about something in Africa, and his love for Africa," Gayle said. "The story doesn't make any sense about going to Elvis Presley's home. . . . I understood 'Bridge over Troubled Water.' That made sense."

"Gayle, it does," Oprah said. "He obviously liked Elvis Presley, and he's finding some solace there."

After a lengthy disagreement, Oprah says she was very frustrated with her friend. "What I wanted to do was stop the car, open the door and get out," she says. Instead, Oprah took a few "cleansing breaths" and continued on toward Tulsa.

Even with a copy of Paul Simon's lyrics, Oprah and Gayle couldn't agree on the meaning of his song "Graceland." Who did they find to settle their dispute? The songwriter himself!

"Let me see if I can clarify the issue a little bit," Paul says. "Oprah, you're right. The song is about a real trip that I took to Graceland. It's not really autobiographical, although there are elements that are. It is about a trip there with a father and his 9-year-old son trying to find some kind of solace from a loss of love."

Before Oprah can gloat, Paul says that Gayle's interpretation is also right! "The song is also about Africa," he says. "The song was made in South Africa, and the musicians were South African. . . . The South Africans were going through a time when they went through the reconciliation with their past, and in that way, that's what the father was looking for in his trip to Graceland and hoping to find there. So in a sense, you're both right!"

Now that the spat is settled, Gayle says she's never discussing "Graceland" ever again!

From the transcript for "Oprah and Gayle's Big Adventure, Part 4" (October 10, 2006) and the online rendition of the discussion, posted at www.oprah.com/dated/oprahshow/oprahshow_20061010.

35. Theodore Gracyk, *I Wanna Be Me: Rock Music and the Politics of Identity* (Philadelphia: Temple University Press, 2001), 145.

36. Louise Meintjes, "Paul Simon's *Graceland*, South Africa, and the Mediation of Musical Meaning," *Ethnomusicology* 34:1 (Winter 1990), 55–56, 66, 67.

37. Jacqueline Warwick, review of *I Wanna Be Me* and *Disruptive Divas*, from *Journal of the American Musicological Society* 57:3 (Autumn 2004), 706.

38. Alison Samuels, "Oprah Goes to School," *Newsweek* (January 8, 2007).

39. Quoted in Robert, *American Women in Mission*, 59.

40. Nick Stevenson, "Globalization, National Cultures and Cultural Citizenship," *Sociological Quarterly* 38:1 (Winter 1997), 42.

41. Rajagopalan Radhakrishnan, "Ethnic Identity and Post-Structuralist Difference," *Cultural Critique* 6 (Spring 1987), 208.

42. Oprah Winfrey, "What I Know for Sure," *O, The Oprah Magazine* 8:1 (January 2007), 218.

43. Oprah Winfrey, "What I Know for Sure," *O, The Oprah Magazine* 7:12 (December 2006), 360.

44. Gien, "Building a Dream," 160.

45. Winfrey, "What I Know for Sure," 7:12 (December 2006), 360.

46. Samuels, "Oprah Goes to School."

47. "Despite Allegations, Oprah's School Supported," CNN.com (October 31, 2007).

CONCLUSION

1. This is an exchange from the Logo Network's reality competition *RuPaul's Drag Race*. RuPaul, "the world's most famous drag queen," hosts a weekly drag contest in which nine of the top American queens "vie for drag stardom" through weekly "challenges." In the third episode of the second season, "Queens of All Media," the contestants were challenged to prepare a performance of Oprah Winfrey. Shanell (age twenty-nine, Las Vegas, Nevada) is a "fierce" white girl with "a killer body, dazzling wardrobe, sickening makeup skills." Bebe (twenty-eight, Minneapolis, Minnesota), a "native of the West African republic of Cameroon," possesses an "exotic dignity and sophistication [that] set her apart from the other contestants."

2. Quoted in Kimberly Wallace-Sanders, *Mammy: A Century of Race, Gender, and Southern Memory* (Ann Arbor: University of Michigan Press, 2008), 1.

3. Thomas Dumm, *Loneliness as a Way of Life* (Cambridge, MA: Harvard University Press, 2008), 29. An article in *O* magazine argues that loneliness produces symptoms aching to be diagnosed. Loneliness "can make you sick, destroy your sleep, raise your blood pressure, and shorten your life. Loneliness isn't just a momentary pang—it's a chronic emotional ache that affects up to 15 percent of us. So who are all the lonely people, and where do they all come from? Answers are finally on the way, now that loneliness is beginning to get the

research attention it deserves." Mamie Healey, "1 Is the Loneliest Number," *O, The Oprah Magazine* (June 2006), 252. Another piece also assesses loneliness as a problem in specific circumstances: Gretchen Reynolds, "Feeling Adrift," *O, The Oprah Magazine* (December 2004), 208–11.

4. "Loneliness is the experience of the pathos of disappearance." Dumm, *Loneliness as a Way of Life,* 34.

5. Susan Douglas, "Narcissism as Liberation," in *The Gender and Consumer Culture Reader,* ed. Jennifer Scanlon (New York: New York University Press, 2000), 268, 277, 278.

6. Veronica Chambers, "Behind Every Great Woman . . . ," *O, The Oprah Magazine* 3:6 (June 2002), 110.

7. www.livingoprah.com/. Okrant's posts became a book. Robyn Okrant, *Living Oprah: My One-Year Experiment to Walk the Walk of the Queen of Talk* (New York: Center Street, 2010).

8. Jessica Grose, "Life in the Time of Oprah," *New York Times* (August 17, 2008); Rupa Shenoy, "The Great Commander," *Chicago Reader* (July 10, 2008).

9. Noreen O'Leary, "O Positive," *Brandweek* (March 5, 2001).

10. John T. Cacioppo and William Patrick, *Loneliness: Human Nature and the Need for Social Connection* (New York: W. W. Norton, 2008), 269.

11. O'Leary, "O Positive," 53.

12. Aaron Curtis, "The Order of Saint Oprah," *Sightings* (July 31, 2008), http:// divinity.uchicago.edu/martycenter/publications/sightings/archive_2008/0731 .shtml.

13. Alina Tugend, "Putting Yourself Out There on a Shelf to Buy," *New York Times* (March 28, 2009).

14. Affluenza has been described as "a painful, contagious, socially transmitted condition of overload, debt, anxiety and waste resulting from the dogged pursuit of more." John De Graaf, David Wann, and Thomas Naylor, *Affluenza: The All Consuming Epidemic* (San Francisco: Berrett-Koehler Publishers, 2002), 2. See also Clive Hamilton and Richard Deniss, *Affluenza: When Too Much Is Never Enough* (Crows Nest, New South Wales: Allen and Unwin, 2005). On the encouragement of expenditure in the financial crisis, see Eric Wilson, "Irresistible and Affordable," *New York Times* (April 2, 2009). On Michelle Obama's European tour, see Carola Long, "Michelle, Ma Belle: A Tour of the First Lady's Wardrobe," *The Independent* (April 4, 2009). Oprah's 2008 Favorite Things episode was aptly titled "How to Have the Thriftiest Holiday Ever!" *The Oprah Winfrey Show* (November 26, 2008).

15. Lee Siegel, "Thank You for Sharing: The Strange Genius of Oprah," *New Republic* 234:21–22 (June 5 and 12, 2006), 23.

16. Lauren Berlant, *The Female Complaint: The Unfinished Business of Sentimentality in American Culture* (Durham, NC: Duke University Press, 2008), 263.

17. Philip Slater, *The Pursuit of Loneliness* (Boston: Beacon Press, 1990), xv. Recent survey results suggest that American women's self-reported happiness has actually decreased even though they are healthier, wealthier, and better educated than they were thirty years ago. "Women: The Happiness Gap," *The Week* (June 26, 2009), 17.

18. "To suggest that most people will never change, no matter how much they want to, seems almost, well, un-American." Alex Williams, "New Year, New You? Nice Try," *New York Times* (January 1, 2009).

19. Maureen Callahan, "Bloated, Depressed—As O Goes, So Goes the Nation," *New York Post* (January 24, 2009).

20. Ofhir Avtalion, Letter to the Editor, *New York Times* (November 8, 1998).

21. Rosieindiana, posted April 19, 2008, at 10:11 A.M., to an article by Claire Hoffman, "Who Are you? Oprah Knows!" WashingtonPost.com (April 14, 2008). On another message board, a viewer asks, "Why would you try to take someone that is only trying to do good things on this planet and make a mockery of her?" Quoted in Curtis, "The Order of Saint Oprah." An article that conveys this same affirming impression of Winfrey's work in response to critical observation can be found by Trudy S. Moore, "How the Oprah Winfrey Show Helps People Live Better Lives," *Jet* 85:24 (April 18, 1994), 56–60.

22. In her examination of Alice Kaplan, Laura Levitt puts well my own resistance to naming first-person "feelings" within a text so obviously devotional to its object. Channeling Kaplan's perspective, Levitt writes, "She is fully absorbed in this work. Given this, she seems to choose not to talk back." Levitt, "Embodied Criticism: A French Lesson," *ARIEL: A Review of International English Literature* 39:1–2 (January–April, 2008), 234.

EPILOGUE

1. In a 2004 interview, Obama and Oprah discussed the similarity between their names: "Oprah Talks to Barack Obama," *O, The Oprah Magazine* 5:11 (November 2004), 288. For more on the branding of the Obama campaign, see Steven Heller, "The 'O' in Obama," *New York Times* (November 20, 2008); Hendrik Hertzberg, "Comment: Obama Wins," *New Yorker* (November 17, 2008), 39; Philip Kennicott, "The Power of Brand-Old Message Art," *Washington Post* (January 13, 2009); "Selling the President: Get Your Obama Hot Sauce," *The Week* (January 30, 2009), 17.

2. On the life stories that Oprah and Obama tell about themselves, see Jennifer Buckendorff, "The Oprah Way," Salon.com (January 24, 2005); Jodi Kantor, "A First Family That Reflects a Nation's Diversity," *New York Times* (January 21, 2009); David Remnick, "The Joshua Generation," *New Yorker* (November 17, 2008), 72; and Brian Stelter, "Following the Script: Obama, McCain, and the *West Wing*," *New York Times* (October 30, 2008).

3. For the religious and cultural communities of Oprah and Obama, see "Bill Cosby Mulls His Show's Possible Impact on Obama's Election," Associated Press (November 12, 2008); John Blake, "Black First Family 'Changes Everything,'" CNN.com (January 15, 2009); Caitlin Flanagan and Benjamin Schwarz, "Showdown in the Big Tent," *New York Times* (December 6, 2008); Michelle Goldberg, "Obama's Divisive Choice of Rick Warren," ReligionDispatches.org (December 18, 2008); James Hannaham, "Obama: Don't Pander to Homophobes," Salon.com (October 26, 2007); "How They See Us: An African President for America," *The Week* (February 6, 2009), 16; Allison Samuels,

"Something Wasn't Wright, So Oprah Left His Church," *Newsweek* (May 12, 2008), 8; Marjorie Valbrun, "The Trouble with Transcending Race," TheRoot .com (April 30, 2008); and Jeff Zeleny, "A New Wind Is Blowing in Chicago," *New York Times* (November 20, 2008).

4. On the styles of Oprah and Obama, see John Dickerson, "Professor Obama's First Seminar," Slate.com (February 10, 2009); Maureen Dowd, "The First Shrink," *New York Times* (April 5, 2009); Jodi Kantor, "The Long Run: Teaching Law, Testing Ideas, Obama Stood Slightly Apart," *New York Times* (July 30, 2008); Lisa Miller, "Is Obama the Antichrist?" *Newsweek* (November 24, 2008), 18; Amy Sullivan, "An Antichrist Obama in McCain Ad?" *Time* (August 8, 2008); and Fareed Zakaria, "The Global Elite: Barack Obama," *Newsweek* (December 29, 2008–January 5, 2009), 37.

5. In a 2004 interview, Obama demonstrated his religious amalgamation in response to the question, "What do you believe?"

> I am a Christian. So, I have a deep faith. So I draw from the Christian faith. On the other hand, I was born in Hawaii where obviously there are a lot of Eastern influences. I lived in Indonesia, the largest Muslim country in the world, between the ages of six and 10. My father was from Kenya, and although he was probably most accurately labeled an agnostic, his father was Muslim. And I'd say, probably, intellectually I've drawn as much from Judaism as any other faith. So, I'm rooted in the Christian tradition. I believe that there are many paths to the same place, and that is a belief that there is a higher power, a belief that we are connected as a people. That there are values that transcend race or culture, that move us forward, and there's an obligation for all of us individually as well as collectively to take responsibility to make those values lived. And so, part of my project in life was probably to spend the first 40 years of my life figuring out what I did believe—I'm 42 now—and it's not that I had it all completely worked out, but I'm spending a lot of time now trying to apply what I believe and trying to live up to those values.

From "Obama's Fascinating Interview with Cathleen Falsani," BeliefNet .com (November 11, 2008).

6. Jon Meacham, "Who We Are Now," *Newsweek* (January 26, 2009), 40; Judith Warner, "Tears to Remember," *New York Times* (November 6, 2008).

7. Portions of this essay initially appeared in Kathryn Lofton, "The Oprah-fication of Obama," posted to *The Immanent Frame* (http://blogs.ssrc.org/tif/) on January 19, 2009.

8. Quoted in "Race: Has America Entered a New Era?" *The Week* (November 21, 2008), 8.

9. Kinney Littlefield, "Oprah Winfrey Is Tired and Tearful but Still Enjoying Her TV Power," *Pittsburgh Post-Gazette* (May 19, 1997), D2.

10. Quoted in "Gossip," *The Week* (February 6, 2009), 10.

11. "Is War the Only Answer?" *The Oprah Winfrey Show* (October 1, 2001).

12. "Vice President Al Gore," *The Oprah Winfrey Show* (September 11, 2000). For a discussion of Oprah's interviews with Bush, Clinton, Gore, and Kerry, see Lee Siegel, "Thank You for Sharing: The Strange Genius of Oprah," *New Republic* 234:21–22 (June 5 and 12, 2006), 20.

13. "Oprah Talks to Barack Obama," 250. Fareed Zakaria invoked Max Weber to explain Barack Obama's charisma, writing that he is "set apart from

ordinary men and treated as endowed with supernatural, superhuman, or at least specifically exceptional powers or qualities." With Weber on his side, Zakaria writes that for some supporters Obama is "the One" whose "birth, background and eloquence . . . give him almost magical qualities." Zakaria, "The Global Elite: Barack Obama," 37.

14. "Oprah Talks to Barack Obama," 290.

15. Jeff Zeleny, "Oprah Winfrey Hits Campaign Trail for Obama," *New York Times* (December 9, 2007).

16. In "The Role of Celebrity Endorsements in Politics: Oprah, Obama, and the 2008 Democratic Primary," University of Maryland economists Craig Garthwaite and Timothy J. Moore argued, "Our results suggest that Oprah Winfrey's endorsement of Barack Obama prior to the 2008 Democratic Presidential Primary generated a statistically and qualitatively significant increase in the number of votes received as well as in the total number of votes cast." Currently posted at http://econ-server.umd.edu/~garthwaite/celebrityendorsements _garthwaitemoore.pdf (see p. 3).

17. Quoted in Remnick, "The Joshua Generation," 80.

18. "Oprah Talks to Barack Obama," 251.

19. Katharine G. Seelye, "The Oprah Party Wants You," *New York Times* (December 2, 2007).

20. Zadie Smith, "Speaking in Tongues," *New York Review of Books* 56:3 (February 26, 2009).

21. Jann S. Wenner, "A Conversation with Barack Obama," *Rolling Stone* (July 10–24, 2008), 72–73.

22. Aside from the comparisons to charismatic individuals from religious contexts cited in chapter 4, Ronald Reagan, especially in his careful self-invention, supplies a strong parallel to Barack Obama. On the conscientious construction of the Reagan iconography, see Will Bunch, *Tear Down This Myth: How the Reagan Legacy Has Distorted Our Politics and Haunts Our Future* (New York: Free Press, 2009); and William Kleinknecht, *The Man Who Sold the World: Ronald Reagan and the Betrayal of Main Street America* (New York: Nation Books, 2009).

Index

TEXT
10/13 Sabon Open Type

DISPLAY
Sabon Open Type

INDEXER
Kevin Millham

COMPOSITOR
BookComp, Inc.

PRINTER/BINDER
Maple-Vail Book Manufacturing Group